Groves Rd

January 3rd

Spurs to Soul Winning

Spurs to Soul Winning

531 Motivations for Winning Souls

By

Frank R. Shivers

LIGHTNING SOURCE
1246 Heil Quaker Blvd.
La Vergne, TN

Unless otherwise noted, Scripture quotations are from
The Holy Bible *King James Version*

Library of Congress Cataloging-in-Publication Data

Shivers, Frank R., 1949-
Spurs to Soul Winning / Frank Shivers
ISBN 978-1-878127-13-6

Library of Congress Control Number:
2010943451

Cover design by
Tim King of Click Graphics, Inc.

For Information:
Frank Shivers Evangelistic Association
P. O. Box 9991
Columbia, South Carolina 29290
www.frankshivers.com

To

Robert A. Varn
An encouraging and enduring friend
who has enabled my work
in the harvest field since college days.

Spur one another on…
Hebrews 10:24 (NIV)

CONTENTS

PREFACE

Fulfilling the Great Commission in bringing the lost to Christ is not only about money and manpower, but also about message and motivation. Herb Miller, a church-growth analyst, states that the average church member has listened to 6,000 sermons, heard 8,000 prayers, sung 20,000 hymns over and over and asked zero people to trust Christ as their Savior.[1]

Why such a failure regarding the primary mandate of Scripture for the Christian to win souls? I believe it has far more to do with the believer's "want to" than the "how to." To win souls requires intentionality. Christians do not drift into soul winning; they are motivated to do it. Soul winners are enlisted.

In *Spurs to Soul Winning,* I purpose to provide both seasoned and novice soul winners with incentives and motivations to consistently seek to win the unsaved. I will use biblical examples, soul-winning stories, sayings of great winners of souls, and compelling scriptural challenges. Freely I have incorporated the most striking appeals and incentives for soul winning from the pen of men like W. B. Riley, J. Wilbur Chapman, R. A. Torrey, D. L. Moody, C. H. Spurgeon, Adrian Rogers, C. E. Autrey, John Bisagno, General William Booth, L. R. Scarborough and John R. Rice. *Spurs to Soul Winning* is a sequel to *Soulwinning 101,* in which the primary focus is the "how to" of soul winning.

These simple and concise challenges are designed to assist the believer in developing and maintaining a "soul focus" and to be a continuous spur to his heart to witness. The format of this volume is designed so that the reader, if he chooses, may read one a day for a year (plus) to keep his heart aflame for souls. "I am made all things to all men that I might by all means save some" (I Corinthians 9:22).

---

[1] Miller, H., newsletter.

"I am very tired, but must go on....A fire is in my bones....O God, what can I say? Souls! Souls! Souls! My heart hungers for souls!"[2]—General William Booth

"The typical churched believer will die without leading a single person to a faith in Christ."[3]—George Barna

"Oh, to realize that souls—precious, never dying souls—are perishing all around us, going out into the blackness of darkness and despair, eternally lost. And yet to feel no anguish, shed no tears, know no travail! How little we know of the compassion of Jesus!"[4]—Oswald J. Smith

"The best way to begin in this work is to begin. The best time to begin is now. The only mistake we need really fear is the mistake of holding off."[5]—Charles G. Trumbull

"It is the cooping yourselves up in rooms that has dampened the work of God, which never was and never will be carried out to any purpose without going into the highways and hedges and compelling men and women to come in."[6]—Jonathan Edwards

"It's not Good News if you don't hear it. It's not Good News if you hear it too late."[7]—Jay Strack

---

[2] Morgan, R., *Stories, Illustrations,* 85.

[3] Barna, *Revolution,* 32.

[4] Smith, *Revival We Need,* Chapter 3.

[5] Trumbull, *Taking Men Alive,* 184.

[6] Edwards, Christianquotes.

[7] Strack, "Tradigital Strategy."

1   Never!

Some question the merit of soul winning, wondering when it will stop. The answer is never, by the designed will of God. Never—as long as one lost soul remains! Never—as long as souls are perishing! Never—as long as the Lord's edict remains to evangelize the world! Never—as long as the day of grace continues for the unsaved! Never—until the saint stands in the presence of God in Heaven! Never—despite suffering, sacrifice and sorrow for telling! Never—despite new trends that espouse that it's outdated and too intrusive! Never—as long as Satan wages war against God for the soul of man! Never—as long as the tongue can tell of a sinner's danger of eternal Hell! Never will we quit, shut up, tone down, go away, alter the message or give up.

You ask if ever the devout believer will stop efforts to win souls. I answer, and may all saints answer in one gigantic chorus, "Never!" We are determined to do MORE—more one-to-one soul winning; more evangelistic preaching; more distribution of evangelistic gospel tracts and books; more television, radio and Internet gospel presentations; more revival, harvest days, crusades; more recruiting and training of new soul winners. Stop? Never! The church is pressing to do MORE! Why not join us?

2   What Is Soul Winning?

Spurgeon stated, "What is it to win a soul? I hope you believe in the old-fashioned way of saving souls. Everything appears to be shaken nowadays and shifted from the old foundations....We drive at something more than temperance; for we believe that men must be born again...that the dead in sin should live, that spiritual life should quicken them, and that Christ should reign where the 'prince of the power of the air' (Ephesians 2:2) now has sway....We are aiming at a miracle....We are sent to say to blind eyes, 'See'; to deaf ears, 'Hear'; to dead hearts, 'Live'; and even to Lazarus rotting in that grave...'Lazarus, come forth' (John 11:43)."[8]

Adrian Rogers said the following words from an unnamed writer answer the questions: What is evangelism? What is soul winning? "It is the sob of God; it is the anguished cry of Jesus as He weeps over a doomed city. It is the cry of Paul: 'I could wish myself a curse for Christ or wish myself a curse from Christ for my brethren.' It is the ringing plea of Moses: 'Forgive their sin, and if not, blot me out of the book which Thou hast written.' It is the cry of John Knox: 'Give me Scotland or I die.' It is the declaration of John Wesley: 'The world is my parish.' It is the prayer of Billy Sunday:

---

[8] Spurgeon, *Soul Winner,* 156–157.

'Make me a giant for God.' It is the sob of a parent in the night, weeping over a prodigal child. It is the secret of a great church; it is the secret of a great preacher and a great Christian."[9]

John R. Rice declared, "By saving souls we do not mean getting people to join the church or to be merely reformed or to go through certain religious rites. We believe the whole world lies in sin. People are all undone, lost, ruined sinners who cannot save themselves. Not an outward change in the life, but an inward change in the heart, a new birth by which one becomes a born-again child of God with all sins forgiven—that is what every man and woman and every child who has reached the age of accountability needs....So to be a soul winner means to cause people to realize their need of Christ as personal Savior and to lead them to commit themselves wholly to Him, with heart faith....One who leads the sinner to make this heart decision is a soul winner."[10]

Henry C. Mabie declared, "Winning souls is not a perfunctory undertaking. The soul winner is not a recruiting sergeant nor a mere zealot gaining adherents to a sect. He is rather one who seeks to add 'to the Lord' as men were 'added' at Pentecost or, as expressed in Hosea's word, 'betrothed' unto the Lord forever."[11]

Samuel Chadwick said, "Soul winning is acknowledged to be as exacting as it is glorious. It is a work that makes demands upon brain and heart and soul. No work requires such tactful wisdom, diligent labor, and earnest prayer."[12]

Based upon these definitions of soul winning, much of what is counted as such, in fact is not. The essential element in soul winning that sets it apart from church visitation or witnessing is the intentional purpose to lead a sinner to make a decision for Christ.

3   The Saint's Report Card

It was report card time, and Jimmy watched intently as his father noticed he had made an F in spelling, an F in math, an F in history, and an F

---

[9] Rogers, "Master Soul Winner," accessed March 26, 2010.

[10] Rice, *The Soul Winner's Fire*, 8–9.

[11] Mabie, *Method in Soul Winning,* 11.

[12] Kemp, *Soulwinner and Soulwinning*, 29.

in English; however, he made an A in citizenship and deportment. He looked up to his son and said, "Great, Jimmy. It looks like you're a neat, well-mannered, stupid kid."[13]

Christians, I fear, are making 'A's' in secondary subjects while making an 'F' in their primary subject, soul winning. It's report card time. What grade has the Master Teacher given you in the subject of soul winning? Work hard today to bring that grade up!

Dick Lincoln, in his sermon "The Chief Mission of the Church," stated, "It is empty worship, teaching, Sunday school, fellowship, caring, steward-ship if we are not engaged in winsome ways to witness....This is why we do all this stuff. What we do here on Sunday morning is not the point. The point is winning people to Christ....We must be serious about evangelizing the world."[14]

4   Soul Winning Is Dead

In research for this writing, I ran across an article with the title, "Soul Winning Is Dead." Though I chose to read only the caption, the author added the following subtitle: "And I am glad." Obviously the author was lost or a liberal.

If soul winning is dead, don't tell me, for I am enjoying the labor and fruit of it now more than ever. If soul winning is dead, don't tell men like Dave Walton, John O'Cain, Scott Eadie, Junior Hill and Bailey Smith, who personally are winning hundreds to Christ. I don't know where the author got his information, but it's bogus. Soul winning is as much alive as ever. Glowing reports of souls saved by such labor are absolutely astonishing, to the glory of God!

Though soul winning is alive and well corporately, it may not be alive individually for you. Are you a soul winner, or is the article's title true, as far as you are concerned? It's not dead to Jesus. He is still seeking to save that which is lost. It's not dead to the Scripture. It yet commands, 'Go ye therefore into all the world...making disciples.' It's not dead to the Holy Spirit, for He continuously is convicting man of sin, judgment, righteous-ness and things to come, showing the need of salvation. It must not be dead to you nor to any believer, for to win souls is the top priority the Lord assigned to the church (Acts 1:8). Soul winning isn't dead and remains the vital means of doing today what the church did in the first century.

---

[13] Smith, Bailey, *Real Evangelism*, 163.

[14] Lincoln, "Chief Mission," accessed June 27, 2010.

5   The Lost

J. Wilbur Chapman stated, "My text this evening is one word. Ever since I have been a minister, I have asked God to help me say two words and say them properly. It is said that Whitefield used to say 'Oh!' in such a fashion that his hearers were convicted of sin, and some of them would cry out for mercy. The first word that I would like to say properly is 'lost.' I have never yet spoken it as it ought to be uttered. I have tried my best and failed. If I could say it as the Son of God appreciated it when, fainting beneath the weight of the Cross, He staggered up Calvary's hill, I would not need to preach. To me it is the most striking word in the English language."[15]

What is the condition of the unsaved? According to Luke 19:10, he is lost; according to John 3:16, he is perishing; according to Ephesians 2:1, he is dead in trespasses and sins; and according to John 3:18, he is condemned. Burn into your heart the reality of man's condition—his restlessness, emptiness, meaninglessness, insignificance, loneliness, hurting, and his being just a heartbeat away from Hell, until you can't wait to share the way to salvation. Feed this flame in your heart constantly, and it will be manifested clearly in sowing and reaping. R. A. Torrey declared, "I would rather win souls than be the greatest king or emperor on earth; I would rather win souls than be the greatest general that ever commanded an army; I would rather win souls than be the greatest poet or novelist or literary man who ever walked this earth. My one ambition in life is to win as many as possible. Oh, it is the only thing worth doing, to save souls and men and women—we can all do it!"[16] Indeed we all can do it, and we all *must* do it.

6   Bring the Fire Back

R. A. Torrey faced a day in which he felt his heart cold toward lost souls. He wrote, "I was so deeply disturbed that I had so little love for souls, that I could meet men and women who were lost and be so little concerned about it, that I could preach to them and had so little inclination to weep over them. I went alone with God and prayed, 'O God, give me a love for souls.' Little did I realize how much the answer to that prayer involved.

"The next day there came into my Bible class a man who was the most distressing picture of utter despair I ever saw. At the close of my Bible class, I walked down the aisle. I saw him in the last seat. His face haunted

---

[15] Chapman, "Eternity," accessed May 20, 2010.

[16] Martin, R., *R. A. Torrey*, 156.

me. I was burdened. I could not lose sight of him. I cannot tell the pain I had for hours and days as I cried to God for his salvation, but I had the joy of seeing him profess to accept Christ.

"Love for souls is one of the costliest things a man can have, but if we are to be like Christ, and if we are to be successful in His work, we must have it. But don't pray for it unless you are willing to suffer."[17] Will you do as he did to bring the fire back into your heart for lost souls?

7 The Sower, the Seed, the Soil

In the parable of the sower (Matthew 13:18–23), Jesus teaches that the soul winner will meet with mixed results as he sows the seed of the Gospel. Not all the seed sown will take root unto genuine salvation. He specifically teaches that soul winners will encounter four responses in witnessing to the lost.

First, there is the response from *the unready heart* (v. 19). These individuals, in hearing a witness, trample it beneath their feet, for they do not see the relevancy of the Gospel or the need for it. The "soil" in their soul is unbroken and has not been plowed by the tiller of the Law of God; and until it is, their hearts will remain as hard as concrete. Cultivation of this field is imperative before one sows the seed of redeeming grace there.

Second, there is the response from *the impetuous heart* (v. 20–21). The response from these type hearers is one of immediate and sincere acceptance to the sower's message. These may experience euphoria accompanied with shouting and crying in their decision for Christ. All outward evidence will indicate these people got saved. However, when affliction, persecution or tribulation occurs due to their interest expressed in the Word, these return to their former sinful lifestyle, revealing they had not been saved. John declares, "They went out from us, but they were not of us; for if they had been of us, they would no doubt have continued with us: but they went out, that they might be made manifest that they were not all of us" (I John 2:19). Their experience was superficial. The seed, though received intellectually and emotionally, never penetrated the soil of their soul. Soul winners must be alert to this type of hearts, granting time for additional contact before pressing for a decision.

The third class of respondents of which Jesus speaks is that of *the unrepentant heart* (v. 22). These respondents to the gospel seed receive it, but not with genuine sincerity. Their hearts are yet preoccupied with thorns, cares and love for the sinful pleasures of this world. These thorns choke out

---

[17] Torrey, *Anecdotes*, 156–157.

the gospel seed before it can germinate. This certainly was the case with the rich young ruler who desired to be saved, and to whom Jesus witnessed; but upon hearing of the cost involved in following Jesus, he walked away sorrowfully, "for he was very rich" (Luke 18:23). The message of repentance must be sounded by the soul winner if genuine fruit is to be harvested (Acts 20:21; Matthew 6:24).

To this point in the parable of the sower, the soul winner has struck out three times in his effort to win a soul—but he's still at bat. Looking at the fourth type of respondent to the sowing of the gospel seed, one sees *the ready heart* (v. 23). This heart has been plowed, broken up, fertilized and is prepared to receive the gospel message with understanding. Matthew Henry stated that this hearer deeply ponders what he hears and chews on it until he understands it sufficiently to be saved. "Intelligent hearers—they hear the word and understand it. They understand not only the sense and meaning of the word, but their own concern in it. They understand it as a man of business understands his business. God in His Word deals with men as men, in a rational way, and gains possession of the will and affections by opening the understanding."[18] Soul winner, be encouraged with this home run. Don't allow what appears to be a strikeout to stop you from going and sowing.

8   Throwing Stones at Birds

Years ago in Kentucky resided two families, one of which had the only radio for miles. This family heard that a tornado was heading straight for their neighbor's house, so the father sent his son Merle to give warning.

Merle darted out the door to do just that, but a bird landed on a limb, and he stopped to throw a stone at it. He missed. He then started running to fulfill his mission again, when the bird flew back to another limb close to him. This time his rock was right on target, and the bird fell to the ground.

As he picked up the bloody bird, he heard a rushing sound coming from the direction of the Renfro family's home in the valley—the family he was to warn. He looked toward it just in time to see their four bodies thrust to death. He rushed back to tell his father what had happened.

In the midst of the story, his father noticed blood on his hands and asked him what that was. Merle told him it was the blood of the bird he killed. His father replied, "No, son, that's not the blood of the bird you killed. It is the blood of the Renfro family you failed to warn."[19]

---

[18] Henry, *Commentary*, Matthew 13:18.

[19] Smith, Bailey, *Real Evangelism*, 163–164.

Most believers are guilty of throwing stones at birds while people all around them die and go to Hell. And their hands are wringing wet with their blood! Look at your hands. Do you see the blood of a friend, an acquaintance, a stranger or a family member dripping from them? God states that one day believers will be held accountable for those to whom they had the chance to witness but didn't (Ezekiel 33:7–9). That is unalterable. A Christian can, however, determine that no one else's blood will be required at his hand.

Are you guilty of throwing stones at birds while people perish? Though well intentioned, as Merle was, are you ever distracted from actually making face-to-face presentations of the Gospel? Satan doesn't care how well intentioned believers are to witness to a doomed soul, as long as they never quite get around to it.

God sees through the empty excuses of Christians for not soul winning, as Merle's dad saw through his excuse for not obeying. He has clearly commanded the saved to warn the entire world of impending divine judgment upon sin and to realize man's only way of escape is through Jesus Christ (Matthew 28:18–20).

C. H. Spurgeon was asked, "Do you believe the heathen who never heard the Gospel are really lost?"

Spurgeon replied, "Do you believe the ones who have heard the Gospel and never shared it are really saved?"[20]

9   Confronting and Conquering Fear

Do you fear that in sharing the Gospel someone will catch you ill prepared? Is it that you feel inadequate to tell others of Christ? This fear paralyzes soul-winning efforts. The solution to this fear is learning how to effectively share the Gospel. Take time to work at learning how to be a master soul winner like Jesus was.

Thomas Edison worked hard on inventing the phonograph. He had grave difficulty in perfecting the sound. He said, "I would speak into the machine the word 'specia,' and the hateful thing would answer back 'pecia.' I worked on that difficulty eighteen hours a day for seven months, until finally I conquered it."[21]

If Edison valued the invention of such a machine that much, how much more should believers value the winning of souls? Christians should be

---

[20] Smith, Jack, *Motivational Sermons*, 36.

[21] Leavell, *Winning Others,* 25.

willing to go without sleep, if need be, to practice, study, practice, study how to win souls until they perfect the right "sound."[22] The knowing how of soul winning produces a confidence that destroys the fear of fumbling the ball.

Do not be afraid to tell the Good News. When I was a high school athletic trainer, the coach surprised me when he informed me I would be dressing out for the homecoming football game. As I hit the field, I was obviously fearful that I would foul up; but after the first play, that fear vanished.

Similarly, the Lord has told every believer to dress out for soul winning, and for most of us that creates nervousness and fear. Rest assured, Trembling Heart, that once you knock on that first door and talk to that first person about Christ, fear will dissipate; and the more you "stay on the field," the less fear will surface.

The Lord has promised to be with your every step and immerse each soul-winning contact with the power of His Holy Spirit (Acts 1:8). In Matthew 28:20, He promised, "Lo, I am with you alway, even unto the end of the world."

"What a promise! If you obey Jesus' 'go,' you can claim His 'lo.' Now we know Jesus is with us always. But here He is making a special promise that when we go, when we witness, when we seek to win people to faith in the Lord Jesus, in a special way He's with us—always, all the days of our life."[23]

Don't allow fear to keep you on the sideline. Jeremiah feared he could not do God's work due to his timidity, but he did. Moses feared his lack of ability to deliver the Israelites out of captivity, but he did it anyway. You may fear dressing out and making that first contact, but this is possible by the Lord's grace. Many fears are only conquered through confrontation; they cannot be overcome simply by reading a book or receiving classroom instruction.

On *The Mark Gallagher Show* for October 19, 2004, Mark Twain was cited as saying, "I know a man who grabbed a cat by the tail and learned forty percent more about cats then the man who didn't." Experience certainly is one of the soul winner's greatest teachers and one of fear's greatest conquerors.

---

[22] Dobbins, *Winning Witness*, 84.

[23] Draper, *Preaching with Passion*, 494.

10   Seeking Souls or Sleeping on the Job

Feel the passion for souls in a prayer by Horatius Bonar and be stirred to win souls: "Lord, let that mind be in us that was in Thee! Give us tears to weep; for, Lord, our hearts are hard toward our fellows. We can see thousands perish around us and our sleep never be disturbed, no vision of their awful doom ever scaring us, no cry from their lost souls ever turning our peace into bitterness. Our families, our schools, our congregations, not to speak of our cities at large, our land, our world might well send us daily to our knees; for the loss of even one soul is terrible beyond conception. Eye has not seen, nor ear heard, nor has entered the heart of man, what a soul in Hell must suffer forever. Lord, give us bowels of mercies! What a mystery! The soul and eternity of one man depends upon the voice of another!"[24]

Meditate upon these words of C. H. Spurgeon's sermon, "What Have I Done?": "Are there not many Christians now present who cannot recollect that they have been the means of the salvation of one soul during this year? Come, now; turn back. Have you any reason to believe that directly or indirectly you have been made the means this year of the salvation of a soul? I will go further. There are some of you who are old Christians, and I will ask you this question: Have you any reason to believe that ever since you were converted, you have ever been the means of the salvation of a soul?

"It was reckoned in the East, in the time of the Patriarchs, to be a disgrace to a woman that she had no children; but what disgrace it is to a Christian to have no spiritual children—to have none born unto God through his instrumentality! And yet, there are some of you here that have been spiritually barren and have never brought one convert to Christ; you have not one star in your crown in Heaven. Come, Christian, what have you done?"[25] What have you done with regard to Jesus' lofty command to be a 'fisher of men?' What do you plan to do with it today?

11   No Oil in the Lantern

A railroad employee had the responsibility of warning automobile drivers of approaching trains by waving a lantern at the railroad crossing. One night a train collided with a vehicle, and lives were lost. This employee was taken to court, accused of gross neglect in not giving a warning. The prosecutor at the trial asked if he waved a lantern at the crossing, and he testified that he did. Upon his acquittal, he yet was distraught. His attorney, believing he was just feeling bad for what had happened, tried to calm him

---

[24] Bonar, *Winners of Souls*, 23–24.

[25] Spurgeon, *Sermons Vol. 4*, 265.

by asking, "You were at the crossing in time to warn of the coming train correctly?"

He answered, "Yes, I was."

"You waved your lantern at the crossing, did you not?"

He again replied, "Yes, I did."

"Then what is troubling you."

The man answered, "It is true that I was at the crossing and that I was waving my lantern, but my lantern was not lit."

Soul winners must be certain that there is oil in their lantern—biblical truth about how one is saved—as they seek to warn the lost, or else their effort is meaningless and eternally futile. O Christian, wave the Gospel Lantern constantly and keep "ringing the bell," warning the lost of their impending doom and need of Jesus Christ.

12   Unfit to Win Souls

Ralph Connors wrote of two rival university football teams in Canada. On one of those teams was a player by the name of Cameron. He was agile, strong and quick on the field. His team was assured victory merely by his playing in that big game. However, the night before the game, he broke training rules and got drunk. The next day, instead of being the help of his team, he was their hurt, and they lost. That game went down in the annals of that school's record books as a game they had every right to win, but they lost because Cameron was unfit.

Concerning your opportunities to win a soul to Christ, how often is it written in God's record books that you failed because of being spiritually "unfit"?

It has been said that God can use a tall vessel and a small vessel, a weak vessel and a strong vessel, but He cannot use and will not use a dirty vessel. Dr. L. R. Scarborough, past president of Southwestern Baptist Seminary, said, "'Holiness unto the Lord' must be on the skirts of God's spiritual priesthood today."[26]

Speaking of John Hyde ("Praying Hyde," who won four souls a day to Christ for a period of his life), E. G. Carre declared, "His power as a soul winner was due to his Christlikeness....without holiness, no man shall be a great soul winner."[27]

---

[26] Scarborough, *With Christ,* 19.

[27] Carre, *Praying Hyde,* 58.

Scripture commands, "Be ye clean, that bear the vessels of the LORD" (Isaiah 52:11). You and I who have been entrusted with the eternal treasure of salvation that the entire world needs must stay clean morally and mentally. Nothing will sap one's desire to witness like sin. Nothing will rob us of power in witnessing like sin. Nothing will cause fruitlessness in soul winning effort like sin. Murray Downey underlines this point, stating that in soul winning, it is more important to be clean than to be clever.[28]

The psalmist asked a question of the soul winner: "Who shall ascend into the hill of the LORD? or who shall stand in His holy place?" Then he answers it for him: "He that hath clean hands, and a pure heart." (Psalm 24:3–4).

Paul exhorts the soul winner: "Wherefore come out from among them, and be ye separate, saith the Lord, and touch not the unclean thing; and I will receive you" (II Corinthians 6:17).

John reminds the soul winner: "Love not the world, neither the things that are in the world" (I John 2:15).

The writer of Hebrews exhorts the soul winner: "Let us lay aside every weight, and the sin which doth so easily beset us" (Hebrews 12:1).

Paul reminds the soul winner that his "body is the temple of the Holy Ghost" (I Corinthians 6:19).

Indulgence in sin, the condoning of sin in one's life, kills one's influence with the lost and quenches the Holy Spirit's power from flowing through the life. If the saved are to impact lost friends and others for Christ, it is imperative that, though they be *in* the world, they never become *like* the world. Soul winners must stay pure and clean before the Lord, ever determining to be a Romans 12:1–2 Christian.

D. L. Moody said, "Despite all of our faults, weaknesses and inabilities, there really is NO LIMIT to what God can do with us, if we will simply turn our lives completely over to Him and be willing to let Him make us what HE wants us to be!"[29]

A continual prayer of the soul winner is, "Search me, O God, and know my heart…And see if there be any wicked way in me" (Psalm 139:23–24).

---

[28] Downey, *Art of Soulwinning*, 17.

[29] Berg, "There Is No Limit," accessed May 21, 2010.

13   Power of Prayer

John Piper said, "The aroma of God will not linger on a person who does not linger in the presence of God."[30]

The London pastor C. H. Spurgeon said, "The longer I live, the more sure do I become that our happiness in life, our comfort in trouble, and our strength for service all depend upon our living near to God—nay, dwelling in God, as the lilies in the water....I would rather spend an hour in the presence of the Lord than a century in prosperity without Him."[31]

Prayer and soul winning are intricately linked. Prayer spurs soul winning. Prayer supports soul winning. Prayer strengthens soul winning. Prayer sustains the soul winner. The apostle Paul knew what it was to pray for the unsaved. He declared, "Brethren, my heart's desire and prayer to God for Israel is, that they might be saved" (Romans 10:1). The soul winner must be a man of earnest, passionate and consistent prayer.

"A little bedridden boy I knew," D. L. Moody writes, "kept mourning that he couldn't work for Jesus. The minister told him to pray, and pray he did; and the persons he prayed for one by one felt the load of their sins and professed Christ. When he heard that such a one had not given in, he just turned his face to the wall and prayed harder.

"Well, he died, [and] by his little memorandum it was found that he had prayed for fifty-six persons daily by name, and before he was buried, all of them had given their hearts to Jesus. Tell me that little boy won't shine in the kingdom of God! These little ones can be used by God."[32]

God said, "Ask of me, and I shall give thee the heathen for thine inheritance" (Psalm 2:8). The winning of souls, according to this verse, is linked to prayer. James stated, "Ye have not, because ye ask not" (James 4:2).

As a soul winner, claim souls upon your knees before you passionately plead with them. Prepare a prayer list of names of the unsaved and faithfully pray for their conversion. This prayer list may be entitled "My Ten Most Wanted," providing a space beside each name for the date of entry, a scriptural promise to claim, dates of personal contact, and date of conversion. A second option is to write the initials of the lost (one per day) in a monthly calendar as a reminder to pray for them. It's time to break out

---

[30] Fabarez, *Preaching That Changes Lives*, 72.

[31] Hayden, *Unforgettable Spurgeon*, 212.

[32] Rost, *Evangelical Teaching*, Chapter Seven: Part Three.

the pencil and notepad or calendar and scribble down names of the lost for which you will now pray regularly.

14   Statue Saints

The German philosopher and poet Heinrich Heine, in a time of distress, stood before the statue of Venus of Milo and cried, "Ah, yes! I suppose you would help me if you could, but you can't. Your lips are still, and your heart is cold."[33]

I wonder how many hurting, lonely, troubled, doubting and discouraged people look to Christians and say the exact same thing. Sadly, many believers are unable to help them because they lack the compassion required. All too often believers' lips are still, and their hearts are cold. Southey said, "No man was ever yet deeply convinced of any momentous truth without feeling in himself the power as well as the desire of communicating it."[34]

If you and I are earnestly convinced of man's desperate need of God, it will be manifested in both our desire and our power to reach him. E. J. Daniels wrote, "A passion for souls must possess us, overwhelm us, burden us, break us, or we will never be great soul winners. This possessing passion is, in my opinion, the greatest need of every evangelist, pastor, teacher, church member and soul winner. The lack of it explains our lack of prayer and personal effort to win souls."[35]

Oh, for a passion for souls like that of Paul, who declared, "Brethren, my heart's desire and prayer to God for Israel is, that they might be saved" (Romans 10:1)! Again, feel Paul's burden for the unsaved when he declared, "I say the truth in Christ, I lie not, my conscience also bearing me witness in the Holy Ghost, that I have great heaviness and continual sorrow in my heart. For I could wish that myself were accursed from Christ for my brethren, my kinsmen according to the flesh" (Romans 9:1–3).

Oh, that the soul winner might know the passion of a Jeremiah who wished his head were waters and his eyes a fountain of tears so he could weep for Israel's restoration (Jeremiah 9:1)!

---

[33] Harrison, *How to Win Souls*, 23.

[34] Ibid., 14.

[35] Daniels, *Dim Lights,* 23.

Oh, for a burden for souls like that of George Whitefield, who said to the people of his day, "I am willing to go to prison or death, but I am not willing to go to Heaven without you"![36]

Oh, may a passion for souls well up within the soul winner like that of William Burns, who stated, "The thud of Christless feet on the road to Hell is breaking my heart"![37]

May a passion for souls possess the soul winner like that of C. H. Spurgeon, who said, "My main business is the saving of souls. This one thing I do."[38]

With John Wesley, may those who seek souls for the Savior declare, "I desire to have both Heaven and Hell ever in my eye."[39]

Hear the heartbeat for souls that possessed D. L. Moody when he declared "The monument I want after I am dead is a monument with two legs going around the world—a saved sinner telling about the salvation of Jesus Christ."[40]

William Booth, founder of the Salvation Army, was once commended by the King of England for his good work. Booth wrote in the King's autograph album, "Your Majesty, some men's ambition is art; some men's ambition is fame; some men's ambition is gold. My ambition is the souls of men."[41]

Oh, Christian, is that your ambition? Oh, that one would say of us what John Wesley's biographer said of him—that he was "out of breath pursuing souls"![42]

---

[36] Lee, "Is Hell a Myth?" accessed June 19, 2010.

[37] Ravenhill, "Billy Nicholson," accessed May 21, 2010.

[38] Zenor, "Spurgeon Gold," accessed July12, 2010.

[39] Unknown Author, "Two Judgments," accessed April 9, 2010.

[40] Moody D. L., "Inspiring Quotes," accessed March 1, 2010.

[41] Atkinson, "William Booth," accessed April 14, 2011.

[42] Unknown Author, "Burning Heart," accessed May 31, 2010.

15   Believe His Power to Save

"Without faith it is impossible to please [the Lord]" (Hebrews 11:6). In soul winning, the saint must exhibit faith, believing the Lord to honor and bless his efforts.

L. R. Scarborough declared that faith "puts iron in the blood and steels the soul for battle. It made a Moses laugh at the Pharaohs, at the barriers of sea and desert. For a Joshua, it bridged swollen Jordans and demolished Jerichos and held back setting suns that victory might crown his day while fighting God's battles. It takes the rage out of the lions' dens and makes them a safe place for a Daniel and takes the destroying elements out of fire when the Hebrew children stood true to their God. It makes heroes like John the Baptist, Paul, Luther, Knox and thousands of others. With it, weaklings are conquerors; and without it, giants are pygmies. It is a divine necessity to all who would win for God."[43]

The Gospel is the power of God to all that believe. In soul winning, you are sharing that power. Donald S. Whitney stated, "Sharing the Gospel is like walking around in a thunderstorm and handing out lightning rods. You don't know when the lightning is going to strike or whom it will strike, but you know what it's going to strike—the lightning rod of the Gospel. When it does, that person's lightning rod is going to be charged with the power of God, and he or she is going to believe."[44]

16   Work of the Holy Spirit

A person with a third grade education can be just as powerful a soul winner as a seminary professor. Why? It is because the power in witnessing is not in man's intellectual ability or technique or even experience, but in the indwelling power of the Holy Spirit in him. "This is the word of the LORD unto Zerubbabel, saying, Not by might, nor by power, but by my spirit, saith the LORD of hosts" (Zechariah 4:6).

Jesus declared, "It is the Spirit that quickeneth; the flesh profiteth nothing" (John 6:63). The degree to which the soul winner is empty of self and filled with the Holy Spirit will be the measure of success he will experience in witnessing. R. A. Torrey declared, "The Holy Spirit is given to the individual believer for the definite purpose of witnessing for Christ."[45]

---

[43] Scarborough, *With Christ*, 22–23.

[44] Whitney, *Spiritual Disciplines*, 102.

[45] Hutson, *Preaching on Soul Winning*, 64.

Scripture states, "But ye shall receive power, after that the Holy Ghost is come upon you: and ye shall be witnesses unto me both in Jerusalem, and in all Judæa, and in Samaria, and unto the uttermost part of the earth" (Acts 1:8).

It is of the Holy Spirit that Jesus declared, "Nevertheless I tell you the truth; it is expedient for you that I go away: for if I go not away, the Comforter will not come unto you; but if I depart, I will send him unto you. And when he is come, he will reprove the world of sin, and of righteousness, and of judgment: Of sin, because they believe not on me; Of righteousness, because I go to my Father, and ye see me no more; Of judgment, because the prince of this world is judged. I have yet many things to say unto you, but ye cannot bear them now. Howbeit when he, the Spirit of truth, is come, he will guide you into all truth: for he shall not speak of himself; but whatsoever he shall hear, that shall he speak: and he will shew you things to come. He shall glorify me: for he shall receive of mine, and shall shew it unto you" (John 16:7–14).

In this passage, Jesus states that the Holy Spirit is the believer's Paraclete, one called alongside of believers to help and plead their cause. The soul winner who is filled with the Holy Spirit never witnesses alone, because He is ever "alongside" pleading His case. It is the Holy Spirit who through the soul winner 'convicts of sin'; that is, "presents or exposes facts to convince of the truth."

"The mighty working of the Holy Spirit is necessary to convince and convict people of their desperate plight."[46]

Samuel Hopkins said, "If all the angels and saints in Heaven and all the godly on earth should join their wills and endeavors and unitedly exert all their powers to regenerate one sinner, they could not effect it; yea, they could do nothing toward it. It is an effect infinitely beyond the reach of finite wisdom and power."[47]

David Brainerd understood the soul winner's utter dependence upon the Holy Spirit, for he wrote in his journal, "I was exceeding sensible of the impossibility of doing anything for the poor heathen without special assistance from above, and my soul seemed to rest on God and leave it to Him to do as He pleased in that which I saw was His own cause."[48]

---

[46] Walvoord and Zuck, *Bible Knowledge Commentary, Vol. 2*, 378.

[47] Pink, *Holy Spirit*, 48–49.

[48] Edwards, *Life of David Brainerd*, 111.

W. A. Criswell declared, "Without the presence of the Spirit, there is no conviction, no regeneration, no sanctification, no cleansing, no acceptable works....Life is in the quickening Spirit."[49]

Dick Anthony wrote:

No power of my own; I have no power of my own.
I confess to you, Holy Spirit, I have no power of my own.
So I claim the promise of God's Word,
And I yield myself to Your control.
For I need your holy filling;
Yes, I want your holy filling.
I expect your holy filling,
For I have no power of my own.

17   Cultivation of the Soil

Paul instructed Timothy that the farmer who labors in the field will be a partaker of its fruits (II Timothy 2:6). Farming is extremely hard and tiring work. Just ask any farmer. He will testify that long before a harvest, there must be the painstaking task of breaking up and preparing the soil, the sowing of the precious seed, the removal of obstacles to crop growth such as various insects, times of disappointment and setback and constant cultivation of the field through tilling and watering. Paul's point to Timothy is that soul winners are to work like farmers in the field of the world, diligently preparing the soil of man's heart for the sowing of the "precious seed" (Psalm 126:5–6).

In Amsterdam '83, Billy Graham stated that witnessing was like a chain with several links, all of which must be connected before true conversion occurs. Link A soul winners share an initial introduction to the Christian faith to those who are completely ignorant. Link B soul winners connect to what the soul winners in Link A shared and lead the person a little closer to salvation. Link C soul winners then connect to what Link B soul winners shared and hopefully are able to draw the person into the net of salvation. Soul winners (Links A and B) in this witnessing scenario simply are cultivating the soul for a harvest by Link C soul winners.

Granted, this is not always the case in soul winning, because sometimes a person is saved through Link A or Link B soul winners, but in most cases some measure of cultivation of the lost must be engaged in to bring them to Christ. Take heart in knowing that regardless of the link role assigned by the Holy Spirit, it is an indispensable necessity in bringing a soul to Christ.

---

[49] Sproul, *New Genesis*, accessed May 21, 2010.

SPURS TO SOUL WINNING

18   Stand or Run

A holy boldness infused by the Holy Spirit must consume the soul winner. The soul winner must be courageous enough to witness to king or pauper, rich or poor, educated or illiterate, black or white regardless of cost or consequence.

He who would win souls must possess boldness like that of John the Baptist, who fearlessly spoke the truth to King Herod about his adultery; like that of Paul, who, after being stoned and left for dead for witnessing in Lystra, returned to that city declaring the Gospel; like that of Martin Luther at the Council of Worms, who, when asked to recant his stand on the Word of God, replied, "Here I stand; I can do none other"; like that of Polycarp, who declared as he was about to be burned at the stake for his faith, "Eighty and six years have I served Him, and He never did me any injury. How then can I blaspheme my King and my Savior?"[50] and like that of John Huss, who, before being burned at the stake for his stand for Christ, said, "In Thee, O Lord, do I put my trust; let me never be ashamed."[51]

May we stand shoulder to shoulder with Paul and look the world in the face and say, "I am not ashamed of the gospel of Christ: for it is the power of God unto salvation to every one that believeth; to the Jew first, and also to the Greek" (Romans 1:16).

It is said that John Knox feared no face except the face of God. May that be so with every believer.

19   Every Christian's Job

I recall a fellow student from my college days stating that the only soul winning one was to do was that prompted by the Holy Spirit. Such an attitude is theologically flawed and opens the door to feeling guiltless about inactivity in soul winning. The Scripture clearly commands the believer to win souls (Acts 1:8; Matthew 28:18–20) as much as it does for him to pray, to be faithful to the church, and to live a holy life. The believer does not have to feel led by the Spirit to read his Bible or pray, and neither does he have to feel led by the Spirit to talk to people about Christ. It should be automatic.

Don't misunderstand me. It is in a general sense every Christian's job to win souls. No amount of praying or waiting on the leadership of the Spirit can alter this. However, there will certainly be specific times when the Holy

---

[50] Wiersbe and Perry, *Wycliffe Handbook,* 214.

[51] Unknown Author, "I Peter 1:7," accessed May 21, 2010.

Spirit will lead the believer to talk to a person at a particular time and place, such as with Phillip and the Ethiopian Eunuch (Acts 8). These specific and definite soul winning encounters are "divine appointments" which God clearly orchestrates.

"Fortunately, no Christian," states William Evans, "however insignificant he may feel himself to be or however limited his talents are, is shut out from the opportunity of soul winning. Inasmuch as God holds all Christians responsible for this work, it must be possible for all to do it.

"Aquila and Priscilla (Acts 18:26–28) are good illustrations of the opportunities that are afforded every individual Christian. Philip (Acts 8) and Paul (Acts 20:31) show us how preachers may engage in this work. Second Kings 5:1–5 tells of a housemaid doing this kind of work. It is said that Lord Shaftesbury was led to Christ through one of his housemaids.

"John 1 gives a picture of a teacher leading his pupil (v. 29); a brother, his brother (vs. 40, 41); and a friend, his friend (vs. 43–45) to Christ as the Saviour of the world. Second Timothy 1:5 and 3:15 afford us a splendid example for parents to lead their children to Christ."[52]

C. H. Spurgeon said, "What did Paul mean by saying that he desired to save some? What is it to be saved? Paul meant by that nothing less than that some should be born again; for no man is saved until he is made a new creature in Christ Jesus. There must be a new nature implanted in us by the power of the Holy Ghost, or we cannot be saved. We must be as much new creations as if we had never been....The great Teacher's words are, "Except a man be born again (from above), he cannot see the kingdom of God." This, then, Paul meant, that men must be new creatures in Christ Jesus, that we may never rest till we see such a change wrought upon them. This must be the object of our teaching and of our praying, indeed, the object of our lives, that 'some' may be regenerated."[53]

Every Christian should be a personal worker for Christ, just as every sinner is a worker for Satan. No one is excluded from this great work. "No one escapes the general call to missions. No one can say, 'Witness is not for me.' The critical question is not whether we're called, for we are. The critical question is 'Where am I called to?' The answer may be to serve Jesus right where we are already, among those we live with and work beside. That is a wholly legitimate calling."[54]

---

[52] Evans, "Instructions," accessed May 22, 2010.

[53] Spurgeon, *Soul Winner*, 243.

[54] Brown, "Call of God," accessed June 28, 2010.

20   Ability with Availability

A skeptic had argued with and won out over every preacher for miles around his town. In this town was a blacksmith who loved souls. One night God laid the infidel upon the heart of the blacksmith so heavily he could not sleep for thinking and praying for him.

That night as he was wrestling with God in prayer for this man's soul, he begged God to send someone who had the wisdom and power to win over his arguments to witness to him and lead him to Christ. It was then the Lord spoke to him saying, "You go—go now at the midnight hour."

He tried to plead with God to send someone more gifted in soul winning, because he felt he was no match for a man who talked down the ministers. The call of God was relentless, saying, "Get up and go see the man and tell him about My love for him."

At three o'clock in the morning, the blacksmith finally went to this man's house, awakening him out of sleep. When the skeptic asked the blacksmith his purpose for coming, he responded, "God has so disturbed me about your lost soul that I just had to get up and come over and beg you to be saved."

This so shocked the infidel that he forgot all about his arguments and was noticeably moved as the blacksmith shared Scripture. At the invitation of the blacksmith to kneel with him to be saved, he fell to his knees and cried out to God for salvation. What the trained preachers could not do, the unlearned blacksmith did with his love and passion for this man.[55]

Oh, soul winner, doubt not that God will use you to win souls as He did this blacksmith, regardless of knowledge or experience. A soul winner who has ability with availability will win souls, but one who has ability without availability never will. Though you lack ability as great as you count others to have, stay available, and God will use you to win souls.

21   Show Them the Door

Helen Smith Shoemaker wrote, "People are lost and need to be found. They search for God, ultimate reality and faith, but they cannot by themselves find 'the most important door in the world,' which is 'the door through which people walk when they find God.'"[56]

Poetically, Samuel Moor Shoemaker, Jr., describes this truth,

---

[55] Daniels, *Dim Lights,* 100–101.

[56] Hunter, *Reach Secular People*, 53–54.

So many…crave to know where the door is,
And all that so many ever find
Is only the wall where a door ought to be.
They creep along the wall like blind men
With outstretched, groping hands,
Feeling for a door, knowing there must be a door;
Yet, they never find it.…
Men die outside that door, as starving beggars die
On cold nights in cruel cities in the dead of winter—
Die for want of what is within their grasp.
They live on the other side of it—because they have found it."[57]

It is the believer's duty to show the lost how to find the door. How? My father often took me fishing when I was a child. He was a master at it, and, as a novice, I earnestly looked to him for direction as to how to catch fish. He would tell me when to use crickets, earthworms, or catawbas on my hook, and which kind of fishing pole or rod to use. I learned that the type of bait and pole used is all-important in catching fish.

As fishers of men, there is only one bait to be used, and that is "Jesus Christ, and Him crucified" (I Corinthians 2:2). No other bait can attract, convict, and then convert the sinner. This is why our "fishing" must be always Christocentric. Jesus said, "If I be lifted up from the earth, [I] will draw all men unto me" (John 12:32).

A fishing and tackle shop posted a card that read, "Flies with which to catch fish in this locality."[58] In fishing, various types bait are necessary for different regions to catch fish—but not so in fishing for men. The gospel bait is effective, regardless of the locale. It need not and must not be altered.

There can be and should be many different rods or poles (methods) the soul winner uses on which to place the bait. The choice of fishing pole used is determined by the fishpond in which one is fishing (campus, community, prison, mission field), the type of fish one is trying to catch (students, adults, children), and one's ability to use it to catch fish (a rod and reel in the hands of my father could be used to catch large bass, but in my hands nothing but grass).

One fishing tackle supplier boasts of its ability to access 252 different types of rods alone. They state, "Carp and pike fishing demands fishing powerful rods." There are likewise many different types of spiritual fishing

---

[57] Shoemaker, "Stay Near the Door," accessed June 1, 2010.

[58] Jowett, *Passion for Souls,* 68.

poles available, but "heart and soul fishing demands fishing powerful rods." Exercise spiritual discretion in their selection and use.

22   An Infidel Unwittingly Instructs the Saint

Robert Dale Owen, a noted infidel, said, "Were I a religionist, did I truly, firmly, consistently believe, as millions say they do, that the knowledge and the practice of religion in this life influences destiny in another, religion should be to me everything. I would cast aside earthly enjoyments as dross, earthly cares as follies, and earthly thoughts and feelings as less than vanity.

"Religion would be my first waking thought and my last image when sleep sank me in unconsciousness. I would labor in her cause alone. I would not labor for the meat that perisheth, nor for treasures on earth, but only for a crown of glory in heavenly regions where treasures and happiness are alike beyond the reach of time and chance. I would take thought for the morrow of eternity alone. I would esteem one soul gained for Heaven worth a life of suffering.

"There should be neither worldly prudence nor calculating circumspection in my engrossing zeal. Earthly consequences should never stay my hand nor seal my lips. I would speak to the imagination, awaken the feelings, stir up the passions, arouse the fancy. Earth, its joys and its grief, should occupy no moment of my thoughts; for these are but the affairs of a portion of eternity—so small that no language can express its comparatively infinite littleness.

"I would strive to look but on eternity and on the immortal souls around me, soon to be everlastingly miserable or everlastingly happy. I would deem all who thought only of this world, merely seeking to increase temporal happiness and laboring to obtain temporal goods—I would deem all such pure madmen. I would go forth to the world and preach to it, in season and out of season; and my text should be: 'What shall it profit a man, if he shall gain the whole world, and lose his own soul.'"[59]

This infidel unknowingly has revealed the heart of Christ for lost man and His desire for His disciples.

23   "We Cannot Keep Quiet"

"We cannot keep quiet. We must speak about what we have seen and heard" (Acts 4:20 NCV). The very etymology of the word *witness* tells of the cost its practice requires. It is derived from the Greek word *martus,*

---

[59] Sanders, *Divine Art*, 13–14.

from which we get the word "martyr." Soul winning is costly business. He that gives himself to the task of bringing others to Christ can expect suffering, persecution, hardship, and even death. There have been 69,421,230 martyrs from A.D. 33 to the year 2000.[60] Granted, not all of these martyrs were killed for soul winning, but all were killed for professing their faith with relentless courage.

Every day in our world, Christians are being persecuted for their faith and endeavors to bring others to the saving knowledge of Jesus Christ. Soul winners must take the witness stand of the world, declaring the Truth, the whole Truth, and nothing but the Truth, so help them God, without thought to personal comfort, possessions, inconvenience, financial cost, slight, personal loss of life itself. The soul winner must count his life as "dung" that he may win the approval of Christ (Philippians 3:8). Jesus said, "If any man come to me, and hate not his father, and mother, and wife, and children, and brethren, and sisters, yea, and his own life also, he cannot be my disciple" (Luke 14:26). C. H. Spurgeon said, "Are you not willing to pass through every ordeal if by any means you may save some? If this is not your spirit, you had better keep to your farm and your merchandise, for no one will ever win a soul who is not prepared to suffer everything within the realm of possibility for a soul's sake."[61]

John MacArthur wrote, "Many of us will never taste the kind of persecution that the apostles or the brothers overseas have known. But the willingness to endure sacrifice for the sake of Christ should never be far from our thinking."[62]

Rachel Scott, Columbine martyr, wrote in her journal, "I have no more personal friends at school. But you know what? I am not going to apologize for speaking the name of Jesus. I am not going to justify my faith to them, and I am not going to hide the light that God has put into me. If I have to sacrifice everything, I will. I will take it. If my friends have to become my enemies for me to be with my best Friend, Jesus, then that's fine with me."[63] Rachel paid the cost for sharing her faith. Every believer must.

---

[60] DC Talk, *Jesus Freaks*, 352.

[61] Spurgeon, *Soul Winner*, 180.

[62] MacArthur, *Follow Me*, 72.

[63] Comfort, *Evidence Bible*, 799.

24   No Other Plan to Save the World

There is an old story about Jesus' return to Heaven. He meets the angel Gabriel and tells him of His work on earth and about the price He paid to purchase man's salvation through His death, burial, and resurrection. Now seated at the right hand of the Father, Jesus tells Gabriel He is interceding for those who receive Him as Lord and Savior. In conclusion, He tells this angel of His desire for all men to hear the message of what He had done. Gabriel asks, "And what is Your plan for getting this done?"

Our Lord replies, "I have left the message in the hands of a dozen or so men. I am trusting them to spread it everywhere."

Gabriel, somewhat surprised, asks, "Twelve men! What if they fail?"

Jesus responded, "I have no other plan."[64]

Jesus has left the work of telling the message of His redemptive work at Calvary in the hands of His saints. They are His plan for world evangelization. This task is so overwhelming that every Christian must urgently and faithfully go and tell. Soul winning is every man's ordained business. Adrian Rogers said, "There are two classes of Christians: soul winners and backsliders."[65]

C. H. Spurgeon said, "If I never won souls, I would sigh till I did. I would break my heart over them, if I could not break their hearts. Though I can understand the possibility of an earnest sower never reaping, I cannot understand the possibility of an earnest sower being content not to reap. I cannot comprehend any one of you Christian people trying to win souls and not having results and being satisfied without results."[66]

25   Did I Do My Best?

On September 8, 1860, the *Lady Elgin* en route for Chicago from Milwaukee, encountered gale-force winds in Lake Michigan. The schooner *Augusta,* sailing without lights at 2:30 A.M., rammed the *Lady Elgin.* Believing the *Lady Elgin* was not damaged, the *Augusta* sailed on to Chicago. The captain of the *Augusta* was sadly wrong in that assumption, because the *Lady Elgin* within twenty minutes broke apart and sank. At

---

[64] Coleman, *Master Plan,* 168.

[65] Rogers, "Sin of Silence," accessed June 10, 2010.

[66] Whitney, *Spiritual Disciplines,* 111.

daybreak, between 350 and 400 passengers and crew were floating in the water, holding onto anything they could.[67]

Word came to a local college about this wreck, and students hurried to the shores of Lake Michigan. Ed Spencer, a famous swimmer, stripped down to the bare essentials and tied a rope to his waist. Tossing the other end to fellow students on the shore, he swam out to the wreck. Grasping a drowning person, he would then give the sign for the students to pull him ashore. Spencer did this time and again, rescuing person after person, until he had brought ten people to shore. Exhausted, scarcely able to stand, he warmed his body by a fire others had ignited. As he looked back into the waters toward the *Lady Elgin,* he saw men and women still drowning. He said to fellow students, "Boys, I am going in again."

They replied, "No, no, Ed. It is utterly vain to try; you have used up all your strength. You could not save anybody; for you to jump into the lake again will simply mean for you to commit suicide."

"Well, boys," he cried, "they are drowning, and I will try anyhow."

As Spencer walked toward the cold waters of Lake Michigan, his friends said, "No, no Ed; no, don't try."

His reply was, "I will." This young man battled the currents and breakers, bringing person after person to the shore, until they counted fifteen. When they pulled him in to shore, he could hardly stand by the fire to warm himself due to intense fatigue. Looking back out into the waters, Ed exclaimed, "Boys, there's a man trying to save himself; boys, there's a man trying to save his wife." He then declared, "Boys, I am going to help him."

"No, no, Ed," they exclaimed. "You can't help him. Your strength is all gone."

Saying, "I will try anyway," he dove back into the waters, summoning all of his remaining strength and rescuing the man and woman. Later, Ed asked his brother, "Will, did I do my best?"

Will responded, "Why, Ed, you saved seventeen."

Ed replied, "I know it; I know it. But I was afraid I didn't do my very best. Will, do you think I did my very best."

Will said, "Ed, you saved seventeen"; to which Ed responded, "I know it, Will; I know it. But, oh, if I could have saved just one more."[68]

---

[67] Unknown, "Lady Elgin," accessed May 19, 2010.

[68] Torrey, *Anecdotes,* 166.

SPURS TO SOUL WINNING

Do you see the unsaved drowning in the ocean of eternal darkness at work, school, neighborhood, marketplace and home? Are you doing your best—your very best—to win as many as possible? As Ed did, let's not count our lives dear to us for the sake of rescuing souls. Oh, believer, keep soul winning; keep going back into the water time after time to rescue more and more, even when strength has all but been exhausted. And then, as death opens the portals of Heaven for your entrance, with weeping eyes wail, "Oh, if I could have saved just one more." May God help us to do our very best to win all we can and "save just one more" before its time to go Home!

26   Must I Go Empty-Handed?

Charles C. Luther heard Reverend A. G. Upham speak of a young man who was dying after having been a Christian for only a month. This young man was sad because he had so little time to serve the Lord. He said, "I'm not afraid to die; Jesus saves me now. But must I go empty-handed?"

This story led Luther to write the song "Must I Go and Empty-Handed" in 1877. This song serves as both a call to serious examination about and prompt commitment to the task of soul winning.

"Must I go and, empty-handed,
Thus my dear Redeemer meet?
Not one day of service give Him,
Lay no trophy at His feet?

"Must I go and empty-handed?
Must I meet my Savior so?
Not one soul with which to greet Him—
Must I empty-handed go?

"Not at death I shrink or falter,
For my Savior saves me now;
But to meet Him empty-handed,
Thought of that now clouds my brow.

"Oh, the years in sinning wasted,
Could I but recall them now,
I would give them to my Savior;
To His will I'd gladly bow.

"O ye saints, arouse; be earnest.
Up and work while yet 'tis day.
Ere the night of death o'er take thee,
Strive for souls while still you may."[69]

The only possessions you can take to Heaven are souls. Determine not to show up "empty-handed."

27   Laughing at the Clown

In England, a man was to be hung. His mother interceded on his behalf before the king, and she prevailed in getting a pardon. The page commissioned to deliver the pardon stopped to watch a clown performing and then hurried to fulfill his errand. He arrived minutes too late. While accounting to the king, he said, "I laughed with the crowd at the clown, and the time slipped away." Many Christians are laughing at the clown and enjoying life and its pleasures as time slips away and souls die without Jesus.

I have been guilty of such delay. I discerned my barber was not a Christian, so I shared Christ while in the chair, but not in a soul winner's manner. I gave her a copy of one of my books that addressed one's relationship with Christ, but put off speaking a direct evangelistic word. I falsely assumed ample time was available for cultivation and then Gospel presentation. I was so wrong, for she died at an early age unexpectedly. I will never forget the invaluable lesson I relearned from this tragic delay. "How do you know what your life will be like tomorrow? Your life is like the morning fog—it's here a little while; then it's gone" (James 4:14 NLT).

28   Spinning Our Wheels

E. J. Daniels tells the story of an oil factory which describes the problem in many churches. This factory, in its second year of operation, was visited by a man who wanted to purchase a few quarts of oil. The manager told this man, "We don't have any oil to sell."

"But," said the man, "you've been running this factory for two years now. You manufacture oil by the barrel every day, and you mean to tell me that you don't have any oil for sale."

The manager replied, "No, it takes all of the oil we make to oil the machinery to make more oil." They were getting nowhere fast!

---

[69] Luther, "Must I Go," accessed April 14, 2011.

Daniels remarks, "Sit down and analyze that, brother, and you may hang your head and say, 'God, forgive us. In our church, we're spinning our wheels making oil to oil the machine to make more oil. But we're not getting men saved.'"[70]

Are the monies, programs, personalities and staff the church is using to oil the "machinery" that was designed to win souls spent almost exclusively in upkeep and maintenance of the "machine"?

29   Reflective Mirrors

The 455 residents in the Austrian mountain village of Rattenberg suffer from a lack of sunshine in the winter, and this is responsible for the mild-to-severe depression some experience. To rectify this problem, scientists are installing thirty eight-foot mirrors in a sunnier spot across the valley. These bounce sunlight back to a rocky outcrop near Rattenberg, where a second bank of mirrors will reflect it down upon the people sitting in darkness. The mayor of this city stated, "Just across the river, we can see the sun shining in its full glory; but here in the village, during these months, we get no direct sunshine, and it takes the pleasure out of life for many people."

Markus Peskoller, a scientist at the Bartenbach Light Laboratory in Aldrans, believes the system will serve as a model for other cities. He states, "I am sure we will soon help other mountain villages see the light."[71]

The spiritual condition of the inhabitants of our world is like the physical condition of those at Rattenberg. They live in darkness without hope and peace. They can see the Sun of Righteousness (Malachi 4:2) shining "in full glory just across the river" but need help in receiving it for themselves. It is every Christian's task to be a reflective mirror of Jesus Christ, the Light of the World, relaying His "true light" unto the ends of the earth.

Scientists state it will take only thirty mirrors to accomplish the Rattenberg project. To accomplish the Acts 1:8 mission, *every* Christian is needed. "Ye shall be witnesses unto me." Clean the dirt and dust of sin off your mirror through repentance unto God, and start reflecting His love to lost people.

Can you imagine the bright "Sonshine" that would be in evidence across our dark world if the millions who profess Christ began mirroring His

---

[70] Daniels, *Why Jesus Wept*, 26.

[71] Stockbower, "Piping in Sunlight," accessed June 27, 2010.

message? Today we can help many "mountain villagers" (sinners) see the light.

30   Just Needed Someone to Explain It

While I was leading a revival in Augusta, Georgia, a fourteen-year-old boy was attending church for the first time in his life. In the aftermath of the service, I asked permission to talk to him about his need of salvation. Upon conclusion of my presentation, the boy looked up to me and said, "That's simple. I just needed someone to explain it to me." He then received Christ into his life. There are people all about you who would be saved if you would take the time to "explain it."

31   Others

It is said that when General William Booth lay dying, he was asked for a message to send around the world. With his dying breath, he uttered that the message should be—"Others." This one-word message summed up the life and ministry of this great soul winner.[72]

Others need our witness. Others need to be reached for Christ. Others need to hear the Gospel of the Lord Jesus Christ. Others need cleansing of sin. Others need peace with God. Others need meaning and fulfillment in life. Others must be warned about the reality of Hell. Others must be told of the hope of Heaven. It is when we shift our eyes from self to others that God can use us to win souls.

R. A. Torrey, as a Yale Seminary student, heard D. L. Moody preach. Afterward, he and others asked the renowned evangelist, "Tell us how to win people to Jesus Christ."

Moody replied, "Go at it. That's the best way to learn."[73]

32   Don't Just Talk It; Do It

There was a group of fishermen who met every week, month after month, year after year to discuss when, where and how to fish successfully. These men constructed large, beautiful buildings to serve as their fishing corporate office. They enjoyed and loved fishing so much that their goal was to have everyone become a fisherman. However, they were so consumed with writing, talking and reading about fishing, that they neglected

---

[72] Bales, *Revival Sermons*, 172.

[73] Unknown, "R. A. Torrey," accessed April 15, 2010.

to do the one essential thing—fish. How like these fishermen most Christians are!

En route to preach at a church in Manning, South Carolina, I saw a truck pulling a pontoon which had inscribed on one rear side "Go" and on the other side "Fish." The owner of the fishing boat did not simply advocate fishing but was en route to fish. The believer must be careful to do the same.

33   Follow Me and Fish for Men

Spurgeon writes, "When Christ calls us by His grace, we ought not only to remember what we are, but we ought also to *think of what He can make us*. It is, 'Follow me, and I *will make you.'* We should repent of what we have been but rejoice in what we may be. It is not, 'Follow Me, because of what you are already.' It is not, 'Follow Me, because you may make something of yourselves,' but 'Follow Me, because of what I will make you.'...O you who see in yourselves at present nothing that is desirable, come you and follow Christ for the sake of what He can make out of you. Do you not hear His sweet voice calling to you and saying, 'Follow me, and I will make you fishers of men'?[74]

"How is a person to be useful? 'Attend a training class,' says one. Quite right; but there is a surer answer than that—follow Jesus, and He will make you fishers of men. The great training school for Christian workers has Christ as its head; He is at its head not only as a tutor, but as a leader. We are not only to learn of Him in study, but to follow Him in action. '*Follow me,* and I will make you fishers of men.'...The Lord Jesus, who knew all about fishing for men, was Himself the dictator of the rule, 'Follow me, if you want to be fishers of men. If you would be useful, keep in My track.'"[75]

John Rice stated, "One of the best ways to be an evangelist is to go with an evangelist. But the very best way to be a soul winner is to follow the Master Soul Winner and get His passion, His burden for dying sinners, and be led by His Holy Spirit in winning them. No one really follows Jesus unless he becomes a soul winner. Jesus makes every true disciple, every learner, everyone who follow in His steps into a soul winner. If you, then, are not a soul winner, you are not following Jesus."[76]

---

[74] Spurgeon, *Sermons on Soul Winning*, 30–31.

[75] Ibid., 32.

[76] Hutson, *Preaching on Soul Winning*, 32.

34 The Lost Are among Us

The lost are among us. There is no locale, despite how rural, in which lost souls cannot be found. They, like the prodigal of Luke 15, are lost to God's plan, provision and pardon, because they left Him for the "far country" of worldliness. These will remain lost for all eternity unless led back "home" to the Father through a personal relationship with His Son, Jesus Christ. Who is assigned the task of telling them the way back home? It is to you and me, brother and sister in Christ, that this monumental work is commissioned. "Ye shall be witnesses unto me both in Jerusalem, and in all Judea, and in Samaria, and unto the uttermost part of the earth" (Acts 1:8).

Then why don't we do it? Is it that we really don't believe it is our task to tell others of Christ (despite plenteous biblical texts to substantiate that it is)? Is it that we really don't believe that Jesus Christ is man's only way to be reconciled with God (though Jesus Himself attested that He was)? Is it that we believe others will do it (though "others" are not do it)? Or is it that we fail to tell due to fear or just plain unconcern?

No excuse is valid for disobeying the command of our Lord to introduce others to Him. It's time to lay aside the excuses and get to the task of winning souls. The lost are among us. Look for them. Love on them. Tell them.

35 The Heartache of Heaven

Hyman J. Appelman stated, "The passion of the soul winner is twofold: a burning passion of love for the blessed Redeemer; a burdening compassion of longing for the souls of men. Jesus kept sweet in our souls will strengthen us in sorrows, sustain us in toil, supply us with the peace of God which passeth all understanding. Our passion for Christ will generate within us a compassion for the souls of men. The two are inseparable. They ever go together.

"Dry-eyed, dry-hearted, dry-tongued preaching, praying and personal work will never win souls for Christ. Someone has well said, 'It takes a broken heart to preach a bleeding Cross.' Cry unto God, beloved. Cry unto God for the gift of passion, the gift of tears. Compassion for souls must be developed, or our work will become matter-of-fact and mechanical. A passionless Christian is a bitter anomaly. A passionless Christian is the heartache of Heaven. A passionless Christian is the laughingstock of Hell."[77]

---

[77] Appelman, *Savior's Invitation,* 35–42.

31

36   No Man Cared for My Soul

"Some years ago, in Jacksonville, Florida, a policeman served for twenty years as a traffic officer. His business was to keep traffic in that great city moving by directing and signaling the many tourists and travelers who passed his street intersection constantly. During these twenty years, he was asked all sorts of questions about all sorts of matters by thousands who passed that way. He was asked the direction and mileage to thousands of places, his opinion about hundreds of questions, about his own personal health, the welfare of his personal family, and a multitude of other things.

"One day, after the policeman had spent twenty years directing traffic and being quizzed by thousands of people, one man came and asked if he was a Christian. This question, asked concerning his soul's welfare by one who cared, made him think. As he thought, his soul was aroused and moved toward God. He confessed his Lord, followed him in baptism and was a faithful and loyal deacon in the great Main Street Baptist Church of that city.

"Yes! The last question one is ever asked is that about his soul. No wonder David cried out in his distress, 'No man cared for my soul.'"[78]

The circumstances may be different from those of the policeman, but by whom have you passed for months or years regularly without referencing their need of Christ due to unconcern or a false assumption that others already have done so? Who will stand before Christ at the Judgment Bar saying that you did not care for their souls?

37   He'd Point toward Heaven; He'd Point to
His Heart and Their Hearts

Dr. Jerry Vines shares the following story. "There was a little deaf boy named Bud Walker who did not have the opportunity to have interpreters and all of these things that our deaf people have today. And so he reached his teen years and was not a Christian. They had tried every means possible to get the Gospel across to him, but without interpreters, they were unable to do so. Somehow, the Holy Spirit of God was eventually able to break through. God touched his heart early in the week in a revival meeting. And so Bud Walker came walking down the aisle and bowed upon his knees. They prayed around him, and in a little while, the Lord Jesus came into his heart.

"Bud was so thrilled that Jesus was in his heart, but he couldn't articulate it. He began to point to his heart and point toward Heaven. He'd

---

[78] Bales, *Revival Sermons*, 57.

then point to Heaven and point to his heart. He smiled, and they knew that Jesus had come into his heart.

"But that's not the end of the story. Throughout the rest of that week, Bud Walker was used of God to win more people to Christ in that revival than any other person in the building. And here's what he would do. During the invitation, Bud Walker, who could not talk, would walk to people in the congregation who knew and loved him; he'd put his arms around them and press them for just a little bit. He'd point his hand toward Heaven, he'd point toward his heart, he'd point toward the person's heart, and then he'd point toward the aisle. There they'd go down the aisle, receiving Jesus. One after one, he'd deal with people in this manner.

"I read that story, and I thought to myself, *Lord, here I am with a good voice; here I am with a mind that's able to think; here I am with a body that is healthy. O God, help me to engage in the ministry of admonition to the lost. Help me get into the hearts of lost people and take the love of Jesus which is in my heart and put it into their hearts.*"[79]

38 A Pep Rally for a Game Never Played

During the time of forced consolidation of high schools, the students of a small East Texas school joined the student body of a larger one. This was to the sorrow of the cheerleaders of the smaller school. They were prepared to cheer their football team to victory. These young ladies sought out the principal of the new school and pleaded their case. He felt for them and authorized a pep rally every week just for those who came from that student body. In these rallies, they would shout cheers something like, "All the way to state boys; all the way to state," and "Hold that line, boys; hold that line!"[80]

The students would be worked up into a frenzy of excitement. The irony of the whole matter, though, was that these cheerleaders were having pep rallies for a game that never would be played. Not once would one of those players from the smaller school ever dress out for a game. Never would any one of those players take the ball over the goal line to score a touchdown.

I fear oftentimes that books and studies on witnessing are like those pep rallies—pep rallies for a game we never get around to playing. It's high time every believer dressed out for the game, heeded the instruction of the

---

[79] Vines, "How to Recognize," accessed April 14, 2011.

[80] Smith, Bailey, *Real Evangelism*, 49.

Coach, utilized teamwork, and hit the field with resolved determination to carry the "ball" across the goal line, winning souls to Christ.

D. L. Moody had posted on the exit doors of his church in Chicago the words, "You are now entering the mission field of the world; go soul winning." May each believer post such words over the doors of his home, car and business as a reminder to actually "play in the game." It is so easy to get used to boys and girls dying and going to Hell that such reminders are imperative. Unless we are intentional about witnessing, it never will happen.

39   Just Do It for Love's Sake

In a time when every second nearly three souls die without Christ and plunge into Hell, believers must be compelled to open their mouths wide and passionately to persistently and boldly declare the Gospel to the lost. In a day when 187 million souls are lost in America, it takes 47 Southern Baptists to add one member to the church annually. More then 10,000 Southern Baptist churches failed to baptize a single convert in 2009.

Every Christian must care enough to share. The time for timidity is over. The time for passive evangelism is gone. You and I must be aggressive, for not only is obedience to God at stake, but the temporal and eternal state of friends, classmates, neighbors and family members as well. One day they will breathe their last and eternity will greet them. What if that happened today?

Oh, may we so live today as if this day was their last chance to be saved. It boils down to how much we love Jesus, doesn't it? Do you really love Jesus? Are you willing to forgo the big game, skip class, miss work or a meal to redeem perhaps a once-in-a-lifetime opportunity to speak to a person about Christ?

It may be awkward; you may stumble with your words. That's all right. Just do it for love's sake. Love covers a multitude of the soul winner's mistakes. Risk showing and sharing God's love to someone today, everyday. God is counting on you. Heaven is counting on you. Friends and families are counting on you. Souls are counting on you. For love's sake, do it.

40   Sin of Silence

Failure to witness is, first, a sin against the *Savior*. In Matthew 28:18–20, Jesus commands the believer to witness and win the unsaved. In Acts 1:8, the summons again is trumpeted loud and clear. He that Jesus saves, He subpoenas to take the witness stand of the world and tell the truth about who He is and what He has done to provide for man's salvation. He that

Jesus converts, He consigns the task to win souls. And he that Jesus regenerates, He expects to reproduce. There is nothing that we can do to make up for not obeying Christ in this matter—no sacrifice, service, stewardship or study is sufficient. The sin of not witnessing is a sin against the heart of Jesus.

Failure to witness is a sin against the *Scripture.* Not to win souls is to rebel against the Bible. Throughout the pages of the inerrant and infallible Word of God, the believer is told to tell of Jesus to others. Mark 16:15 says, "Go ye into all the world and preach the gospel to every creature." Jude tells us, "And others save with fear pulling them out of the fire" (v. 23). In Revelation, we read, "And the Spirit and bride say come. And let him who heareth say come" (22:17). Peter exhorted, "But you are a chosen generation, a royal priesthood, a holy nation, His own special people, that you may proclaim the praises of Him who called you out of darkness into His marvelous light" (I Peter 5:9 NKJV). In his sermon entitled "Get Real," Alvin Reid makes this shocking observation: "More people are amazed at our silence than offended at our witness."

Failure to witness is a sin against the *Sinner.* It is a sin against the value of the sinner's soul and the desperate need of his heart. How valuable is a soul? Jesus stated the soul is more valuable than the entire world (Matthew 16:26). D. L. Moody said, "I believe that if an angel were to wing his way from earth up to Heaven and were to say that there was one poor ragged boy, without father or mother, with no one to care for him and teach him the way of life, and if God were to ask who among them was willing to come down to this earth and live here for fifty years and lead that one to Jesus Christ, every angel in Heaven would volunteer to go. Even Gabriel, who stands in the presence of the Almighty, would say, 'Let me leave my high and lofty position, and let me have the luxury of leading one soul to Jesus Christ.' There is no greater honor than to be the instrument in God's hands of leading one person out of the kingdom of Satan into the glorious light of Heaven."[81]

"'Oh!' says one, 'I am not my brother's keeper.' No? I will tell you your name; it is Cain. You are your brother's murderer, for every professing Christian who is not his brother's keeper is his brother's killer. And be you sure that it is so, for you may kill by neglect quite as surely as you kill by the bow or by the dagger."[82]

---

[81] Bright, *Steps to Maturity*, 342.

[82] Allen, *Exploring the Mind*, 454.

Failure to witness is a sin against the *Saved*. The believer who neglects to witness hinders the progress of his church, for such disobedience grieves the Holy Spirit, hindering His power from being fully manifest. The believer's disobedience also promotes complacency about soul winning in the lives of fellow saints.

Failure to witness is a sin against *Society*. The only cure for the moral and social ills of society is Jesus Christ. The saints' neglect of soul winning allows the world to become bleaker and darker morally and spiritually. Robert Louis Stevenson told about his fascination as a child with the gas lamp lighter. He stated that as the lamplighter lit the lamps in his community, he would rush to his mother, exclaiming, "Come see a man who is punching holes in darkness." The born again of God must punch holes in spiritual darkness one person at a time; and, in doing so, he will bring His Light into society's deep darkness.

Failure to witness is a sin against one's own *Soul*. Failure to be a soul winner hurts the saint personally. It stagnates his soul, steals his power, stunts his growth, softens his burden and stains his hands with the blood of those he refused to tell of Jesus.

Refuse to commit these six horrible sins by failing to witness. Determine by God's grace to be a consistent soul winner.

41   The Cheap Violin

The story is told about a master violinist who publicized that in an upcoming concert he would use an unusually expensive violin. People packed into the hall on that designated day to hear the great violinist play that expensive violin. The crowd applauded the violinist for a most excellent performance.

He then startled everyone when he took the violin and threw it upon the floor, stamping it to pieces, and walked off the stage. A few moments later, the stage manager said to the crowd, "Ladies and gentlemen, the violin that was just destroyed was only a twenty-dollar violin. The maestro will now return to play on the advertised instrument." He did so, and few could discern any difference between the two musical instruments.

It's not the violin, but primarily the violinist that makes the music. Most of us are twenty-dollar violins or less, but the Master can use us to sound forth beautiful music, touching many lives for His Glory and Honor.[83]

Don't discount your usefulness and potential as a soul winner, for in the hands of God, you become a mighty tool for winning others.

---

[83] MacArthur, *Follow Me*, 101–102.

42   The Human Thumb Mark

Andrew Bonar declared that there will not be a redeemed soul in Heaven who has not a human thumb mark upon it. He is biblically correct in making that assertion. Frankly put, if you and I fail to tell, men and women will die and go to Hell.

Charles G. Trumbull states, "It may be a small matter for you to speak the one word for Christ that wins a needy soul—*a small matter to you,* but it is *everything to him.*"[84]

"Some of the greatest trophies that have been won for Jesus Christ have not been reached by planned evangelism, but by casual conversation with a keen Christian. When in the course of life's daily contacts we use opportunities to speak a word for our Master, we can never tell what the consequences may be. It is expected of the preacher in the pulpit that he will plead with souls to accept Christ. But when a housewife speaks to the milkman of his need of salvation, when a passenger shows interest in the spiritual welfare of the taxi driver, or when the store clerk asks her fellow employee to go to church with her, that is unexpected—and the result may be unexpected, too....and what could make Heaven more heavenly than to find people there who trusted the Savior because of something we said?"[85]

43   Yes I Can; Yes I Can

Oswald Chambers stated, "When it is a question of God's almighty Spirit, never say, 'I can't.'"[86]

Believers can certainly say, "I can do all things through Christ which strengtheneth me" (Philippians 4:13)—even confront the lost with the Gospel. "For with God nothing shall be impossible" (Luke 1:37).

John MacArthur exhorted, "Start looking beyond the minutiae to the Eternal Christ who can take even your weak faith and use you for His kingdom purposes."[87]

Chambers also remarked, "If Jesus ever commanded us to do something that He was unable to equip us to accomplish, He would be a liar. And if we make our own inability a stumbling block or an excuse not to be obedient, it

---

[84] Trumbull, *Herald of His Coming*, 4.

[85] Ackland, *Joy in Church Membership*, 125–126.

[86] Chambers, *My Utmost,* April 20 entry.

[87] MacArthur, *Follow Me*, 42.

means that we are telling God that there is something that He has not taken into account. Every element of our self-reliance must be put to death by the power of God. The moment we recognize our complete weakness and our dependence upon Him will be the very moment that the Spirit of God will exhibit His power."[88]

God will enable and empower you to be a successful witness.

44 Spiritually Barren

C. H. Spurgeon wrote, "Oh, that every one of you might 'save some.' Yes, my venerable brethren, you are not too old for service. Yes, my young friends, ye young men and maidens, ye are not too young to be recruits in the King's service.

"If the kingdom is ever to come to our Lord, and come it will, it never will come through a few ministers, missionaries or evangelists preaching the Gospel. It must come through every one of you preaching it—in the shop and by the fireside, when walking abroad and when sitting in the chamber. You must all of you be always endeavoring to 'save some.'

"How many others have you brought to Christ? You cannot do it by yourself, I know; but I mean how many has the Spirit of God brought by you? How many, did I say? Is it quite certain that you have led any to Jesus? Can you not recollect one? I pity you, then! Your children are not saved, your wife is not saved, and you are spiritually childless. Can you bear this thought? I pray you, wake from your slumbering and ask the Master to make you useful."[89]

45 Throw Out a Longer Rope

A father and son were fishing when the son fell into the water and began to drown. Struggling for life, he cried to his father, "Throw me a rope." The father hurriedly cut the rope attached to the anchor of the boat and threw it to his son. However, it was too short.

The son cried, "Dad, the rope is too short. Throw me a longer rope." The dad frantically but unsuccessfully looked for another rope. The last words this father heard from his son were, "Dad, the rope is too short; throw me a longer rope."

---

[88] Chambers, *My Utmost*, May 5 entry.

[89] Spurgeon, *Evangelism*, 198–199.

In a day in which ten thousand Southern Baptist churches failed to win and baptize one soul in an entire year, and in which it takes 47 Southern Baptists an entire year working together to win and baptize one soul, and when 92 percent of Southern Baptists will die without witnessing to another person,[90] God is truly crying out to evangelists, pastors, missionaries, student ministers, music leaders, teachers, children and youth workers, and layman at large to throw out a longer rope in soul winning.

Sadly, most believers must confess that they either have failed to throw out the rope of soul winning or have done so with passionless inconsistency. It's time that Christians "lengthen thy cords, and strengthen thy stakes" (Isaiah 54:2), rescuing as many souls from the plight of eternal darkness and dam-nation as possible. Today, throw out a longer rope by increasing the number of gospel tracts distributed, personal contacts made, time spent in soul-winning prayer, cultivation of the unsaved, and direct personal soul-winning encounters.

46   Not Willing One Should Perish

I don't know of a more exacting song that depicts the Christian duty regarding the lost than *O Zion, Haste,* written by Mary A. Thompson in major part during the grave illness of her son in 1868. This hymn pulsates with the urgent and compelling need to tell the unreached people of the world "of the Savior's dying, or of the life He died for them to win." Why? "He who made all nations is not willing one soul should perish, lost in shades of night."

Ponder that statement: "Not willing one soul should perish." Sound familiar? Peter uttered the same (II Peter 3:9). God is not willing for *anyone* to perish—not your spouse, not your child, not your parent, not your sibling, not your friend, not the elite, not the poor, not the Hitlers or the Mansons—not anyone.

O Zion, haste, thy mission high fulfilling,
To tell to all the world that God is light,
That He who made all nations is not willing
One soul should perish, lost in shades of night.

Publish glad tidings, tidings of peace,
Tidings of Jesus, redemption and release.

---

[90] Sjorgren, Ping, and Pollock, *Irresistible Evangelism*, 38.

Behold how many thousands still are lying
Bound in the darksome prison house of sin,
With none to tell them of the Savior's dying,
Or of the life He died for them to win.

Proclaim to every people, tongue, and nation
That God, in Whom they live and move, is love;
Tell how He stooped to save His lost creation
And died on earth that we might live above.

'Tis thine to save from peril of perdition
The souls for whom the Lord His life laid down;
Beware lest, slothful to fulfill thy mission,
Thou lose one jewel that should deck His crown.

Give of thy sons to bear the message glorious;
Give of thy wealth to speed them on their way;
Pour out thy soul for them in prayer victorious.
O Zion, haste to bring the brighter day.

He comes again! O Zion, ere thou meet Him,
Make known to every heart His saving grace.
Let none whom he Hath ransomed fail to greet Him,
Through thy neglect, unfit to see His face.[91]

47   Mission of the Church

The mission of the church can be summed up in four words (Matthew 28:18–20).

The Mission of the Church is *Introduction:* "Go ye therefore." The business of the church is to tell the lost of Christ, locally and globally, without discrimination as to race or status or lifestyle. This assignment is not only for the ministerial staff, but every member. The challenge of every pastor is to get his people to open their mouths and speak of Jesus to the unsaved. If we fail here, we utterly fail.

The Mission of the Church is *Invitation:* "Make disciples" (NIV). Coupled with introduction must be invitation. It's not enough to tell man of Christ and his need of salvation. A way must be opened in the pulpit and in personal witnessing for man to respond to Christ's offer of salvation. We must call for a "verdict."

---

[91] Thompson, "O Zion, Haste," accessed April 14, 2011.

The Mission of the Church is *Induction:* "Baptizing them in the name of the Father and of the Son and of the Holy Spirit" (NIV). Not only are we to introduce man to Christ and then invite Him to be saved, but we are to induct him into the church through baptism once he believes.

The Mission of the Church is *Instruction:* "Teaching them to observe all things." What are we to teach them? "Whatsoever I have commanded you." That covers the whole Bible. We are to teach them the doctrines of the faith. We are to teach them what it means to love Jesus with all the heart, soul, mind and strength. We are to teach them absolute surrender to the will of God. We are to teach them absolute obedience to the Word of God. We are to teach them how to be soul winners.

L. R. Scarborough wrote, "The evangelism that stops at conversion and public profession is lopsided, wasteful, incomplete. It should go on to teach, to train and to develop and utilize the talents and powers of the new convert. This educational phase of evangelism is transcendently important." He continued, "Modern evangelism finds here its greatest leakage and waste."[92]

Albert Simpson composed the hymn *The Regions Beyond* (1904) that resounds with the mission of the church and of every believer.

> To the regions beyond I must go, I must go,
> Where the story has never been told;
> To the millions that never have heard of His love,
> I must tell the sweet story of old.

> *To the regions beyond I must go, I must go,*
> *Till the world, all the world,*
> *His salvation shall know.*

> To the hardest of places He calls me to go,
> Never thinking of comfort or ease;
> The world may pronounce me a dreamer, a fool—
> Enough, if the Master I please.

> Oh, you that are spending your leisure and powers
> In those pleasures so foolish and fond,
> Awake from your selfishness, folly and sin,
> And go to the regions beyond.

---

[92] Scarborough, *With Christ,* 107–108.

There are other "lost sheep" that the Master must bring,
And to them must the message be told;
He sends me to gather them out of all lands
And welcome them back to His fold.

48   Lost, Lost, Lost

Jesus testified that He came "to seek and to save that which was lost" (Luke 19:10). *Lost*—do you understand its meaning? Do you comprehend the problem and peril of the lost?

L. R. Scarborough, in describing man's lostness, underscores the urgency in soul winning: "There is no way of understanding that Scripture (Luke 15:11–24), unless you say that God is there trying to tell and describe the spiritual condition before God of every unsaved man. He said the boy was 'dead.' There is no evidence in that parable that the boy had been actually dead and buried. He is talking about the condition of his soul. He said he was 'lost' and is found. There is no evidence in the parable that the boy was lost from human habitation. The fact is that he had too much company of the bad sort. He is describing the spiritual condition of his son.

The word I want to talk to you about tonight, descriptive of the spiritual condition of every man and woman who has not trusted Jesus Christ as his Savior, is that little word 'lost'—L-O-S-T—'Lost.'…It means separation from God. It means eternal dwelling in the land of eternal punishment. It means the opposite of Heaven. It means the extreme opposite of righteousness. It means Hell. It means no peace. It means no happiness, no joy. It means separation from the good and companionship with evil. It means all there is that is wrapped up in darkness into which no sun shines. It means the starless night of eternity. It means sunless day forever and ever. It means all there is in the punishment of sin, in the wrath of God, in the indignation of a wrathful sovereign. Lost! Lost! Lost!"[93]

And Jesus said His sole purpose for leaving Heaven and coming to earth was "to seek and to save that which was lost." If that is His supreme passion, what ought yours to be as His disciple?

General William Booth commented that he would like to send all his candidates for officership to Hell for twenty-four hours as part of their training. "Why? Because it is not until we have a vital conviction of the irrevocable doom of the impenitent that our belief will crystallize into action."[94]

---

[93] Scarborough, "Lost!" 1.

[94] Sanders, *Art of Soul Winning*, 15

49   His Work Lives On

D. L. Moody stated, "If we only lead one soul to Jesus Christ, we may set a stream in motion that will flow on when we are dead and gone....So if you turn one to Christ, that one may turn a hundred; they may turn a thousand, and so the stream, small at first, goes on broadening and deepening as it rolls toward eternity. In the book of Revelation, we read: 'I heard a voice from heaven saying unto me, Write, Blessed are the dead which die in the Lord from henceforth: Yea, saith the Spirit, that they may rest from their labours; and their works do follow them.' There is one thing you cannot bury with a good man; his influence still lives."[95]

C. H. Spurgeon was buried, but his influence lives on. W. A. Criswell and Adrian Rogers were buried, but that has not silenced their ministries and witnesses. D. L. Moody and Billy Sunday have long since been buried, but their labor for souls yet continues. Daniel spoke a certain truth in declaring, "They that be wise shall shine as the brightness of the firmament; and they that turn many to righteousness as the stars for ever and ever" (Daniel 12:3). Hear Moody again: "Let us go on turning as many as we can to righteousness. Let us be dead to the world, to its lies, its pleasures and its ambitions. Let us live for God, continually going forth to win souls for Him."[96]

Death soon will be your lot. Determine that death to the flesh will not mean cessation of your influence for the winning of the lost.

50   Intentionality

Be intentional in winning souls to Christ. William Borden was a young millionaire who graduated from Yale University in 1909. He determined to witness to his entire class before graduation. He would go to the rooms of his unsaved classmates, study with them, talk with them, wrestle with them, and then pray with them. One by one, he did this until all were saved.[97] He knew what it was, not only to have a passion for souls, but to have a goal to win souls.

At the death of a young man who had unusual power to win souls, a small box was opened, which contained among his treasures a list of the names of forty boys. This young man had prayed for each one of these forty

---

[95] Hutson, *Preaching on Soul Winning*, 235.

[96] Ibid., 235.

[97] Leavell, *Winning Others*, 81.

boys regularly, gave them books to read, showed them Scripture texts until the Lord awakened them spiritually; and the whole forty had been converted to Christ.[98] John Hyde (Praying Hyde) determined to lead no less than four souls to Christ daily. Each of these men was intentional about sharing Christ. Are you?

51   Getting the Passion

How can one obtain the flame for souls? Charles G. Finney advises the seeker of this soul passion to "look, as it were, through a telescope into Hell and hear their groans; then turn the glass upward and look into Heaven and see the saints there in their white robes and hear them sing the song of redeeming love; and ask yourself: 'Is it possible that I should prevail with God to elevate the sinner there?' Do this, and if you are not a wicked man, you will soon have as much of the spirit of prayer as your body can sustain."[99]

Wilbur Chapman suggests: "Take your New Testament and go quietly alone and read a sentence like this: 'He that believeth not is condemned already.' Then sit and think about it for ten minutes. Put your boy over against it—your girl, your wife, your husband, yourself. Then take this: 'He that hath not the Son of God, hath not life, but the wrath of God abideth on him.' I know that a soul thus burdened generally gains its desire."[100]

John Stott states, "What impels the Christian to be active in witness? The basic motive is plain obedience. Every Christian is a servant of Christ. He has been 'bought with a price' and is now attached to his master by the bonds of a grateful obedience. The love of Christ controls us. It has us in its grip. Indeed, since our new life is due entirely to Christ's death, His love hems us in and leaves us no choice but to live for Him (II Corinthians 5:14–15). In seeking to live for Christ, we are concerned to do His will and keep His commandments—all of them. We are not at liberty to pick and choose. Nor do we wish to. So we do not overlook His last commandment—to 'go...and make disciples.'"[101]

---

[98] Andross, "Prevailing Prayer," accessed May 19, 2010.

[99] Sanders, *Art of Soul Winning*, 22.

[100] Ibid., 22.

[101] Stott, *Guilty Silence*, 14.

John R. Rice wrote, "Our fathers were accustomed to pray, 'Lord, roll on us the weight of immortal souls.' Again and again I have heard that heartfelt petition as men besought God to give them a Heaven-born concern for the salvation of sinners. That prayer I heard often in my childhood, and I make it my own again today."[102]

The Holy Spirit creates spiritual interest for the lost in the believer. We cannot create it; we can only discover it.

52   Winnie the Pooh and Eeyore

"And of some have compassion, making a difference: And others save with fear, pulling them out of the fire; hating even the garment spotted by the flesh."—Jude 22–23.

Winnie the Pooh had a donkey friend named Eeyore. Playing too close to the water's edge, Eeyore fell in and began to drown. Unable to get to the bank, he began to float downstream on his back, anticipating this ride would be his last. He knew that the river ended in a waterfall. As Eeyore floated underneath a bridge, he saw Winnie standing upon it, and a conversation was engaged.

Winnie said to Eeyore, "Seems like you've got yourself in a spot of trouble."

"Yes," Eeyore replied.

Winnie then said, "And it looks like you are going to drown."

Eeyore again answered sadly, "Yes." Then, with a pleading cry, Eeyore said to Winnie the Pooh, "If it wouldn't be too much bother, would you mind rescuing me?"[103]

All around us are friends, family members and classmates who are floating downstream—not toward a waterfall, but toward eternal destruction in Hell—in need of rescue. They are inapt to rescue themselves. You and I stand on the bridge like Winnie the Pooh and hear their cry, "If it wouldn't be too much bother, would you mind rescuing me?"

53   Divine Appointment

R. A. Torrey wrote, "One evening when Mr. Alexander and I were in Brighton, England, one of the workers went from the afternoon meeting to a restaurant for his evening meal. His attention was drawn toward the man

---

[102] Rice, *Soul Winner's Fire*, 11.

[103] Orr, "Will You Rescue Me?", accessed April 4, 2011.

who waited upon him, and there came to his heart a strong impression that he should speak to that waiter about his soul, but that seemed to him such an unusual thing to do that he kept putting it off.

When the meal was ended and the bill paid, he stepped out of the restaurant but had such a feeling that he should speak to that waiter that he decided to wait outside until the waiter came out. In a little while, the proprietor came out and asked him why he was waiting. He replied that he was waiting to speak with the man who had waited upon him at the table. The proprietor replied, "You will never speak to that man again. After waiting upon you, he went to his room and shot himself."[104]

The waiter, clerk, teacher, student, bus driver or employee you encounter today may be a "divine appointment." If you fail to recognize it as such, a soul may eternally be lost. Sometimes you will have only one time to make an impression upon a soul for Christ. Make it the best possible.

54   Delay May Mean Doom

If you fail to witness of Christ at the first opportunity, another may never arise. As I write these words, my heart smites me for the multiplied times I shamefully neglected to speak to someone of Christ. In those instances, I thought, *This is not the time to make a witness,* or *I don't have a tract with me,* or *There are too many people present,* or *He doesn't appear receptive.* Sadly, I have to attest that more often than not these opportunities never reappeared. They were lost forever.

God will hold me accountable. He will hold every believer accountable for opportunities to witness to the lost that are neglected. Ezekiel frankly states that God will require their blood at our hands (Ezekiel 3:17–18). Whatever else this statement may entail, it certainly means God will hold the Christian who fails to witness guilty of criminal neglect!

55   Two-by-Two Telling

Individual soul winning is definitely biblical. Phillip, without assistance, won the eunuch. But Scripture seems to emphasize a "two-by-two" approach, and this seems more productive. Jesus sent the seventy out two-by-two (Luke 10:1). Jesus used Peter and John to witness to the lame man at the Gate Beautiful. He used Paul and Silas to witness to the Philippian jailer in the jail, and later to his family, after he had won the demon-possessed girl on the streets of Philippi.

---

[104] Walden, *Sword Scrapbook,* 41.

G. S. Dobbins stated, "There was divine wisdom in this arrangement. We work best for Christ when we work with others. One person by himself will not ordinarily win many people to Christ."[105]

Two-by-two witnessing is profitable in regard to partner accountability. Every believer from time to time needs someone to "spur" him onward in soul winning.

It is profitable in regard to protection from slander or false accusation.

It is profitable with regard to prayer. As one shares the Gospel, the other prays for the sinner's enlightenment and conversion.

It is profitable with regard to proof. "At the mouth of two witnesses..." (Deut. 17:6).

It is profitable with regard to pattern. Two-by-two witnessing provides the opportunity of training soul winners.

Who will be your partner at the outset?

Again the "two-by-two" method does not negate the great importance of personal soul winning; it simply provides an additional plan by which you can win souls.

56   Rescuing the Captive

Jeremiah was captive in a dungeon pit (Jeremiah 38:1–13). Upon learning of the plight of this prophet, Ebed-melech took steps to rescue him. Unraveling this narrative, one discovers what it takes for a Christian to become a soul winner.

It takes *Information* (v. 7). It was not until Ebed-melech "heard that they had put Jeremiah in the dungeon" that he took immediate steps to rescue him. Christians will not make any serious soul rescue attempt until they are clearly and convincingly made aware of man's hopeless and helpless estate apart from God.

It takes *Intercession* (v. 9). Ebed-melech boldly, courageously entered the king's presence to plead for the salvation of Jeremiah. The soul winner must boldly enter into the throne room of the thrice-holy God and plead vigorously by name for the souls of the eternally damned.

It takes *Cooperation* (v. 10–11). The King authorized Ebed-melech to recruit thirty men to assist in the rescue of Jeremiah. Partnership in soul winning is advantageous.

---

[105] Dobbins, *Winning Witness*, 110.

It takes *Authentication* (v. 11). Look with me and see Ebed-melech making a rope out of "old cast clouts" and yanking on each section to make certain of its strength. The soul winner must be certain of the means which he employs to win the lost. He must from personal experience (salvation) and Scripture know that the sinner's only hope is "repentance toward God, and faith toward our Lord Jesus Christ" (Acts 20:21).

It takes *Compassion* (v. 12). "And Ebed-melech the Ethiopian said unto Jeremiah, Put now these old cast clouts and rotten rags under thine armholes under the cords." Matthew Henry makes the point that it was an act of great tenderness and compassion on Ebed-Melech's part to provide soft rags for Jeremiah to put under his armpits to prevent them from being irritated by the rope.[106] The soul winner in his rescue attempts must ever be respectful, courteous, considerate and compassionate, making it as easy as possible for the sinner to be saved.

It takes *Instruction* (v. 12). "And Ebed-melech the Ethiopian said unto Jeremiah, Put now these old cast clouts and rotten rags under thine armholes under the cords." Ebed-melech instructed Jeremiah in exactly what he needed to do to be saved. It is expedient and imperative that the soul winner know how to win a soul.

It takes *Volition* (v. 12b). Ebed-melech did not and could not force Jeremiah to do as he instructed and thus be rescued. The decision was up to Jeremiah. The soul winner can only make his best effort in seeking to win souls. Ultimately it's up to the sinner whether or not he will be saved. Jesus allowed the rich young ruler to walk away from him unsaved.

It takes *Determination* (v. 13). Ebed-melech did not rest until Jeremiah's feet were out of the miry clay and upon solid rock. It is essential that the soul winner refuse to quit in the rescue effort.

57   "Shall Your Brethren Go to War, and Shall Ye Sit Here?"

The children of Gad and Reuben preferred to remain in their comfort and safety zone at home while their "brethren" went to war. Moses called their hand on this great sin through a question. I choose to adapt this question and apply it to the battle for souls, which many saints neglect, by asking, "Shall other believers engage in the battle for souls, and shall ye sit here while they do?" (Numbers 32:6).

This question was directed specifically to the children of Gad and Reuben. It was these believers who refused to join other saints in the war, opting to stay where they were. The question of the hour is for saints who

---

[106] Henry, *Commentary*, Jeremiah 38:1–13.

are Gadites and Reubenites who neglect soul winning. It doesn't apply to those who are passionately and faithfully soul winning, leaving the place of their comfort zone by making sacrifices and taking risks.

Are you a Gadite and Reubenite, relying upon others to go to the front line for Jesus at your school or job while you stay where you are? The question is relevant because God did not exempt these two tribes from fighting in the battle for His cause and glory. Nor has God exempted any in the church from working for souls. There is no more pertinent question to ask of the Gadites and Reubenites from our churches regarding soul winning than this one. "Shall your brethren go to war, and shall ye sit here?"

This question led the Gadites and Reubenites to declare to Moses, "We will build sheepfolds here for our cattle, and cities for our little ones: But we ourselves will go ready armed before the children of Israel, until we have brought them unto their place: and our little ones shall dwell in the fenced cities because of the inhabitants of the land. We will not return unto our houses, until the children of Israel have inherited every man his inheritance. For we will not inherit with them on yonder side Jordan, or forward; because our inheritance is fallen to us on this side Jordan eastward....And the children of Gad and the children of Reuben spake unto Moses, saying, Thy servants will do as my lord commandeth" (v. 16–19, 25).

Moses' question obviously accomplished profitable results. Such a question regarding soul winning is intended to accomplish the same—the prompting of saints who have been negligent in soul winning to make commitments to join in the battle for souls. "Shall your brethren go to war, and shall ye sit here?" How shall you answer this paramount question?

58   Hand-to-Hand Work

D. L. Moody regarded his pulpit soul winning appeal only as preparatory to personal soul winning. "To him, pleading with individual souls in the inquiry room was of more importance than his appeal before the great audiences. Moody knelt by, pleaded with, prayed for, and won personally seven hundred fifty thousand people to Christ."[107]

Speaking to a group of young men, Moody commented, "Plenty of men are willing to get on a platform and preach and exhort and do that kind of work, but workers are scarce who will labor with a drunkard or deal with men one at a time."[108]

---

[107] Autrey, *You Can Win Souls*, 5.

[108] Dorsett, *Moody*, 399.

Moody, believing in the supremacy of personal soul-winning work, stated, "We must have personal work—hand-to-hand work—if we are going to have results."[109]

Billy Graham remarked, "God has a lot of preachers but few soul winners."

Lead me to some soul today;
Oh, teach me, Lord, just what to say.
Friends of mine are lost in sin
And cannot find their way.
Few there are who seem to care,
And few there are who pray.
Melt my heart and fill my life;
Give me one soul today.[110]
—Will Houghton

59   Won by Example

At the time that David Livingstone was lost in Africa, the *New York Herald* sent H. M. Stanley to find him. This he did and chose to spend several months with him prior to his return. In this time, Stanley observed Livingstone's habits, patience, sympathy and love for the natives, which he could not understand. Stanley said: "When I saw that unwearied patience, that unflagging zeal, that eager love spending itself for those unenlightened sons of Africa, I became a Christian at his side, although he never spoke to me directly about it."[111]

Russell H. Conwell stated, "The faithful and silent witnessing of John Ring saved me from a life of folly to a life of faith in Christ. He was my orderly during the Civil War. On his first night in my tent, he read the Bible and knelt and prayed. I was an agnostic and ridiculed him. Thereafter he went outside to read his Bible and pray. One day he was mortally wounded. 'Twas then I surrendered myself to Jesus Christ."[112]

---

[109] Ibid., 399.

[110] Jenkens, *Brands*, 114.

[111] Leavell, *Evangelism*, 170.

[112] Knight, *Illustrations for Today*, 326.

Lee Strobel states, "It was my agnostic wife's conversion to Christianity and the ensuing positive changes in her character that prompted me to use my legal training and journalism experience to systematically search for the real Jesus. After nearly two years of studying ancient history and archaeology, I found the evidence leading me to the unexpected verdict that Jesus is the unique Son of God who authenticated his divinity by returning from the dead."[113]

L. R. Scarborough was conducting a revival during which in one service he invited the people to thank the person(s) present who most influenced them to be a Christian. "Pupils went to their teachers. Some went to the Sunday school superintendent. A number came to the pastor. Husbands put their loving arms about their wives. Noble sons and daughters fell in the arms of their parents. Joy abounded.

"There sat to my left an aged woman, quiet, modest, wearing a sunbonnet. She had never spoken in public, never led in public prayer. She was not a teacher. She was not an officer in any departments of the church life, but a faithful, modest, consecrated mother and wife. She was more than seventy-five years of age. I noticed that a long line went to where she sat. Some took her by the hand, some softly enfolded her in their arms, all were weeping, and all were triumphant in the joys of salvation. They said, as they silently and in tears took her hand, "Your quiet, faithful, consecrated life and persistent work and testimony for Christ when I was in your home or under your influence led me to find Christ as my Savior."

That noble woman was the mother of George Truett. Not only has she blessed the world through the ministry of her children, but her own marvelous and beautiful life constantly won people to know the Savior. A responsibility rests upon every soul winner to live his or her best before a lost world."[114]

Never underestimate the power of the life to speak loudly for Christ.

60   Persistent Praying for the Lost

George Müller stated, "In November 1844, I began to pray for the conversion of five individuals. I prayed every day without a single intermission, whether sick or in health, on land or at sea, and whatever the pressure of my engagements might be.

---

[113] Strobel, *Real Jesus*, 13.

[114] Scarborough, *Search for Souls*, 45–46.

"Eighteen months elapsed before the first of the five was converted. I thanked God and prayed on for the others. Five years elapsed, and then the second was converted. I thanked God for the second and prayed on for the other three.

"Day by day I continued to pray for them, and six years passed before the third was converted. I thanked God for the three and went on praying for the other two. These two remained unconverted....

"The man (Müller referring to himself) to whom God in the riches of his grace has given tens of thousands of answers to prayer in the selfsame hour or day in which they were offered has been praying day by day for nearly thirty-six years for the conversion of these individuals, and yet they remain unconverted...But I hope in God, I pray on and look yet for the answer. They are not converted yet, but they will be."[115]

Müller lived to see four of these men converted, and the last man was saved shortly after Müller's death. God honored his trust and perseverance in prayer for them.

Courtland Meyers declared, "God's greatest agency in winning men back to himself is the prayer of other men. How few enter into the positive, practical power of prayer."[116]

> Oh, for a passionate passion for souls;
> Oh, for a pity that yearns!
> Oh, for a love that loves unto death;
> Oh, for a fire that burns!
>
> Oh, for a pure prayer power that prevails,
> That pours itself out for the lost—
> Victorious prayer, in the Conqueror's Name;
> Oh, for a Pentecost![117]

Pray for the unsaved expectantly and continuously. No man is beyond the grasp of our omnipotent God who desires for all to be saved.

---

[115] Miller, B., *George Müller,* 146.

[116] Lee, *Seven Swords*, Orlando, 53.

[117] Sanders, *Art of Soul Winning*, 10.

61   Failure to Mail the Invitations

Oscar Wilde wrote of his Aunt Jane that she died of mortification that no one attended her grand ball. She died without realizing she failed to mail the invitations.[118] We build our grand church buildings and provide the best in music and preaching and programming. And yet they do not come for failure to mail out the "invitations."

Despite the grandeur of the worship complex, exemplary worship or excelling preaching, the "invitation" must be delivered by the people to those outside, lest the church become consumed with its own and gradually die. This invitation is not merely "Welcome to our church on Sunday," but "God welcomes you to become a member in His family." Amidst the necessary preparation for church, don't fail to deliver the invitations.

62   An Unlikely Soul Winner

R. A. Torrey tells the conversion account of Fred, a young, illiterate man who then wanted to assist the evangelist Charlie Alexander in his evangelistic endeavors. Mr. Alexander, citing the man's inability to read, refused. Fred responded, "Oh, I could take care of the tent, black your boots, do anything; but I must go with you." Alexander finally agreed to allow the man to assist. He surprised everyone, for not only did he do his janitorial work of the tent, but he proved to be a great soul winner. Fred's earnestness and spiritual power were so tremendous that people overlooked his ungrammatical speech, and he succeeded in winning souls where everyone else had failed. In five years, the Lord used this young man to win 1,200 persons. Why did God so use him? It was due to his total surrender to Christ (Romans 12:1–2).[119]

God is constantly using the weak vessels of this world to win souls in order to showcase His glory and power. God says "I know thy works: behold, I have set before thee an open door, and no man can shut it: for thou hast a little strength, and hast kept my word, and hast not denied my name" (Revelation 3:8). God is mindful of your spiritual weakness and will turn it into a torrent river of strength as you but keep His Word and honor His name.

---

[118] Sweazey, *Effective Evangelism*, 22.

[119] Torrey, *Anecdotes*, 31.

"God stands in no need," D. L. Moody said, "of our strength or wisdom, but of our ignorance, of our weakness; let us but give these to Him, and He can make use of us in winning souls."[120]

63   Tell Because of Hell

Why bother to tell others of Christ and seek their salvation? One big reason is the reality of Hell. The narrative of the rich man and Lazarus told by Jesus reveals Hell's sordid nature (Luke 16:19–31).

Hell is a place of *Pain* (v. 23–24). Physical and mental torment unimaginable will be experienced in Hell. Scripture makes clear that there will be varying degrees of punishment inflicted in Hell (Matthew 10:15; 11:22, 24; Mark 6:11; Hebrews 10:29).

Charles Finney stated that if the believer had the power to heal all the sufferings of all the people in the world for all time, he would not remove as much suffering as he would in the saving of just one lost soul from Hell.[121]

C. H. Spurgeon, with great conviction, said: "Hell is not metaphorical fire. Who cares for that? If a man were to threaten to give me a metaphorical blow on the head, I should care very little about it. He would be welcome to give me as many as he pleased. There is a real fire in Hell—as truly as you now have a real body."[122]

Hell is a place of *Passion* (v. 24). Insatiable appetites and desires plague the inhabitants of Hell forever and ever.

Hell is a place of *Parting* (v. 26). The unsaved are forever separated from the redeemed.

Hell is a place of *Prayer* (v. 27). The eternally damned will come to see the need of God, but woefully too late. Hell is a domain in which men with weeping, wailing and gnashing of teeth cry out to God for salvation, but in vain.

Hell is a place of *Permeating Darkness*. Jude describes Hell as "the blackness of darkness forever" (Jude 13). Utter blackness makes relationships impossible in Hell. C. S. Lewis declared Hell is a place of "nothing

---

[120] Moody D. L., "Inspiring Quotes," accessed May 31, 2010.

[121] Whitesell, *New Testament Evangelism*, 179.

[122] Lee, *Seven Swords*, Orlando, 51–52.

but yourself for all eternity!"[123] The inhabitants of Hell know only isolation and utter loneliness; there are no friendships and no fellowship.

Hell is a place of *Permanence* (v. 26). Hell hath no exits. There is no way out of Hell, so there is no hope for its inhabitants. This is one of the worst things about Hell. It is a place where one will be absolutely without hope, for not even God can grant deliverance. One can purchase a shirt in the country store in Hell, Michigan, which states, "I've been to Hell and back"; but a person cannot purchase such a shirt in Satan's domain of eternal darkness.

In England, a man preached a sermon on the horrors of Hell and its only escape. An atheist in attendance said, "If I believed that, I would crawl on my hands and knees all over England to tell men how to be saved from Hell."[124]

I am certain that if the saints believed in Hell as the Scripture teaches, more would be about the task of winning souls. Awaken your conscience to the reality of Hell that awaits the lost by musing over sermons on the subject, studying biblical texts regarding it and asking God to enlighten your mind.

64   "Not Heard the Call"

William Booth, Salvation Army founder, said "'Not called!' did you say? 'Not heard the call,' I think you should say. Put your ear down to the Bible and hear Him bid you go and pull sinners out of the fire of sin. Put your ear down to the burdened, agonized heart of humanity and listen to its pitiful wail for help. Go stand by the gates of Hell and hear the damned entreat you to go to their father's house and bid their brothers and sisters and servants and masters not to come there. Then look Christ in the face—whose mercy you have professed to obey—and tell Him whether you will join heart and soul and body and circumstances in the march to publish His mercy to the world."[125]

65   The Soul Winner's Mightiest Weapon

Prayer is the soul winner's mightiest weapon in winning souls. Dr. J. Hudson Taylor, writing of his conversion, said: "Little did I know at that

---

[123] Little, *What You Believe*, 199.

[124] Ford, *Heaven, Hell and the Judgment*, 54.

[125] Booth, "Missions Slogans," accessed March 5, 2010.

time what was going on in the heart of my dear mother, 70 or 80 miles away. She rose from the dinner table that afternoon with an intense yearning for her boy's conversion, and feeling that a special opportunity was afforded her of pleading with God on my behalf, she went to her room and turned the key in the door, resolved not to leave that spot until her prayers were answered.

"Hour after hour that dear mother pleaded for me, until at length she could pray no longer but was constrained to praise God for that which His Spirit had taught her was already accomplished—the conversion of her only son. When our dear mother came home a fortnight later, I was the first to meet her at the door and to tell her I had such glad news to give. I can almost feel that dear mother's arms around my neck as she pressed me to her bosom and said: 'I know, my boy; I have been rejoicing for a fortnight in the glad tidings you have to tell me.'

"'Why,' I asked in surprise, 'has Amelia broken her promise? She said she would tell no one.' My dear mother assured me that it was not from any human source that she learned the tidings and went on to tell the little incident above. You will agree with me that it would be strange indeed if I were not a believer in the power of prayer."[126]

Oswald Sanders writes, "It is by believing prayer alone that the strong man can be bound and souls delivered. 'They overcame him by the blood of the Lamb, and by the word of their testimony' (Revelation 12:11). The prayer warrior must learn how to plead the victory of Calvary, for the blood of the Lamb has forever broken the power of the Devil and robbed him of his prey. Plead the blood of the Lamb for the liberation of the soul for whom you pray."[127]

S. D. Gordon states, "The enemy yields only what he must. He yields only what is taken. Therefore the ground must be taken step by step. Prayer must be definite. He yields only when he must. Therefore the prayer must be persistent. He continually renews his attacks; therefore, the ground taken must be *held* against him in the Victor's name."[128]

---

[126] Sanders, *Art of Soul Winning*, 42–43.

[127] Ibid., 40–41.

[128] Wilkerson, *Bring Your Loved Ones*, 116.

66   Changing the Message

The concept of easy-believism has a stranglehold upon the church. According to Scripture, the condition for salvation is more than mental assent that Jesus is the Savior of the world, a resolve to do better or uniting with the church by baptism. The Bible makes plain that the means of salvation is "repentance toward God, and faith toward our Lord Jesus Christ" (Acts 20:21).

Nothing short of Jesus' death, burial and resurrection can atone for (forgive) man's sin. It is when man repents of sin (expresses godly sorrow for the sin of rejecting Christ and changes his mind about the role of Christ in his life) and exhibits faith (personal trust) in Jesus Christ that he is saved. Salvation is a free gift of God available to all people that cannot be merited, earned or deserved (Ephesians 2:8–9).

In witnessing, it is imperative that knowledge be instilled regarding the message, means and must of salvation before calling for a decision. After all, how can a person choose to do something about which he knows nothing or at best very little? Frankly, I believe this is why many "decisions" are merely "still births" and not new births.

67   Flowers in Gratitude

H. C. Coleman was a successful businessman who contributed large sums of money to Hardin Simmons University. On one occasion, he asked the president of the school, Dr. Sandifer, to accompany him on a trip to California. In the midst of the trip, Mr. Coleman had his chauffeur stop at a florist shop so he could purchase some flowers. Dr. Sandifer wondered about their purpose but did not ask. Later, the chauffeur stopped the car on a hill at a cemetery. Mr. Coleman asked Dr. Sandifer to wait for him as he placed the flowers on a lonely grave. He stood there and prayed for a long time. Upon returning to the car, Dr. Sandifer inquired, "Is a member of your family buried there?"

Mr. Coleman responded, "No, an old lady by the name of Mrs. Smith lies buried there. Once she lived in Philadelphia and ran a little mission there. I was a wayward boy on the streets, and she invited me in and led me to know Jesus Christ as my Savior. I never come to California without putting some flowers on her grave in gratitude for what she did for me."[129]

Corrie ten Boom had a God-given desire to win the lost. One of her poems says,

---

[129] Ford, *Christian Life*, 65.

When I enter that beautiful city
And the saints all around me appear,
I hope that someone will tell me,
"It was you who invited me here."[130]

Who is or will be in Heaven because of you?

68   Stay the Course

Soul winning doesn't just happen. The tendency is to drift away from it, never toward it. Intentionality is imperative if one is to be a consistent soul winner. Adapt several hints with regard to staying the course in witnessing.

Fasten it. Make it a sure discipline of life, as that of prayer, Bible study or church attendance. Focus on it as a daily duty.

Fuel it. Read sermons that stir the soul regarding the sinner's temporal and eternal estate. Study sin and sinners. Meditate upon Scripture texts that speak of man's gloom and doom apart from Christ. Converse with soul winners. Pray for a passion for souls.

Facilitate it. A major credit card markets itself with the motto, "Don't leave home without it." In soul winning, don't leave home without gospel tracts and Bible in hand. Plan to witness in departure for school, work or play.

Force it. Compel yourself to overcome fear and the flesh to witness. Don't force a witness, but force the effort.

Faith it. Doubt not God's desire to save the lost (II Peter 3:9; Psalm 2:8). Rely upon His promise to enable, empower and embolden for the task (Acts 1:8). Claim the promise of Isaiah 55:11, "So shall my word be that goeth forth out of my mouth: it shall not return unto me void, but it shall accomplish that which I please, and it shall prosper in the thing whereto I sent it."

Fortify it. Solicit a believer to hold you accountable on a weekly basis.

Fix it. At the first sign of spiritual coldness toward the lost, take action to rekindle the flame.

69   Tracts Make It Easy

A friend introduced me to the Gospel Tract Ladder thirty-seven years ago. It is a simple but effective approach to sharing the Gospel with tracts.

---

[130] ten Boom, "Words of Wisdom," accessed May 19, 2010.

It begins with the elementary stage in sharing the Gospel and progresses to the most difficult. Picture a ladder with six rungs.

Rung One is *Leave a Tract*. This first step in witnessing through tracts requires no courage, for it can be done in secrecy. It simply requires the soul winner to distribute gospel tracts in places like restrooms, phone booths, bus stations, restaurant menus or magazines.

Rung Two is *Mail a Tract*. This rung demands some boldness but not a heaping amount. The soul winner simply inserts a gospel tract with payment of bills or in correspondence.

Rung Three is *Pin and Tract*. This step involves a large, bold-colored badge that the soul winner wears to prompt others to inquire of its meaning. In response to this inquiry, the soul winner responds, "Oh, it is to remind me to give you this tract that tells how much God loves you."

Rung Four is *Hand a Tract*. This rung involves simply handing a tract to someone, asking that person to read it at his or her leisure.

Rung Five is *Lend a Tract*. The soul winner using this method actually loans a tract or book to an unsaved person, asking that it be read and returned as soon as possible. This applies pressure on the unsaved person to read the material and provides an opportunity to discuss it with that person upon its return.

Rung Six is *Share a Tract*. The soul winner utilizing this rung walks up to a stranger, asking if he might give him a tract. Once the person accepts it, the soul winner proceeds to share exactly what the tract states, seeking to bring the person to a decision for Christ then and there.

Choose tracts wisely. Make sure the tracts distributed are biblically sound and are spiritual dynamite.

70   But How?

How are the saved to accomplish the monumental task of telling the entire world of the Good News of Jesus Christ? More specifically and personally, how are you to win friends, relatives and acquaintances to Jesus Christ? It is through the same Person and power through which the apostle Paul did it.

Let me first hasten to state what this power source God has made available for the work of soul winning is not. It is not intellectual power.

It is not oratory power. Men may speak with the golden tongue of a Chrysostom, causing people to be spellbound, but one's flowery vocabulary and oratory ability cannot convict or save.

It is not debating power. A man convinced against his will is unconvinced still.

It is not salesmanship power. The former Saturn automobile dealerships built their businesses on letting the Saturn car sell itself rather than depending upon salesmen. GMC believed this product was so great that once a prospect seriously considered it, he would buy one. The Christian's task is to present Christ to the unsaved in all His beauty and glory and let Him sell Himself. In reality, Christ is the Soul Winner; believers are just His agents or representatives.

It is not booklet power. Mere mental assent to words of Truth printed in a booklet fail to genuinely convict or convert the sinner.

It is not personality power.

Oswald Chambers stated, "When we say 'What a wonderful personality, what a fascinating person, and what wonderful insight!' then what opportunity does the Gospel of God have through all that? It cannot get through, because the attraction is to the messenger and not the message. If a person attracts through his personality, that becomes his appeal. If, however, he is identified with the Lord Himself, then the appeal becomes what Christ can do."[131]

What is the power source of the soul winner in his effort to win men? A man asked a friend, "Do you know what the greatest untapped source of power is in the world?" He then led him to the foot of the Niagara Falls, pointed at it and said, "There it is."

The wise friend countered, "No, the greatest untapped power in all the world is the power of the Holy Spirit."

Your source of power in witnessing is the Holy Spirit. Jesus promised that the Holy Spirit would infill the believer, enabling him in this great task. "But ye shall receive power, after that the Holy Ghost is come upon you" (Acts 1:8). The word translated power in this text is *dunamis*, from which comes the English word "dynamite." It expressed the greatest power known to the people of Jesus' day. The Holy Spirit is God's "dynamite" for the Christian in witnessing. It is He who convicts of sin, judgment and right-eousness, tears down satanic strongholds, opens blinded eyes, liberates the captive in Satan's prison camp and saves the soul.

The reason why so few believers are soul winning powerfully is the lack of Holy Spirit control. The infilling of the Holy Spirit is a prerequisite to soul winning (Ephesians 5:18; Acts 1:8).

E. J. Daniels said, "When we are willing to be done with our sins, to give up, to clean up, to let Almighty God take over, we can have God's power. Perhaps you have heard the true story about D. L. Moody. One day

---

[131] Chambers. *My Utmost*, November 9 entry.

after a great sermon he had delivered, someone came up to him and said, 'Mr. Moody, I'd give the world if I had your power.'

"To this Moody replied, 'Friend, that is just what it cost me. I had to surrender the world to have power.'

"The reason millions of church members have no power with God and men is that they are holding on to many sins—or at least questionable things—of the world. You must surrender these things if you want to be filled with the Holy Spirit."[132]

D. L. Moody well stated, "It would be foolish to try to do the work of God without the power of God."[133]

71   Not All Will Be Saved

A woman was stranded by an open window on the top floor of a burning building. A fireman climbed a ladder to that window and, with arms outstretched, sought to make the rescue. The woman, out of fear or panic, retreated back into the building and perished. Upon his return to the ground, the fireman, with tears in his eyes, could only say, "I tried to save her, but she wouldn't let me. I tried to save her, but she wouldn't let me."

The soul winner will make many rescue attempts to save people from a life wrapped up in self, sin and the world. Sadly, he will not always be successful and will lament repeatedly, "I tried to save her, but she wouldn't let me. I tried to save him, but he wouldn't let me."

Make the rescue attempt speedily, thoroughly and compassionately, but refuse to let Satan browbeat you over those who choose to remain as they are. Ultimately, it is the sinner's decision to live or die spiritually. Sorrow over those who refuse to be rescued from the captivity of Satan, but never allow such rejection to discourage you from continuing in soul winning. Keep in mind that Jesus did not win all He encountered.

72   Don't Cower Down

Persecution will be the occasional lot for the soul winner. Jesus said, "Blessed are ye, when men shall *[not might]* revile you, and persecute you, and shall say all manner of evil against you falsely, for my sake" (Matthew 5:11). In persecution for the Faith, you stand shoulder to shoulder with the disciples, patriarchs, prophets and church of ancient days, even until today.

---

[132]   Daniels, *Dim Lights*, 80.

[133]   Rice, *Grand Success*, 193.

Seventeen Christians die daily for their faith, while thousands suffer imprisonment.

In the early 1900s, Chinese rebels sought to expel from their land the Christian witness. One attack of the rebels was on a missionary training school that housed youth preparing for ministry. The rebels blockaded all but one exit from the school. In front of that exit, a cross was laid. The students were informed that if they would trample the cross beneath their feet, no harm would come to them; but if not, it would mean immediate death.

The first seven students to exit walked upon the cross to their free-dom. However, the eighth student, a teenage girl, knelt at the cross and then walked around it, where a firing squad took her life. The following ninety-two students followed her bold example. They walked to the cross, knelt to pray and then walked around it to their death. Oh, the strength of the ninety-two that was infused by the courage of that one girl.[134]

Expect and prepare for persecution due to standing boldly for Christ. Resolve to stand firm in the Faith, refusing to be silenced in the face of suffering, and in so doing, infuse strength and boldness into the lives of weaker believers to do the same.

73   Value of One Soul

Contemplate the value of just one soul. R. G. Lee stated, "One may be many. Andrew brought Simon—just one. But that one won many; for under God, Simon brought 3,000 in one day. Jack Stratton, a waiter in a restaurant, brought John Gough to Christ—just one. And Gough brought many to Christ. Ezra Kimball, a Sunday school teacher, brought Moody to Christ—just one. But that one won many, for Moody reached two continents for God. But why say more? Just as one digit is valuable in the multiplication table, and one letter in the alphabet, far more valuable is just one soul in God's sight."[135]

A young college evangelist brought George W. Truett to Christ—just one. But that one became a powerful voice of God in the church and across the land in crusades winning multitudes.[136]

---

[134] Tan. *7700 Illustrations*, #3343.

[135] Knight, *Master Book*, 644.

[136] Bales, *Revival Sermons*, 168–169.

And J. D. Prevatte, counselor in the Mordecai Ham crusade in Charlotte, North Carolina, in 1934, brought Billy Graham to Christ—just one. But that one has won millions to Christ.[137]

A shoe cobbler brought C. H. Spurgeon to Christ on a snowy day in London—just one. But that one has impacted more preachers and Christians with regard to preaching and soul winning than any other. A Salvation Army worker witnessed to Billy Sunday on the streets in Chicago—just one. But that one was responsible for thousands of converts to Christ.

D. L. Moody said, "If you win only one soul to Christ, you may set a stream in motion that will flow long after you are dead and gone."[138]

When you win someone to Jesus Christ, you have no idea of the domino effect it will set in motion.

74   How Do You Spell "Go"?

Jesus instructs the believer in Matthew 28:19 to "go" and make disciples. I think for many this word has been misspelled in terms of application. How do you spell "go"?

Do you spell it "pray"? Clearly the saint is to pray for the unsaved, but there comes a time when he must leave off praying and begin telling.

Do you spell it "giving"? Financially investing in evangelism is of tremendous importance, something the believer ought to do, but he must remember this command cannot be obeyed by proxy.

Do you spell it "visitation"? Extending a kind invitation to another to attend church is commendable, but this in itself does not replace personal witnessing to the death, burial and resurrection of Jesus Christ and man's need to be saved.

Do you spell it "pastor"? Witnessing is every man's responsibility, not just that of the ministerial staff.

"Go" can only be spelled "g-o"; that is, get out and get telling people about the wonderful Savior, Jesus Christ, endeavoring to bring them to Him. "Go out into the highways and hedges, and compel them to come in" (Luke 14:23). "Therefore go and make disciples of all nations" (Matthew 28:19 NIV). "Son, go work to day in my vineyard" (Matthew 21:28).

You may not be comfortable with the word "go." You may wish Jesus had excluded it. But it is what it is, and therefore you must do what it

---

[137] Shivers, *Evangelistic Invitation*, 60.

[138] Hutson, *Preaching on Soul Winning*, 235.

commands. Encompassed in the word "go" is the promise that "lo, I am with you alway, even unto the end of the world" (Matthew 28:20).

75 "I Made a Difference to THAT One!"

A man was walking along the beach when he saw in the distance a young boy throwing something into the water. As he got closer, he asked the boy, "What are you doing?"

The boy answered, "I'm throwing these starfish back into the water. The tide is going out. If they don't get back into the water, they will die."

Looking around, the man literally saw thousands of stranded starfish on the beach and said, "Son, there are thousands of starfish here. What makes you think you can make a difference?"

The boy stooped down, picked up another starfish and flung it into the water; and with a smile, he said, "I made a difference to THAT one!"

With the millions of the unsaved in our world, "What makes you think you can make a difference?" I trust your answer parallels that of the boy in the story: "I made a difference to THAT one!" Don't be overcome with discouragement in soul winning by looking at the multitudes on the "sand" that are lost, but rather focus upon "THAT one" to whom you can make a difference in Jesus' name.

76   How Much Do You Value Souls?

"For what shall it profit a man, if he shall gain the whole world, and lose his own soul?" (Mark 8:36).

"Do you want to know how much a soul is worth? Then tell me how much Jesus suffered at Calvary, and I'll tell you the value of a soul. At Calvary, Jesus suffered all the Hell that I would have to suffer if I died without Him and went to Hell forever. He suffered that much for me alone. He suffered all the Hell that you would have to suffer just for you alone....

"The human mind cannot possibly grasp the immeasurable sufferings of Jesus Christ on Calvary....His body was beaten with a scourge until He had 195 furrows plowed through His back....They plucked out His beard until His face bled and didn't even look like a human face.

"I'm just saying that all the suffering that Jesus did at Calvary, He would have done for ONE SOUL. He would have suffered that much for a little boy over behind the railroad tracks who hadn't eaten a decent meal since his birth. He would have suffered that much for one little fellow."[139]

---

[139] Hutson, *Salvation Crystal Clear,* 177–178.

How valuable is one soul? C. H. Spurgeon answers, "If there existed only one man or woman who did not love the Savior, and if that person lived amongst the wilds of Siberia, and if it were necessary that the millions of believers on the face of the earth should journey thither and every one of them plead with him to come to Jesus before he could be converted, it would be well worth all the zeal and labor and expense of all that effort. One soul would repay the travail in birth of myriads of zealous Christians....

"We have not yet sufficiently learned the value of an immortal soul, if we do not feel that we would be willing to live, say, seventy years to be the means of saving one soul and be willing to compass the whole globe and preach in every city and town and village, if we might only be rewarded at the last with just one convert."[140]

The value you place on lost souls will be manifested in the extent to which you are willing to go to win them.

77   "My Word Will Not Return Unto Me Void"

"For as the rain cometh down, and the snow from heaven, and returneth not thither, but watereth the earth, and maketh it bring forth and bud, that it may give seed to the sower, and bread to the eater: So shall my word be that goeth forth out of my mouth: it shall not return unto me void, but it shall accomplish that which I please, and it shall prosper in the thing whereto I sent it" (Isaiah 55: 10–11).

William Evans shares a story to illustrate this text. "A Christian worker once met a man who was hardened in sin and skepticism. After the worker had spoken to him about becoming a Christian, the skeptic said, 'I do not believe in the Bible or in God or in Heaven or in Hell. I am a skeptic.'

"The worker took no notice of the man's confession but quoted to him this passage: 'Except ye repent, ye shall all likewise perish' (Luke 13:3).

"'But,' the skeptic said again, 'did I not tell you that I did not believe in the Bible? Why do you quote it to me?'

"The Christian again quoted the same verse, and again the skeptic gave the same reply. After repeating that same verse about a dozen times, adding no words of his own to it, the worker said to him, 'Now, my friend, I do not remember half of what you have said to me; but you cannot forget the passage of Scripture I have quoted to you, and I am going to pray that God will, through that passage of Scripture and His Holy Spirit, cause you to realize its truth.'

---

[140] Allen, *Exploring the Mind*, 453.

"'But,' he replied, 'I do not believe it.'

"Then the worker quoted Romans 3:3–4: 'For what if some did not believe? shall their unbelief make the faith of God without effect? God forbid.' The Christian then left the skeptic in the hands of God.

"The next night, the skeptic sought him and confessed that he had spent a miserable night. He said, 'That verse you quoted so often has haunted me ever since; it will not leave my memory. Won't you show me how to find rest for my soul?' What a joy it was to point him to John 1:29, leave him in Acts 13:52 and commend him to Jude 24. Thus, you see, God will honor His own Word."[141]

The great weapon the believer has at his disposal in soul winning is the double-edged Sword of the Word of God, an indispensable resource promised by God never to fail.

78   Praying for Souls

"Ask of me, and I shall give thee the heathen for thine inheritance" (Psalm 2:8). How might you pray for the lost?

Pray for *Cultivation* prior to the witness, that the soil in the soul of the sinner may be broken up, seeded and prepared for the presentation of the gospel (Hosea 10:12).

Pray for *Orchestration* of the witness, that the Holy Spirit will lead the right soul winner to this person at the most opportune time to share the Gospel (Matthew 9:38).

Pray for *Reception* to the witness, that the sinner will be open to the soul winner's presentation (II Thessalonians 3:1).

Pray for *Illumination* in the witness, that the Holy Spirit will open blinded eyes that divine truth may be revealed and received (Acts 26:18; Acts 16:14).

Pray for *Liberation* in the witness, that every satanic stronghold in the heart would be destroyed, resulting in total deliverance (Matthew 12:29).

Pray for *Conviction* in the witness, that the sinner will see his disobedience (failure to keep the Ten Commandments) toward God (John 16:8).

Pray for *Conversion* in the witness, that the lost person may express godly sorrow regarding his crime against God and in faith receive Jesus Christ as Lord and Savior (Acts 20:21).

---

[141] Evans, "Personal Worker," accessed May 22, 2010.

It has been stated that the soul winner's prayer is, "Lord, help me be a nobody who will tell everybody about Somebody who can save anybody."[142]

79   Baby Jessica's Rescue

In 1987, Jessica, an 18-month-old baby, fell twenty-two feet into an unused Texas well. Emergency teams spent fifty-eight hours in an effort to rescue her until paramedic and rescuer Robert O'Donnell wriggled into the passageway and slathered a frightened Jessica in petroleum jelly before sliding her out into the bright television lights. "A poll taken by the Pew Research Center for the People and the Press in 1997 that measured coverage of Princess Diana's death earlier that year found that in the previous decade, only Jessica's rescue rivaled the Paris car accident in worldwide attention."[143]

We count the value of one baby girl such that no machinery, manpower or monetary cost would prevent her rescue. In fact, I dare say that had you been the first passer-by to hear of Jessica's plight that dreadful day, nothing would have hindered you from reaching down into the well to make the rescue attempt.

Jesus states that the soul is of greater value than the body. "What shall it profit a man, if he shall gain the whole world, and lose his own soul?" (Mark 8:36). Is it not the sensible thing, therefore, to be more concerned for the soul of man than his body?

Scripture makes plain that man has carelessly fallen into the well of sinful degradation, depravation and destruction and is separated from God. He cannot rescue himself. He is entrapped. He will die in his sin unless delivered. Believers must come to his aid, sparing no expense or effort to rescue him. Every believer is on the Rescue-Recovery Team and is dispatched to save everyone possible.

80   Hypocrisy

Robert A. Laidlaw shares the following allegory showing the sinfulness of failing to pray for the lost. "In one of our munitions plants employing 500 men, there was an excellent canteen and lounging room. After the men had lunched each day, they developed an informal open forum where for the balance of their lunch period they discussed topics of general interest.

---

[142] Smith, Jack, *Motivational Sermons*, 52.

[143] Unknown Author, "Baby Jessica," October 17, 2007.

One day their discussion centered on Christianity and hypocrisy. Some very harsh and cruel things were said about Christians. In the company was a Christian fellow named William James.

"When Bill could stand it no longer, he rose to his feet and said, 'Men, you have been saying some very hard things about Christians. Now I admit that there are hypocrites in the church, but I also want you to know that there are quite a lot of sincere Christians, and I myself very humbly claim to sincerely believe in Jesus Christ as my personal Lord and Savior.'

"He was about to sit down, when a man said, 'Just a minute, Bill. I would like you to answer some questions. I take it from what you have said that you believe the Bible to be the Word of God?'

"'I certainly do,' said Bill. 'I believe it from cover to cover.'

"'Then do you believe that all men out of Christ are lost and on their way to outer darkness?'

"'Yes, I do.' And so the dialogue proceeded:

"Question: 'Do you think most of us men are out of Christ and therefore lost?'

"Bill: 'Yes, boys, I am very sorry indeed to say I do believe that.'

"Question: 'Do you believe in the efficacy of prayer?'

"Bill: 'Yes, I have had many answers to my prayers in the past.'

"Question: 'How long have you worked with us?'

"Bill: 'Four years.'

"Question: 'How often in that period have you spent a night in prayer for our lost souls?'

"Bill: 'I am sorry, boys, but I cannot say I ever spent a night in prayer for you.'

"Question: 'Well, Bill, how often have you spent half a night in prayer for us, say from 8:00 to 12:00?'

"Bill (whose head was going lower): 'I am sorry, but I cannot say I ever spent half a night in prayer for you.'

"Question: 'Well, Bill, we'll take your word for it—quickly add together all the time you've spent in prayer for us during the last week; how much would it be, all told?'

"Bill: 'I am sorry, fellows, but I cannot say that I have spent any time in prayer for you this last week.'

"Questioner: 'Well, Bill, that is just the kind of hypocrisy we've been talking about.'"[144]

If such a scenario would unfold regarding you in the workplace or schoolhouse, would the outcome be any different?

81   The Winning of a Soul

Charles Cowman wrote regarding the millions in Japan, "By the help of God, they shall hear, if it costs every drop of my life's blood. Here I am, Lord; send me! Send me!"

It was said of Cowman, "The winning of a soul was to him what the winning of a battle was to a soldier, what the winning of a bride is to a lover, what the winning of a race is to an athlete. He lived for just one thing—to win souls for Christ. This was his soul passion, and in a very extraordinary manner, God set His seal upon it. Whenever the evangelization of the Orient was mentioned, his soul took fire, and you felt he would die a martyr through his own ferventness before he reached the sunset of life—and it was even so. He belonged to the class of early martyrs whose passionate souls made an early holocaust of the physical man."[145]

Do you possess the soul winner's passion as Cowman did? If not, pray incessantly until you get it.

82   Hard Work

Billy Sunday, preaching in Richmond, Indiana, in 1922, declared, "Winning souls is a difficult form of work. It is more difficult than preaching; it is more difficult than attending conventions or giving goods to the poor. You can pin on a badge, usher people to their seats, pass the collection plate, be an elder or deacon or a steward; you can go to church, sing in the choir, be a member of a home or foreign missionary society—the Devil will even let you attend Bible conferences—but the minute you begin to do personal work, to try to get somebody to take a stand for Christ, all the devils in Hell will be on your back, for they know that is a challenge to the Devil and to his forces. The work of leading people to Christ by personal effort [is]...hard. 'He that winneth souls is wise.'"[146]

---

[144] Laidlaw, *Prayerlessness*, 5.

[145] Duewel, *Ablaze*, 3.

[146] Sunday, "Present-Day Proverbs," 20.

Indeed, it is hard work and that to which satanic opposition will arise from every front. Knowing this, ever remember as you go and tell, "we are more than conquerors through him that loved us" (Romans 8:37) and "he that winneth souls is wise" (Proverbs 11:30).

Lanny Wolfe captures in his song *My House Is Full but My Fields Are Empty* (Benson Music) the prevalent state of the church regarding personal evangelism. Far too many believers have become content with the "feeding trough" and fellowship time within the walls of the church, to the neglect of those without. As the song says, God's house is full, but His fields are empty, because His children want to stay around His table, rather than go to work in His fields. It is time to go to work in His field, for it is ripe unto harvest.

83   The Power of the Pen

A minister in England asked a dying woman how she came to know Christ as Savior. She handed him a piece of paper torn from an American journal which included part of a sermon by C. H. Spurgeon. The sermon "scrap" had been wrapped around a package she received from Australia and was the means the Holy Spirit used to bring her to Christ.

One commented on this incident: "Think of it—a sermon preached in England, printed in America, in some way coming to Australia, a part of it being used as wrapping paper there, coming back to England was the means of converting this woman."[147]

In a professional diver's home, showcased upon his chimney, hangs an unusual ornament—the shells of an oyster holding tightly a piece of printed paper. This diver was diving off the coast, when he noticed at the bottom of the sea this oyster on a rock with the piece of paper in its mouth. This paper was a Gospel tract, which he read through his goggles, and there in the depth of the ocean, he repented of his sin and was saved.[148]

Mitsuo Fuchida, the Japanese Commander who shouted the war cry "tora, tora, tora" at Pearl Harbor, became a Christian through reading the New Testament. It was a simple gospel tract, however, that prompted him to purchase the New Testament. What if Jacob DeShazer had not handed him the tract?[149]

---

[147] Tan. *7700 Illustrations*, #3164.

[148] Ibid., #3158.

[149] Fuchida, "Pearl Harbor, accessed March 12, 2010.

Gospel tracts written through the leadership of the Holy Spirit, distributed by the guidance of the Holy Spirit under the power of the Holy Spirit will be used by the Holy Spirit to quicken the spiritually dead to new life in Christ. Gospel tracts need a vehicle to get into the hands of the lost—this vehicle is you.

84   Fuel for the Soul Winner's Fire

How can you get a passion for the lost? It is not produced by simple resolve or decision.

It will take *Praying*. Earnestly and continuously ask the Lord to fire your heart for the unsaved. "And I will give you a new heart, and I will put a new spirit in you. I will take out your stony, stubborn heart and give you a tender, responsive heart" (Ezekiel 36:26 NLT). The mighty evangelist E. J. Daniels stated that he cried out to God for a deep burden for souls more than anything else, with perhaps the exception of the infilling of the Holy Spirit.[150]

It will take *Pruning*. "Every branch in Me that does not bear fruit, He takes away; and every branch that does bears fruit, He prunes, that it may bear more fruit" (John 15: 2 ESV). In response to praying, God will *cut* from your life the hindrances to bearing soul-winning fruit. What might these hindrances be that need pruning? It is essential that the believer 'abide in Christ' (John 15:5).

It will take *Pondering*. David, the psalmist, declared, "My heart was hot within me, while I was musing the fire burned: then spake I with my tongue" (Psalm 39:3). Mediate upon the scriptural picture of the lost until soul winning coals are flamed in the soul.

It will take *Piercing*. Not until you bleed for the unsaved will you plead with the unsaved. "When he (Jesus) saw the crowds, he had compassion on them, because they were confused and helpless, like sheep without a shepherd" (Matthew 9:36 NLT). This compassion is birthed through the believer's ability to identify with the heartache, havoc and Hell of a life separated from God. Don't live in isolation from the lost. Avoid the sanctuary of the safe cocoon where only believers dwell. Rub shoulders with the lost, and this friction will enhance soul passion to win them.

It will take *Pumping*. Satan will endeavor to hinder witnessing at every turn; therefore, keep handy scripture texts, literature, stories and hymns that will propel you in doing it. Align with a soul winning partner who will be an impetus for witnessing.

---

[150] Daniels, *Soul-Stirring Sermons*, 114.

It will take *Pleading.* Shake off the dread, distaste and fear of witnessing, and just do it! The engagement in witnessing will fuel the flame to witness.

C. H. Spurgeon declares, "I cannot believe that you will ever pluck a brand from the burning without putting your hand near enough to feel the heat of the fire. You must have, more or less, a distinct sense of the dreadful wrath of God and of the terrors of the judgment to come, or you will lack energy in your work, and so lack one of the essentials of success."[151]

85   Souls Slipping through Our Hands

E. J. Daniels recounts the story of a teenage girl who was accidentally killed. "The sadness was made greater for the family because they had no knowledge of the girl's conversion. The mother was a professing Christian but had made no effort to witness to her daughter and win her to Christ. With heavy heart, she went to the daughter's Sunday school teacher, hoping she could gain some assurance of the girl's salvation.

"'I am ashamed to admit,' said the teacher, 'that I talked about the Bible lessons, about socials, about many things to Mary; but I never tried to win her to Jesus. Maybe one of the teachers who taught her through her four years in the Junior department won her to the Lord.' They went to all of her teachers from the time she had reached the age of accountability, but none of them had won her. All admitted that they 'just taught the lesson' but failed to make an honest effort to win the girl to Jesus.

"'I'll go to our pastor,' the mother said. 'He is a good man and is interested in souls. I know he must have tried to win Mary; maybe she professed salvation to him.'

"When they talked to the minister, he shamefully said: 'I meant many times to talk with Mary but allowed the press of other duties to keep me from it. There have been so many calls to visit the sick and so many details in the business of the church that I just did not get around to it. I kept putting if off day after day until she was gone. I have failed her and my God.'

"All the group said, 'We let her slip through our hands into Hell. May God have mercy!'"[152]

Bailey Smith declares, "The other things we have to do may be called important by those around us, but there is nothing on earth more important

---

[151] Allen, *Exploring the Mind*, 453.

[152] Daniels, *Dim Lights*, 31–32.

to do than to win a person to Jesus Christ."[153] God help you not to allow souls that you have every opportunity to win to Christ to "slip through your hands into Hell."

86   The Level of Pain

The Apostle Paul experienced pain for the unsaved. He cried, "Brethren, my heart's desire and prayer to God for Israel is, that they might be saved" (Romans 10:1). He labored for souls night and day (Acts 20:31). He experienced great distress and pain sharing the Gospel (II Corinthians 11:23–28). He was willing to be *anathema* (cut off from God) for the salvation of the Jews (Romans 9:3). He was ready to die for the cause of Christ (Acts 21:13).

When speaking to his team about losing a game, NBA coach Hubie Brown said, "When your level of pain reaches my level of pain, then we can do something." It is only when the Christian's level of pain for the lost reaches Paul's level that he or she will engage in soul winning as passionately and persistently as Paul did.

Luis Palau at Urbana 1976 said, "Do you know how I get compassion? I remember that in Latin America, every two months an average of 500,000 people die. Every two months! And my heart breaks when I think of it. I have a book with pictures of Latin America—the Indians and city people, rich people and poor people. When I begin to feel that my heart is getting hard, I go through this book and look at the old people and the poor people and the blind, and I begin to cry almost every time. We must not be embarrassed to cry a little bit for those who are lost. Compassion in my mind has got something to do with crying. When people are suffering and dying and lost and there are so many millions of them that we cannot even imagine what 2.7 billion is, how can we not cry?"[154]

William Burns said, "The thud of Christless feet on the road to Hell is breaking my heart."[155] David Brainerd declared, "I cared not how I lived or what hardships I might go through, as long as I might win souls." Do you identify with the level of pain for the lost manifested by the Apostle Paul and these men?

---

[153] Smith, Bailey, *Real Evangelism*, 118.

[154] Palau, *Unfinished Task*, accessed March 15, 2010.

[155] Unknown Author, "Sunday Bulletin," accessed August 9, 2010.

87   Fish but Feast

"You may have a widespread net cast into the great sea and no end of fishes all around you, and yet you may take nothing—that night's work yielded nothing but splash and haul, disappointment and fatigue. If you are in that condition, you evidently need encouragement. Times of refreshing from the presence of the Lord will be your present want. The Savior calls to you, 'Come and breakfast. Leave the boat and the nets and forget the night's vain toil and come and commune with Me.'

"Weary worker, worried and weeping, cease your complaining and come to the fire and the food which Jesus provides for you. You will remind me that before the breakfast, the disciples had taken a great number of fish and had counted them. And that is another reason for calling them to feast with Jesus. Catching fish is a fine business, but being fed is equally needful. No fisherman can live on catching and counting. It is a very deceptive thing for a man to sustain his faith upon the success of his labors.

"Our tendency in a revival is to rejoice over converts and count them 'an hundred and fifty and three.' It is not wrong to count your converts if Christ gives them to you. The awkward part of it is that you are apt to count in with the fish a number of frogs—I mean a sort of convert that Jesus never sent. You may, if you please, count every convert and say, 'an hundred and fifty and three.' But do not think that this will nourish your own soul. You cannot sustain the life of divine grace upon the grace received by others.

"Believe me, you must in secret draw from the divine storehouse your personal supplies, or you will be famished. You will find it very hungry work if you try to live on catching and counting! You must be yourself watered, or your watering of others will dry up your soul. The most successful evangelist, if he attempts to live on his own work, will suck up the wind. If a teacher of children or a conductor of young men's classes makes the food of his soul to be his success in the service of God, he will feed on ashes.

"Oh, you that have had grand times in preaching or teaching, do not be content with these! Grace for your office is one thing—divine grace for yourselves is another. It is well to catch fish, but even that would be sorry work if you perished with hunger yourselves."[156]

88   What Preaching Could Not Do

Following a church service, Dr. Courtland Myers said to a young man departing, "I hope you are a Christian."

---

[156] Spurgeon, "Breakfast with Jesus," accessed March 13, 2010.

The young man responded to the amazement of Dr. Myers, "No, I am not a Christian, but I know you and have heard you preach for seven years." Myers had a heart-to-heart talk with the young man and led him to Christ. Myers said later, "What seven years of preaching Sunday after Sunday had failed to do was accomplished by a few minutes of personal contact."[157]

Dr. George W. Truett stated, "One evening, as I sat on the platform with the pastor of a prominent church, an influential citizen entered the church. The pastor whispered to me, 'For twelve years I have tried to win that man to Christ. I have preached to him so long that I find myself doing it almost unconsciously.'

"'How many times have you gone to him and lovingly said, "I want you to become a Christian?"'

"The pastor replied, 'I must confess that I have never spoken to him personally concerning his salvation.'

"'Then,' I said, 'a loving personal appeal may be all that is needed to bring him to the Savior.'

"At the close of the service, the pastor personally pleaded with the man to receive Christ as his Savior. The next night that man was among the first to come forward to confess Christ as his Savior."[158]

Personal appeal from minister or layman is by far the most effective means to bring a soul to Christ. Guard against allowing public appeal to sinners from the classroom or the pulpit to replace that of the private wherein there is no mistake when it is said, "Thou art the man."

89   Not Required to Be Successful, but Faithful

Dr. A. T. Pierson stated, "We are not responsible for conversion, but we are responsible for contact. We cannot compel any man to decide for Christ, but we may entreat every man to decide one way or the other. We may so bring others the gospel message that the responsibility is transferred from us to them. God will take care of the results, if we do our part: 'He that goeth forth and weepeth, bearing precious seed, shall doubtless come again with rejoicing, bringing his sheaves with him' (Psalm 126:6)."[159] God has not called us to be successful, but faithful in witnessing.

---

[157] Knight, *Illustrations for Today*, 320.

[158] Ibid., 320.

[159] Ibid., 318.

Paul Little said, "We do not measure our spirituality by how many scalps we have. At the same time, we are alert to issue the invitation at every possible opportunity."[160]

90 The Hero of the Titanic—the Rest of the Story

On April 14, 1912, at 11:40 P.M., the Titanic hit an iceberg, which ripped open six water-tight compartments, allowing the water to pour in. As the gigantic ship began to lurch upward, John Harper was seen making his way up the deck yelling, "Women, children and unsaved into the lifeboats!" As the huge ship made a loud rumbling sound as she was literally breaking in half, 1,528 people jumped from the deck into the frigid waters. John Harper was among them. It is documented that John Harper was seen swimming frantically to people trying to lead them to Christ before hypothermia became fatal.

Harper swam to a young man upon a piece of debris asking him between breaths, "Are you saved?" The young man said he was not, so Harper did his best to lead him to Christ, but without success. Harper removed his life-jacket and threw it to the man and said, "Here then; you need this more than I do," and swam away to witness to others. A few minutes later, Harper swam back to this young man and this time was successful in winning him to Jesus.

Only six of the 1,528 people in the water that night were rescued, one of whom was the young man on the debris. In 1916, at a survivors' gathering, this young man shared the story of how John Harper won him to Christ. He further shared that after Harper had led him to Christ, he tried to help other people, but his strength soon gave way. Harper's last words prior to death were, "Believe on the name of the Lord Jesus Christ and you will be saved."[161]

John Harper is an prime example of what it means to love souls above self. He gave up his life that others might be saved.

91 Blood on My Hands

Luis Palau said, "When you win someone to Christ, it's the greatest joy. Your graduation is exciting; your wedding day is exciting; the birth of your first baby is exciting. But the most thrilling thing you can ever do is to win someone to Christ. Yet today, in an effort to be sophisticated and contem-

---

[160] Little, *Guide to Evangelism*, 14.

[161] Unknown Author, "True Hero on the Titanic," accessed March 19, 2010.

porary, many Christians have stopped trying to persuade others to follow Christ. There's an underlying feeling in our society that nice people just don't go around persuading other people to do things. We don't want to offend people, appear strange or lose our newfound status. So we do nothing.

"I, too, have been guilty of this. When I lived in Mexico City, my next-door neighbor was a young television personality. We would chat from time to time, and he even mentioned that he listened to our radio program occasionally. But I didn't share the Gospel with him. *After all,* I thought, *he seems completely immune to the problems of life.*

"Eventually, though, my neighbor changed. The joy seemed to have left his face. He and his wife started driving separate cars to work. I could tell their marriage was souring, and I felt the need to talk with him, but I didn't want to meddle in his life. I went about my business and headed off for an evangelistic crusade in Peru. After all, that was the polite thing to do.

"When I returned home, I learned my neighbor had killed himself. I was heartbroken. I knew I should have gone to him and persuaded him to repent and follow Christ. But because of false courtesy, because I followed a social norm, I didn't do it.

"It's very convenient to make excuses for not persuading others to follow Christ. We may say we don't want to be overbearing or offensive. We may think we can't possibly witness to someone, because he or she will become angry. But over the years, I have learned that some of the people I thought would be most closed to the Gospel often are the most receptive. Although they may outwardly fear it, in their hearts they welcome the message of the Gospel."[162]

An ancient Greek sculptor entitled a piece of his work "Opportunity." A visitor in his studio viewing the sculpture inquired "Why is its face veiled?"

"Because men seldom know her when she comes to them," was the reply.

"And why does she stand upon her toes, and why the wings?"

"Because," said the sculptor, "when once she is gone, she can never be overtaken."[163]

The message of this sculpture is never truer than in regard to witnessing. Delays in telling men about Jesus often result in irretrievably lost opportunities to win them to Christ.

---

[162] Palau, "Telling Others," accessed March 15, 2010.

[163] Sanders, *Art of Soul Winning*, 68.

92   We Must Tell of Our Find

The walled city of Samaria lay under siege, and its inhabitants were starving for want of food. The enemy encamped without the city was caused by God to hear the noise of many armies preparing an attack upon their camp. The soldiers panicked and fled, leaving all their food and possessions. Four lepers, ignorant of the enemies' departure, decided to go to their camp to beg for food. Surprisingly, upon arrival, they discovered that the camp was deserted. The lepers plundered the tents, taking food and clothing, silver and gold. Suddenly it dawned on them that it was wrong not to share such a find with the perishing people within the city wall. "We do not well: this day is a day of good tidings, and we hold our peace" (II Kings 7:9). The lepers shared the good news with the king, and the famished people received plenteous food and were saved.

Regarding this story, W. A. Criswell remarks, "I don't know of a finer illustration of what it is to be a preacher and what it is to be a witness and what it is to be a Christian than just that thing. We are not men who are theorizing. And we are not philosophizing. We are saying to sinners that there is a way that a man can be saved. And we are saying to those who are dying that there is a way that they can live. And we are saying to those who face eternity, 'Come. There is a great triumphant hallelujah God hath set before those who will trust in Him.'

"That's what it is. We are witnesses. We are heralders. We are proclaimers. We are not philosophizers and metaphysicians and speculators. We are announcing the great Good News of the love and mercy and forgiveness of God in Christ Jesus. Come. Come. Come.

"Why, how many, and especially of our religious intellectuals, how many speculate on religion? And they handle it like they would some kind of a philosophical proposition. And how many of them are like scientists who seek to analyze the blood of Christ and seek to put in some kind of test tube the Bread of Life? And how much of religion is somehow esoteric or peripheral, speculative? 'Oh!' said these lepers. 'Come. Come. Come. There's bread enough and to spare.'"[164]

The saved have made the glorious discovery in Jesus Christ of the source of plenteous supply of all that is needed to sustain life and save the soul. It is unthinkable, utterly selfish not to share this Good News with those who around us are perishing. We who have 'tasted that the Lord is gracious' (I Peter 2:3) have a debt to pay; we owe it to our friends and others to share our find of Jesus with them. We must not remain silent in this day of Good News!

---

[164] Criswell, "Four Lepers," accessed March 19, 2010.

93   The Farmer Won Him

"I went to hear D. L. Moody preach when I was a country minister. He so fired my heart that I went back to my country church and tried to preach as he preached, and we had really a great work of grace. It did not start immediately; and I was so discouraged, because things did not go as I thought they ought, that I called my church officers together and said, 'You will have to help me.'

"They promised to do so, and finally an old farmer rose and said, 'I have not done much work in the church, but I will help you.'

"One of the officers said to me afterward, 'Do not ask him to pray, for he cannot pray in public'; and another said, 'Do not ask him to speak, for he cannot speak to the edification of the people.'

"The next morning, we had one of those sudden snowstorms for which that part of the country is famous, and this old farmer rose and put his horse to his sleigh and started across the country four miles to a blacksmith's shop. He hitched his horse on the outside and went into the shop all covered with snow and found the blacksmith alone. The blacksmith said, 'Mr. Cranmer, whatever brings you out today?'

"The old farmer walked up to the blacksmith's bench and, putting his hand upon the man's shoulders, said, 'Tom!' and the tears started to roll down his cheeks. Then with sobs choking his utterance, he said, 'Tom, when your old father died, he gave you and your brother into my guardianship, and I have let you both grow into manhood and never asked you to be Christians.'

"That was all. He did not ask him then; he could not. He got into his sleigh and drove back home. And he did not go out again for months; he almost died from pneumonia.

"But that night in the meeting, the blacksmith stood up before my church officers and said: 'Friends, I have never been moved by a sermon in my life, but when my old friend stood before me this morning with tears and sobs, having come all through the storm, I thought it was time I considered the matter.' We received him into the church, and he is a respected church officer today. *Preaching fails, singing fails, but individual concern does not fail.*"[165]

94   Laborers, Not Experts

G. S. Dobbins said, "One of the Devil's best tricks is to delude Christians into the belief that they are not fitted to be soul winners and that this

---

[165] Sanders, *Art of Soul Winning*, 17–19.

delicate and difficult business must be left to a small group of 'experts.' True, soul winning is an art, but it is an art which any Christian can learn."[166]

Jesus told the believer, "Pray ye therefore the Lord of the harvest, that he will send forth labourers into His harvest" (Matthew 9:38). Note the word "labourers" rather than "experts." Soul winning is not restricted to ministers or religious professors or deacons but is assigned to all the redeemed.

It is undeniable that some believers are more apt to win souls than others, but this in no wise exempts the less effective from soul winning. Frankly, all you can do is develop the art of witnessing to the best of your ability, present yourself available and usable unto God, rely upon the Holy Spirit's guidance and power, pray earnestly as you go to the lost, be intentional about sharing Christ, and leave the results up to God. Vance Havner said if there was an eleventh commandment, it would be, "Thou shalt not compare." In witnessing according to your potential in the Spirit, don't compare souls won with those who win more; this will open the door for discouragement and derailment.

95   Pray for the Fire to Rekindle

As a vocational evangelist who regularly preaches to win the lost, at times I must come before the Lord and cry, "Lord, don't let me get used to boys and girls, men and women dying and going to Hell." If it is easy for one who has given his life to evangelistic service to get "used to it," how much more is this a danger for the laity? Guard the passion for souls, or it will gradually disappear.

When you first notice in yourself the absence of a soul winner's passion, ask God to restore it. He will, you know. The scripture states, "And this is the confidence that we have in him, that, if we ask any thing according to his will, he heareth us: And if we know that he hear us, whatsoever we ask, we know that we have the petitions that we desired of him" (I John 5:14–15). And certainly it is His will that you possess a grave concern for the unsaved and are intentional about winning them. Go to God with words like, "Father, I know I should be concerned for the unsaved, but, frankly, I am not. I am ashamed at my lack of concern for the lost. But I want to care, love them and tell them of You. Please help me, Lord, to manifest Your heart to them, starting today."

---

[166] Dobbins, *Winning Witness*, 79–80.

96   By Any Road, at Any Cost, by Any Means

A man came to Dr. George W. Truett in one of his revivals and said, "Dr. Truett, there is a neighbor of mine whose wife recently died after a long illness. His crops are behind. I'm going out to his farm in the morning to see if he will let me plow for him while he comes to hear you preach. If I am not here and a stranger is, please pray that he will be saved."

The next morning, the merchant went out to the farm. He went to the farmer in the field plowing corn. Going up to him, he said, "Neighbor, I know that your crops are behind and you feel that you cannot take time to attend our revival. I have come out to see if you will let me plow your corn while you go to hear Dr. Truett preach."

The farmer looked at him with astonishment and said, "Do you mean to tell me that you would plow my corn in those good clothes for me to go hear a preacher?"

"I would do anything to get you saved," was the reply. "You know that I have talked with you often about your eternal destiny when you have come to the store. Won't you allow me to do your work while you hear Dr. Truett?"

With tears in his eyes and a sob in his voice, the farmer said, "Friend, if you are that much interested in my soul, I guess it is time I was interested in it myself. I'll take you up on it."

When Dr. Truett gave the invitation at the close of his message, the farmer stepped forward to accept Christ. He later said, "Dr. Truett, it was not your sermon that won me to Christ. In fact, I did not hear much you said. But while you were up there preaching, I could see a neighbor of mine walking up and down my corn rows plowing while I came to hear you preach. I figured that if he was that much interested in my soul, I must really need to be saved and should get right with God."[167]

Oh, for more Christians as this merchant who are willing to plow for souls, babysit for souls, mind the store for souls. Fill whatever gap necessary to make it easier for the lost to hear the Gospel presented.

97   Spiritual Birth Pangs

Before I witnessed the birth of my daughter, the doctor said to me, "Watch real close, preacher. You can get a sermon out of this." And, boy, did I! As my wife travailed in excruciating pangs to give birth to Stephanie, I recalled that the prophet Isaiah declared, "As soon as Zion travailed, she brought forth her children" (Isaiah 66:8). How the soul winner needs to

---

[167] Daniels, *Dim Lights*, 36–37.

travail in spiritual pangs through intense prayer for the lost until they are born into God's eternal family.

David Brainerd gave the church the secret of reaching the unsaved when he exhorted, "Travail, travail, travail until you prevail, prevail, prevail." He testifies, "Near the middle of the afternoon, God enabled me to wrestle ardently in intercession for my friends. But just at night, the Lord visited me marvelously in prayer. I think my soul never was in such an agony before. I felt no restraint, for the treasures of Divine grace were opened to me. I wrestled for my friends, for the ingathering of souls, for multitudes of poor souls, and for many that I thought were the children of God, personally in many different places. I was in such an agony from sun, half an hour high, till near dark that I was all over wet with sweat."[168]

Likewise may we travail in prayer for the unsaved. Prayer can be the means of tearing down strongholds and setting the captive free. Never underestimate its power. "With God all things are possible" (Mark 10:27). No man is beyond the reach of God, not even the chief of sinners whose life is dedicated to the persecution and eradication of Christians. Just ask the Apostle Paul.

With great soul wrestling, souls are won. Alvin I. Reid told of a picture he saw in a pastor's study that depicted a man prostrate on the floor praying. The caption, in large letters, declares, "MAKE WAR ON THE FLOOR."[169]

The soul winner must make war on the floor in prayer for the sinner's *revelation* of need of salvation, *reception* of the presentation of salvation, *release* from hindrances to salvation and *response* to the invitation of salvation.

Prayer blasts satanic strongholds in the sinner's life, granting deliverance from the blindness of the flesh, the pride of life and the shackles of sin (II Corinthians 10:4). R. A. Torrey declared, "It is doubtful if even a single soul is born again without travail of soul on the part of someone."[170] C. H. Spurgeon declared, "Let us never venture to speak for God to men until we have spoken for men to God."[171]

---

[168] Smith, Oswald, *Revival We Need*, Chapter 3.

[169] Reid, *Radically Unchurched*, 51.

[170] Barlow, "Travail for Souls," 20.

[171] Spurgeon, *Evangelism*, 201.

98   Such by Prayer and Fasting

Fasting and prayer are necessary to win some to Christ (Matthew 17:14–21). In the failure of the disciples to deliver a child from demonic possession, they inquired of the Lord, "Why could not we cast him out?" (v. 19). Jesus answers that it was due to their unbelief (v. 20) and failure to pray and fast (Mark 9:29).

Undoubtedly these devoted followers of Christ were not maintaining a habit of prayer and fasting which would have prepared them for this unexpected encounter. The lesson to the disciples then and every believer now is to engage in the discipline of prayer and fasting faithfully so as to be prepared for the unexpected encounter to be used of God in transforming a life. Once faced with such an encounter, it is too late to fast or even pray with the intensity and duration it deserves or demands. Isaiah, in describing the purpose of the fast, includes that it is to be practiced to liberate souls from the yoke of sin's mastery (Isaiah 58:6).

Arthur Wallis remarked, "Fasting is calculated to bring a note of urgency and importunity into our praying and to give force to our pleading in the court of Heaven. The man who prays with fasting is giving Heaven notice that he is truly in earnest....Not only so, but he is expressing his earnestness in a divinely appointed way. He is using a means that God has chosen to make his voice to be heard on high."[172]

Fasting combined with prayer and proper motive makes it acceptable unto the Lord and a mighty force to be reckoned with by the enemy. Fasting with prayer needs to be engaged in while seeking the salvation of the unsaved that are shackled with many chains in Satan's prison camp. "This kind can come forth by nothing, but by prayer and fasting" (Mark 9:29).

99   Wearing Gospel Shoes

"And your feet shod with the preparation of the gospel of peace" (Ephesians 6: 15).

The Gospel shoes speak of the believer's assurance of salvation and disposition to recognize immediately his duty, with a readiness to plunge into it. It is important the Christian soldier walk in full confidence of salvation so that in the time of doubt or temptation he will not stumble and fall. Confidence of salvation enables a life of peace in every circumstance of life, whether good or bad. Further, Gospel shoes emphasize the need for saints to share the Good News of the Gospel with the unsaved.

---

[172] Whitney, *Spiritual Disciplines*, 164.

Jon Courson comments, "Having my feet shod with the Gospel of peace doesn't means I don't walk on people, but that I get to share with people. The word *gospel* means 'good news.' Therefore, as I walk through my day, it is my privilege to say to those in my path, 'Good news! The Lord loves you. He knows what you're going through. He can set you free.'"[173]

John R. Rice wrote regarding Ephesians 6:15, "First, I think this means that you need a new dedication to soul winning every day....So if you want to win souls, put your shoes on your feet every day. That means to store your mind and heart with Bible verses that you can take to those whom you seek to win. That means to plan your work. Depend upon the Holy Spirit to direct where you should go, whom you should see and what you should say.

Watch for the 'breaks' in the game. Many a football game has been decided because an alert player blocked a punt or fell on the ball or snatched a pass not intended for him....The Christian's mind should be so set on soul winning and his heart so prepared for soul winning and his will so surrendered to the Spirit's leadership that he can win souls at every opportunity."[174]

Go into the "closet" and retrieve your gospel shoes. Polish them, and start wearing them today!

100 Keep Knocking on Heaven's Door

David Wilkerson stated, "As a younger Christian, I was often confused by some teaching and preaching that said, in essence, 'God's Word cannot lie. If we ask *anything* in His name, He will do it. God is bound to His Word. He will answer us.' I believed this. However, when it came to praying for unsaved loved ones, I wondered about it in light of the teaching regarding the free will of man. I thought, *If my prayers can cause a person to turn to Christ, doesn't this trespass man's free will?* I have learned to accept both truths as being possible, yet not contradictory.

"Through prayer, we can move men toward God. Through prayer, we can see our loved ones come to Christ. I also believe the unsaved have a free will of their own, and they may resist the conviction of the Holy Spirit which comes as a result of our prayers....We are to pray 'without ceasing' and leave the ultimate outcome in the hands of God and within the decision-making prerogative of the unsaved."[175]

---

[173] Courson, *Application Commentary*, 1265.

[174] Rice, *Soul-Winner's Fire*, 95–97.

[175] Wilkerson, *Bring Your Loved Ones*, 116–117.

S. D. Gordon said, "Man is a free agent, to use the old phrase, so far as God is concerned—utterly, wholly free. *And*, he is the most enslaved agent on earth, so far as sin and selfishness and prejudice are concerned. The purpose of our praying is not to force or coerce his will—never that. It is to *free* his will of the warping influences that now twist it awry. It is to get the dust out of his eyes so his sight shall be clear. And once he is free, able to see aright, to balance things without prejudice, the whole probability is in favor of his using his will to choose the only right."[176]

'Keep on asking, and you will receive what you ask for; keep on seeking, and you will find; keep on knocking, and the door will be opened to you,' says Matthew 7:7. It has been said that believers spend more time praying to keep saints out of Heaven than they do to keep sinners out of Hell. Determine to personally change that! Prayer gives God a foothold on the battlefield in the soul of the lost. Therefore, don't relent in incessant praying for them.

101 The "Light" on George Street

Reverend Francis Dixon was having a testimony time in Lansdowne Baptist Church in Bournemouth, England. A young man whom he had led to Christ told of an incident from when he had been a sailor in Sydney, Australia. In George Street, an elderly man had asked him, "If you were to die tonight, where would you be—in Heaven or in Hell?" He was deeply affected and upon returning to England sought spiritual help, which resulted in his salvation. Another former sailor in the meeting recounted nearly the identical story from when he was in Sydney.

Soon afterward, Francis Dixon had some preaching engagements in Australia and decided to check out the reports firsthand. His first preaching was to be done in Adelaide, and while speaking there, he mentioned the strangely coinciding stories of the two former sailors in England. Surprisingly, upon sharing the story, he learned that his host had also been started on the road to Christ by the same unknown man. He had been approached while running to catch a train, but through the impression the man made upon him, he had received Christ two weeks later in his barracks.

While preaching next in Perth, Dixon repeated the stories as he had done in Adelaide. After his message, a man who had become a Christian leader in Australia said that he too had come to Christ after hearing the brief challenge from this preacher on George Street in Sydney. Upon arrival in Sydney, Dixon asked a local Christian minister if he knew who the man was. The minister replied, "I know him well. His name is Frank Jenner.

---

[176] Ibid., 117.

Like me, he works with the Forces, and he is a sailor himself. He worships at one of the Christian Brethren assemblies in Sydney."

Dixon visited in Jenner's home and learned that he had been a sailor with a gambling habit who had been saved and set free. With joy, Dixon told him the stories he had accumulated of people who had been saved through the witness he gave to them on George Street and how they were fruitfully serving the Lord to that day. The faithful soul winner said, "You know, I never heard that anyone I ever spoke to had gone on for the Lord. Some made professions of salvation when I spoke to them, but I never ever knew any more than that."

At the time of the visit, Frank Jenner had been telling at least ten people a day about Christ for sixteen years, and he had kept going despite not knowing of lasting fruit from his efforts. He continued his practice several more years until the Lord brought this shining example for all soul winners to Heaven, where he will shine as the stars forever (Daniel 12:3).[177]

102 Calling Too Late

Franklin Graham said, "Our Rapid Response team went to Virginia Tech. In August, 2007, thirty students were murdered on this campus in Blacksburg, Virginia. A lot of these kids didn't have ID on them. They had grabbed their backpacks and schoolbags and gone to class. It took a while for the first responders to identify some of these kids. The media and the first responders were all investigating as to why this happened. The police could not move the bodies out of Norris Hall, because it was a crime scene investigation. Almost all of these kids had cell phones, and they began to ring.

"The police said that they were standing there by a dead body lying on the floor with a cell phone in its hand, and it began to ring. It rang and rang, and no one answered. Families were calling to warn these kids that there was danger on campus—but they were calling too late.

"Do you want to win souls for Christ? What's stopping you? Would you say, 'Lord, with Your help, I will endeavor to win at least one soul for You this year'?"[178]

---

[177] www.wordsoflife.co.uk/FrankJenner/FrankJenner.htm. Accessed March 23, 2010.

[178] Fordham, Personal Correspondence, March 23, 2010.

103 The Soul Trap

C. H. Spurgeon said, "They called Mr. Whitefield's chapel at Moor-fields 'The Soul Trap.' Whitefield was delighted and said he hoped it always would be a soul trap. Oh, that all our places of worship were soul traps and every Christian a fisher of men, each one doing his best, as the fisherman does, by every art and artifice to catch those he fishes for! Well may we use all means to win so great a prize as a spirit destined for eternal weal or woe. The diver plunges deep to find pearls, and we may accept any labor or hazard to win a soul. Rouse yourselves, my brethren, for this God-like work, and may the Lord bless you in it!"[179]

104 A Bolt of Lightning Made Him a Soul Winner

C. E. Matthews was one of Southern Baptists' greatest soul winners and evangelism leaders. This account depicts what God used to propel him into being such.

Mr. Cooper gave Charlie Matthews a class of seven fourteen-year-old boys. Charlie was a success in a business office, so he made sure he had his lesson prepared. On the first Sunday, he stepped into a new venture. He stepped before the class and felt scared out of his wits. In ten minutes, he had run out of anything to say. He said, "My knees were knocking so that I could hardly stand, so I sat down." The boys looked at him with seeming pity and amazement. But a beginning had been made, and Charlie launched forth in active religious service.

What God had wrought was the beginning of a life which is more amazing as it unfolds before us. Charlie did not figure that he was very smart. He did not know what to do, but he was too smart to be caught like that again as a teacher. The next Sunday, he arrived early in his department at Sunday school. He went straight to Mr. Cooper and asked to be relieved of the class. He said, "I cannot teach, but I can push a pencil. Let me be department secretary. Let Dr. Graham teach, and let me push that pencil."

Mr. Cooper just laughed and walked off. Charlie went home that day and spent much time in deep meditation over his predicament. He did not have it in him to give up. He decided to solve the problem by sitting in imagination in the class as though he were a fourteen-year-old boy. He asked himself, *What kind of a teacher would I want if I were a fourteen-year-old boy?* Thereupon he began to pray and to think.

After that, the preparation of lessons became easy. He thought out a program of social life for his boys. The boys began to give evidence of

---

[179] Spurgeon, *Soul Winner*, 264.

liking their teacher, and he found himself able to spend the entire thirty minutes giving the lesson to his boys. Mrs. Matthews helped Charlie between Sundays with the social program for his boys. Everything was moving forward, and Charlie was becoming a real teacher of intermediate boys.

Arthur Flake, the famous author of the book *Building a Standard Sunday School* as well as other books, was approaching his prime and was the educational director of the First Baptist Church in Fort Worth where Charlie was teaching intermediate boys. Mr. Flake himself had been a businessman in Winona, Mississippi. He sold his business because he believed God wanted him in full-time religious work and went to work with the Sunday School Board in Nashville, Tennessee. He relinquished that position to accept the great challenge of educational director in Fort Worth.

He had his keen eyes upon this young teacher of fourteen-year-old boys. Mr. Flake observed that Charlie's class had organized itself into a Boy Scout troop and that Charlie had gone with them in scout work by becoming their Scout Master. With good teaching, a social program, and Boy Scout work all combined under Charlie's leadership, the class mushroomed in its growth. Soon there were twenty-four boys enrolled.

Those were happy days for the class, the troop, Charlie, and his wife. He went on hikes with them, and they had parties in his home. Mrs. Matthews found great delight in helping to entertain those boys. The boys seemed to enjoy most the delicious fudge which she served them, and often they expected to see a boy so full of fudge that he could not budge. Charlie truly was growing as a Christian and was master of those twenty-four boys in that Sunday school class. He strove well to entertain them with God's truth on Sunday as well as to entertain them between Sundays. The sheer joy of it was most stimulating.

God was not through. He was standing in the edge of the sunshine circle and preparing to use a strange circumstance to change the entire situation. After a while, he would change Charlie Matthews. The hour had come. He was about to begin to make Charlie an evangelist. The God of this universe is infinite in every way. He is infinite in his authority to convict men of their sins. He is infinite in the variety of ways he calls men to preach. God did not use a brilliant light surpassing the noonday sun, as he did in the case of Saul of Tarsus, to bring Charlie Matthews to begin as a soul winner. He used a bolt of lightning.

One morning on his way to work, Charlie bought a Fort Worth newspaper. On the front page was a glaring headline: "Boy Killed by Lightning—Sister Unconscious." Charlie quickly looked upon the picture accompanying the headlines. He was startled to recognize the face of one of the boys of his Sunday school class. This boy was returning from school with his sister as an electrical storm was raging. The boy carried a pair of roller skates over his shoulder and was leading his sister by the hand. Lightning struck and killed the boy instantly, knocking his sister to the ground and rendering her unconscious.

This story was such a shock to Charlie that he had to talk to someone. He talked to a companion on the way to work. "That boy is in my Sunday school class," he said. It was then that Charlie realized that although the boy had been in his home often and in his class regularly, he had never been in the boy's home. He determined to attend the funeral that afternoon.

Upon arrival at the house, he met the father of the boy for the first time as he was walking in his grief in the yard. Charlie was not in the habit of attending funerals or of speaking words of comfort in bereavement. He stopped the father in the shade of a peach tree in the yard and simply said, "I am Charlie Matthews."

Quickly the father recognized him and said, "Oh, you are Grady's Sunday school teacher. Grady really loved you. He was always talking about his class. He would quote what you said and refer to the good times he had in your home."

As the two men stood silently in the shade of the peach tree, the people were gathering for the funeral. Finally Charlie said to the father, "Are you a Christian?"

He answered, "Not a very good one. I am a member of the Methodist church in Burleson, Texas. I operate a dairy here in Fort Worth and have never moved my church membership. I am not much of a Christian."

It was then that Charlie asked, "Was Grady a Christian?"

That question startled the father. He jumped and said, "Brother Matthews, I do not know. Do you?"

"No," was Charlie's sad reply. Thus stood the father of a fourteen-year-old son and the teacher of that boy, while the boy lay cold in death inside the house. Neither knew whether Grady was saved or lost.

The time had arrived for the funeral service. The father invited the teacher to sit with the family. A Methodist minister conducted the rites. As the custom was, following the service, the long line of friends marched by to pay silent tribute to the dead and to view the body for the last time. The family came last to the casket. Charlie stood by that grief-stricken father and has never forgotten his words. Grady was a wonderful boy, well built, with red hair and freckled face. But Grady was dead, and neither father nor Sunday school teacher knew if it was well with his soul. If anguish could kill, both men would have died there. The father wept, disconsolate; and Charlie wept with him.

SPURS TO SOUL WINNING

Before nightfall of that dreadful day, Charlie was on the phone. Before Sunday, he had talked over the phone or in person in their homes with the twenty-three remaining boys. No longer could doubt be tolerated. Charlie had to know. He asked every one of the twenty-three, "Are you a Christian?" Thirteen rejoiced in saying, "Yes." Ten truthfully said, "No."

The Sunday following Grady's death, twenty-three fourteen-year-old boys sat before Charlie. The class had a new teacher. Until then, his aim had been simply to please the boys and to keep their attention while he convinced himself that he could go on for the thirty-minute lesson period. Their teacher's name was still Charlie Matthews, but today he was different. He turned that teaching period into an opportunity, and then grasped it, to tell them about Jesus, about the necessity of salvation, about the love of God. Finally, he said, "Let's all stay for church and sit together." It was easy. In the balcony sat twenty-three fourteen-year-old boys and their teacher, every one of them conscious of an empty chair in the midst. The pastor preached and gave the invitation. Seven boys walked to the front to confess saving faith in Jesus.

The pastor was overwhelmed, the people were profoundly touched, but that teacher up there in the balcony felt that he could never breathe again if that were all. No, it could not be. God could not be stopped here. He would help in their salvation, so he turned to Claude Howard, one of the three remaining who had said "I am not a Christian," and said, "Don't you want to trust Jesus and be saved?"

He pleaded, "Will you go with me, Brother Matthews?" As they started, the two remaining unsaved boys followed. No one had ever seen such a sight even in the First Baptist Church of Fort Worth. There stood ten fourteen-year-old boys and their teacher rejoicing in "so great salvation"— but Grady was dead. All were baptized, but no one knew how it was with Grady and his God. Charlie never forgot Grady.

God had wrought again. That bolt of lightning started Charlie in the work of soul winning. On the pen-written page upon which Charlie handed this story to the writer is a series of splotches. Could they be tear marks? They are mute evidence that Charlie never forgot another lesson he had learned as God wrought through him. It was his first time to taste the unbounded, unspeakable joy of knowing that he had won a soul to salvation in Christ. Instantaneously his whole life was changed.

Charlie was convinced that the Gospel is the power of God unto salvation to everyone that believeth, and he was awakened to the fact that he was personally responsible for winning the lost to Christ. From that dramatic hour forward for months there was a growing desire in the hearts of Charlie and Mrs. Matthews to win the lost to Christ. There was in their services through their church a faithfulness which had not been there before. More and more they became burdened for lost people.[180]

105 Potential Brother or Sister

A man driving a speed boat hit a pylon under the bridge and was thrown into the water. Emergency personnel rescued him, and once they got him to the shore, paramedics began CPR. Another man driving a car on the bridge, seeing what was happening, stopped out of curiosity to get a better look. The paramedics rolled the victim's face toward the bridge, and the driver discovered it was his brother. He immediately did all he could to assist the paramedics and even rode in the ambulance to pray as they transported him to the hospital.

At the first, the man on the bridge saw the driver of the boat who was being rescued only in the "flesh." Later, he saw him as his brother, which made all the difference. Look upon the lost who are shipwrecked in the lake of condemnation as your potential brother or sister in Christ, and launch an all-out rescue attempt to save them.[181]

106 One Man Responsible for Nearly Ninety-one Souls Saved

C. E. Matthews recounts a revival meeting experience involving a banker who took soul winning seriously. One Wednesday night the sermon subject was "The Sin of Indifference." The chief usher in the church was present. This man was president of a bank, a position he had held for twenty years. He was a fine Christian gentleman, highly respected in his city as a businessman and a citizen loyal to his church and faithful in church attendance. Something was said in the sermon that brought self-condemnation to this banker's heart because of his neglect in trying to win his many lost friends to Christ. Here is the banker's testimony as to what he did, given after the close of the revival.

"The next morning after hearing the sermon, I went to my office and told my secretary that I would be away from the bank most of each day during the revival. Then I made a list of names of lost men in my city with whom I had business dealings. I then contacted each of them in person. What I said and did in these personal calls was practically the same in each case.

---

[180] Wilbanks, *What God Hath Wrought*, 36–37.

[181] Fordham, Personal Correspondence, March 23, 2010.

"Upon entering the place of business, I would ask my friend if I could see him privately. Then I would say, 'I have come to make an apology to you. I have known you and have had business dealings with you for a number of years. In all of these years during which I have known you, I have been an active deacon in my church, but not one time have I sought to help you become a Christian. I want you to forgive me, for that is far more important than all the business dealings I have had with you. Because you knew I was an active churchman, I am quite sure that you wondered why I failed to manifest an interest in your spiritual welfare.'

"In several cases, the prospect would say, 'Yes, I have expected you to say something to me about religion.'

"Then I would ask, 'Would you permit me to read a few verses of Scripture and pray?' In every instance, permission was granted. At the close of the prayer, I would ask the prospect if he believed that Jesus was the Son of God and if he believed that He died to save us from our sins. Then I would ask if he would take my hand and say that he would trust Christ as his Savior. Several men did this. In every case, the prospect promised to attend the revival services."[182]

At the conclusion of the revival, ninety-one persons were baptized into the church. The largest percentage of these was men. Almost all of them were the fruits of this Christian banker's effort.

Have you been guilty of "The Sin of Indifference" regarding the lost as this businessman was? Make a list of the names of people with whom you have business dealings and determine without delay personally to share Christ today.

107 Spurs to Soul Winning

The Bible is replete with spurs that ought to incite you to win the lost to Christ.

(1) The Spur of Conversion. In knowing what it is to be lost, shackled to the chains of eternal darkness, and then to be rescued should prompt every believer to want to tell others of their Deliverer. "The love of Christ constraineth us" (II Corinthians 5:14).

(2) The Spur of Conviction. One ought to win souls based upon the fact that it is the will of God. It may be difficult to ascertain the will of God for some things, but not for this. The Bible makes it clear that it is God's will for the believer to be His witness (Acts 1:8).

---

[182] Matthews, *Every Christian's Job*, 83–84.

(3) The Spur of Compassion. Compassion motivated Jesus to seek and to save that which was lost, and it must do the same for the believer (Matthew 9:36). Look at the damnable plight of men apart from Christ and be moved with sympathy and deep concern to rescue them. Remember what it was like to be lost, and this will fill your heart with compassion for those yet without Christ.

(4) The Spur of Constraint. The inner promptings of the Holy Spirit should incite the believer to witness. As the believer walks under the controlling influence of the Holy Spirit, he will be led to share with the lost, as was Philip at the Gaza Strip (Acts 8:29). He realizes that not heeding the divine nudges of the Spirit to share his faith is disobedience that blocks the blessings of God upon him and others. The soul winner under the guidance of the Holy Spirit is confident that all power will be at his disposal to tear down strongholds and to set the captive free.

(5) The Spur of Condemnation. Knowing that man apart from Christ will be separated from God and saved loved ones for eternity in Hell prompts the believer to go and tell.

(6) The Spur of Consecration. Soul winning enables spiritual growth "in grace, and in the knowledge of our Lord and Savior Jesus Christ" (II Peter 3:18) and enhances a surrendered, separated life unto Christ (Romans 12:1–2). Faris Whitesell comments, "This state of spiritual maturity will be accelerated more by soul winning efforts than by any other thing."[183] The prospect of such growth in godliness should spur the believer to engage in the task of soul winning.

(7) The Spur of Crisis. Jesus states there is a crisis demand for more laborers in the harvest field of evangelism. "The harvest truly is great, but the labourers are few: pray ye therefore the Lord of the harvest, that he would send forth labourers into his harvest" (Luke 10:2). The insufficiency of the number of soul winners calls every believer to get his sickle immediately and get into the field. Time is of the essence. Souls are ready to be won, but reapers are needed.

(8) The Spur of Celebration. The fact that the believer can create joy in the presence of the angels in Heaven by leading a soul to Christ should stir him to action (Luke 15:7).

Likewise, there is joy for the soul winner. Leonard Sanderson said, "One of the joys that flood the soul winner's heart is that God brings success to his efforts. Sometimes when one thinks he has made a miserable failure, God takes over and saves the soul in spite of it. When one sees another soul come to the Savior, all the bells of his heart begin ringing in a

---

[183] Whitesell, *New Testament Evangelism*, 177.

melody similar to that on the day of his own salvation. When a Christian beholds the transformation of a newborn soul, his own faith is greatly confirmed. When he feels the warm handclasp of the one who has just said, 'I do,' it is like an electric current that connects with Heaven for a time. Joy inexpressible in human language is experienced. There is the joy that comes to the soul winner in the gratitude and the affection expressed by those who have been brought to Christ. There is a tie between those saved and those who won them that is somehow unmatched in the present life."[184]

C. H. Spurgeon testified, "Even if I were utterly selfish and had no concern but for my own happiness, I would choose, if I might, under God to be a soul winner, for never did I know perfect, overflowing, unutterable happiness of the purest and most ennobling order, until I first heard of one who had sought and found a Savior through my means. I recollect the thrill and joy that went through me! Oh! the joy of knowing that a sinner once at enmity has been reconciled to God by the Holy Spirit through the words spoken by our feeble lips."[185]

(9) The Spur of the Cross. Knowing the ultimate sacrificial price Jesus paid for the salvation of man at Calvary ought to propel the redeemed to carry on His mission of evangelizing the world. The Cross speaks of the magnitude of God's great love for the world, in that He would allow His only Son to die such a horrendous death in order to reconcile man to Himself (II Corinthians 5:19). The Christian is His ambassador bearing the message of reconciliation to God through the Cross. "Therefore, we are ambassadors for Christ, as though God were making an appeal through us; we beg you on behalf of Christ, be reconciled to God" (II Corinthians 5:20 NASB).

(10) The Spur of Commendation. The reward of the soul winner is cited in the following biblical passages: "Brethren, if any of you do err from the truth, and one convert him; Let him know, that he which converteth the sinner from the error of his way shall save a soul from death, and shall hide a multitude of sins" (James 5:19–20). "And they that be wise shall shine as the brightness of the firmament; and they that turn many to righteousness as the stars for ever and ever" (Daniel 12:3). "For what is our hope, or joy, or crown of rejoicing? Are not even ye in the presence of our Lord Jesus Christ at his coming?" (I Thessalonians 2:19). The believer is not to win souls for the sake of the reward, but Christ graciously offers such as inducement.

---

[184] Sanderson, *Personal Soul Winning*, 7–8.

[185] Spurgeon, *Sermons on Soul Winning*, 11.

(11) The Spur of Coming Judgment. The knowledge that the believer will certainly give an account for soul winning neglect should incite its engagement (Romans 14:10; II Corinthians 5:10). Junior Hill said, "The thought that motivates me so heavily (to win souls) is the passage from Ezekiel which says, 'Their blood will I require at your hand.' That is a powerful and sobering reminder of our responsibility to share the Word with those we meet."[186]

Surely at least one of these spurs for soul winning resonates within your heart and motivates its practice.

108 The Domino Effect of Winning Just One Soul

Edward Kimball, a Sunday school teacher, won a shoe clerk named D. L. Moody to Christ. Moody, in ministering in England, impacted F. B. Meyer. F. B. Meyer, in preaching at Furman University, refueled the flame in a student named R. G. Lee, who had decided to drop out of the ministry. Meyer then preached at another location where a young man named J. Wilbur Chapman caught fire and began to evangelize. Chapman eventually needed someone to help him in his ministry and recruited a young baseball player convert named Billy Sunday. Sunday, influenced greatly by Chapman, entered evangelism and went to Charlotte, North Carolina. A group of laymen were so inspired that they decided to invite Mordecai Ham from Louisville, Kentucky, to preach in a crusade. It was in that meeting that Billy Graham was saved. Graham became a mighty vessel throughout the world for God, because Edward Kimball—a nobody—won a young shoe clerk and started a series of dominoes falling that produced millions saved under Moody, hundreds of thousands in Meyer's ministry, hundreds of thousands in Chapman's ministry, hundreds of thousands more in Lee's ministry, hundreds of thousands in Sunday's ministry and millions in Graham's.[187]

All this occurred because one Sunday school teacher took time to win one soul to Christ. He certainly did not know the eternal impact of winning that one soul. Nor will you know the full impact of those you win.

109 Go Back Up There and Knock Again

A certain Christian would knock on a door, and when someone arrived to open it, he would smile, hand them a gospel tract and say, "I would be

---

[186] Hill, Personal Correspondence, March 23, 2010.

[187] Hutson, *Preaching on Soul Winning*, 202–203.

very grateful if you would read this." At one house, no one answered his first knock, so he knocked again, still without success. He knocked a third time without response and put the tract in the screen door and started to leave. But the Holy Spirit arrested him, forbidding him to walk away. It was as if He were saying, *Don't go off this porch! Go back up there and knock again.* This he did, yet again without response. As he started to walk away, the impulse not to give up was greater, so he knocked on the door again.

The door suddenly opened, and a man asked, "What do you want?"

The man replied, trembling, "I got the wrong house," and handed a tract to the man, saying, "Sir, would you please read this?" The man snatched the tract and slammed the door. This experience unnerved the tract distributor, but after knocking on a few more doors, he was calm. He finished knocking on doors on that block and then hit another block before calling it a day.

That evening, the tract man received a phone call from a man who inquired, "Sir, are you the man who was giving out the little papers over in [a certain area] today?"

"Yes, I was," he replied.

"Is it possible for you to come by and talk with me?"

"Sure. Give me the address," he answered. He immediately made his way to this home and, upon approaching it, recalled that it was the very house where he had felt impressed to keep knocking earlier in the day.

"Come in. I want to show you something," the man said and led him to the attic. On the rafters in the attic hung a hangman's noose with a basket beneath it. The man explained, "This afternoon I heard your knock. I was standing on that basket with that rope around my neck, planning to end it all. When I heard you knock the second time, I thought, *I'll wait just a moment; and when the man goes away, I'll jump.* You knocked a third time. Then it got quiet. I was ready to jump, when I heard you knock again! I figured I better go see who it was. After you gave me that tract, I sat down and read it in its entirety. I must have read it fifty times this afternoon before calling you. I need what that is talking about."[188]

Thank God this tract man was sensitive to the leadership and prompting of the Holy Spirit. The Holy Spirit will guide you equally in soul winning, if you remain in a position to hear Him. "Do not quench the Spirit" (I Thessalonians 5:19 NASB).

Oswald Chambers comments, "The voice of the Spirit of God is as gentle as a summer breeze—so gentle that, unless you are living in complete fellowship and oneness with God, you will never hear it. The

---

[188] Ibid., 204–205.

sense of warning and restraint that the Spirit gives comes to us in the most amazingly gentle ways. And if you are not sensitive enough to detect His voice, you will quench it, and your spiritual life will be impaired."[189]

And I may add that the lives of others also will be impaired.

110 Special Blessings for the Soul Winner

John R. Rice states, "The Christian who wins souls has special blessings which other Christians who do not win souls never have. The Christian who does not obey God's commands to win souls is not as good a Christian, does not have as many promises, does not have as much joy, does not have as many answers to prayer, does not know Christ as well as ones whose life is centered on soul winning.

"To be a Bible scholar is not as good as being a soul winner. To be separated from worldly habits, amusements, and company is not as good as being a soul winner. To be a defender of the faith is not as good as being a soul winner.

"To be a martyr, to suffer persecution and death for your convictions is not as good as being a soul winner. No, there are special blessings of God for soul winners which are not given in like degree to anyone who does not win souls....Other Christian virtues and values are secondary to the one great end of keeping souls for whom Christ died out of Hell. So the soul winner is the best Christian, has the best promises, has the most happiness here and has the greatest rewards hereafter."[190]

One never knows when he may, as Moody states, "put a stream in motion" in soul winning. A highlight of my soul winning is the salvation of "Coca-Cola Buster" in Conway, South Carolina, shortly after graduation from seminary. Buster worked for the Coca-Cola Company and was therefore affectionately given this name. I can recall as though it were yesterday the drive to his farm to speak to him of Christ, his gracious welcome and receptiveness to the Gospel. He came forward publicly confessing Christ in the revival and hasn't missed a beat since then in walking with Christ. I bumped into Buster at the hospital in Myrtle Beach, South Carolina, a few years back, and he testified humbly of the many souls he had won to Christ. Little did I know that in 1975 when I led Buster to Christ, he would in turn lead so many others to the Savior. Moody is correct—in leading a soul to Christ, we do put a soul-winning stream in motion that will flow for time

---

[189] Chambers. *My Utmost*, August 13 entry.

[190] Rice, *Golden Path*, 275–276.

and eternity. Go and put such a stream in motion today. One lighted torch serves to light another.

111 Go without the Feeling

A champion of soul winners, Curtis Hutson cautions believers about waiting for a feeling before they go soul winning. "Too many Christians are sitting around waiting for a mystical feeling while souls are dying and going to Hell....When I was a boy, it was my duty to feed the chickens, and my father raised hundreds of them. Suppose before going to work one morning my father gave me an order to feed the chickens, told me how much to give them and the time they should be fed. During the day, I got busy playing and neglected the duty. That night when my father returned, he discovered several dead chickens. Immediately he calls for me and asks, 'Curtis, did you feed the chickens?'

"Sadly I reply, 'No, sir.'

"'Why didn't you?'

"I answer, 'I didn't feel led.'

"'What do you mean, you didn't feel led? Did I tell you to feed the chickens?'

"'Yes, sir.'

"'Did I tell you how much to give them?'

"'Yes, sir.'

"'And when they should be fed?'

"'Yes, sir.'

"'Then what were you waiting for?'

"'Well, Dad, I was waiting for a feeling!'

"Brother, my father would have given me feeling enough to put me in the chicken-feeding business for the rest of my life! And what will our Heavenly Father say at the Judgment Seat of Christ when we tell Him we never led a soul to Christ because we were waiting for the feeling? How can we give such a silly excuse in light of the clear command of Scripture!

"The greatest soul winning experiences have come when I went without a feeling. As a matter of fact, there have been very few times I really wanted to go soul winning. On the other hand, it has been my experience that, after winning several people to Christ, I wanted to continue visiting with people and sharing the Gospel."[191]

---

[191] Hutson, *Preaching on Soul Winning*, 245.

Setting specific times with a partner to go soul winning will aid you in overcoming the "I don't feel like it" syndrome.

112 The Meyer Challenge

F. B. Meyer met with the deacons of the church and rendered his resignation after serving only a year. He said the reason for this decision was that in the space of a year, not one person outside the church had been saved, and, as a result, he couldn't continue. The deacons felt his service was not up and pleaded with him to stay. Meyer then asked each deacon one by one if he had ever won a soul to Christ. Each man answered that he had not. Meyer then said that he would remain as pastor upon the condition that each of them would lead a soul to Christ within the next thirty days. This they agreed to do. One can only imagine the revival that broke out in that church!

The deacon, the pastor and every other church leader should be soul winners. What if every pastor would make the Meyer challenge to the deacons of the church he served!

113 Going and Winning

Coach Mark Richt was on the coaching staff of Bobby Bowden when one of the team members died. Coach Bowden called the coaches and team members together and told them how to be saved. He asked, "If that boy had been you, would you be in Heaven or Hell now?" It was that day Mark Richt got saved.[192]

Jerry Vines, commenting on Richt's conversion, wrote, "You probably are never going to have the chance to witness to a football team. You probably are never going to have the opportunity to move in certain circles that other people will move in. But as you go, wherever you are, do whatever you can to obey the Great Commission of our Lord to get involved in this 'going' business of making disciples.

"Not only is there going; there is also *winning*. What does it mean to 'make a disciple'? To make a disciple means to win someone to faith in the Lord Jesus Christ. Then this person begins to follow Jesus Christ as his Lord and Master. That's what it means to make a disciple. Go and make disciples.

"This is the job of every believer—going, winning. I'm here to tell you that a church that does not win souls does not deserve the land on which the building stands. I'm here to tell you that a Bible class that does not win

---

[192] Draper, *Preaching with Passion*, 490.

souls is not worth the electricity, the heat, the lights, the carpet, and the paint that goes into that room. Are you winning people to Christ in your Bible class? If not, get busy. It's time for you to do that. Put an empty chair in your class. Say to the members of your class, 'This chair represents some person who needs to know Jesus Christ. Get him here next Sunday.'"[193]

114 Dave Walton's Motivation

Dave Walton is an exemplary soul winner. Walton shares, "On September 7, 1975, I came to salvation through the prayers of a man who had fasted and prayed for me. I immediately became strongly involved with the church where I met Jesus. Pastor Rupert Guest was always challenging his congregation to pray and witness.

"It was at this time that I developed my first 10 Most Wanted List. My heart was burdened for my lost loved ones and friends. I began to pray with faith, believing that these that I was praying for would be saved. This pushed me into being a faithful intercessor. In due time, I became conscious of God's favor and power and presence with me.

"On December 7, 1983, I had an encounter with God's Holy Spirit. It was a brokenness of heart that is impossible to describe. I was in prayer, and all of a sudden, I could hear the cries of loved ones and friends crying for help. These were lost and headed to a Devil's Hell. In that moment, there was a fresh river of divine power flowing through me as I wept out of control for lost souls. The anguish of prayer had hit its mark. From that day forward, the Lord has made me a 'Fisher of Men.'

"From that day even until now there is a River of Living Water flowing out of my belly for lost souls. In my heart, I know that the Spirit of Jesus Christ is with me every moment, inspiring and fulfilling His assignments in my life. It is not always easy, but I am convinced that His power and presence are always with me.

"The more I pray from the secret place, the more I see God with me in the marketplace as I share my personal salvation story. I remain relentless at reaching people for the Kingdom of God. My example is Jesus. I am deeply moved as I read of Jesus on the Cross. What is He doing with His last breath? Winning a thief to the Kingdom of God. This inspires and motivates me to do the same."[194]

---

[193] Ibid., 491–492.

[194] Walton, Personal Correspondence, March 27, 2010.

Prayer in the secret place is absolutely imperative for soul winning passion. Prayer spurs soul winning. Prayer strengthens soul winning. Prayer sustains soul winning. Prayer sharpens soul winning. But a lack of prayer siphons the heart of passion and stops soul winning. Not soul winning? Take a serious look at your prayer life.

115 The First Great Essential in Soul Winning

John R. Rice states, "The first great essential in soul winning is to go after sinners! This is the simplest part of soul winning but the one on which most people fail. Most people do not win souls simply because they do not work at it. They do not go after sinners.

"One may cry and pray and read his Bible and go to church and have family altar and give his tithes and pay his honest debts, and yet his own family may go to Hell and all his friends around him, because he simply does not go after them, does not take the Gospel to them, does not try to urgently win them to Jesus Christ. No one ever becomes a soul winner who does not work at it. Aggressive efforts are blessed in soul winning. One who does not make the effort will not get people saved.

"The 'Go' is first (Mark 16:15). Going is before preaching. Going is before baptizing. The Bible command is not, 'Build a church house and preach.' The command is not, 'Settle down and preach.' The Bible says, 'Go...and preach.' Preaching without an earnest effort to reach sinners and get them to hear the Gospel does not fulfill the plain command of Jesus Christ."[195]

Preacher and church member need to get going after souls.

116 Keep Ringing the Bell

I read the story of a father who took his son to the church where he was saved many years earlier through loud Gospel preaching. Inside the church, the boy noticed a rope hanging from the ceiling and asked his dad what it was. The father shared that it was the rope that pulled the bell in the steeple that called the people to church to hear the Gospel and to get saved. The boy looked up to him and said, "Daddy, ring it again!" O Christian, ring the bell of salvation. Ring it again and again and again.[196]

---

[195] Rice, *Golden Path*, 89–90.

[196] Roloff, "Family Altar News," 8.

SPURS TO SOUL WINNING

Don't cower down. Don't cool down. Don't come down. Don't back down. Keep ringing the bell of salvation from pillar to post until the whole world hears.

"The Ninety and Nine"

There were ninety and nine that safely lay
In the shelter of the fold;
But one was out on the hills away,
Far off from the gates of gold—
Away on the mountains wild and bare,
Away from the tender Shepherd's care.

"Lord, Thou hast here Thy ninety and nine;
Are they not enough for Thee?"
But the Shepherd made answer, "This of Mine
Has wandered away from Me.
And although the road be rough and steep,
I go to the desert to find My sheep."

But none of the ransomed ever knew
How deep were the waters crossed,
Nor how dark was the night the Lord passed through
Ere He found His sheep that was lost.
Out in the desert, He heard its cry,
Sick and helpless and ready to die.

"Lord, whence are those blood drops all the way
That mark out the mountain's track?"
"They were shed for one who had gone astray
Ere the Shepherd could bring him back."
"Lord, whence are Thy hands so rent and torn?"
"They are pierced tonight by many a thorn."

And all through the mountains, thunder riven,
And up from the rocky steep,
There arose a glad cry to the gate of Heaven,
"Rejoice! I have found My sheep!"
And the angels echoed around the throne,
"Rejoice, for the Lord brings back His own!"[197]

---

[197] Clephane, "The Ninety and Nine," accessed April 14, 2011.

117 How to Conquer Negligence in Soul Winning

John R. Rice makes some suggestions as to how one may conquer the sin of not soul winning and become an alert, always-at-it soul winner.

(1) Face your sin and failure honestly. In a quiet time before God, confess that sin. Accept as a basic part of your Christian philosophy that soul winning is the first duty of every Christian....See your excuses for what they are. Make honest confession of your sin and failure to God and, pleading for His constant help, set out to be a consistent, daily, working soul winner.

(2) You should give soul winning priority. The preacher should face the fact that winning souls is more important than preaching a sermon that would not win a soul. The Sunday school teacher should face the truth that to win one of his pupils is more important than teaching the lesson. The church attender should face it that it is far more important to win a soul than it is to get someone to attend a service or join a church.

(3) You should definitely schedule a time for soul winning. One should have a time he gives to seeking sinners as regularly as he eats or goes to his job or attends church services. Every consecrated Christian hopes to do soul winning. But it is often left to convenience....But the Christian should set aside a certain evening every week or certain morning or other time when he definitely sets out to win somebody to Jesus Christ.

(4) Be soul conscious, always alert to find a lost sinner. Every morning, you ought to pray for an open heart so that, as Jesus found the woman by the well of Samaria and as He found the man born blind and the poor cripple by the pool of Bethesda, you can win souls.

(5) Daily, constantly pray that you may find the right person.[198]

118 Nonprevalence of Soul Winning

In my lifetime, I recall only three occasions in which someone confronted me about salvation. The first was at a barber shop in St. George, South Carolina, as I was waiting to get a haircut. A man getting a haircut, Charlie Thompson, frankly asked me if I was saved. The second occasion was at a McDonald's in Camden, South Carolina. A stranger approached me asking if I knew Jesus as my Savior. The third occasion happened at New Orleans Seminary as I was visiting the campus to make a decision regarding graduate studies. A student squarely looked me in the eyes and asked if I knew for sure I was saved.

---

[198] Rice, *Golden Path*, 82–85.

SPURS TO SOUL WINNING

Despite the hundreds of places I have been, the tens of thousands of people with whom I have crossed paths, and the hundreds of pastors whom I have met, only three times was I confronted with the greatest issue and need of life! Sixty-two years on this earth, and only three people have shown eternal interest in my soul.

If this is true of someone like me, sadly it is the case of multiplied thousands of men and women, boys and girls who declare, "No man cared for my soul" (Ps. 142:4). Don't assume another has already spoken to a person about Christ; the chance for that to be true is extremely small.

It is good to do humanitarian deeds, but that is not soul winning. It is awesome to visit the elderly and care for the sickly, but that is not soul winning. It is great to invite people to church, but that is not soul winning. And it is tremendous to visit hospitals and prisons teaching Bible studies, but that is not soul winning.

Soul winning is the express task of purposely and pointedly talking to a person about Christ, seeking a salvation response or decision. Acts 1:8 can only be obeyed by actually going and telling, not of one's great pastor, church or program (though this may be included), but of Jesus Christ, who died, was buried and raised from the dead to secure man's redemption.

119 They Won More One-on-One

Dr. Charles G. Trumbull, who preached for years to congregations, had for twenty years written weekly and edited a religious paper with a circulation of 100,000 copies, and was the author of thirty books, states that, to his knowledge, he had won more people to Christ in private than through any other means. Dr. A. C. Dixon, who replaced C. H. Spurgeon at the Metropolitan Tabernacle in London, declared that he also had won more to Christ in private than through preaching.[199]

"D. L. Moody stated that if he had to win one thousand souls in order to make sure of Heaven himself, he would certainly choose to risk it by personal soul winning without public preaching rather than to attempt it by public preaching without personal soul winning."[200]

With but few exceptions, I believe the preacher will bear greater fruit for his labor in personal soul winning than simply by mounting a platform to preach. This in no wise is to diminish the importance of preaching the Gospel, but to undergird the fact that preachers ought not simply to rely

---

[199] Rice, *Grand Success*, 201.

[200] Rice, *Personal Soul Winning*, 4.

upon preaching to win souls. This same truth may be carried over to the Sunday school teacher, children and youth minister.

A. T. Pierson wrote, "Upon this primitive evangelism God set His seal, confirming it with signs following and adding to the church daily. To such preaching we trace the most rapid and far-reaching results ever yet known in history. Within one generation, with no modern facilities for travel and transportation and for the translation and publication of the Word, without any of the now multiplied agencies for missionary work, the gospel message flew from lip to ear till it actually touched the bounds of the Roman Empire. Within one century," Pierson said, "the shock of such evangelism shook paganism to its center, the fanes of false gods began to fall, and the priests of false faiths saw with dismay the idol shrines forsaken of worshippers."[201]

120 Soul Winning Cures a Cold Heart

"A preacher who preaches to crowds and lives in pleasant places among generous and kindly people is often not right with God nor happy nor victorious. I know, for I have been there. But the man who has the continuous evidence of God's blessing on his ministry in personally winning the lost may be sure he is on the right track.

"How often I have tried to preach when words were hollow, the sky was brass, and weighty words went from a cold heart to colder ears. How often the Book had no message, and there was no joy in prayer. How often the weight of a service was breaking my heart, and I had no victory for the sermon.

"Then I slipped away to a neighbor, or more often to boys and girls, privately sought the appointed one with hungry heart and told again the sweet story that lived again in my heart with the telling, saw tears flow, heard the confession, felt the angels rejoicing again. Then I have gone again to public ministry and found that the Holy One had taken an ember from dead ashes in my heart, lighted a coal from the Book of God, and fanned it with His heavenly presence to a holy, blessed flame.

"O brethren, personal, heartbroken seeking of the lost by us preachers, not as preachers but as Christians, will fix our ministries, will fix our temptations, will fix our prayers, as nothing else will, because God will see to it that we can win souls only in proportion as we are right."[202]

---

[201] Pierson, *Evangelistic Work*, 32.

[202] Rice, *Grand Success*, 202–203.

"How many times I have been almost defeated, discouraged, down-hearted, without a message to preach; but when I gave myself to personal soul winning and had the joy of seeing some saved, what joy, what close touch with God!

"How much easier it is to pray when you win souls! How much easier it is to resist temptation when your feet are shod with the preparation of the Gospel of peace! The only safe place for a Christian is in the line of duty, and that is always in a path of soul winning."[203]

121 Soul Winning Piggyback Style

Be alert for what I count "piggyback" invitations from people to share Jesus. At this writing, Bojangles Restaurant employees wear a ribbon that states, "Ask me anything." In seeing this, I asked a waitress, "Can I really ask you anything?"

She answered, "Yes, as long as it's not immoral or unethical." I then asked her if she knew Jesus Christ as her Lord and Savior.

Similarly, in a family restaurant in Manning, South Carolina, a waitress wore a button that simply stated, "Ask me." So I did. I asked her if she was saved, a child of God.

When driving on an unfamiliar road, I asked a farmer in the field the shortest direction to the town of Eastover. In thanking this man for his directions, I asked if anyone had ever given him directions to Heaven, to which he replied no. This provided me with the opportunity to tell this man how one can enter Heaven.

The cashier at a carwash was reading a book as I approached to pay. I inquired about the book, and she began telling me the various subjects it covered. I was able to piggyback her response into a discussion of some of the various subjects of the Bible.

A nurse at a doctor's office, while taking my blood pressure, commented that we shared the same birthday. I immediately responded, "I have two birthdays; how about you?"

She was puzzled for a moment and then replied, "You mean born again?"

"Yes," I replied and then gave a witness.

I was at a restaurant mentoring a "preacher boy," and the waitress asked if he were my son. I replied that he wasn't my son but my brother in Christ. I told her that if she was a Christian, she was our sister. She wasn't, but she

---

[203] Rice, *Soul Winner's Fire*, 101.

said her mother and pastor had been talking to her much about becoming one, and just the night before she tried to pray about it. Realizing God was at work in this encounter, I shared what was necessary for salvation, gave her a tract pinpointing the sinner's prayer, and instructed her to find a quiet place to pray that prayer if she indeed wanted to become a Christian. This she joyously did.

I was mailing book orders at the post office prior to Easter, and each one cost $3.16. I said to the clerk that 316 reminded me of John 3:16, the message of Easter. He replied, saying, "For God so loved the world..." This opened the door to share a brief witness to the postal clerk and others nearby.

My cell phone died, and in having it replaced, I shared with the clerk that the first wireless connection invented was prayer, seeking to open the door to present a witness.

In a coffee shop, a young man ahead of me in line wore a shirt that stated, "Sky Diving Saved My Life." I asked what was meant by that statement.

"Actually, a parachute saved my life," he replied. I then shared how Jesus Christ had saved my life.

In a hospital waiting room, I noticed that a three-year-old girl's hair was braided with what I call witnessing bracelet beads. I shared that observation with the mother and proceeded to share what several of the colors meant, speaking of man's sin and Jesus' shed blood. I had a receptive audience, not only from that mother, but others seated nearby.

Stay alert to share a nugget of gospel truth in every venue. It is amazing how many doors people unwittingly open for us to do that comfortably and easily.

122 Have You Wept Lately?

Prior to a revival service, C. E. Matthews met a gentleman who had resisted previous soul-winning attempts by others. Matthews presented the plan of salvation, but the man insisted on not responding to Christ's invitation. "Finally, Brother Matthews burst into tears. That broke the man's resistance. He received Christ as his Savior and later that evening made his public profession of faith....Have you wept over a lost soul lately?"[204]

"When William C. Burns, so greatly used in revival work in Murray M'Cheyne's parish, and later in China, was commencing his ministry, his

---

[204] Hobbs, *Favorite Illustrations*, 64–65.

mother met him one day in a Glasgow close. Seeing him weeping, she said: 'Why those tears?'

"He answered 'I am weeping at the sight of the multitudes in the streets, so many of whom are passing through life unsaved.'…Oh, for tear-filled eyes! Oh, for sleepless eyes because of the imminent danger and doom of the unsaved! Do the tears ever start unbidden from *our* eyes as we behold our city filled with sin and suffering and shame? Does sleep ever flee *our* eyes because of our concern for the souls around? How cold and callous and benumbed are our souls!"[205]

123 Professor, President, but above All a Soul Winner

L. R. Scarborough was known better than anything else for his personal soul winning. He practiced what he preached. Scarborough declared, "I have won someone to Christ every way Jesus did except up a tree and on a cross. And the first chance I get, I am going after them. I think I probably won some where He didn't. I would not boast about it. I have tried to make it a habit to pick up men for Christ."

Sixteen years before his death, he wrote, "Oh, the joys and rich experiences of those who win souls. As I look back across the fifty-five years of my little life, I remember a happy home, though it was a log house on the frontiers of Texas, the joy of a gloriously good father and mother, and remember the joys of my own happy home through now twenty-five years with my blessed companion and our six children….As I look back over the years of study and recount the intellectual joys and the comradeships of my friends and remember the social joys, shining and rising above them all is the oft repeated joy of my heart when I have been permitted by the same Savior to bring to Him scarlet women, infidels, atheists, gamblers, murderers, whoremongers, moralists, and all sorts, thousands and thousands of them. There is no joy like the joy of soul winning."[206]

As I write this entry, my heart is smitten with deep soul agony as I contrast my soul winning with that of Scarborough. Oh, for a passion like unto his for the souls of the lost!

124 "Pushed" into Soul Winning

Charles Alexander was not only a superior music evangelist working alongside of R. A. Torrey, but also a great soul winner. He personally led to

---

[205] Sanders, "Passion for People," accessed April 12, 2010.

[206] Barlow, *Profiles in Evangelism*, 165–166.

Christ all of his associates who were not Christians—pianists, soloists, and secretaries. Alexander was not only a soul winner, but he enlisted others to win souls.

Dr. T. B. Davis, a biographer of Alexander, was literally "pushed" into soul winning by Alexander during a crusade. Davis, a syndicated religious reporter, was covering the crusade and was studying the crowd during the invitation in order to write a story. The altar was full of souls seeking salvation, and the number of counselors was insufficient. Alexander, seeing Davis on the platform, inquired, "What are you doing here, Davis, while people are down there waiting to be led to Christ?"

Davis replied, "I'm watching for an incident for my articles."

With a firm, gentle push, Alexander said, *"Get off the platform and lead some of these people to Christ, and you'll have some firsthand incidents to tell."*[207]

As a soul winner, enlist others to win souls. You may have to "push them into the water" the first time to witness, as Alexander did Davis, but that may be the very thing needed to boost their confidence that they can do it! Everyone you enlist to win souls multiplies your witness, enabling more of the lost to hear the Gospel.

Helen, Alexander's wife, testified, "To Charles Alexander, every new soul with whom he came in contact thrilled him with an ardor as fresh as if it were the first with whom he had come into contact to lead to Jesus."

Fred Barlow sums up Alexander's ministry, "Thus the great platform man witnessed, warned and won the lost to Christ—in meetings, yes, but also on the streets (in Melbourne he walked the streets a whole night seeking to win a man to Christ); in hospitals (he led two nurses to Christ after an appendectomy); in restaurants, cabs, anywhere and everywhere!"[208]

Pray the Lord will raise up more musicians like Charles Alexander.

125 "What's Your Excuse?"

Nell Kerley is a 76-year-old widowed great-grandmother with diabetes, arthritis, non-Hodgkin's lymphoma, no kneecaps, and with screws holding her ankles in place, who loves winning souls. "So," she asks, "what's your excuse?"

---

[207] Ibid., 11.

[208] Ibid., 11.

This woman, who has "been a Sunday school teacher forever," never led a person to Christ until 1998. After having now led more than 2,465 souls to Christ, she isn't slowing down.[209]

So I ask with Nell Kerley, "What's your excuse?"

126   The Loss of Lee

Lee loved to play basketball and would join with others to play at a corner of the parking lot of a Baptist church in Fort Worth, Texas. Dozens of boys would play basketball daily at this church lot well up into the night. Nobody ever walked out of the church to invite these boys to Sunday school. Worse, no one ever walked out to tell these boys of their concern for them or of Jesus' great love and concern.

A few years later, Lee moved from the neighborhood and got involved with some bad company. Eventually, he was lured into a socialistic, communistic style of life. Once discharged from the army, Lee spent time in Russia. In the autumn of 1963, just a few months after his return from Russia, the newspapers carried the headline: "Lee Harvey Oswald Shoots President John F. Kennedy."[210]

Reverse the hand of the clock back to the days when Lee was playing basketball at the corner of that Baptist church parking lot. Had a Sunday school teacher, a deacon, the pastor or any church member just taken the time to share Jesus with Lee, to show some love and care for Lee, this story might have ended so much differently. Who is outside now playing ball at your church?

127   How to Keep Your Courage Up

Chuck Kelly shares the story of an evangelist friend who approached a table of drinking men in a restaurant, presenting a quick witness. Kelly said to himself, *Can you believe this guy and his boldness? I wish I had that kind of courage.*

Outside the restaurant, the evangelist said to Kelly, "I find I have to do that to keep my courage up." Kelly asked for clarification, to which the friend said that the longer he went without telling someone about Jesus, the harder it was for him to open his mouth.[211]

---

[209] House, *2,000 and Counting,* accessed April 12, 2010.

[210] Smith, Jack, *Motivational Sermons*, 280–281.

[211] Ibid., 288–289.

The same is true for you. The longer you go without speaking to some-one about Christ with the specific goal of leading him or her to salvation, the more difficult it will become. That is why it is expedient for the believer to witness habitually.

128 He Knew How to Get Hold of God

Lewis Drummond tells the story about a great Christian named Brother O'Neal. He was a simple man with only a fifth-grade education but was successful in business. He loved the church and, though he never held a leadership position, was a tremendous soul winner. He constantly sought out people with whom to share the Gospel. Sometimes when he witnessed in homes, entire families were saved. He witnessed of Christ in restaurants and in businesses. As Brother O'Neal shared Jesus under the power of the Holy Spirit, lives would melt in conviction.

One day, he became seriously ill and was hospitalized. As the nurse was preparing him for surgery, he did his best to win her to Christ. This would be O'Neal's final witness. His last full conversation in life was an effort to win a soul.

Drummond asks, "What undergirded his life?" and answers, "He was a man who knew how to get hold of God, ask for a blessing, and see God do things. Prayer is effective in the ministry of Christ's witnesses."[212]

129 The Lost Ring

When I was the pastor of a church, I discovered, prior to leaving to attend my weekly classes at seminary, that my college ring was lost. Believing it might be in my car, I searched high and low but without success. I left my car at the church for the week and asked a dear Christian, Aunt Ida, to continue the search. This she did but again without success.

The entire week, while at seminary, my mind kept returning to the lost ring. Upon my return to the church, I made another search, and this time I was successful. When I shared the news with Aunt Ida, we both rejoiced.

How thorough has been your search for the lost son, lost daughter, and lost Sunday school member or friend? Are you gravely concerned about them? Diligently search and recruit others to assist, so that these may be "found" before it is too late. Once they are found, then it is "party time," time to celebrate that he who was lost is now found.

---

[212] Drummond, Lewis and Betty, *Spiritual Woman*, 219.

SPURS TO SOUL WINNING

130 Testimony of O. J. Peterson

"I was raised in Phoenix, Arizona, just four blocks from a Southern Baptist church. My parents were not church members and had their problems with alcohol and its effects. No one from that church or any other church ever knocked on our door. We were never invited to Sunday school, Vacation Bible School or revival meetings.

"As an unrestrained, curious kid, I experimented with alcohol and then drugs. In my teens, I became hooked on drugs. I heard you could get them easier in California than anywhere else, so I made my way there.

"It was there that I met Arthur Blessitt. He told me about Jesus, who saved me. I'm saved. I've been saved from sin. I've been saved from Hell. I've been saved from alcohol. I've been saved from drugs. I've been saved from a wasted life. I've been saved."[213]

How many O. J.'s live within sight of a church without having any member ever once share the Gospel with them! The blood of those which the church member fails to warn and win will be 'required at their hands' (Ezekiel 3:18).

131 "I Am Ready"

The apostle Paul testified, "I am ready" (Romans 1:15). This Christian servant was always ready to share the Gospel. If you were to awaken him in the middle of the night, immediately he would point the way of salvation. Upon entering towns, he would find a soapbox, as in Lystra, stand upon it, and preach Jesus. He was ready to witness the Gospel at the riverside to Lydia, in a jailhouse to a chief jailer, in a courthouse to King Agrippa, in leg irons to his Roman guards in Rome, to a fortuneteller in Philippi, to the household of the Philippian jailer at midnight. This man refused to be silenced. He was ever ready to open his mouth and tell of the Savior who saved him.

Can you say the same? Are you ready today, tonight or tomorrow to witness of Christ, despite possible injurious consequences? Then why don't you do so? "I am not ashamed of the Gospel of Christ: for it is the power of God unto salvation to every one that believeth" (Romans 1:16).

What is required for you to be ready to share Christ? Seminary education? No. F.A.I.T.H.? No. Certification in soul-winning training? No. Scripture memorization of multiple verses? No.

---

[213] Smith, Jack, *Motivational Sermons*, 219.

Though these things will certainly enhance soul winning, all that is necessary for you to witness is to know Jesus as Lord and Savior. In reality, you *are* ready to share Christ with others now; so do it.

132 A Soul-Longing

L. R. Scarborough stated, "A soul-longing to see the lost saved and to have a share in their salvation…is essential in successful soul winning. Jesus had compassion on the multitudes wherever He saw them. His loving heart poured forth tears as from Olivet He looked out upon rebelling Jerusalem, and in a deep spiritual compassion, He longed to see the city saved by the grace of God. The successful soul winner must catch from Christ this burden of soul if he is to win in this triumphant trail after the lost."[214]

Pray unto the Lord, pleading for such a "soul-longing."

133 Do You Get It?

I read the story of a theater manager instructing a new usher, pointing out the exits in case of an emergency. The usher replied, "Don't worry about me. I will get out." He missed the whole point. He was to be the guide to lead occupants in the theater to safety.[215]

Do you get it? You are not to simply sit back relishing in salvation, but be busy guiding others from the "fire" to the only escape exit in Jesus Christ.

134 Three Keys to Enable Witnessing

Thad Hamilton cites three keys that will enable you to witness to others, based upon II Timothy 1:7: "For God hath not given us the spirit of fear; but of power, and of love, and of a sound mind."

(1) Accept His authority over you. God is the absolute owner of the Christian; therefore, acknowledge His right to mandate soul winning. In times of fear in witnessing, recall His authority, saying, "Lord, take control. Have control of me—what I say, what I do, and what I think."

(2) Accept His appointment for you. Did you know that God makes appointments for you? The biggest appointment He has made is for you to

---

[214] Scarborough, *Search for Souls*, 14.

[215] Smith, Jack, *Motivational Sermons*, 124.

share the Gospel with others (Matthew 28:19). This should be the goal of your life. Have you ever accepted such appointments?

(3) Accept His ability in you. Here's the principle: God's Spirit, when He has authority over us and when we have accepted His appointment for us, will operate His ability through us. The Bible says, "Faithful is he that calleth you, who also will do it" (I Thessalonians 5:24).

In your witnessing, the Holy Spirit will give you all that is necessary to be successful—power, love, and a sound mind.

Power (God's "dynamite") to witness is not restricted just to preachers or Sunday school teachers, but is available to each believer.

The Holy Spirit will give you love to be a witness. "The love of God is shed abroad...by the Holy Ghost" (Romans 5:5) in the life of the believer and from the lips of the believer. He will help you to love as Jesus loves.

The Holy Spirit will give you a sound mind to witness. The Holy Spirit will work in the believer's mind, giving good sense and the good actions that result from the good sense. The Holy Spirit will grant you good sense about preparation to witness, personal life in witnessing, presentation of the witness, and praise in witnessing.[216]

135   Don't Be Arrogant

C. H. Spurgeon warns, "If we have brought many to Christ, we dare not boast, for we are humbled by the reflection that more might have been done had we been fitter instruments for God to use."[217]

"When we are successful, we must long for more success. If God has given us many souls, we must pine for a thousand times as many. Satisfaction with results will be the knell of progress. No man is good who thinks he cannot be better."[218]

"Stand and look that matter over and see if you are at all able, in and of yourself, to work the conversion or regeneration of a single child in your Sunday school. My brethren, we are at the end of ourselves here....If we aim at the new birth of our hearers, we must fall prostrate before the Lord in conscious impotence, and we must not go again to our pulpits till we have

---

[216]   Ibid., 71–74.

[217]   Allen, *Exploring the Mind*, 548.

[218]   Spurgeon, *All-Round Ministry*, chapter 11, accessed April 4, 2010.

heard our Lord say, 'My grace is sufficient for thee: for my strength is made perfect in weakness.'"[219]

136 "Take It to the People"

"A new theory has lately been started which sets forth as its ideal a certain imaginary kingdom of God, nonspiritual, unscriptural, and unreal. The old-fashioned way of seeking the lost sheep, one by one, is too slow. It takes too much time and thought and prayer, and it does not leave space enough for politics, gymnastics, and sing-song."[220]

These words were spoken over a hundred years ago by the London pastor C. H. Spurgeon but are just as timely and truthful today. Christians are forever trying to find the easier and less costly method in winning the unsaved. Anything but door-to-door or person-to-person witnessing seems to be the attitude of the day. But it is the Master's model and the believer's mandate (John 4:10). The apostle Paul was the champion soul winner he was due to taking the Gospel to the people (Acts 20:20). Remember the soul winner's motto: "Take it to the people."

137 Extraordinary Power Needed

C. H. Spurgeon declared, "Ask an ungodly man whether he will take up the humble, often abused and persecuted position of a lowly follower of Christ, and he scorns the idea. If it were possible for him to get into that position for a time, how gladly would he shuffle out of it! He likes to be 'in the swim' and to side with the majority, but to be a live fish and to force his way up the stream is not according to his desire. He prefers a worldly religion with abundant provision for the flesh. Religious worldliness suits him very well, but to be out-and-out for Jesus, called out from the world and consecrated to obedience is not his ambition.

"Do you not see in this your need of an extraordinary power? To call men out to a real separation from the world and a true union with Christ, apart from the power of God, is an utterly futile effort. Go and whistle eagles into an English sky or beckon dolphins to the dry land or lure leviathan till thou canst play with him as with a bird, and then attempt this greater task. They will not come; they have no wish to come. Even so our Lord and Master warned the Jews when He said, 'Ye will not come to me, that ye might have life.'

---

[219] Ibid., chapter 11, accessed April 4, 2010.

[220] Ibid., chapter 11, accessed April 4, 2010.

"They will read the Bible: 'Ye search the Scriptures; for in them ye think ye have eternal life'; but they will not come to the Lord Himself. That is too spiritual a matter for their tastes. No, the command 'Repent ye, and believe the gospel' is too hard, too sharp, too humbling for them. Is not this enough to appall you? Dare you go forward unless your Lord shall gird you with heavenly power? 'Who is sufficient for these things?'

"We are weak, exceedingly weak, every one of us. If there is any brother here who is weaker than the rest and knows that he is so, let him not be at all cast down about that; for you see, brethren, the best man here, if he knows what he is, knows that he is out of his depth in his sacred calling.

"Well, if you are out of your depth, it does not matter whether the sea is forty feet or a full mile deep. If the sea is only a fathom deep, you will drown if you be not upborne; and if it be altogether unfathomable, you cannot be more than drowned. The weakest man here is not, in this business, really any weaker than the strongest man, since the whole affair is quite beyond us and we must work miracles by Divine power or else be total failures."[221]

138 Converts Like Money Put in a Bag of Holes

The soul winner can never know for sure the sincerity and understanding of the lost at that moment in time when they pray for salvation. Sadly, no doubt, some counted as conversions were not. As Spurgeon says, "We may announce them as our converts, we may associate with them as workers and feel thankful for them as fellow-heirs, and yet bitter may be our disappointment when all comes to all and they turn aside unto perdition. How grievous to be, to all appearance, rich in usefulness and on a sudden to find that our converts are like money put into a bag that is full of holes and that our treasured converts fall out, because they were not truly gathered to the Lord Jesus after all!"[222]

Take encouragement and faint not. Jesus had his Judas, and Moody his drunk; but this, though grievous, did not prevent their continued soul winning. You will have yours also. All the believer can do is to go to man in the Holy Spirit's control (discernment, power, leadership), making plain the message, means, and must of salvation, seeking their salvation. Salvation decisions made can only be trusted as genuine at that moment.

---

[221] Ibid., chapter 11, accessed April 4, 2010.

[222] Ibid., accessed April 4, 2010.

139 Success in Soul Winning

"What is success in evangelism? Is it when the person you witness to comes to Christ? Certainly that's what we want to happen. But if this is success, are we failures whenever we share the Gospel and people refuse to believe? Was Jesus an evangelistic 'failure' when people like the rich young ruler turned away from Him and His message? Obviously not. Then neither are we when we present Christ and His message and people turn away in unbelief. We need to learn that sharing the Gospel is effective evangelism. We ought to have an obsession for souls and tearfully plead with God to see more people converted, but conversions are fruit that God alone can give."[223]

Your role is to go and tell under the power of the Holy Spirit, leaving the results up to God. If you are faithful in this, then you are successful, regardless of outcome.

140 I Corinthians 13 Adaptation

The following is a paraphrase of I Corinthians 13 by Dr. Joseph Clark, quoted in Don Whitney's *Spiritual Disciplines for the Christian Life.*

Though I speak with the tongues of scholarship, and though I use approved methods of education, and fail to win others to Christ or build them up in Christian character, I am become as the moan of the wind in a Syrian desert.

And though I have the best of methods and understand all mysteries of religious psychology, and though I have all biblical knowledge, and lose not myself in the task of winning others to Christ, I become as a cloud of mist in an open sea.

And though I read all Sunday school literature and attend Sunday school conventions, institutes, and summer school, and yet am satisfied with less than winning souls to Christ and establishing others in Christian character and service, it profiteth nothing.

The soul-winning servant, the character-building servant, suffereth long and is kind; he envieth not others who are free from the servant's task; he vaunteth not himself, is not puffed up with intellectual pride.

Such a servant doth not behave himself unseemly between Sundays, seeketh not his own comfort, is not easily provoked, beareth all things, believeth all things, hopeth all things.

---

[223] Whitney, *Spiritual Disciplines*, 103.

And now abideth knowledge, methods, the Message, these three; but the greatest of these is the Message.[224]

141 The Supreme Weapon

Joseph Ton was Pastor of Second Baptist Church, Oradea, Romania, until he was exiled by the Romanian government in 1981. In *Pastoral Renewal*, he writes of his experience:

"Years ago I ran away from my country to study theology at Oxford. In 1972, when I was ready to go back to Romania, I discussed my plans with some fellow students. They pointed out that I might be arrested at the border. One student asked, 'Joseph, what chances do you have of success-fully implementing your plans?'

"Ton asked God about it, and God brought to mind Matthew 10:16: 'I send you as sheep in the midst of wolves,' and seemed to say, 'Tell me, what chance does a sheep surrounded by wolves have of surviving five minutes, let alone of converting the wolves? Joseph, that's how I send you: totally defenseless and without a reasonable hope of success. If you are willing to go like that, go. If you are not willing to be in that position, don't go.'"

Ton writes: "After our return, as I preached uninhibitedly, harassment and arrests came. One day during interrogation, an officer threatened to kill me. Then I said, 'Sir, your supreme weapon is killing. My supreme weapon is dying. Sir, you know my sermons are all over the country on tapes now. If you kill me, I will be sprinkling them with my blood. Whoever listens to them after that will say, "I'd better listen. This man sealed it with his blood." They will speak ten times louder than before. So, go on and kill me. I win the supreme victory then.'"

The officer sent him home. "That gave me pause. For years I was a Christian who was cautious because I wanted to survive. I had accepted all the restrictions the authorities put on me, because I wanted to live. Now, I wanted to die, and they wouldn't oblige. Now I could do whatever I wanted in Romania. For years I wanted to save my life, and I was losing it. Now that I wanted to lose it, I was winning it."[225]

Jesus said, "For whosoever will save his life shall lose it: and whosoever will lose his life for my sake shall find it" (Matthew 16:25). The apostle Paul stated, "For me to live is Christ and to die is gain" (Philippians 1:21).

---

[224] Ibid., 114.

[225] Larson, *Illustrations for Preaching*, 202.

Jim Elliot declared, "He is no fool who gives what he cannot keep to gain what he cannot lose."[226]

Personally apply these statements to soul winning.

142 Fishing with a Rod or a Net

You cannot win the world at one time—but you can help the process by winning one person at a time. Alexander Maclaren stated, "It is better for most of us to fish with the rod than with the net, to angle for single souls rather than to try to enclose a multitude at once. Preaching to a congregation has its own place and value, but private and personal talk honestly and wisely done will effect more than the most eloquent preaching."[227]

143 Lifeboat No. 14

April 14, 1912, the unthinkable happened to the unsinkable Titanic when it struck an iceberg at 11:40 P.M. and began sinking. Twenty lifeboats, most of which were only half filled, were lowered into the water. These lifeboats waited a safe distance away for fear that those drowning would cling to their craft, eventually swamping it. As 1,528 people struggled for survival, all but one of these lifeboats chose to play it safe. Lifeboat No. 14 rowed back to the place of the sinking at 2:20 A.M. alone, chasing the cries in the darkness, seeking and saving precious lives.[228]

Far too many whom Jesus has delivered from the sinking vessel of self, sin and Satan want to play it safe for fear someone or something will rock the boat (ridicule, discrimination, ostracism, inconvenience). It's time you join believers aboard Lifeboat No. 14, jeopardizing your own life if need be, to save those drowning in the sea of eternal condemnation.

144 Who Is Holding the Rope?

In a fishing village that was located at the mouth of a turbulent river, a scream was heard, "Boy overboard!" The strongest swimmer in the village tied a rope around his waist, threw the other end among the crowd gathered, and plunged in the river. He gallantly fought the tide until he reached the

---

[226] Elliot, *Through Gates of Splendor*, 172.

[227] Green, *Illustrations for Biblical Preaching*, 126.

[228] Larson, *Illustrations for Preaching*, 67.

young boy, and a great cheer went up when he grasped him in his arms. He then shouted, "Pull in the rope!"

Each one upon the shore looked at the others, inquiring, "Who is holding the rope?" Sadly no one was. In the excitement of watching the rescue effort, the rope slipped into the water. Unable to help, they watched two lives drown because no one made it their business to hold the end of the rope.

Believers ought to hold the end of the "evangelistic rope" financially, encouragingly, prayerfully, and supportively for others who are winning souls. Are you willing to hold the shore end of the rope for others as they seek to rescue the unsaved at home and around the world? This is a method of soul winning all can and should do.

145 The Rope

A medical missionary performed surgery on a poor blind man and restored his sight. The man disappeared for a few days and then appeared at the missionary's door. In opening the door, the missionary saw this man holding one end of a rope. On that rope were ten more blind people.

If Jesus has opened your spiritual eyes to the truth about salvation and has saved you, grab a rope and bring as many "blind" people to the Cross as possible.

146 He Gave Up His Freedom for Lost Souls

Stephen Olford told the story of a 19th century missionary in the West Indies who worked tirelessly night and day seeking to win the natives, to no avail. This man's passion was so intense for the souls of the people that in desperation he sold himself into slavery to become one of them. Though he forfeited his freedom to work side by side with these natives, he won many to Christ. What price are you willing to pay to win souls?

147 Why Didn't We Join Hands Sooner?

A child was lost in a vast wheat field. Friends and rescue helpers searched diligently until the dark forced them to halt for the night. The next morning as they resumed their search, the suggestion was made that they join hands and form an unbroken human chain across the field in search for the child. In doing this, they found the lost child, but tragically it was too late. The child's mother walked back and forth wringing her hands and crying, "Why didn't we join hands sooner? Why didn't we join hands sooner?"

The lost are all about us. It is high time believers join hands in rescuing them before it is eternally too late. Will you join hands with fellow believers in this soul-saving rescue attempt?

148 Save One More for Jesus

Rick Warren's father, in the final days of life, semiconsciously spoke twenty-fours a day of church-building projects. One night as he tried to get out of bed, Rick's wife asked him, "Jimmy, what are you trying to do?"

He replied, "Got to save one more soul for Jesus! Got to save one more soul for Jesus! Got to save one more soul for Jesus!" He repeated that phrase probably a hundred times over the next hour. As Dr. Warren began to thank God for his dad's faith, his father placed his frail hand upon his head and said, as if commissioning him, "Save one more for Jesus! Save one more for Jesus!"[229]

May you be on the lookout to "save one more for Jesus!"

149 That Kind We Don't Need

A man shouted out in one of D. L. Moody's meetings, "Brother Moody, for twenty years I have been living on the Mountaintop of Transfiguration."

Moody replied, "Have you ever won a soul to Christ?" The man answered that he had not. "Well," responded Moody, "we don't want that kind of a mountaintop experience."[230]

150 Love Sinners for Jesus' Sake

A little girl returned from play with a small kitten that was the dirtiest, filthiest, and most unpleasant kitten one could imagine. The little girl loved that kitten, while her siblings kicked it and tossed it outside the house at every opportunity.

One day this girl became sick and eventually died. In the aftermath of her funeral, the family returned home only to see the scrawny kitten walking across the yard. All the children ran into the yard, took the little kitten unto their arms, and said, "Bless you, kitten; sister loved you." From

---

[229] Warren, *Purpose Driven Life*, 287–288.

[230] Ford, *Special Days and Occasions,* 34.

then on, their attitude toward that kitten was changed. They loved the kitten, nursed the kitten, fed the kitten—for little sister's sake.[231]

What changed the children's attitude about the scrawny little kitten? It was the fact that their sister who died loved it, and in loving what she loved, however unpleasant it was, they would be honoring her. These girls were saying by their action, "Sister, we love you enough to take care of what you loved."

How can you love some of the dirtiest, filthiest, most vulgar and unpleasant people in the world? You can do so by recalling how much God loves them. He loved them so much that He sent His only son, Jesus, to rescue them. Jesus loved them to the death. Your love for Jesus should change your attitude about vile and vulgar sinners, knowing that as you love them, Jesus is honored and glorified.

Do you love Jesus enough to take care of what He loves?

151 "You Never Asked Me"

Henry Ford purchased a large insurance policy, and it was blazoned in the Detroit newspapers. A friend of Ford who was in the insurance business and read the story confronted him for its truthfulness. Ford assured him it was true. The friend then inquired why he did not purchase the policy from him, since he was a personal friend and had sold insurance for years. Ford responded, "You never asked me."[232]

How many classmates, business associates, neighbors, teammates or friends can say to you, "You never asked me," as it relates to becoming a Christian?

152 "I Want to Point Out My Rescuer"

As a Mississippi River captain's boat was passing another boat, he grabbed the first passenger he saw, shouting: "Look, look over there on the other boat. Look at its captain." The passenger inquired as to the reason to look, and the captain then told him the story of how he was thrown overboard when his ship collided with another ship, and as he was drowning, the captain of the other vessel dove into the water and saved him.

---

[231] Daniels, *Why Jesus Wept*, 76–77.

[232] Green, *Illustrations for Biblical Preaching*, 124–125.

After telling the story, the captain then turned to the man and said, "Ever since that day, I want to point out my rescuer to others."[233]

Don't you really want to do the same? Doesn't love for your Rescuer, Savior, Deliverer constrain you to tell one and all of Him who saved you?

153 How Can You Eat or Sleep While Loved Ones Are Unsaved?

John R. Rice tells of a revival service at Shamrock, Texas, wherein a young woman, amidst sobs, testified that her husband was unsaved. "When I want other things, I go after them," she said, "and I have decided this morning that I want my husband saved more than anything else in the world."

The next day Rice had lunch with the couple, and the wife said, "Brother Rice, Charles is not a Christian. I want you to read and pray with him now that he will be saved." Rice did so, but the young man refused to be saved.

Following the meal, he heard the wife say to her husband, who was to take her to work before going to his own job, "Charles, I am not going to work this afternoon. Tell Mr. Forbis that I will not be there." Puzzled, the man left for his job.

As Rice was departing, the wife with tears said, "Brother Rice, how can I stand behind a counter, measure goods, sell hose, ribbons or gloves, knowing that my husband is lost and may die at any moment and go to Hell? I must get hold of God today. My husband must be saved!"

When Charles returned home from work that evening, only one plate was on the table, but he asked no questions. That evening he wanted to rest, but his wife said, "No, Charles, you must go with me to church." And he did.

Rice preached and pleaded for souls. Others were saved, but not Charles. In the aftermath of the service, Rice talked and prayed with Charles but to no avail. The church was about to be shut down for the night, but Mrs. Jessie stood in the center of the floor weeping. When Charles suggested they depart, she shook her head and sobbed the more. Charles walked to and fro, disturbed and distressed, and burst into tears when Rice touched him on the shoulder. Charles got saved that night![234]

---

[233] Ibid., 127–128.

[234] Hutson, *Preaching on Hell*, 40–41.

Jessie won her husband because she made it a priority. Realizing something of the terrible danger and punishment of a lost soul, she sought her husband's salvation with hot pursuit. How desperate are you for your husband, wife, father, mother, brother, sister, or friend to be saved? Don't sit back idly while loved ones die without Jesus and go to Hell!

154 "Until He Find It"

Spurgeon proclaims, "Christ, the Good Shepherd, first will seek the lost sheep 'until he find it.' It is a long reach 'until he find it.' The Lord Jesus did not come down to earth to make an attempt to find men; He came to do it—and He did it. He tarried here, seeking the lost sheep until He found it; He never gave over until His work was done.

"And mark, for a shepherd there is no giving up. That sheep has wandered now for many hours. The sun has risen, and the sun has set—or at least it is just going down—but as long as the shepherd can see and the sheep is still alive, he will pursue it 'until he find it.' He has been disappointed a great many times; and when he thought that he should have found it, he has missed it; but still, he will never give up. He is impelled onward by irresistible love, and he must continue his weary search 'until he find it.'

"It was precisely so with our Lord Jesus Christ. When He came after you and after me, we ran from Him, but He pursued us. We hid from Him, but He discovered us. He had almost grasped us, but so long as we eluded Him, He still pursued with love unwearied until He found us.

"Oh, if He had given up after the first ten years, if He had ceased to care for us after fifty different occasions in which we had choked conscience and quenched the Spirit, then we should have been lost. But He would not turn away. If He determines to save, He continues to pursue the rambling sheep until He finds it. He cannot, He must not, He will not cease from the work of seeking and finding 'until he find it.'...

"If you seek the conversion of any man, follow him up until you find him. Do not be discouraged. Put up with great rebuffs and rebukes; you will have him yet.…Whisper to yourself, *If He persevered with me even to the death, I may well persevere as long as I live in seeking and finding a soul.* Persevere with loving entreaties! Until you bury your unsaved ones, do not consider them dead; do not bury them spiritually until they are dead really.

"Some are easily baffled. They have written the death warrant of a friend by ceasing to pray for him, and yet that death warrant will never be written in the records of Heaven, for the friend will be brought to the Savior's feet.

"'Until he find it'—now nail your colors to the mast. 'Until he find it'—go out, undershepherds for Christ. Wear this motto on your right hand: 'Until I find it.' Live or die or work or suffer, whether the time be short or long or the way be smooth or rough, let each one of you be bound to seek a soul 'until he find it.' You will find it then, even as Christ found you."[235]

155 You Do Identify with the Sower

"A sower went forth to sow" (Matthew 13:3). The text does not reveal if he was an experienced sower or a novice sower. It does not reveal if he was a minister or layperson. It does not indicate the type of clothing worn by the sower or his race. It is silent about the method he used in sowing, whether it was conventional or radical. Nothing is mentioned regarding boldness or timidity or whether he spoke fluently or stammered. In fact, we know nothing of the sower outside of the fact that he went into the field to sow. I am glad this is the case, for it opens a wide door for every believer to identify with him and join him in the work.

Vance Havner stated, "If there was an eleventh commandment, it would be, 'Thou shalt not compare.'" Don't compare your ability to win souls with that of the experienced and polished.

Spurgeon stated, "Just feel that you have to sow the good seed of the kingdom; and, if you have not so big a hand as some sowers have and cannot sow quite so much at a time, go and sow with your smaller hand. Only mind that you sow the same seed, for so God will accept what you do.

"You are grieved that you do not know so much as some do and that you have not the same amount of learning that they have. You regret that you do not have the poetical faculty of some or the holy ingenuity of others. Why do you speak about all these things? Our Lord Jesus Christ does not do so; He simply says, 'A sower went forth to sow.'"[236]

Being very aware of men who are much more apt to win souls effectively than I am, I intentionally thank God for them, learn from them, fuel my passion with them, but ever refuse to be intimidated or discouraged because of them. Every believer would be wise to do the same.

In the final analysis, it is really irrelevant whether a man is a preacher or a layman, refined or rustic, educated or illiterate, rich or poor, bold or shy in soul winning. What matters is that he gets into the harvest field and sows the good seed!

---

[235] Spurgeon, *Sermons on Soul Winning*, 125–127.

[236] Ibid., 68.

SPURS TO SOUL WINNING

156 The Bottom Line in Soul Winning

Ultimately it is going to take enormous discipline to habitually share the faith one-on-one. Spurgeon advised, "We must school and train ourselves to deal personally with the unconverted. We must not excuse ourselves, but force ourselves to the irksome task until it becomes easy. This is one of the most honorable modes of soul winning, and if it requires more than ordinary zeal and courage, so much the more reason for our resolving to master it. We must win souls. We cannot live and see men damned; we must have them brought to Jesus! Oh! Then be up and doing and let none around you die unwarned, unwept, uncared for....Get a hold of the man alone, and in love, quietly and prayerfully, talk to him."[237]

Donald Whitney asks, "Isn't the main reason we don't witness because we don't *discipline* ourselves to do it? Yes, there are those wonderful, unplanned opportunities 'to give the reason for the hope that you have' (I Peter 3:15) that God brings unexpectedly. But I maintain there is a reason for most Christians to make evangelism a spiritual discipline....Unless we discipline ourselves for evangelism, it is very easy to excuse ourselves from ever sharing the Gospel with anyone."

Whitney shares this view in light of the fact that some believers are not associated with the lost, and those who are in the workplace do not have ample opportunity to seriously share a Gospel witness with them. The believer therefore must be disciplined to "invent" ways to get into the circle of the unsaved privately for the purpose of evangelism (private lunches with neighbors or coworkers, dialog during informal times while traveling on business with coworkers, meals in your home with unsaved neighbors or others, in athletic events or church social functions).[238]

157 Rescue 911 for Souls

As I write this, news is forthcoming regarding a major mine explosion at the Upper Big Branch Mine, Whitesville, West Virginia, in which twenty-five have died and four remained trapped. It is the worst mine disaster in twenty-five years. An all-out effort is underway to rescue the four trapped in hopes they are yet alive. On national television, the governor of the state has asked prayer for these men. There is grave concern and compassion exhibited both for the families of the miners and their loved ones trapped. Everything that can possibly be done, without thought of cost or sacrifice, is underway to seek and save these miners before it is too late.

---

[237] Ibid., 18.

[238] Whitney, *Spiritual Disciplines*, 106–109.

Life is precious, and one ought to do all that is possible, when it is in jeopardy, to save it. I am grateful for the hundreds of mine rescue workers who are giving their best effort to save these men.

The soul of man is likewise precious, and one ought to do all possible, when it is jeopardized, to save it. The Bible makes clear that man's soul is presently in jeopardy of eternal separation from a Holy God. He is entrapped and held captive by Satan and cannot free himself. An all-out effort must be launched in grave concern and compassion to search him out and to bring him out (Acts 1:8). If a soul rescue is beyond one's reach, then others must be asked to assist. Time is of the essence. Delay may mean his doom.

Privately pray for man's soul rescue. Publicly urge prayer that these trapped in the darkness and deceit of depravity will be freed. Give your best effort, without thought of cost or consequence, to reach the lost trapped deep in the mine of sin TODAY. A soul is worth it. Jesus said, "For what shall it profit a man, if he gain the whole world, and lose his own soul?" (Mark 8:36).

158 Soul Sharpshooters

"So, try to get close with sinners. Talk gently to them until you have whispered them into the kingdom of Heaven and have told into their ears the blessed story that will bring peace and joy to their hearts. We need in the church of Christ a band of well-trained sharpshooters who will pick the people out individually and always be on the watch for all who come into the place—not annoying them, but making sure that they do not go away without having had personal warning, invitation, and exhortation to come to Christ."[239]

Such sharpshooters should find this focused task simple and fruitful, for they labor for souls in an evangelically conducive, nonhostile place to a captive audience. This Sunday take aim at the lost and pull the gospel trigger.

159 Payment Enough for Soul Winning

What is your motivation to witness? Is it applause and honor of man, numerical increase in the church, the approval of the senior pastor, or pressure from others? Hopefully, it is none of the stated. James cites the proper motive in witnessing: "Brethren, if any of you do err from the truth, and one convert him; Let him know, that he which converteth the sinner from the

---

[239] Spurgeon, *Soul Winner*, 127.

error of his way shall save a soul from death, and shall hide a multitude of sins" (James 5:19–20).

Spurgeon comments, "Do observe here that the apostle offers no other inducement to soul winners. He does not say, 'If you convert a sinner from the error of his way, you will have honor.' He does not say, 'If you convert a sinner from the error of his way, you will have the respect of the church and the love of the individual.' Such will be the case, but we are moved by nobler motives. The joy of doing good is found in the good itself. The reward of the deed of love is found in its own result. If we have saved a soul from death and hidden a multitude of sins, that is payment enough, even though no ear might ever hear of the deed and no pen ever record it. Let it be forgotten that we were the instruments if good is effected. It will give us joy, even if we are not appreciated....It will be joy enough to know that a soul has been saved from death and a multitude of sins has been covered."[240]

D. L. Moody once said, "My purpose in life is to go to Heaven and take as many people as possible with me."[241]

160 Lifestyle Coupled with "Lipstyle"

A young man saved in a Billy Graham meeting rushed back to inform his roommate with whom he had shared an apartment for several years of this decision. "I must tell you something," he told his friend. "Tonight I invited Christ to be my Savior, and He has changed my life."

The friend smiled and replied, "Wonderful. I have been hoping you would do that. I have been living the Christian life before you all these years hoping that you would trust Christ as your Savior."

Surprised greatly, the new believer said, "You lived such a perfect life that I kept trying to do it without Christ, inasmuch as you seemed to be doing it without Christ. Tonight, I invited Him to become my Lord and Savior because I failed to live up to your standard. You should have told me why you lived the way you live. Why didn't you tell me how I could know Christ too?"[242]

Jon Courson writes, "Sometimes we think that by being nice—mowing our neighbor's lawn, baking him cookies, or smiling when he drives by—

---

[240] Ibid., 294.

[241] Douglas, *Work of an Evangelist*, 163.

[242] Bright, *Steps to Maturity*, 343.

we will convert him. This is not true. There was no lovelier person than Jesus Christ; yet, His brothers did not believe on Him until the cross and the resurrection. That is why it is imperative to preach Christ crucified (I Corinthians 1:23). You can wave to your neighbor for twenty years and wave him right into Hell. Or you can take the time at some point to say, 'You know what? Jesus Christ died for your sins and rose from the dead, and you must believe on Him.'"[243]

Lifestyle evangelism is only effective when it is coupled with "lipstyle evangelism." People can easily misinterpret the reason for the change in our lives (the church, resolution, Buddha, or Christ), so we must clearly tell them. John Stott well said, "Words without works lack credibility; works without words lack clarity."[244]

161   There Was No Intercessor

"He saw that there was no man, and wondered that there was no intercessor" (Isaiah 59:16).

Andrew Murray declared, "From of old God had among His people intercessors to whose voice He had listened and given deliverance....Of what infinite importance is the place the intercessor holds in the Kingdom of God!...God rules the world and His church through the prayers of His people. That God should have made the extension of His Kingdom to such a large extent dependent on the faithfulness of His people in prayer is a stupendous mystery and yet an absolute certainty. God calls for intercessors. In His grace, He has made His work dependent on them; He waits for them."[245]

The Place of Prayer
There is a place where thou canst touch the eyes
  Of blinded men to instant, perfect sight;
There is a place where thou canst say, "Arise"
  To dying captives, bound in chains of night.

---

[243] Courson, *Application Commentary*, 1647.

[244] Stott, *Contemporary Christian*, 345.

[245] Murray, *God's Best Secrets*, 46.

There is a place where thou canst reach the store
  Of hoarded gold and free it for the Lord;
There is a place—upon some distant shore—
  Where thou canst send the worker and the Word.
Where is that secret place—dost thou ask, "Where?"
  O soul, it is the secret place of prayer!
—Alfred Lord Tennyson[246]

One testifies of John Smith, "I have often seen him come downstairs in the morning after spending several hours in prayer with his eyes swollen with weeping. He would soon introduce the subject of his anxiety by saying, 'I am a brokenhearted man; yes, indeed, I am an unhappy man—not for myself, but on account of others. God has given me such a sight of the value of precious souls that I cannot live if souls are not saved. Oh, give me souls, or else I die!'"[247]

162 Keeping the Net in Good Repair

The believer is to cast his net into the stream of lost humanity, seeking to win them to Christ. O. S. Hawkins states, "When the pastor publicly preaches the message of Christ, he is casting the net. When the layman personally shares his or her faith, he or she is casting the net."[248]

Hawkins cites that it is important to *mend the net* when it becomes full of holes; *wash the net* when it becomes dirty, so that we stay clean before the Lord; *cast the net* out of the boat into the world, for it is impossible to be a fisher of men if we do not; and *draw the net* by inviting the lost to become Christians.[249]

Look at your "net." Is it in good repair, or does it need mending or cleaning? Maybe it just needs to be thrown out of the boat to others at work, at school, on the athletic team, in the neighborhood, or at church. Or perhaps it has been cast into the water but never drawn back.

---

[246] Bright, *Steps to Maturity*, 248.

[247] Smith, Oswald, *Revival We Need*, Chapter 3.

[248] Hawkins, *Drawing the Net*, 15–16.

[249] Ibid., 15–16.

163 No Honor to the Soul Winner

"The inspired writer of Hebrews tells us that for the joy that was set before Him, Jesus endured the cross and despised the shame. He looked forward to the joy in Heaven, so He despised the shame of the cross and endured it gladly (Hebrews 12:1–2). The soul winner must have the same wisdom.

"I well know the course of a soul winner will not bring me the wealth of this world. I once thought that if I won many souls I would gain the fame and honor of Christian people everywhere. Alas, I find that is not true. The churches honor the scholar more than the soul winner. In denominational councils, the man who can raise money for schools and hospitals is more valued than he who can keep the drunkard and the harlot out of Hell.

"The pay of the world for soul winning is not large. But, thank God, I can take the 'long look,' as Moses did when he led the children of Israel out of Egypt and was content not be called Pharaoh's daughter's son; or be like Paul, who gave up his place as a blameless Pharisee, a leader of the Sanhedrin at Jerusalem, and became the despised but soul-winning apostle to the Gentiles. Moses had insupportable burdens. Paul so suffered that he said, 'If in this life only we have hope in Christ, we are of all men most miserable.'

"Both endured as seeing Him who is invisible. They knew there is a life beyond the grave when the soul winner will have his payday. 'He that winneth souls is wise,' and there will be eternal glories and rewards for the one who has the wisdom to turn many to righteousness."[250]

Rice's observation is true. Man does not honor the soul winner, so be not disappointed when others criticize or scorn instead of rejoicing in the news of souls won that you report. Jesus paid a huge price to be a soul winner, and so will all His disciples.

"My Christian friends, if the cost of soul winning seems too great, then I urge you to take private lessons from the Holy Spirit (I Corinthians 2:14)....The Holy Spirit can show you the things of God, the worth of a soul, and help you to be a soul winner. No one ever wins souls except by the power of the Holy Spirit."[251]

---

[250] Rice, *Soul-Winner's Fire*, 19

[251] Ibid., 19.

SPURS TO SOUL WINNING

164 Witnessing in the Church

A major New York life insurance company invited all of its agents to its corporate office for a conference. In the midst of that conference, one of the company's agents insured the elevator man, a barber and a waiter, all of whom had been employed at the corporate office for many years. No one thought to seek to sell a policy to these men in the corporate home office![252]

Witnessing must not be neglected within the walls of the "corporate office," the church. Never assume that janitors, daycare workers, maintenance personnel and Sunday school class attendees are Christians.

"The close of the regular church service affords a splendid opportunity for speaking to souls. Already hearts have, in all probability, been touched by the preached word and may be longing to have someone deal definitely with them and point them individually to Jesus Christ. It was at the close of a great service that Philip won his convert (Acts 8:37–38)."[253]

165 Spiritual Amnesia

Are you suffering from spiritual amnesia? Have you forgotten what it is like to be lost? Stir the pot of memory of your pre-Calvary life. Review the brokenness, hopelessness, emptiness and loneliness. Recall what it took to awaken you to the solitary solution in Jesus Christ from the heartache and havoc; wantonness and wastefulness. Reminisce about the sweeping transformation that happened at salvation.

Multitudes yet are as you once were. Joel attests, "Multitudes, multitudes in the valley of decision: for the day of the LORD is near in the valley of decision" (Joel 3:14). Identify with them. Empathize with them. Share Jesus with them. You once sat where they now sit. Having been there and having left there, you know how to tell the way to freedom. Since you know what the lost endure and the incomparable joyous estate of one who is saved, of all people in the world, you should be a soul winner.

---

[252] Tan. *7700 Illustrations*, #5902.

[253] Evans, "Instructions," accessed May 22, 2010.

Remind Me, Dear Lord
Roll back the curtain of memory now and then;
Show me where You brought me from and where I could have been.
Remember, I'm human, and human's forget;
So remind me, remind me, dear Lord.
—Dottie Rambo

166   The Soul Winner's Fire

John R. Rice cites the source of the soul winner's fire. "That passion, that compassion was wrought in the heart of Paul by the Holy Spirit, as it was in the heart of Jeremiah. Without some of that, no man or woman is fit to win souls nor able to do much of that holy work....This is a divine matter about which I write. We did not save ourselves, call ourselves, nor equip ourselves. We need to wait before God until the dross is burned out of our lives, until self-will is dead and the self-life is conformed to the death of Christ, before we can wholly follow the Lord.

"I say frankly that the passion for soul winning—that holy, loving, tearful 'MUST' that has burned with consuming flame in the heart of soul winners—is a supernatural enduement from God. Schools do not give this. Organizations cannot build it. It is supernatural, not natural; divine, not human. What we need is to tarry before God and so confess and forsake our sins until we are anointed from Heaven. Then the Word of God will be in our hearts like a fire in our bones, as it was with Jeremiah.

"O Thou holy God, Thou dying, risen, living Savior, Thou seeking Spirit, give us this holy passion for sinners, this compelling Gospel, this fire from Heaven."[254]

167   Discriminatory Witnessing

The style of dress, hairdo, or wearing of body rings in uncommon places by the people we meet must not deter the soul winner from his mission to give all men everywhere the opportunity to be saved. In visiting a dying teenage boy at a hospital, I was deeply saddened by what his mother shared concerning a prior visit by a minister. Seeing a ring in her son's ear, this minister commented on it and walked out never to return. These types of ministers need to reread Paul's and James's admonitions, "For there is no respect of persons with God" (Romans 2:11) and "But if ye have respect to persons, ye commit sin, and are convinced of the law as transgressors" (James 2:9).

---

[254] Rice, *Soul-Winner's Fire*, 54.

SPURS TO SOUL WINNING

The soul winner must look through the lenses of Jesus at people, looking beyond the external to the internal need. Do not be discriminatory or prejudicial when sharing the Gospel.

168 Avoid Shrinking Back

Regarding soul winning—"just do it." Don't shrink back. Don't turn back at the prospect's door and head for home. Lee Strobel states, "Almost every day, we come to evangelistic turning points. We make choices whether to help rescue these people from danger or to walk the other way. We make spur-of-the-moment decisions whether to heroically venture into their lives and lead them to a place of spiritual safety or merely hope that someone else will do it. We make split-second decisions all the time to play it safe or tilt the conversation toward spiritual topics, and many times we shrink back."[255]

A retracing of our steps today would probably shockingly reveal just how many times in fact we chose to shrink back from a witness. Brazen up and determine to redeem the golden opportunities to share Christ that surface today.

169 No Training Necessary, Though Beneficial

Neither God nor man expects the Christian just starting to witness to be thoroughly polished in presentation and technique. The blind man Jesus saved immediately gave testimony without any training period. He immediately testified, "Whether he be a sinner or no, I know not: one thing I know, that, whereas I was blind, now I see" (John 9:25). The adulterous woman converted at Jacob's Well left her water pot immediately and entered into the town broadcasting, "Come, see a man, which told me all things that ever I did: is not this the Christ?" (John 4:29). This woman had no instruction in soul winning, but that didn't stop her from telling others of Christ. She had no prior experience, yet, "many of the Samaritans of that city believed on him for the saying of the woman, which testified, He told me all that ever I did" (John 4:39).

Don't let books or clinics on soul winning intimidate you or cause you to develop "soulwinophobia." You can win souls apart from instruction from man. You possess enough knowledge and power to lead a soul to Christ if you have been saved. Soul winning clinics and training books simply are intended to serve as "iron sharpeneth iron" (Proverbs 27:17), enabling the soul winner to witness better and more effectively.

---

[255] Fay, *Share Jesus*, 143.

170 The Gospel Was Born in a Day Like Ours

Jimmy Draper, using Paul's aggressive pursuit to reach the immoral society of his day, said, "One's environment should never be a deterrent for witnessing. The Gospel was born in a day just like ours—a heretic, immoral environment. The Gospel exploded in that kind of culture."[256]

A pastor who had begun to believe that the day of door-to-door visitation was past excitedly shared with me the great results his church was experiencing in using that approach in reaching souls for Christ. Often the sinner's hardness of heart is blamed for the lack of soul winning, when in reality it is the saint's hardness of heart.

"Answer me this question," states J. Wilbur Chapman. "Do you really think that men at heart are indifferent? Let your mind run over the list of men you know. Do you think that they are indifferent? I do not. I know men fairly well. I know what they sometimes say with their lips. If I were to go through your shops and some of the workmen would tell me they were not interested in God, I should know they were not speaking the truth. If I were to go through your college halls and some student would say that he was not interested in spiritual things, I should know that he was speaking falsely. They are not indifferent."[257]

171 Just Do What You Can

The soul winner should be confident in knowing that whether he succeeds in his soul winning effort or not, he is successful in God's eyes. Jesus did not win every person to whom He witnessed. Arthur Archibald stated, "No one fails in this work except the one who does not make the attempt."[258]

A Sunday school teacher asked her class of junior boys to bring an object the following Sunday that would illustrate a Scripture verse. One boy brought a salt shaker, saying, "Jesus said, 'Ye are the salt of the earth.'"

A second boy brought a candle, saying, "Ye are the light of the world."

The third boy brought a bantam egg. The teacher was confused and asked, "Is that an egg?"

The boy replied, "Yes, it is a bantam egg."

---

[256] Draper, "Grasp Opportunity," accessed May 13, 2010.

[257] Chapman, "Eternity," accessed May 20, 2010.

[258] Autrey, *Basic Evangelism*, 89.

The teacher then asked, "And what Scripture does it illustrate?"

The boy said, "She hath done what she could."[259]

Soul winner, under the leadership of the Holy Spirit, just do what you can do, the best you can, and leave the results to God.

Santus Real, a Christian band, in sharing the inspiration behind writing the song "Forgiven," provides encouragement for every Christian who feels inadequate in any form of ministry, including soul winning. "As a band, we've often felt that we don't measure up—that someone else would be more suited for this job than we are. Second Corinthians 8:12 says, 'For if the willingness is there, the gift is acceptable according to what one has, not according to what he does not have' (NIV). God doesn't use us for what we can't do—He uses us for what we can do. We realized that this struggle of not measuring up is just a form of pride cloaked in insecurity. 'Forgiven' was the song that came out of our prayer and repentance."[260]

Don't compare. Others may be more suited for the task of winning souls, but that is God's business. The focus must not be on them, but upon using your full potential in the Lord to win as many as possible. That's all God expects!

172 He Didn't Wait Until He Got Around to It

Upon arriving home from a revival meeting one night, Don Womack was asked to see a young man in the hospital who had been in an auto accident when he got around to it. Womack did not wait until he got around to it but went immediately to see him. He shared Christ with the boy and urged acceptance of Christ as Savior and Lord. The boy replied, "Mr. Womack, this is not the time nor place for this." Womack pressed the matter again to the boy's heart. Once again he responded, "Preacher Womack, this is not the time nor place for this." Knowing nothing else to do, he prayed with the young man and departed. Sadly, during the night this young man was rushed into intensive care and died.

Don Womack responded promptly to an opportunity to win a soul, regrettably without success. Such is all any man can do. Had Womack waited until he got around to it, the opportunity would have been eternally lost.

---

[259] Martin, G., *Evangelistic Preaching*, 88.

[260] Scott Osterbind, "Forgiven," June 29, 2010.

Upon the Holy Spirit's prompting to witness to someone, immediately go and share Christ. Failure to do so may forever shut the door of salvation for that person.

173 Keys to the Sinner's Heart

G. S. Dobbins stated, "It is a truism that as a rule, we must first win the lost to ourselves before we can win them to our Savior. If the unsaved person in whom I am interested does not believe in me, does not like me, or holds himself aloof from me, it is next to impossible to influence him to accept Christ. Someone else may do it, but I cannot. It is therefore of utmost importance that we seek to be winsome, friendly, attractive in manner and personality. If I can convince anybody that I am interested in him, that I like him for his own sake, that I believe he has possibilities; if I can get him to talk about himself, to reveal his aspirations and ambitions, to confide his hopes and fears, then he will assume toward me a friendly attitude."[261]

Lewis Drummond wrote, "The person-to-person ministry must be utilized, and members can be educated to perform it. Witnessing in the context of meeting pressing needs often opens the door for a reception of the Gospel. To repeat John Stott, 'A hungry man has no ears.'

"Personal witnessing is often the most effective way to confront the postmoderns with the Gospel. This calls for building relationships, which can often be done by the meeting of needs. Relatively few postmoderns are now attending church. The factory worker speaking about Christ to his coworkers, the young person giving the Good News to his or her friends— these are the ones who will make the greatest impact on contemporary society.

"It will take time, effort, and sacrifice. Relationships are costly. It hardly seems an overstatement to say that either the mouths of God's people will be opened and relationships established, or the church may well slip into even more serious decline."[262]

174 Feeble Witnesses

"Every member of Christ's church ought to be a witness for Him. Today, as at all other times, the crying need of the Christian church is for witnesses. In our day and generation, the Christian message often seems to be outmoded, outdated, and generally irrelevant. Consequently, in self-

---

[261] Dobbins, *Winning Witness*, 83–84.

[262] Drummond, *Reaching Generation Next*, 150.

conscious weakness we refrain from speaking the word that God would place in our mouths.

"First of all, and of fundamental importance, is the fact that God calls these feeble witnesses. Paul begins by saying that the early Christians did not appoint themselves. It was God that determined that they should bring Christ to the world, and this must always be the case.

"Again and again Christian history has illustrated the truth of our text. In the Early Church, God's feeble witnesses often came from among slaves and other social outcasts. Through such lowly agents, many of whom encountered persecution, torture, and death, the church conquered large parts of the Roman Empire. During the Reformation, Luther, Calvin, and other men on whom the Roman Church looked down, won for the evangelical cause large portions of Europe. In Victorian England, such a scholar as William Robert Dale stood amazed at the outpouring effects of the Gospel as spoken by such an unlearned man as Dwight L. Moody. Likewise in our own century, with all its materialism, sophistication, and secularism, the Lord blesses personal work by countless inconspicuous saints.

"Many times the believer may feel that his testimony is feeble, foolish, and ineffective. Still he is to continue bearing witness, knowing that he is not the one to decide whether or not his words will win a soul for Christ."[263]

175 The Promise to the Soul Winner

"Shall doubtless come again with rejoicing, bringing his sheaves with him" (Psalm 126:6).

Hyman Appelman declared regarding this text, "This is the guarantee of God. God's promise has never failed. The going, weeping, sowing Christian will become the reaping Christian. Where Jesus goes, there is joy. Where Jesus goes, there is victory. Where Jesus goes, there is fruitfulness. This promise has never fallen short of fulfillment. Our going, our weeping, our sowing shall not be in vain. All the power in Heaven and earth is at the command of those who do the will of God in this most sacred task to be performed by the children of God.

"The joy of the soul winner is beyond description. It outstrips and outweighs any and every other benediction and pleasure that comes to the human heart. Nothing on earth can compare with it. To know that you have been instrumental in the hands of the Holy Spirit in rescuing a brand from

---

[263] Blackwood, *Evangelical Sermons*, 272–278.

the burning will compensate for every tear, for every toil, for every trial, for every trouble that may come your way in this greatest of all pursuits.

"This very day, this very hour, this very moment, let us determine in our hearts that we shall be in the ranks of the soul winners. Let us dedicate ourselves to the task with all that we are and have. Let us count no cost too great, no sacrifice too extensive, no toil too arduous, no task too exacting to accomplish this great duty."[264]

176 The Story of Peter Apples

Gipsy Smith tells the story of a Civil War soldier named Peter Apples. He didn't know much about being a soldier except to obey the order of the ranking officer to proceed to battle when he said, "Charge," and not to retreat until ordered.

One day his regiment was ordered to charge the enemy, and he did. The battle was so intense that the officer ordered a retreat, a word Apples did not hear. He continued across "no man's land" into the thick of enemy territory. He saw a ditch filled with enemy soldiers and grabbed one by the back of the neck, drug him out and headed for camp. The enemy soldiers tried to shoot Apples, but their own soldier was in the way. Finally, he crossed "No man's land" to the safety of the camp and dropped the soldier off at the commanding officer's feet. The officer looked at him and said, "Where in the world did you get him?"

He replied, "I got him over there in a ditch. There are plenty of them over there, and all of you could have had one if you had wanted one."[265]

There are plenty of unsaved people in your city, community, school, and workplace. "All of you could have had one if you had wanted one." The trouble is that not many do.

177 A Most Unlikely Prospect

Leonard Sanderson comments, "If a soul winner waits for some dramatic moment or some sensational event, he will miss many opportunities to win the lost. The opportunities are all about him—on the bus, on the train, on the plane, at the desk, at the next machine, in the store, in the home, around the corner, or across the fence.

---

[264] Appelman, *Saviour's Invitation*, 42.

[265] Hutson, *Soulwinning*, accessed April 7, 2010.

"Since Jesus 'knew what was in man,' He knew all about the Samaritan woman. Many would not feel that she was a very good prospect. She was of a different race, and therefore most soul winners would not consider her their responsibility. She was a woman, and it was not the usual thing for a man to speak to a woman when the two were alone. She had lived a life of gross immorality. There was every evidence that she was not a good prospect.

"It would have been very easy for Jesus to say, 'This woman is not a good prospect; she is of a different race and morally unclean. After all, I sat down here to rest, and if I am to render the best service, if I am to carry the load of the heavy responsibilities assigned to me, I must get my rest. After all, one person cannot do everything. Not only am I not expected to speak to this woman, but it would be an innovation if I did so. I will completely ignore her.' Such rationalizations were completely foreign to Jesus."[266]

Watch for the most unlikely prospect for you to lead to Christ, and when he or she surfaces, refuse to rationalize the opportunity away! Imagine how the story for this woman at Jacob's Well would have ended had Jesus ignored her, dismissing her as a good prospect.

178 Soul Winners Who Don't Win Souls

At a person's conversion, the Holy Spirit plants in his soul the amber of soul winning. The believer must stoke this amber unto full flame with meditation upon the estate of the lost as revealed in Scripture, heartfelt prayer, worship and witnessing. It is on this basis that I state that every Christian is a soul winner, whether he is winning souls or not. The soul winner's seed is in him, sown there by the Holy Spirit.

The type of soul winner the Christian chooses to become is up to him. He may remain a soul winner simply in name without bearing any fruit, or he may wholeheartedly engage in the task bearing much fruit. The former is to live in hypocrisy, while the latter is to live in blessed obedience.

So the question is not, "Are you a soul winner?" but rather, "What kind of soul winner are you?"

179 The Soul Winner's Critics

Soul winning is not without its critics. At one point in my ministry, a fellow minister spoke disparagingly of my witnessing of Christ to people in places like parks, restaurants or sporting events and pressing for a decision. I respected this servant of God, and his condemnation at the first staggered

---

[266] Sanderson, *Personal Soul Winning*, 48–49.

me, until I was overwhelmed with God's assurance that I was doing the right thing in the proper manner. As I have matured in the faith, I can honestly say it doesn't bother me if a saint or sinner disapproves of my soul winning methods.

Mark it down. You will have critics. Ridicule goes with the territory. Stand firm in sure confidence that you are doing the greatest work on earth, refusing to allow any critic to discourage or sidetrack you from winning souls passionately.

Spurgeon remarked, "He who actually, really, and truly turns men from the error of their ways to God, and so is made the means of saving them from going down to Hell, is a wise man; and that is true of him, whatever his style of soul winning....He may be a Paul, deeply logical, profound in doctrine, able to command all candid judgments...an Apollos, grandly rhetorical, whose lofty genius soars into the very heaven of eloquence...or a Cephas, rough and rugged, using uncouth metaphor and stern declamation; but if he wins souls, he is no less than his polished brother or his argument-tive friend, but not else. The great wisdom of soul winners, according to the text, is proven only by their actual success in really winning souls. To their own Master they are accountable for the ways in which they work, not to us."[267]

To the persecuted soul winner, Jesus declares, "Blessed are ye, when men shall revile you, and persecute you, and shall say all manner of evil against you falsely, for my sake. Rejoice, and be exceeding glad: for great is your reward in heaven: for so persecuted they the prophets which were before you" (Matthew 5:11–12). Soul winners must have backbone not to allow the objections of others to hinder witnessing efforts.

180 "The Sower Went Forth"

The London pastor C. H. Spurgeon said in regard to the sower of Matthew 13:3, "What did this sower do? He 'went forth.'...He said, 'It is time that I went forth to sow. I have waited quite long enough for favorable weather, but I remember that Solomon said, "He that observeth the wind shall not sow." I feel the sowing time has come for me, and I must set about it.'

"Can I look upon some here who have been members of the church for years but who have never yet done anything for the Lord? Brother or sister, if you have been a servant of God for many years and have never really

---

[267] Spurgeon, *Sermons on Soul Winning*, 9–10.

worked for the salvation of souls, I want you now just to say to yourself, 'Come now, I must get at this work.'

"You will be going home soon; when your Master says to you, 'Did you do any sowing for Me?' you will have to reply, 'No, Lord; I did plenty of eating. I went to the Tabernacle, and I enjoyed the services.'

"'But did you do any sowing?'

"'No, Lord; I did a great deal of hoarding; I laid up a large quantity of the good seed.'

"'But did you do any sowing?' He will still ask, and that will be a terrible question for those who never went forth to sow....Yes, but is it not time for you, Mr. Sower, to go forth? The millions in London are perishing; asylums for the insane are filling, jails are filling, poverty is abounding, and drunkenness is at every street corner. Harlotry is making good men and women to blush. It is time to set about work for the Lord if I am ever to do it.

"What are some of you doing for God? Oh, that you would begin to take stock of your capacity, or your incapacity, and say, 'I must get to work for the Master. I am not to spend my whole life thinking about what I am going to do; I must do the next thing and do it at once, or I may be called home and my day be over before I have sown a single handful of wheat.'"[268]

The ills of society, the depravity of man and the multitudes dying without Christ beckon you to start sowing today.

181 The Absence of Concern

In excess of a hundred years ago, A. T. Pierson stated a truth that is valid today: "Practical indifference as to the peril of lost souls is eating like dry-rot at the very foundation of evangelistic effort."[269]

C. E. Autrey reminds the believer of the need of great concern if souls are to be won. "When the Christian becomes genuinely concerned, the sinner can also be led to concern. 'For as soon as Zion travailed, she brought forth her children' (Isaiah 66:8). The proper atmosphere must exist before souls can be born into the family of God. Concern is one of the vital elements of this atmosphere....Christians must be willing to match their blood and sweat with the sacrifice of Christ upon the cross.

---

[268] Ibid., 71–72.

[269] Pierson, *Evangelistic Work*, 22.

"There is no real evidence of deep concern among God's people today....Who stays awake all night because of the lost? Who prays all night long, as did David Brainerd, the missionary among the Indians in the days of the Great Awakening? Who weeps over the many millions in sin, stupidity, and ignorance on their way to eternal perdition?

"If we are not gravely concerned, why not? Could it be because the rich truths and promises of the Bible are not real to us? Could it be that we do not have the same conviction of the destiny of men that Jesus, Simon Peter, Paul, and others had? Has the flame been quenched in our hearts because of intellectual attitudes? When there is unconcern, there is always a reason."[270]

What is the reason for your unconcern for the lost?

The unconcerned ought to follow the example of B. H. Carroll, the founder of Southwestern Baptist Theological Seminary, who prayed that his last breath be an evangelistic breath. Carroll preached in a crusade in Belton, Texas, to large crowds night by night but with only negligible results. This great preacher became so burdened that sleep was impossible.

Finally, one night he arose from bed and walked about a mile to a cemetery on the side of a hill. Here he fell upon his knees and cried out, "Lord, if you have called me to preach, I want you to show me what Hell is like." C. E. Autrey states, "That night God pulled back the curtains and revealed afresh to the devout preacher the destiny of lost men." The next night as Carroll preached, "he said it seemed to him that flames of Hell leaped up into his face, and he preached as a dying man on his way to Hell." Concern was awakened in the audience, and great was the response to the invitation.[271]

If you are smitten with cold unconcern for the unsaved as a preacher or lay person, why not do as Carroll and beg God to give you a glimpse of the awfulness of Hell?

182 The Guilty Silence

Jesus left Heaven to come to earth "to seek and to save that which was lost." Wherever you trace His footsteps on earth, whether by seaside, roadside, wellside, or hillside, you find Him preaching the Gospel to the unsaved. And Peter admonishes, "For even hereunto were ye called: because Christ also suffered for us, leaving us an example, that ye should

---

[270] Autrey, *Basic Evangelism*, 116–117. (Italics added)

[271] Ibid., 117.

follow his steps" (I Peter 2:21). You are most like Jesus when imparting the Good News to others.

In excess of 150,000 souls die daily without Christ. Yet the Christian is silent. Why do believers hold their tongues when friends, acquaintances, relatives, and employees are in dire need of the touch of Jesus in their lives? What is the cause for your not telling His Story to others consistently—fear of reaction, spiritual indifference, assumption that it's not your responsibility, lack of know-how or of compelling motivation? Identify the cause for failure to witness, and the cure is not far off.

My heart pounds in agreement with C. H. Spurgeon, who declared, "Beloved, we must win souls. We cannot live and see men damned; we must have them brought to Jesus. Oh! then be up and doing and let none around you die unwarned, unwept, uncared for."[272]

All believers are called to this task—minister or layman, educated or illiterate, refined or unrefined, extroverted or introverted, male or female, spiritually mature or new convert, able or unable, famous or infamous, wealthy or poor, professor or student. L. R. Scarborough wrote, "Every Christian is called in the hour of salvation to witness for Jesus Christ. Nothing in Heaven or on earth can excuse him from it. God gives no furloughs from this heaven-born obligation."[273]

Paul Rees said, "A silent discipleship is the first betrayal and the last futility of a movement that began when one hundred twenty Christians, filled with the Spirit of God, took the witness stand to declare 'the wonderful works of God.'...A converted man, armed with two or three Bible promises and overflowing with the rich experience of the forgiveness of sins, will win more converts in six weeks than will be won by a well-read, well-indoctrinated church member who quotes from the creed and the theologians but has no vibrant 'I know' in his testimony."[274]

183 The Gold Apple

The Christian basically may witness in three ways. *By presence*—this is lifestyle evangelism, allowing others to see the difference Christ has made in one's life. *By proclamation*—this is the act of verbally sharing the mes-

---

[272] Spurgeon, *Sermons on Soul Winning*, 18.

[273] Scarborough, *With Christ*, 3.

[274] Rees, *Stir Up the Gift*, 109.

sage of Jesus with the lost. *By persuasion*—this is the act of inviting the sinner to receive Christ as Lord and Savior. This is bona fide soul winning.

It is with the last where most fall short, failing to actually invite a sinner to receive Christ in their presence. A pastor recently stated to me that this was his chief weakness. Likewise it may be yours.

I adapt an illustration by C. H. Spurgeon using a golden apple to show the difference between witnessing by presence or proclamation and witnessing by persuasion. You may pull an apple (the Christian life) out of your pocket and toss it in the air before people, and that visual is the only part of it that is theirs. You may let them smell it and then place it back in your pocket, and the aroma of the apple is all that is theirs. Simply presenting the golden apple of the message of salvation and letting people see it, even letting them smell its luxurious fruit, is a grave injustice. Give the sinner the chance to take the apple and put it in his pocket—the invitation.

In addition to offering the gold apple in person-to-person encounters, the preacher must offer it in pulpit ministry. Spurgeon shared the comment of another minister: "Have you never heard preaching of that sort? 'Here is a precious salvation! I hope you sinners see how precious it is, for that is your share of it.' The minister puts the heavenly fruit back again into his pocket, and the sermon is over; and this is called free grace! The most liberal of those who dare not invite the sinner try to give him a smell of the Gospel by telling him of the peace and joy which it brings."

Then Spurgeon stated, "Now, when I am preaching to sinners, I feel inclined always to beg every one of them to put the golden apple into his pocket, for this choice fruit of the tree of life may belong to millions, and yet the whole of it will remain for millions more. There is not a sinner in the world who is to be told that he may not come to Jesus and receive the whole of the blessings of the Gospel. What a blessing to have a free salvation to preach, as well as a full salvation!"[275]

184   Whose Responsibility Is It to Witness?

A patient in a Kentucky hospital accidentally spilled some water on the floor, and in fear he might slip on it, he asked a nurse's aide to mop it up. The hospital had a policy regarding water spillage cleanup. Small spills were to be cleaned up by the nurse's aide, while larger spills were handled by the custodial staff. The nurse's aide felt the spillage was large and called in the custodial staff to mop it up. The staff personnel from housekeeping arrived and determined it was a small spill and thus the job of the nurse's

---

[275] Spurgeon, *Only a Prayer Meeting*, 206.

aide to handle it. These two individuals got into a heated argument. The nurse's aide said, "It's not my responsibility, because it's a large spill."

Housekeeping said, "Well it's not mine, because the puddle is too small."

The patient, exasperated with the whole ordeal, took a pitcher of water from the nightstand and dumped it onto the floor, saying, "Is that a big enough puddle now for you two to decide?"[276]

The point is that God wants you to do it, to literally tell others the plan of salvation. He doesn't want us to argue about who is to do it—the pastor or evangelist or deacon—but to realize that everybody in the Kingdom is to do it (Matthew 28:19).

185 False Professions

No soul winner, regardless how experienced and masterful in leading men to Christ, bats a thousand in harvesting genuine commitments. Jesus had His Judas, Phillip had his Simon Magus, and D. L. Moody had his drunk. The soul winner certainly must take every step to insure decisions made are based upon genuine repentance and faith in the Lord Jesus Christ (not human manipulation), but then he must rest them in the hands of God.

Don't despair in witnessing due to bitter disappointment with "decisions" experienced in the past. Learn from them, but don't allow the fear of this happening again to hinder soul winning. In times when I am uncertain of a person's genuine desire to be saved, I say, "If I left right now without your praying to receive Christ, would that be okay with you?" Sinners who are convicted of sin and their need to be saved quickly object to my departure.

186 Enemies to Soul Winning

There are seven enemies to soul winning that must be combated.

(1) Misunderstanding. Satan would have the saint believe that winning souls is the task of the minister and church staff, not one discharged by Christ to all the redeemed (Acts 1:8).

(2) Pessimism. The mind-set of many believers regarding witnessing is that it will do no good. Yet our Lord stated that "the fields are white (ripe) unto harvest"; people are hungering and thirsting for that something missing without which there is no real peace or purpose (John 4:35).

---

[276] Exum, "Soul Winning," accessed April 8, 2010.

(3) Busyness. The pastor has sermons to prepare, administrative chores, and hospital visits; and the church member has his job, family engagements, and community calendar. The noble desire to witness is buried beneath the load of daily duties and goes undone. Plan the day around soul winning, not soul winning around the day. Keep it a priority. The great London pastor C. H. Spurgeon made time each day to win a soul to Christ.[277]

(4) Unconcern. Primarily, few Christians win souls due to a lack of passion and compassion for the eternally damned. Pray for a passion for souls as George Whitefield did. He prayed, "O God, give me souls, or take my soul."

(5) Fear. The Apostle Paul experienced it (I Corinthians 2:3). All believers do. It's not unnatural or unspiritual. The key is not to allow fear to paralyze and deter soul winning efforts. Paul didn't. We mustn't.

(6) Carnality. C. H. Spurgeon declared, "Fish will not be fishers. We cannot be fishers of men if we remain among men in the same element with them."[278]

The separated Christian is the soul-winning Christian (II Corinthians 6:17).

(7) Failure to Perceive the Reality of Hell. A failure to grasp the end of the lost lessens soul concern and thus soul winning. Hell is a reality, and it awaits the unsaved at the end of this life. Muse over the nature of Hell until the heart is inflamed to go and tell. The abode of Hell answers soberly the question, "Does it really matter if I try to lead others to Christ?"

187 "It Pays to Be a Witness, Doesn't It?"

A pastor was making an early morning drive to downtown Jacksonville, Florida, for a radio broadcast, when he noticed a man thumbing for a ride on the expressway. The pastor had prayed earlier for an opportunity to witness, and now the Spirit seemed to say, "There's your man." He pulled over and invited the man to get into the car and asked where he was going. "I'm going downtown," he replied.

Bob Gray then said, "I didn't mean where you are going today. Where are you going when you die?"

The man responded, "I haven't given much thought about that." Gray engaged him in conversation about life after death, and the man listened

---

[277] Autrey, *Basic Evangelism*, 67.

[278] Spurgeon, *Sermons on Soul Winning*, 33.

intently. Shortly, he asked the man if he could pull over to the side of the expressway and explain the matter more fully. The man gladly agreed. Gray shared various Scriptures that pointed to man's way of salvation and then invited him to receive Christ, which he did.

Afterward, wiping tears from his eyes, he pulled out a revolver, laid it on the seat, and said to Gray, "Sir, as I hitchhiked, I had determined that whoever picked me up, I would make him pull off the highway. Then I would kill him, steal his car, dump his body, and go on my way to another state. Sir, if you hadn't talked to me about this, you could have been a dead man by now."

Bob Gray later said, "It pays to be a witness, doesn't it?"[279]

Gray not only saved a soul that early morning by being obedient to the Spirit's divine impression to stop and share the Gospel, but he saved the life of another who would have stopped to offer the man a ride had he not. Stay sensitive and obedient to the Spirit's impressions to witness.

188 Excuses Don't Hold Water

In Exodus 3–4, the account of God's call to Moses to be Israel's deliverer is recorded. A frightened Moses responded to this call by stating "O my Lord, I am not eloquent, neither heretofore, nor since thou hast spoken unto thy servant: I am slow of speech and of a slow tongue" (Exodus 4:10). Moses tried to excuse God's call to go to Pharaoh because of his lack of fluent speech and eloquence. In fact he felt so inadequate for the task that he asked God for a replacement, which angered the Lord (vs. 13–14).

God responded to Moses, "I will be with your mouth and with his [Aaron's] mouth, and teach you what ye shall do" (v. 15). In essence, God told Moses, "I can transform your disposition and enable you to do this task effectively. I will make it easier for you by teaming you up with Aaron. You two together can get the job done."

If God can change the disposition of cowardly Moses into a courageous one, He certainly can alter any man's disposition in the same manner. As with Moses, every believer has been called to go into spiritual Egypt to grant deliverance to the captives through the Lord Jesus Christ. Excuses about one's inabilities or shyness don't hold water. Christ will "be with your mouth...and teach you what you are to do" and even team you up with an "Aaron" if necessary. Soul winners must confidently trust the Lord to perform this work in and through them.

---

[279] Hutson, *Preaching on Soul Winning*, 201–202.

In Numbers 22, God used a mule to communicate His message to Balaam, and that mule's talking saved Balaam's life (vs. 27–33). Obviously, if God can use a dumb mule to communicate His Word, He is more than able to use the most feeble and ignorant Christian to speak the gospel message to the saving of the lost.

189 "I Still Feel Hot Tears for the Lost"

"Dr. Rice bared his soul winner's heart in this moving message—a Christmas letter dictated to his friends a few days before his death—when he wrote: 'I still, from my armchair, preach in great revival campaigns. I still envision hundreds walking the aisles to accept Christ. I still feel hot tears for the lost. I still see God working miracles. Oh, how I long to see great revivals, to hear about revival crowds once again! I want no Christmas without a burden for lost souls, a message for sinners, and a heart to bring in the lost sheep so dear to the Shepherd, the sinning souls for whom Christ died. May food be tasteless and music a discord and Christmas a farce if I forget the dying millions to whom I am debtor, if this fire in my bones does not still flame! Not till I die, or not till Jesus comes, will I ever be eased of this burden, these tears, this toil to save souls.'

"Yes—that is the beat of a soul winner's heart! That was not just Christmas season sentimentality. It was the overflow of a bleeding, broken heart for the lost which had been constrained and conquered by this terrible truth: 'If there is a place of eternal torment where damned souls cry in vain for water amid the flames they cannot escape forever, it is the most alarming and terrifying fact in the universe! The very possibility that such a doom may await a sinner is so shocking that no other question can compare with its importance. How can today's feasting or hunger, clothing or nakedness, honor or infamy, pleasure or pain compare in importance with a million years of pain, torment of body, mind and conscience?'"[280]

O God, may I still feel hot tears for the lost upon my deathbed! May I never be eased of a consuming burden to save souls nor relent in sacrificial effort to reach them.

190 Won by a Mother's Love and Tracts

A young man was rebellious and indifferent to his mother's appeal to be saved. This mother was relentless in her effort to win her son to Christ to the point she would put gospel tracts in inconspicuous places, such as under his pillow or cereal bowl. Finally when he was sixteen years old, the tracts

---

[280] Barlow, "John R. Rice," accessed April 9, 2010.

hit home, and he was saved. This young man was Eddie Martin, one of Southern Baptist's greatest evangelists and soul winners, who preached in 1,500 crusades/revivals during his ministry.[281] Heaven only will tell of the thousands this evangelist won to Christ through his preaching and personal soul winning. And it all can be traced back to a saintly mother who refused to accept no from her son regarding salvation.

As a young evangelist, I recall Martin's referring to his mother as a soul winner in a sermon. Despite her hands being crippled with arthritis, she continuously passed out gospel tracts seeking souls for the Master.

191 Interrupted to Win a Soul

"At No. 10 Downing Street, London, early one morning, a timid knock called William Gladstone from the writing of an important speech he was to deliver that day in Parliament. Standing at the door was a boy. Mr. Gladstone had won the friendship and confidence of the boy by little deeds of kindness. Said the boy, 'Mr. Gladstone, my brother is dying. Won't you please come and show him the way to Heaven?'

"Leaving his own important work for the most important work any Christian can do, Gladstone soon arrived at the bedside of the dying boy. In a matter of moments, the little fellow was rejoicing in his newly found Savior! Returning to his office, Gladstone wrote at the bottom of the speech he was preparing, 'I am the happiest man in London, England, today!'"[282]

The day is to be abhorred when the believer places more value and importance upon the writing of a sermon or speech, attendance at a class, appointment with the dentist or doctor, attending a church function or service than on responding to the need of a lost soul about salvation. Sadly this happens all too frequently.

192 Cry "Water! Water!"

In his little book "*And Peter,*" J. Wilbur Chapman told the following story. "A number of travelers were making their way across the desert. The last drop of water had been exhausted, and they were pushing on with the hope that more might be found. They were growing weaker and weaker.

"As a last resort, they divided their men into companies and sent them on, one in advance of the other, in this way securing a rest they so much

---

[281] Curry, "Collection," accessed April 9, 2010.

[282] Tan. *7700 Illustrations*, 1320.

needed. If they who were in the advance guard were able to find the springs, they were to shout the good tidings to the men who were the nearest to them, and so they were to send the message along.

"The long line reached far across the desert. They were fainting by the way when suddenly everyone was cheered by the good news. The leader of the first company had found the springs of water. He stood at the head of his men, shouting until the farthest man had heard his cry, 'Water! Water!' The word went from mouth to mouth until the whole company of men heard the sound, quickened their pace and soon were drinking to their hearts' content!

"I have found the Water of Life. It is flowing fully; it is flowing freely; and so I stand and cry, 'Water! Water!' Take up the cry, everyone, until every thirsty soul shall drink and live."[283]

Isaiah exhorts the saved, "Cry aloud, spare not, lift up thy voice like a trumpet, and shew my people their transgression, and the house of Jacob their sins" (Isaiah 58:1). Jesus declared, "And the Spirit and the bride say, Come. And let him that heareth say, Come. And let him that is athirst come. And whosoever will, let him take the water of life freely" (Revelation 22:17). We have found the Well of Living Water, and now we must tell where it may be found from mouth to mouth until the whole world knows.

193 Go after the Hard Ones

A preacher in Waco, Texas, said to the congregation, "Oh, men, do not go on in the ordinary, commonplace way in the winning of souls. Go after a case difficult. Go after a case long neglected, preoccupied, too busy to come to God; go after him, and if you do not do the extraordinary thing and put forth the unusual effort, you will not arrest his attention. Go after him."

A lawyer, in hearing this appeal, approached some colleagues and said, "If three of you men will join me, we will go after this great lawyer." They did not delay but went that day to see Judge Waller Baker. This attorney was working on a difficult case and requested not to be disturbed. This was not known to the men, for prior to their arrival, the stenographer of the office had stepped out for a minute.

They knocked on the inner door and were received by the judge, who said, "There must be something very serious that can bring you four men here."

The first great Christian lawyer answered, "There is, Mr. Baker, the most serious matter in the world. I want first of all to ask you to forgive me

---

[283] Chapman, *"And Peter,"* 84.

that I have been such a poor Christian that I have not talked with you more earnestly about Christ and His supreme claims and your need of Him. But we have come, we four men, to ask if you won't cease all your procrastination, and if you won't, for your own sake, and for Waco's sake, and the world's sake, and for Christ's sake, today yield yourself to Christ."

Each of the men followed in appeals for the man to be saved. The first lawyer then asked the man to give himself to Christ, and all five of them went to their knees. Judge Baker was gloriously saved because four men were concerned enough for him to go and tell.[284]

Dr. George Truett, who related this story in a sermon, said following it, "I am summoning you this morning to do both the difficult and consistent thing—to go after such cases all about you....I am beseeching you that you will combine with the other man, and you twain will plead the promise of Jesus: 'If two of you shall agree on earth as touching anything that they shall ask, it shall be done for them of my Father which is in heaven.' If you need two, let there be two that go....Let us do the unusual thing, if that be necessary, to get the attention and win the heart of some soul that has missed the upward way. Let us combine and cooperate. Let us pray together and go together, if haply by such earnest effort we may win that difficult case. Pass no case by. Leave no case unapproached, unhelped. Take them as you can see them and bethink you concerning them and do your best to win them to Christ."[285]

Who do you count the most difficult case for salvation? Clothed in His power, courage and confidence, seek him or her out without further delay. Win these, and the community or city will take note that God still is in the soul saving business, revival fires will flame in the church, doors of soul winning will open due to their sphere of influence, and, above all, God will be glorified.

194 Be Soul-Conscious

Most believers have a "church mind"; few have a "harvest mind"—a soul consciousness. It's not easy to obtain or maintain a soul consciousness. I know. As an evangelist for thirty-seven years whose life's work has been to call the lost to salvation, it hasn't always been easy to consistently, passionately pursue souls. I have often been ashamed of my unconcern for souls. You have to stay at it. You have to keep confronting people with the question, "Are you a Christian?" or "Are you certain if you died today you

---

[284] Truett, *Quest for Souls*, 233–234.

[285] Ibid., 235–236.

would go to Heaven?" You must keep interjecting Christ into the conversation with the store clerk, banker, teacher, student, friend, neighbor, and stranger in the marketplace. The more this is done, the more natural and easier it becomes. You must train your eyes to look at people through the lenses of Christ as souls in eternal peril needing salvation. You must come to the realization that D. L. Moody was right when he testified, "It is the only happy life to live for the salvation of souls."[286]

C. H. Spurgeon pleaded, "Dear friends, do try to speak personally to some friends about their immortal souls. I know that it is not easy work for some of you to break the ice and make a beginning in such service, but I can assure you that you will do it better and better the more often you attempt it."[287]

195 "Write You This Man Childless"

C. H. Spurgeon stated, "I would like to stress the question for you who are saved. How many others have you brought to Christ? I know you cannot do it by yourself. But I mean, how many has the Spirit of God brought by you? Is it quite certain that you have led any to Jesus? Can you not recollect one? I pity you, then!

"The Lord said to Jeremiah about Coniah, 'Write ye this man childless' (Jeremiah 22:30). That was considered to be a fearful curse. Should I write you childless, my beloved friends? Your children are not saved, your wife is not saved, and you are spiritually childless. Can you bear this thought? I entreat you, wake from your slumbering and ask the Master to make you useful.

"'I wish the saints cared for us sinners,' said a young man.

"'They do care for you,' answered one. 'They care very much for you.'

"'Why don't they show it, then?' said he. 'I have often wished to have a talk about good things, but my friend, who is a member of the church, never broaches the subject and seems to study how to keep clear of it when I am with him.'

"Do not let them say so. Do tell them about Christ. Make this your resolve, every one of you, that if men perish, they will not perish for lack of your prayers or for the lack of your earnest and loving instructions. May

---

[286] Moody D. L., "Inspiring Quotes," accessed April 10, 2010.

[287] Spurgeon, *Sermons on Soul Winning*, 84.

God give you grace, each one of you, to resolve by all means to save souls, and then to carry out your resolution."[288]

196 "He Must Needs Go through Samaria"

Jesus encounters the woman at Jacob's Well with the Gospel. This woman gets gloriously saved and immediately becomes an evangelist going through the city shouting, "Come, see a man, which told me all things that ever I did: is not this the Christ?" (John 4:29). John tells us that because of the testimony of this woman, many believed on Jesus (John 4:39). The text states emphatically that Jesus "must needs go through Samaria" (John 4:4). He *had* to go that way, plain and simple; the reason is obvious. A lost soul was waiting to be won.

God has prearranged divine appointments for the soul winner to witness to a "woman at Jacob's Well." Today that "woman" is a friend at the end of class, a waiter at the restaurant, someone in the apartment or at the game, a person on the bus, or a fellow employee at work.

Often, we too "must needs go through Samaria" (be detoured, have plans interrupted and end up where we didn't intend to go) to get to that person at the right time to share the message of Christ! Stay sensitive to such assigned appointments and do whatever is necessary (miss class, skip lunch, arrive late at work) to show up for them, for such an opportunity may not arise again.

En route to church, I passed a bus stop where two people were seated. I was strangely moved to turn my car around and make a gospel presentation. Both individuals received my witness and invited Christ into their lives. Certainly, this was a divine appointment.

Traveling from Dallas to Chicago by car, John R. Rice prayed with his family, "Lord, help me to find someone I can win on the way before I reach Chicago."

"Then he related how he missed a turn at Ardmore, Oklahoma, and drove fifty miles out of the way. At the filling station where he sought directions, he dealt with the attendant—and led him to Christ. Retracing his route and upset with himself because of the unnecessary delay and detour, he was suddenly challenged by the giggle of girls who confronted him: 'Daddy, don't you see? You asked God to lead you to a soul you could win today, so He brought you fifty miles to reach the man who was ready.'"[289]

---

[288] Spurgeon, *Soul Winner*, 251–252.

[289] Barlow, "John R. Rice," accessed April 12, 2010.

197 A Permanent Passion for Souls

Paul was heartbroken over lost souls (Romans 9:1–3). Spurgeon stated, "There was no sham about it. It is pretty easy to work yourself up into a state of feeling, but it was not passing emotion with Paul; it was deep, true, constant grief. He says, 'I say the truth in Christ, I lie not, my conscience also bearing me witness in the Holy Ghost.'…He really felt heartbreakings for guilty souls. He did not sometimes get up into that condition or down into it, but he lived in it.…His was a true heaviness, real sorrow.

"Do we feel the same, or is it only a little excitement at a revival meeting, a chance feeling which passes over us through sympathy with other people who are in earnest? May the Lord plough your soul deep. If He means you to be a soul winner [and He does], He will. May the ploughers make deep furrows upon your heart, as once they did upon your Master's back. You are not fit to carry souls on your heart till it has been bruised with grief for them. You must feel deeply for the souls of men if you are to bless them.

"It is of no use to try to get it by reading books or to pump yourself up to it in private; this feeling is the work of God. A soul winner is a creation.…There has to be a careful preparation, a softening of the soul to make the worker know how naturally to care for the welfare of others. He [Paul] says that his conscience bare him witness that he spake the truth, and then he says the Holy Spirit bore witness with his conscience. May we have such a manifest love for sinners that we can ask the Holy Ghost to bear witness that we have it."[290]

198 We Persuade Men

"Knowing the terror of the Lord," declared R. G. Lee, "we should persuade men—persuade them as a singer singing to reach the soul, persuade them as a lover wooing to win hand and heart, persuade them as a lawyer arguing for a verdict, persuade them as a mother begs her son to turn from evil, persuade them as a statesman pleading for his country, persuade them as a preacher with tongue of fire espousing the cause of righteousness. We must persuade men with recognition of the truth.

"Lyman Beecher once spoke, 'The greatest thing a human being can do is to bring another human being to Jesus Christ as Savior.' The hour when we persuade men is greater than the hour when the surgeon holds a knife at the end of which is life or death for the patient, greater than the hour when a

---

[290] Spurgeon, *Evangelism*, 185–186.

lawyer faces a jury with the conviction that if he makes a mistake an innocent man will hang and a family be disgraced forever."[291]

"I would say that 'persuade' means to win people to make decisions concerning the soul—as to the past, the present, the future—that will stand the test of a lightning-swift accident bringing sudden death; the test of a tediously torturous disease that closes the shutters of all life's windows; the test of the Jeshurun-like prosperity which causes a man to forsake God who made him and esteem lightly the Rock of his salvation (Deuteronomy 32:15); the test of that solemn hour when 'every one of us shall give account of himself to God' (Romans 14:12), when 'for every idle word that men shall speak, they shall give account thereof in the day of judgment' (Matthew 12:36)."[292]

199 Holy Spirit Impressions to Share

Charles Finney advised, "If you have any feeling for a particular individual, take an opportunity to converse with that individual while this feeling continues. If it is a truly benevolent feeling, you have reason to believe the Spirit of God is moving you to desire the salvation of his soul, and that God is ready to bless your efforts for his conversion. In such a case, make it the subject of special and importunate prayer and seek an early opportunity to pour out all your heart to him and bring him to Christ."[293]

What I now relate occurred forty years ago, but it seems like yesterday. I was a student pastor in Century, Florida, while attending seminary in New Orleans. My studies required my being off the field Monday evening through Friday afternoon each week.

Upon arriving back from seminary one week, I learned of a house fire in the community and immediately sought to minister. In this ministry, it was discovered that the son of the couple, named Terry, was not saved. It is almost indescribable how the Holy Spirit pressed me with this young man's soul. I travailed in prayer for his soul while at seminary, wrote him regarding salvation, and, once back on the church field, with grave diligence tried to see him. He avoided my attempts that Friday and Saturday. Sunday he was dead. It all happened so quickly.

---

[291] Lee, *Seven Swords*, Orlando, 45–46.

[292] Ibid., 34.

[293] Finney, *Revivals*, 147.

Finney is right on target when he suggests that should a believer "have any feeling for a particular individual" (burden for their soul), such is of God and must be acted upon immediately. Delay may mean his or her eternal doom.

200 Make It a Constant Study and Daily Reflection

Charles Finney instructed, "Make it an object of constant study and of daily reflection and prayer to learn how to deal with sinners so as to promote their conversion. It is the great business on earth of every Christian to save souls. People often complain that they do not know how to take hold of this matter. Why, the reason is plain enough; they have never studied it. They have never taken the proper pains to qualify themselves for the work.

"If people made it no more a matter of attention and thought to qualify themselves for their worldly business than they do to save souls, how do you think they would succeed? Now, if you are thus neglecting the main business of life, what are you living for? If you do not make it a matter of study how you may most successfully act in building up the Kingdom of Christ, you are acting a very wicked and absurd part as a Christian."[294]

201 Soul Winning Contrasted to an Airplane

In soul winning, one can expect to experience three "sound barriers," much like the sound barrier through which an airplane passes. Each can rattle the nerves and produce stress. The first "sound barrier" is moving the conversation from the physical realm to the spiritual. The second is boldly asking the sinner if he would be willing to receive Christ, and the third is when the soul winner presses for a decision on the spot. The soul winner will face fear and hesitation with each of these "sound barriers" which will grow more intense the further the witness progresses, necessitating a jet propulsion blast of Holy Spirit power to get through.[295]

The Holy Spirit certainly will provide such a blast! "For the weapons of our warfare are not carnal, but mighty through God to the pulling down of strongholds; casting down imaginations, and every high thing that exalteth itself against the knowledge of God, and bringing into captivity every thought to the obedience of Christ" (II Corinthians 10:4). You are the airplane (vehicle) transporting the Gospel to a person, but the Holy Spirit is

---

[294] Ibid., 158.

[295] Bright, *Steps to Maturity*, 352.

the engine (power source) enabling a safe take-off (confrontation), smooth flight (presentation) and successful landing (invitation).

202 Witnessing on the Job

Adrian Rogers stated, "I've heard people say, 'I sure would like to be in a Christian company and be surrounded by Christians. The only time I hear God's name mentioned where I work now is when people are cursing. And you just cannot believe the obscene jokes, gossip, greed, backstabbing, throat cutting, and all of the materialism! Oh, if God would only get me out of this place so I could serve Him!'

"Do you know how I would respond? I would tell them, God put you in that place so you could serve Him. We are to let our light shine in every place where God has placed us! (Matthew 5:14–16). You have been saved out of the world and then sent back into the world to witness to the world, and that's the only business in the world you have in the world till you're taken out of the world! Now, let me give you four rules for witnessing to those with whom you work.

"**Don't Brag.** The Bible says let your light shine. It doesn't say *make* it shine. Your light is to glow, not glare. Also, people are to see the light, not the source of the light. If you go to work with an air of self-righteousness, you're going to make your coworkers sick, and they will not want to even be around you.

"**Don't Nag.** If you're always thumping a Bible or nagging somebody when he gambles, smokes, or curses, you're not going to win that person to Christ. You may think that you're doing a good job, but that person is not going to take a step closer to Jesus Christ through that kind of witness.

"**Don't Lag.** If you're a lazy Christian—not getting to work on time, doing personal stuff on company time, procrastinating on work that you ought to do—then you're a disgrace to grace. It is a sin for a Christian to do less than his best.

"**Don't Sag.** I want to tell you something about those people with whom you work. Most of them are not all that interested in going to Heaven or Hell. They just want to know how to hack it on Monday. And when they see you come in the office without a hangover and with the joy of the Lord Jesus on your face, they're going to ask you, 'What makes you so happy?' And at that moment, you're going to be able to share the Lord Jesus with them because you will have sanctified the Lord God in your heart."[296]

---

[296] Rogers, "Witnessing at Work," accessed April 13, 2010.

531 Motivations for Winning Souls

203 "Open Season" on Lost Souls

Paul instructs, 'Preach the word in season and out of season.' There are two times you are to seek to win souls, "In season, out of season" (II Timothy 4:2). It is "open season" on lost souls! It's just not "open season" during revival meetings, harvest days or special evangelistic events or festivals. It is "open season" for souls TODAY as you go to work, attend class, visit the mall, or check on someone in the hospital or in prison.

There is no limit. You will never hear God say, "John, you talked to way too many people about Me and led far too many to salvation"—never. Rather, you will hear His divine applause for every witness you make.

"Open season" for souls, though open presently, will close without fore-warning, so diligently pursue souls while you may. In Heaven, soul-winning season is closed permanently. Soul winning is the one thing you can do for Christ now that you cannot do in Heaven.

204 No Great Hardship

The soul winner will go to the brink of Hell to rescue a soul from falling into its horrible abode. He will bear reproach, ridicule, sacrifice, and suffering for the sake of winning a lost soul to Christ, and the whole while count it but all joy. The soul winner dittos C. H. Spurgeon's attitude: "To be laughed at is no great hardship to me. I can delight in scoffs and jeers; caricatures, lampoons, and slanders are my glory. But that you should turn from your own mercy, this is my sorrow. Spit on me, but, oh, repent! Laugh at me, but, oh, believe in my Master! Make my body as the dirt of the streets, if you will, but damn not your own souls! Oh, do not despise your own mercies. Put not away from you the Gospel of Christ....I charge you as I shall face you at the judgment bar of the Lord Jesus in the day of judgment, I charge you by your own immortal welfare, lay these things to heart."[297]

205 Winning Souls

"He that winneth souls is wise." The metaphor, so states Joseph W. Kemp, "is a very striking one, and it may be used in a variety of ways.

"Win is a military term and was used in the taking of cities in warfare by warriors. As wisdom was needed by these soldiers, just so it is essential for the soul winner seeking to storm the citadel of man's soul.

"Win is a fishing term used in catching fish. The word 'win' may be translated 'taketh,' which refers to fishing (Matthew 4:19). The fisherman

---

[297] Spurgeon, *New Testament Men*, 132.

fishes in all weathers, calm or rough. You must seek to win souls when easy and not so easy. The fisherman fishes despite possible danger with sea storms and boisterous waters. The fisher of men willingly exposes himself to risks in an effort to win souls. The fisherman fishes patiently and perseveringly. The soul winner does likewise. The fisherman fishes in faith. He cannot see the fish in the sea. They are out of sight, but in faith he lowers the net into the water expecting a catch. 'Soul fishing' is a work of faith. One does not know when a 'fish' will be caught, but he labors believing.

"*Win* also may refer to the captivating of human affections. A bridegroom is said to 'win' his bride, and before the valued heart is won, there have been many wooing acts and pleading words. There are sweet and mysterious ways by which love wins its object. Perhaps this illustration is nearer the mark than the others, for thus may souls be 'espoused unto Christ.'

"These illustrations are helpful in explaining the work of the soul winner. They imply assault and conquest, conviction and persuasion, and at the same time indicate that no rigid method can be followed. What wins one repels another, for no two souls are exactly alike."[298]

206 Keep a Sensitive Conscience for Souls

The great saint Richard Baxter declared, "I confess to all you here my shame, that I remember no one sin in the world that my conscience doth so much accuse and judge me for as for doing so little for the saving of men's souls and dealing no more fervently and earnestly with them for their conversion....I have many excuses come in, from other business and from disability and want of time; yet none of them all do satisfy my own conscience when I consider what Heaven and Hell are, which one of them will be the end of every man's life. My conscience telleth me that I should follow them with all possible earnestness night and day and take no nay of them until they return to God."[299]

Is your conscience sensitive for souls as Baxter's was, or has it become "seared" due to coldness of heart for the lost? Oh, plead unto the Lord for a fresh love for souls and a pricking conscience.

E. J. Daniels warns of the danger of allowing soul winning to become routine. "I believe that I can truly say that I love souls, for I have given my life by day and night to seeking to win them. And yet, it is so easy to

---

[298] Kemp, *Soulwinner and Soulwinning*, 26–28.

[299] Ormer, *Richard Baxter*, 82.

become professional and perfunctory even in so sacred a matter as preaching the Gospel and winning souls. I pray that God will never let this happen to me. I want a missionary passion, a missionary heart, a missionary burden for the lost. I want the kind of passion for lost souls that brought the Lord Jesus Christ out of the Ivory Palaces into this world of woe to seek and to save the lost. May God grant it to me and to you."[300]

207   God Never Gives Any One Man a Whole Soul

W. Y. Fullerton stated, "A great many agencies are used in the conversion of a soul, and much humility is needed when we speak of our little service. A Puritan writer has said, 'God never gives any one man a whole soul.' We must be ready to reap the harvest that has been sown by others, and to acknowledge their sowing; we must equally be ready to sow the seed for others to reap. It is a great art to drop a sentence in the midst of a conversation and to pass on without waiting for a response, without demanding an answer or starting a discussion, simply just trusting the seed. There is much condensed wisdom in the Northern proverb: 'Keep aye stickin' in trees; they will grow while you are sleepin'.' The expert in the quest for souls will often be content to plant an acorn without expecting to see the tree grow."[301]

Today, look for opportunities to sow seed in lost souls through a gospel tract, witness, or comment. Sowing always precedes reaping.

208   Ready—Set—Go

You are ready to go soul winning. You have been snatched as a brand from the burning by the merciful hand of God and stand ready to so testify to the lost. You have received word of deployment from God to immediately go into the enemies' camp to set the captives free. You are prayed up and powered up.

You are set to go soul winning. You have gospel tracts in your pocket and a New Testament in the hand eagerly awaiting the Holy Spirit's signal to whom to go.

You go soul winning. A runner who hears the official say, "Ready—Set—Go," and simply gets ready and set but fails to go never attains the prize. He has to break out of the starting block and literally go. You must do the same. Kyle Yates stated, "If you would become a champion in the rare

---

[300] Daniels, *Soul-Stirring Sermons*, 114–115.

[301] Kemp, *Soulwinner and Soulwinning*, 52.

adventure of soul winning, you must want them, walk with them, warn them, and woo them. Then you'll win them."[302]

All the talk about getting ready and being set is empty apart from actually going after lost souls. Get ready; get set; now go!

209 Benefits of Winning Souls

C. H. Spurgeon proclaimed, "I will not try this morning to sum up in the short time allotted to me the immense benefits which come to a man through laboring for the conversion of others; but I will venture this assertion, that no man or woman in the church of God is in a healthy state if he or she be not laboring to save some.

"To long for the conversion of others makes us Godlike. Do we desire man's welfare? God does so. Would we fain snatch them from the burning? God is daily performing this deed of grace. Can we say that we have no pleasure in the death of him that dieth? Jehovah has declared the like with an oath. Do we weep over sinners? Did not Jehovah's Son weep over them? Do we lay out ourselves for their conversion? Did He not die that they might live? You are made Godlike when this passion glows within your spirit....

"Loving God makes us sorrow that all men do not love him too....Trying to bring others to Christ does us good by renewing us our old feelings and reviving our first love. If we love others, we shall, like Paul, become wise to attract them, wise to persuade them, wise to convince them, wise to encourage them; we shall learn the use of means which had lain rusted by and discover in ourselves talents which else had been hidden in the ground if the strong desire to save men had not cleared away the soil.

"Love to souls will in the end bring to everyone who follows it up the highest joy beneath the stars. What is that? It is the joy of knowing that you have been made the spiritual parent of others. I have tasted of this stream full often, and it is Heaven below. The joy of being saved oneself has a measure of selfishness about it, but to know that your fellowmen are saved by your efforts brings a joy pure, disinterested and heavenly, of which we may drink the deepest draughts without injury to our spirits."[303]

---

[302] Knight, *Illustrations for Today*, 321.

[303] Spurgeon, *Evangelism*, 208–209.

210 Can You Say That You Have an
Intense Burden for Souls?

Francis Dixon said, "Have we a burden for lost souls? Sitting in his office in New Zealand, Mr. Robert Laidlaw turned to me and asked, 'Can you say that you have an intense burden for souls?' What a heart-searching question! What is our answer?

"Many years ago, Dr. Jowett said, 'The Gospel of a broken heart demands the ministry of bleeding hearts. When our sympathy loses its pang, we can no longer be the servants of the passion. We can never heal the needs we do not feel. Tearless hearts can never be heralds of the passion. We must pity if we would redeem. We must bleed if we would be ministers of the saving blood.'

"How much real concern have we for those who are without a knowledge of the Savior? Do we fail to win the lost to Christ because we do not feel the depth of their need? How may we become possessed with a passion for souls?

"We must get a glimpse into eternity. If we are gripped by a realization of the fleeting nature of this life and of the solemn unendingness of eternity, we shall be constrained to 'persuade men' to be reconciled to God (II Corinthians 5:18). Let us take time to meditate upon the truth of E-T-E-R-N-I-T-Y and the future destiny of the saved and of the lost.

"We must be absolutely convinced about the present desperate need of every lost soul and about the future destiny of all the impenitent. If we believe the testimony of the Scriptures concerning the condition of the unregenerate, we shall surely feel drawn to do something for their salvation.

"We must meditate upon the tremendous sacrifice of Calvary where our Lord Jesus gave Himself for our sins, and not for ours only, but for the sins of the whole world (I John 2:2). As we meditate upon His passion and His blood shedding, we shall be filled with a deep desire that after the suffering of His soul, He will see the light of life and be satisfied (Isaiah 53:11); and we shall realize that He has 'committed to us the message of reconciliation' (II Corinthians 5:19).

"We must be much in communion with the Lord Jesus, so that we shall increasingly share His concern for the souls of men. After all, a real passion for souls is not the product of ourselves at all; it is His love and compassion within us that makes us concerned! But how can we be filled with His love and concern for the salvation of the lost?

"We must be filled with the Holy Spirit, so that we are constrained by His love as it is shed abroad in our hearts and flows out from our lives."[304]

---

[304] Dixon, "Passion for Souls," accessed April 14, 2010.

SPURS TO SOUL WINNING

211 Plan to Go

As a fisherman plans to catch fish, an athlete plans to win the race, and a man plans to win a girl's heart, just so the believer must plan to win souls. Plan to win souls in several ways.

Take tracts. Never be caught without a gospel tract in hand, for it is an awesome "bridge" on which to walk to share Christ.

List targets. Keep the names of the lost to win handy for prayer and pursuit.

Show interest. Exhibit genuine interest and concern in the lost, not just in regard for their souls, but for the whole of their lives. How might you do this with those on your target list?

Schedule it. Make an appointment entry in your datebook to see a lost person and then keep it.

Give invitation. Invite the unsaved to a meal and/or to an evangelistic service.

The key is to plan to go and tell. Do you have a plan to tell others of Christ today?

Lord, speak to me that I may speak
 In living echoes of Thy tone;
As Thou hast sought, so let me seek
 Thy erring children lost and lone.

Oh, fill me with Thy fullness, Lord,
 Until my very heart o'erflow
In kindling thought and glowing word,
 Thy love to tell, Thy praise to show.

Oh, use me, Lord, use even me,
 Just as Thou wilt, and when, and where,
Until Thy blessed face I see,
 Thy rest, Thy joy, Thy glory share![305]

212 Absence of Conviction to Witness

Frankly I stand baffled at how few believers actually share their faith or even feel the slightest inclination to do so! I can only deduct that such

---

[305] Havergal, "A Worker's Prayer," accessed May 11, 2010.

"believers" are not genuinely saved or know nothing of the convicting power of the Holy Spirit that incites one to witness. The remedy for the former is for the person to experience the new birth, and for the latter to position the heart to hear from the Holy Spirit.

Absence of conviction to witness is due to a barrier or barriers erected in the heart that shield from the conviction. This barrier may be a feeling of exemption (belief that soul winning is for the ministerial staff and not us), closed-mindedness, indifference, cowardice, disobedience or just plain carnality. Such barriers must be removed through confession and cleansing if the heart is to encounter the convicting power of the Holy Spirit that incites the need and must of soul winning (Psalm 139:23–24).

The absence of conviction to witness should not lead one to believe he is excused from witnessing. The Word of God trumps the conscience, and it clearly mandates all to witness (Acts 1:8). The heart that is free from barriers that block the conviction to witness hears the call of the Spirit to witness.

213 Shall I Sound Alarm?

On the night of the great Yorkshire flood some years ago, a man on the reservoir noted the rise of the water to a dangerous level. He debated for a full twenty minutes whether or not to sound the alarm. Tragically, he never gave warning, and the waters rushed over the banks and spread destruction on every hand. A decision by this person twenty minutes before this occurred would have saved numerous lives.[306]

You are hesitating in talking to someone about Christ, unsure if this is the time to "sound the alarm." Heaven and Hell unite in beckoning you not to procrastinate but to do so without further delay. Record books attest to the many that would have been saved had someone sounded the alarm twenty days, twenty hours or twenty minutes sooner!

214 Catch a Trout Early in Life

J. H. Jowett declared, "'It is a great matter to take a trout early in your trial. It gives one more heart. It seems to keep one about his business. Otherwise you are apt to fall into unproductive reverie.' I know no word more closely applicable to the work of the ministry. If we do not catch men, we are in great danger of losing even the desire to catch them. Our purposed activity is in peril of becoming a dream.

---

[306] Tan. *7700 Illustrations*, 1090.

"Let me counsel my fellow preachers in the lay ministry to make up their minds to catch one soul, to go about it day and night until the soul is won. And when they have gained one man for the Master, I have then no fear as to what will be their resultant mood. The joy of catching a soul is unspeakable! When we have got one soul, we become possessed by the passion for souls. Get one, and you will want a crowd.

"And let me say this further word. Keep a list of the names of the souls you win for the King, and if on any day you are apt to be cast down and the lightness and buoyancy go out of your spirit, bring out that list and read it over, and let the contemplation of those saved lives set your heart a-singing and inspire you to fresh and more strenuous work. It is a good thing to have lists of the Lord's mercies by which to drive away the clouds in a day of adversity. Let your labor be directed to the immediate catching of men for the Lord. 'It is a great matter to take a trout early in your trial.'"[307]

215 "Hopeless" Cases

"Here then, my brethren, is the setting of the divine purpose. Our Lord will work upon the world through us. Through our moral elevation and fine spiritual kinships, He would compel the world into primary and fruitful beliefs. Let us place the matter before us in pertinent application. If the organized worldliness of this city is ever to be disturbed, if worldly men and women are to be startled into wonder and incipient belief, it will have to be done through the unworldliness and fine spiritual fellowships of professed disciples of Christ.

"Are we ready for the Master's use? Do we really believe in the possibility of the world's redemption? How spacious is our belief; how large is the possibility which we entertain? When we survey the clamant needs of the human race, do we discover any 'hopeless cases'? Where have we obtained the right to use the word 'hopeless'? What evidence or experience will justify us in saying of any man, 'He is too far gone'? In what atmosphere of thought and expectancy are we living? Are we dwelling in the Book of Ecclesiastes or making our home in the Gospel by John?

"Let us ransack the city. Let us rake out, if we can find him, the worst of our human race. Let us produce the sin-steeped and the lust-sodden soul, and then let us hear the word of the Master: 'Believest thou that I am able to do this?' The first condition of being capable ministers of Christ is to believe in the possibility of the world's salvation.

---

[307] Jowett, *Passion for Souls*, Mediations #71 & #72.

"Let us become reverently familiar with the glorious evangel until the music of the Gospel rings through every part of our being. Let us ask Him to free us, not only from doubt, but from uncleanness. Let us plead with Him to make us the fitting instruments of His power, that through the beauty and strength of our life and the steady persistence of our faith, the world may be allured into the fellowship of the saints in light."[308]

216 Just Use What You've Got

A seminary professor told our class, "Between the things you cannot do and the things you are unwilling to do, there is a great danger that you will do nothing." This profound truth certainly applies to soul winning.

A young boy was courting a beautiful young lady on the front porch swing of her home. He looked at her and said, "If I had a thousand lips, I would kiss your rosy cheek; if I had a thousand eyes, I would stare into your beautiful blue eyes; if I had a thousand arms, I would embrace you so tight."

The young girl looked at him and said, "Just use what you've got."

In soul winning, don't harp on what you would do if you had the abilities of a Graham or Finney; "just use what you've got."

217 The Primary Objective

L. R. Scarborough wrote regarding the paralytic taken to Jesus by the four men, "Look at the method Jesus used. He first saved the soul of the seeking sinner. He regarded that the lost man's salvation was preeminent above the healing of his body. The interests of the soul are primal with Christ and should be with all His people.

"Hospitals, orphans' homes, rescue stations and other benevolent institutions, social service, the proper housing and feeding and clothing of the poor, all laws governing child labor and such like are important indeed; but the salvation of the souls of the people is the first matter; and in whatever benevolent and social service we render, we must have regeneration as the foremost objective. We must heal and help the bodies of men, train and culture the minds of men, but our primary purpose and objective must be the salvation of the souls of men."[309]

---

[308] Jowett. *Brooks,* 155–156.

[309] Hutson, *Preaching on Soul Winning,* 193.

218 Love 'Em No Matter Which Side of the
Tracks They Live On

"One day a letter came to the church where this writer was pastor (Charles L. McKay). It was signed by twenty-three people. The letter read: 'We hear that the First Baptist Church is interested in lost people no matter where they live or what side of the railroad track they are on. Will you give us a Sunday school?'

"When the pastor read the letter, he went immediately to his study and locked the door. He read the letter again, then got down on his knees and asked God to keep him on his face until he could get up with the conviction that the pastor of that church loved lost people, no matter where they lived or on what side of the railroad track they were. This made the difference. He called the deacons of the church together. Eighteen of them came. They read the letter. Nineteen men got on their knees and pledged God their best in leading their church into a great mission program for Christ."

McKay then challenges, "We must go into regions beyond, and go now. If we fail to warn the multitudes, they will die in their sins, and their blood will be on our hands. Oh, Southern Baptists, multitudes lie in darkness and despair. Will we, at this late hour, rise up and meet the emergency and go into these unchurched areas and provide Bible study and a church program for those who need Christ?...Providing for and reaching these people for Christ is not optional with Christians. It is a divine command....The best-known way we have to reach these people and reach them fast is to go where they are and make Bible study so convenient for them that they cannot reject it....Many of these unreached people will not come to our present churches."[310]

Where might a nonchurch Sunday school or evangelistic Bible study be initiated? Sidewalks, apartment meeting parlors, and homes are possibilities. The place, whatever it may be, needs to be nonthreatening and inviting to the unsaved.

219 "Depraved Indifference"

Charles Spurgeon said, "Have you no wish for others to be saved? Then you are not saved yourself. Be sure of that." He continued, "The saving of souls, if a man has once gained love to perishing sinners and his blessed Master, will be an all-absorbing passion to him. It will so carry him away that he will almost forget himself in the saving of others. He will be like the

---

[310] McKay, *Call of the Harvest*, 118.

brave fireman who cares not for the scorch or the heat so that he may rescue the poor creature on whom true humanity has set its heart.

"If sinners will be damned, at least let them leap to Hell over our bodies. And if they will perish, let them perish with our arms about their knees, imploring them to stay. If Hell must be filled, at least let it be filled in the teeth of our exertions, and let not one go there unwarned and unprayed for."[311]

Kirk Cameron stated, "Hell should be so real to us that its flames burn away apathy and motivate us to warn the lost. Do we understand that sinful humanity is the anvil of the justice of God? Have we ever been horrified or wept because we fear their fate? The depth of our evangelistic zeal will be in direct proportion to the depth of our love. If you are not concerned about your neighbor's salvation, then I am concerned for yours. Remember, if you let a human being die when you have the ability to save him, even man's law will charge you with 'depraved indifference.' How much more does God's Law demand concern?"[312]

220 God's Conception of a Soul's Worth

J. Wilbur Chapman relates the story of the capture of a British subject named Campbell by the Abyssinians and the price paid by Britain for his rescue. Campbell was imprisoned at the fortress of Magdala for six months before Britain discovered his captivity. Immediately they demanded his release, but to no avail. In fewer than ten days, ten thousand British soldiers went by ship to that coast where they disembarked and then marched seven hundred miles in the fierce heat up the mountain heights to the very dungeon where he was imprisoned. A battle ensued, dungeon gates were torn down, and the prisoner was lifted upon the shoulders of fellow soldiers and carried to the ship. It cost Great Britain $25 million to gain the release of that one man. Such was the value Britain placed upon the liberty of one English subject.

"But God puts a greater price," says W. B. Riley, "upon the life and liberty of a single soul. That is why He summoned all Heaven to its redemption and appointed His Son chief Captain and Leader to effect its liberty. When we get God's conception of the soul's worth, no sacrifice will seem too great to make in the effort to save it; when we get God's conception of a soul's worth, no obstacle will seem insurmountable; when we get God's

---

[311] Comfort, *Way of the Master*, 250.

[312] Ibid., 251.

conception of a soul's worth, we will sacrifice, as did Christ, to reclaim it from sin, believing with Solomon, 'He that winneth souls is wise.'"[313]

221   Contrary to Belief, More Won One-to-One

Seventy-five to ninety percent of people come to Christ through a friend or acquaintance who explains the Good News on a one-to-one basis. Only seventeen percent of all conversions come as a result of a Sunday morning sermon, evangelistic crusade, or a Friendship Sunday.[314] The fact that friends and loved ones stand a far better chance of being saved by a personal witness than a sermon ought to prompt believers to prioritize soul winning above invitation to attend church.

222   "Do Something; Do Something"

C. H. Spurgeon, speaking to students at his college, said, "We want facts—deeds done, souls saved. It is all very well to write essays, but what souls have you been the means of saving from going down to Hell? Your excellent management of your school interests me, but how many children have been brought into the church by it? We are glad to hear of those special meetings, but how many have really been born to God in them?...Are sinners converted?

"To swing to and fro on a five-barred gate is not progress; yet some seem to think that it is....God save us from living in comfort while sinners are sinking into Hell!...Brethren, do something; *do something*; DO SOME-THING. While committees waste their time over resolutions, do something. While societies and unions are making constitutions, let us win souls....Too often we discuss and discuss and discuss while Satan only laughs in his sleeve."[315]

223   Plow in Faith

"He that ploweth should plow in hope" (I Corinthians 9:10). The soul winner is a farmer who uses the gospel plow to break up the hard and barren soil in man's soul to plant the precious seed. It is tedious and

---

[313] Hutson, *Preaching on Soul Winning*, 90.

[314] Fay, *Share Jesus*, 12.

[315] Spurgeon, *All-Round Ministry*, chapter 2, accessed April 4, 2010.

difficult work. During the plowing stage, he never knows if the seed planted will germinate but presses forward in "hope."

Herein is a great need in soul winning—the sower must sow the seed in faith, expectantly believing it will be received. He that embraces the attitude, "I will tell him, but it won't do any good," has failed before he even tries. Plow earnestly. Plow consistently. But plow expectantly. The believer will be pleasantly surprised as he but does so at the many so called "unlikely candidates" for salvation who are won!

224 The Need of a Solemn Assembly

C. H. Spurgeon strikes a note in our hearts in stating, "Men are passing into eternity so rapidly that we must have them saved at once. We indulge no secret hope which can make it easy to lose present opportunities. From all our congregations, a bitter cry should go up unto God unless conversions are continually seen."[316]

Believers should weep and wail in great disgust and disappointment when souls are not being saved. But, alas, not only is there no heart disturbance among the saints over its soul barrenness, but no grave concern why this is so! Winning souls is the primary function of the church (its members); and its failure is inexcusable, for the fields are ripe unto harvest in every community. Barren saints and members of barren churches need to declare a "solemn assembly" to repent, fast and pray that soul winning fires will be ignited in their hearts. Many saints are clueless about the solemn assembly. In times of extraordinary spiritual decline, extraordinary steps must be taken for revival.

In I Samuel 7:5–6, Samuel required the people to gather at Mizpeh in a solemn assembly for fasting and confession of sins. Asa called a solemn assembly in Jerusalem, calling on the people to seek God with all their hearts and souls (II Chronicles 15:9–15). A solemn assembly was held at the water gate where the people stood to hear the Book of the Law read and where a written agreement was made to put away sin and seek God with the whole heart (Nehemiah 8:1ff).

Bitter cries ought to be heard from every barren church altar in the land as saints lament their soul neglect and seek renewal. "Sanctify ye a fast, call a solemn assembly, gather the elders and all the inhabitants of the land into the house of the LORD your God, and cry unto the LORD" (Joel 1:14).

---

[316] Ibid., chapter 8, accessed April 4, 2010.

SPURS TO SOUL WINNING

225 Always Be Looking for "Awakened" Sinners

"When the prodigal was a great way off," C. H. Spurgeon states, "his father saw him. Oh, to have quick eyes to spy out the awakened! (*'Awakened' sinners are those in whom the Holy Spirit has wrought conviction of sin and need of salvation*). The father ran to meet him. Oh, to be eager to help the hopeful! He fell upon his neck and kissed him. Oh, for a heart overflowing with love to joy and rejoice over seeking ones! As that father was, such should we be—ever loving and ever on the outlook. Our eyes and ears and feet should ever be given to penitents. Our tears and open arms should be ready for them. The father in Christ is the man to remember the best robe and the ring and the sandals; he remembers those provisions of grace, because he is full of love for the returning one. Love is a practical theologian and takes care to deal practically with all the blessings of the covenant and all the mysteries of revealed truth. It does not hide away the robe and ring in a treasury of theology, but brings them forth and puts them on."[317]

One may identify an "awakened" sinner through his sudden interest in spiritual things, questions and conversations. Stay on the watch for these dear souls in whom the Lord is working and ever be ready to stop what you are doing to lead them to Christ.

226 The King's Business Requireth Haste

Francis Dixon stated, "If a businessman is to succeed, he must be gripped by a threefold conviction—first, that he is an authorized representative of his firm; second, that the goods he has to offer are second to none; and, third, that the public needs what he has to offer.

"If we are to engage in the King's business and win souls for Him, we must be gripped by this threefold conviction. We must be absolutely sure that we are authorized to represent the Lord down here in the world. Can we be sure? Yes (Matthew 28:18–20). Are the "goods" we have to offer second to none? Do we believe implicitly in the Gospel of the saving grace of God? Yes (Romans 1:16). Do men and women stand in desperate need of what we have to offer them? Yes, for they are lost (Luke 19:10), condemned (John 3:18), and under God's wrath (John 3:36). One reason why many Christians are not engaging in the King's business by seeking to save the lost is that they are not gripped by this threefold conviction.

---

[317] Ibid., chapter 8, accessed April 4, 2010. (italicized added for clarification)

"The King's business requires *haste*—there is urgency about it. Souls need to be saved quickly. Why? First, because the time left for trading (soul winning) is brief (I Corinthians 7:29). Second, because the markets are closing down. On every hand, doors for the Gospel that have long been open are being closed, and God's servants are not able to enter in and "trade." The third reason why there is urgency about the task of evangelism is that our King is soon coming (James 5:8)."[318]

227 Hearing God's Voice

A friend visiting Peter Lord's home told him he could hear no fewer than eighteen different kinds of crickets in his garden. This surprised Peter, for he had lived there for years and never heard one. The difference was a trained ear. This friend was a professor of entomology and had learned to distinguish over 200 different cricket calls. Looking back, Peter wrote, "I suddenly understood that a person must want to hear and learn to hear, and there were many sounds I was not hearing."[319] Failure to hear crickets is no big loss, but consider the loss of not hearing the voice of God speak due to an untrained ear (not the audible voice of God, but primarily the still small voice of God to the heart).

"They follow him because they know his voice" (John 10:4 NCV). Hearing God's voice is essential in every facet of the Christian life, but of immense importance in soul winning. Had Phillip not heard God speak to him regarding the searching lost sinner traveling the Gaza Strip, this man would not have been saved. Had Peter not heard God's voice telling him to witness to Cornelius, Cornelius never would have been saved. These men had trained ears to hear the voice of God above the voices of all others clamoring for attention. The believer must discipline himself to learn to hear the still small voice of God, for multiple times in our lives, God will speak with specific soul-winning assignments, saying, "Go here"; "Go there"; or "Speak to him or to her now." Failure to hear God when He speaks will result in failed assignments and lost souls.

228 Fullness of the Holy Spirit to Win Souls

C. H. Spurgeon declared, "But there is another thing to be done as well, and that is to pray; and here I want to remind you of those blessed words of the Master: 'Every one that asketh receiveth; and he that seeketh findeth;

---

[318] Dixon, "King's Business," June 4, 1963.

[319] Unknown author, "Opportunity," accessed June 2, 2010.

and to him that knocketh it shall be opened. If a son shall ask bread of any of you that is a father, will he give him a stone? Or if he ask a fish, will he for a fish give him a serpent? Or if he shall ask an egg, will he offer him a scorpion? If ye then, being evil, know how to give good gifts unto your children: how much more shall your heavenly Father give the Holy Spirit to them that ask him?'

"You see, there is a distinct promise to the children of God, that their heavenly Father will give them the Holy Spirit if they ask for His power; and that promise is made to be exceedingly strong by the instances joined to it. But he says, 'How much *more* shall your heavenly Father give the Holy Spirit to them that ask him?' He makes it a stronger case than that of an ordinary parent. The Lord *must* give us the Spirit when we ask Him, for He has herein bound Himself by no ordinary pledge. He has used a simile which would bring dishonor on His own name, and that of the very grossest kind, if He did not give the Holy Spirit to them that ask Him.

"Oh, then, let us ask Him at once with all of our hearts. Am I not so happy as to have in this audience some who will immediately ask? I pray that some who have never received the Holy Spirit at all may now be led, while I am speaking, to pray, 'Blessed Spirit, visit me; lead me to Jesus.' But those of you that are the children of God—to you is this promise especially made. Ask God to make you all that the Spirit of God can make you—not only a satisfied believer who has drunk for himself, but a useful believer who overflows the neighborhood with blessing. I see here a number of friends from the country who have come to spend their holiday in London. What a blessing it would be if they went back to their respective churches overflowing, for there are numbers of churches that need flooding. They are dry as a barn floor, and little dew ever falls on them. Oh, that they might be flooded!"[320]

"Be not drunk with wine, wherein is excess; but be filled with the Spirit" (Ephesians 5:18). One is Spirit-filled when the Holy Spirit is not simply present but President in his life, when he lives under the controlling influence of the Holy Spirit.

John R. Rice stated, "I was delighted to find what I did not know before, that Spurgeon understood how Jesus our Savior was filled with the Holy Spirit as our example, and how all Christ's marvelous ministry on earth was done in the power of the Holy Spirit, not in His own power. And Spurgeon, I find, understood what I had found from the Scriptures—that the parable of the importunate friend in Luke, chapter 11, begging for bread for a friend

---

[320] Rice, "Great Soul Winners," 23.

who had journeyed to the pleader's house pictured a Christian waiting on God for the power of the Holy Spirit to carry bread for sinners!"[321]

229 What Feeds the Longing to Win Souls?

L. R. Scarborough, writing about one's passion for souls, stated: "It might be worthily asked, what are the spiritual foods on which this longing exists, thrives and flourishes in our hearts? The answer is an easy one.

"(1) Secret and closet prayer, a spiritual intimacy with Christ in secret communion.

"(2) A close and intensive study of God's Word, not controversially but devotionally.

"(3) A review of the sinner's condition before God as revealed in God's Word. I have a marked Bible. Most of the passages speaking of sin—its nature; its guilt; its diabolism; its murderous intent; its extensive and deadly leavening power; its direful results to soul, body, mind, and destiny; its punishments; and all of its long and bloody history—are marked in heavy black lines. Then the passages in the Bible telling of God's remedy for sin, what He does with sin and for the sinner, many scores of them are marked. When my heart is cold and I am apparently far away from God, I can read these passages, and there begins at once a kindling flame of evangelism in my heart, and nothing will satisfy me except an effort at winning a soul to Christ and the joy of seeing him saved.

"(4) An association with God's most consecrated followers, sitting with them in fellowship and hearing them talk of God's dealings with them and recount the triumphs they have witnessed in Christian service. This will start evangelistic flames in our own souls.

"(5) A real sacrificial spirit toward one's own testimony in the use of one's talents, money, and time will feed the fires of soul winning. When we are willing to give of our strength or possessions, or invest our time in the salvation of men, we will probably be greatly strengthened to win others.

"(6) A vital, constant and persistent effort to carry Christ to men and bring men to Christ will rekindle in our hearts the soul winning passion."[322]

---

[321] Ibid., 24.

[322] Scarborough, *Search for Souls*, 55–57.

230 More Laborers Needed

Many are praying for an awakening among saints and a harvest among the lost. But the urgent prayer need of the hour is for God to rise up and send forth workers into the harvest who fear no one but God and relentlessly pursue lost souls. Jesus Himself said, "Pray ye therefore the Lord of the harvest, that he would send forth laborers into his harvest" (Matthew 9:38). Soul winners are to pray for more soul winners. Pray specifically for adults and students to be thrust—pushed (the meaning of "send")—into the thick and thin of witnessing in your church, community, city, country, and the whole world.

C. H. Spurgeon stated, "Brethren, do *you* ever pray God to send such workers into His vineyard? How long since you heard that prayer prayed, except from this pulpit? Pray ye, every one of you. Are you in the habit of doing so every morning and night? Why is there such a dearth of really warm-hearted, loving, earnest evangelists? It is because they are not asked for. God will not give them to us if we do not ask for them....But if you do not pray that God would send forth the laborers, and the laborers do not come, who is to blame? 'Pray ye.'"[323]

231 Asleep in Harvest Time

"He that sleepeth in harvest is a son that causeth shame" (Proverbs 10:5). Regarding this scripture text, R. G. Lee declared, "Why does sleep in harvest cause shame? Because the harvest will not wait. Harvesttime is a crisis time. This crisis must be vigorously and promptly met. Grain once ripe must be gathered in at once, or it will fall to the ground and be lost....Doors once opened but unentered may close again. Minds made susceptible but not won to Christ may turn away and become hardened. Truth resisted once is easier to resist next time, you know. We must strike while the iron is hot. It is now or never—when the harvest is ripe and ready for reaping.

"Why are those who sleep in harvest sons and daughters who cause shame? Because the harvest will not reap itself. The harvest needs men—to reap in the high places. The harvest needs women—to glean in the corners. The harvest needs men and women to gather it in. When the harvest is on, how shameful it is when the Church itself is a cemetery where the living sleep above the ground and the dead beneath the ground. There is not time to play when the harvest is ripe. To sleep in harvest time is to sleep in a time of supreme need....

---

[323] Spurgeon, *Evangelism*, 61.

"Now a man asleep is useless. He toils not, neither does he spin. A man asleep has lost his savor. No use to make an impassioned appeal to him about God's most daring enterprise, for he is asleep. He cannot be used in any program of the Church, for he is deaf to all the holier calls. He is blind to all the loftier visions. He is a spiritual nonentity. He does not count. He weighs nothing on God's scales of requirement. He is powerless as a tombstone, as impotent as spots of dried blood. The church needs him; God needs him; every good cause needs him. But he is asleep.

"Christ is saying with pathos indescribable to you and to me today, 'Can you not arouse yourselves from your sleep, shake yourselves from this lethargy of death and watch with Me in this great harvest night?' Men and brethren, are we acting as we ought to act in the time of harvest?...Are we saying with the disciples of old, 'Four months and then the harvest'? Or are we throwing our God-given energies and resources unreservedly into this great enterprise for God and for souls at this crucial hour? Is the harvest song in our hearts and the harvest blades in our hands while the 'fields are white unto the harvest'? 'He that sleepeth in harvest is a son that causeth shame!' 'Awake, thou that sleepest!'"[324]

232 Your Lost Friends Marvel at Your Silence

Oswald Sanders tells the story of Judge Mingins, an infidel who lived with infidel companions in Philadelphia. Following his conversion, he was visiting one of them, who said: "George, do you believe in God? I hear you are a Christian now. Is that so?"

"Yes," said Mr. Mingins.

"And do you believe in Hell and that all who do not believe in God and in Jesus Christ will ultimately go to Hell?"

"I do, most certainly."

"Well, George," said he, "does Christianity dry up all the milk of humanity in one's body as it has in yours?"

"Why," said Mr. Mingins, "what do you mean?"

"I mean this," he replied, "that here you have been living under my roof for three days and three nights, knowing and believing all this, and yet you never put your hand on my shoulder, or said one word to save me."[325]

Are you a Judge Mingins?

---

[324] Lee, *Feet to Fathoms*, 53–56.

[325] Sanders, "Passion for People," accessed April 12, 2010.

233   All for a Picture of a Bird

"We must persuade men," states R. G. Lee, "with something of the spirit of Audubon, the ornithologist. He counted his physical comforts nothing compared with success in his work. He would rise at midnight, night after night, and go out into the swamps to study the habits of certain night hawks. He would crouch motionless for hours in the dark and fog, feeling himself well rewarded, if, after weeks of waiting, he secured one additional fact about a single bird.

"During one summer he went, day after day, to the bayous near New Orleans to observe a shy waterfowl. He would have to stand almost to his neck in the nearly stagnant water, scarcely breathing, while countless poisonous moccasin snakes swam past his face and great alligators passed and repassed his silent watch. 'It was not pleasant,' he said, as his face glowed with enthusiasm, 'but what of that? I have the picture of the bird.'

"He would do that for the picture of a bird. What are we doing to persuade men already condemned (John 3:18) to accept a pardon that is to last for the eternities?"[326]

234   It's So Easy That a Caveman Can Do It

Dr. Riley reported, "We have known a boy of medium ability at work with his schoolmaster to win more souls between the day of his conversion at seven years of age and the time we parted company with him at twelve years of age than the average president of a Christian college has to his credit."[327] Certainly if a seven year old boy can win souls, there is no excuse for grown adults not to do so!

C. H. Spurgeon stated, "I further address myself to my text. I should like to remind you that the honor (soul winning) does not belong to ministers only; they may take their full share of it, but it belongs to every one of you who have devoted yourselves to Christ. Such honor have all the saints. Every man here, every woman here, every child here whose heart is right with God may be a soul winner. There is no man placed by God's providence where he cannot do some good. There is not a glowworm under a hedge but gives a needed light; and there is not a laboring man, a suffering woman, a servant girl, a chimney sweeper, or a crossing sweeper but has some opportunities for serving God. And what I have said of soul

---

[326] Lee, *Seven Swords*, Orlando, 46.

[327] Ibid., 55.

winners belongs not to the learned doctor of divinity or to the eloquent preacher alone, but to you all who are in Christ Jesus."[328]

235 "Is There Not a Cause?"

The giant Goliath wanted someone from King Saul's army to fight him. The winner of that duel would determine whether the Philistines or the Israelites would be declared the victors. No one wanted to fight Goliath, who stood over nine feet tall and wore heavy battle armor; that is, not until a young man named David arrived willing to do what the experienced soldiers in Saul's army were afraid to do.

When David stepped up to the plate to face Goliath, his eldest brother Eliab rebuked him, but he declared, "Is there not a cause?" (I Samuel 17:29). The cause David was referencing was "that all the earth may know that there is a God in Israel" (v. 46). In facing this big challenge, David refused to let others discourage or stop him. He was determined from the get-go to do what God wanted him to do.

Is there not a cause for you to be a soul winner? Sufficient cause is found in the estimated average of souls that die and go to Hell:

> 1.68 per second
> 101 per minute
> 6048 per hour
> 145,000 per day
> 53,000,000 per year
> 3,700,000,000 per average lifetime (70 years)[329]

To all who would oppose soul winning, answer resoundingly with young David, "Is there not a cause?" ever refusing, as he was, to be discouraged or turned back! As long as there remains one Christless soul, there remains a cause for us to go and tell.

236 The Silo of Sin

E. J. Daniels tells the story of a cow that slipped through a door into a silo. The cow ate her fill of grain and was unable to exit the silo due to her enlarged stomach. News of this event hit the news, and soon the entire

---

[328] Spurgeon, *Soul Winner*, 222–223.

[329] Bronson, "How Many," accessed May 11, 2010.

nation was concerned for "Old Bessie." Newspapers reported on their front pages the suggestions this farmer received about how to free the cow. Interested people wired or called long distance sharing advice on freeing the cow. One man volunteered to book a flight at his own expense to travel the great distance to the farm to assist in getting the cow out of the silo.

Daniels, commenting on this story, said, "I could not help contrasting the concern of the masses—even of Christians—over souls in the silo of sin. I love 'Old Bessie' and do not want any cow to get the idea that I am not appreciative of her kind! But I am compelled to say that we have a distorted sense of values and sympathies when we become alarmed over a cow in a silo but manifest no real burden over the lost in sin. May God open our eyes to see men as they really are—*sin sick unto death!*"[330]

237 The Parable of the Lifesaving Station

An unknown author wrote that on a dangerous seacoast where shipwrecks often occur, there was once a crude little lifesaving station. The building was just a hut, and there was only one boat, but the few devoted members kept a constant watch over the sea; and, with no thought for themselves, they went out day or night tirelessly searching for the lost. Many lives were saved by this wonderful little station, so that it became famous. Some of those who were saved and various others in the surrounding areas wanted to become associated with the station and give of their time and money and effort for the support of its work. New boats were bought, and new crews were trained. The little lifesaving station grew.

Some of the new members of the lifesaving station were unhappy that the building was so crude and so poorly equipped. They felt that a more comfortable place should be provided as the first refuge of those saved from the sea. They replaced the emergency cots with beds and put better furniture in an enlarged building. Now the lifesaving station became a popular gathering place for its members, and they redecorated it beautifully and furnished it as a sort of club. Fewer of the members were now interested in going to sea on lifesaving missions, so they hired lifeboat crews to do this work.

The mission of lifesaving was still given lip service, but most were too busy or lacked the necessary commitment to take part in the lifesaving activities personally. About this time, a large ship was wrecked off the coast, and the hired crews brought in boatloads of cold, wet and half-drowned people. They were dirty and sick, some had skin of a different color, some spoke a strange language, and the beautiful new club was

---

[330] Daniels, *Dim Lights*, 27.

considerably messed up. So the property committee immediately had a shower house built outside the club where victims of shipwreck could be cleaned up before coming inside.

At the next meeting, there was a split in the club membership. Most of the members wanted to stop the club's lifesaving activities as being unpleasant and a hindrance to the normal pattern of the club. But some members insisted that lifesaving was their primary purpose and pointed out that they were still called a lifesaving station. But they were finally voted down and told that if they wanted to save the lives of all various kinds of people who were shipwrecked in those waters, they could begin their own lifesaving station down the coast. They did.

As the years went by, the new station experienced the same changes that had occurred in the old. They evolved into a club, and yet another lifesaving station was founded. If you visit the seacoast today, you will find a number of exclusive clubs along that shore. Shipwrecks are still frequent in those waters, but now most of the people drown![331]

Isn't it easy for the believer and the church to gradually forget their primary purpose? Have you?

238 "What If George Is in Hell?"

E. J. Daniels' flight had landed in Chicago one morning when he received word that his brother had died. "I got on the plane and started flying back to Florida. I was living in hell—constantly crying out in my soul, 'What if George is lost? What if George is in Hell?'

"I finally deplaned and went to where his body was lying in state. As I walked into that room, members of the family were there. I walked over to the casket, and what I said was not intelligent. I fell over his face, and I cried out, 'If George is in Hell, I don't want to go to Heaven. If George is in Hell, I don't want to go to Heaven.'

"It suddenly dawned on me that the brother I had slept with, that furnished me the car to court my wife and helped me go to school might be in Hell. Have you ever thought about somebody that you love being in Hell—your own son or your own daughter, your brother or sister, your husband or wife? My dear friends, since what the Word of God says about Hell is so, let's you and I tonight dedicate ourselves unto God to try and get every possible person saved from Hell.

---

[331] MacArthur, *Bible Studies*, 30–31.

"Do you care whether men go to Hell or not? Honestly, I'm asking you high schoolers—do you really care? Do you adults care if men go to Hell? We don't want to get involved. How many of you are not making phone calls? You're not begging men to come. You just don't want to get involved. Do you really care?

"I don't know how you feel, but I know how I feel. As I prayed about this message, God convicted this poor preacher's heart. Preachers, we need convicting tonight. And God convicted my heart. And God said, 'Daniels, do you care? Do you care whether souls go to Hell or not?' Do we care?

"I want to tell you, my brethren, my sisters, we can have all the religion we want, but if we don't care for souls, we're dishonoring God. We can have all the professional programs we want; we can preach like angels and sing like angels, but if we don't care for souls, we dishonor God. Do you care? How many of you have somebody that you love—it may be a member of your family; it may be a friend—but somebody that you don't want to go to Hell. You want to lift up your hand and say, 'Pray for me, Daniels. I don't want them in Hell. I want them saved.'"[332]

239 The Hardest People to Reach

It is essential in soul winning that the "awakened" heart be recognized so that an opportunity to be saved might be extended with urgency. Such people who are not given the chance to be saved or persuaded to be saved become more difficult to reach.

D. L. Moody commented, "There is not a true minister of the Gospel who will not say that the hardest people to reach are those who have been impressed and whose impressions have worn away. It is a good deal easier to commit a sin the second time than it was to commit it the first time. But it is a good deal harder to repent (salvation) the second time than it was the first."[333]

C. H. Spurgeon stated soul hardness leads sinners to testify, "'Considerations that used to thrill me and make my flesh creep are now put before me, but I seem like a piece of steel. Nay, I do not even rust under the Word; I am unimpressible. Harvests have dried me; summers have parched me; age has shriveled my soul.'…Harvests and summers leave us worse if they

---

[332] Daniels, *Why Jesus Wept*, 33–35.

[333] Moody D. L., "Hardest People," 16.

do not see us mend....Oh, for grace to repent at once, ere yet the wax has cooled and the seal is set forever."[334]

"Strike while the iron is hot"—this adage is never truer than in soul winning.

240 "Give Me Four Souls Every Day"

John (Praying) Hyde "often went into the hills to visit friends and pray. A friend relates, 'It was evident to all he was bowed down with sore travail of soul. He missed many meals, and when I went to his room, I would find him lying as in great agony or walking up and down as if an inward fire were burning in his bones.'

"It was from intense burden that Hyde asked God to give him a soul a day that year. Praying Hyde departed from his friends no ordinary man. He became a burden bearer for mankind. At year's end, four hundred souls had been won to Christ!

"As the New Year came, John Hyde approached God's throne with a greater burden. Now Hyde begged for two souls daily. Twelve months later, more had been won than Hyde anticipated. In fact, some eight hundred souls were claimed that year. This, however, did not satisfy Praying Hyde. Soon we hear him pleading, 'Give me four souls every day.'

"Hyde's intent was not to win these with tent crusades or massive rallies. He went for every soul, one at a time. Conversation ensued, and before long, both would kneel in prayer. Multitudes of souls found Christ when this humble man assumed a burden for the lost."[335]

R. G. Lee declares of this great man, "Think of the man Hyde—a missionary to India. The revival period there extended from 1904 to 1910—six wonderful, soul-saving years. To him fellow missionaries attributed one hundred thousand souls resulting from revivals for which he prayed. He died after a few years of some prayer, his heart having been forced to the right side of his body through the agonizing earnestness of his praying. In his praying, he urged public confession of sin."[336]

---

[334] Spurgeon, *Special Days and Occasions*, 184.

[335] Goll, "Crisis Intervention," accessed April 22, 2010.

[336] Lee, *Seven Swords*, Orlando, 53.

SPURS TO SOUL WINNING

241 Mourning over the Lost

In the beatitudes, Jesus says, "Blessed are they that mourn: for they shall be comforted" (Matthew 5:4). To mourn is to express sorrow and grief of soul that God is being dishonored by either your life or that of others. The strongest word in the Greek language for mourning is used in this verse. It means to mourn as one mourns over the dead. It is the same word that is used to express Jacob's grief when he thought his son Joseph was dead (Genesis 37:34). It is this kind of sorrow the saint should manifest when he engages in sin, just as Isaiah (Isaiah 6:5) and David (Psalms 51:4) did. It is this kind of deep heartache the believer should exhibit regarding the moral, spiritual and political corruption of the world—the millions of souls steeped in stubborn rebellion against a Holy God; the rampage of abortion, murder, suicide, pornography, drugs and alcohol, and sex crimes; the rise of liberal theology denying Christ as the only way to salvation; and politicians who tread upon God's name and Word in a blasphemous manner.

Viewing the condition of the world through the lenses of Heaven, every child of God must testify with David, "Rivers of waters run down mine eyes, because they keep not thy law" (Psalm 119:136). The born again ought indeed to weep and wail, as the unsaved at the death of a loved one, over personal and public sin, crying out to God for divine intervention and deliverance. And "they shall be comforted."

Jeremiah exclaims, "For the hurt of the daughter of my people am I hurt" (Jeremiah 8:21). Spurgeon comments that Jeremiah "was more hurt than they were. The man of God, who personally had least cause to mourn, was filled with heavy grief, while the people who were about to lose their all and lose their lives still remained but half-awakened—complaining, but not repenting; afraid, but yet not humbled before God. None of them uttered such a grievous lament as that which came from the heart and mouth of the prophet. Their heads were full of idle dreams, while his had become waters; their eyes were full of wantonness, while his were a fountain of tears. He loved them better than they loved themselves....

"A preacher (soul winner) whom God sends will often feel more care for the souls of men than men feel for themselves or their own salvation. Is it not sad that there should be an anxious pain in the heart of one who is himself saved, while those who are unsaved and are obliged to own it feel little or no concern? To see a man in jeopardy of his life, and all around him alarmed for his danger, while he himself is half asleep, is a sad sight....

"Such a sad sight we constantly see in our congregations; those who are 'condemned already' on account of sin are altogether indifferent to their awful peril, while their godly parents are greatly distressed for them,

Christian people are pleading with them, and earnest messengers from God are expostulating with them."[337]

242 Gipsy's Trousers' Worn Knees

Gipsy Smith told the story of the conversion of his Uncle Rodney. In the gypsy camp a child was not to speak to an elder unless first addressed, so Gipsy prayed and patiently waited for such an occasion to share Jesus with Uncle Rodney. This uncle, noticing Gipsy's worn trousers, said, "Laddie, how do you account for the fact that the knees of your trousers have worn nearly through, while the rest of the suit is almost like new?"

"I have worn the knees through praying for you, Uncle Rodney," Gipsy answered. Then tearfully he said, "I want so much to have God make you a Christian!" Immediately Uncle Rodney embraced Gipsy, and within a few moments, he fell to his knees receiving Christ as his Savior![338] What do the trouser knees of your pants say regarding prayer for the lost?

Gipsy prayed for and told his Uncle Rodney about Christ. Pray indeed for the unsaved, but then go to them. Spurgeon stated, "Prayer and means must go together. Means without prayer are presumption. Prayer without means is hypocrisy."[339]

243 Most *Know* to Do More Than *Want* to Do

John Bisagno writes, "The problem is that most of us *know* to do more than we *want* to do! While we continue to use new methods, new witnessing ideas, and new ways to teach our people how to be soul winners, the truth of the matter is that most of them simply do not *want* to be soul winners. We have *information,* but not sufficient *motivation.* If they had to, most Christians could probably tell a person how to accept Christ as his personal Savior, but few there be who really do it.

"It is obvious that the reason we do so little is that information (knowing what to do) is not being coupled with motivation (the desire to do what we know). To know what to do is human. To do what we know is divine."[340]

---

[337] Spurgeon, *Special Days and Occasions*, 184. (Italics added by author)

[338] Tan. *7700 Illustrations*, #5878.

[339] Spurgeon, *Soul Winner*, 75.

[340] Bisagno, *Letters to Timothy*, 134.

Bisagno suggests four principles of motivation to soul winning directed to the pastor, which I adapt to make applicable to all who would win souls.

Enthusiasm. Develop a positive attitude toward soul winning—excitedly expect, plan, hope, and dream soul winning.

Repetition. Bisagno shares how that Wrigley Empire was built on five-cent packages of gum—repetition. They sold a lot of them! Continuously keep before you the urgency of outreach, the imperative of winning souls, by talking with others about it, reading sermons and stories about it, listening to music that reminds you of it, and placing post-it notes around the house and in the car to stimulate it. Keep repeating its imperative.

Illustration. Keep a lookout for others who are doing it, and be inflamed by their passion and discipline.

Example. (This principle applies more to motivating others.) Do it yourself. Show them how by doing it with them. Lead the way.[341]

"Motivation is getting people to do what they already know they ought to do, and it is probably 75 percent enthusiasm and 25 percent repetition, illustration, and example."[342]

244 "Daddy, Save Me!"

A public school burned in Camden, South Carolina. Seventy students lost their lives. The father of one was restrained by firemen as his little boy stood at the window and pathetically cried, "Daddy, save me!" Within two years, the father went insane and died. That is nothing to compare with the agony men will experience at the Judgment for allowing their families to go to Hell.[343]

245 Soul Winning: A "Thank You" for Salvation

Oswald Chambers said, "Has it ever dawned on you that you are responsible spiritually to God for other people? For instance, if I allow any turning away from God in my private life, everyone around me suffers. We 'sit together in heavenly places' (Ephesians 2:6). If you allow physical selfishness, mental carelessness, moral insensitivity, or spiritual weakness, everyone in contact with you will suffer....

---

[341] Ibid., 134–136.

[342] Ibid., 136.

[343] McComas, "Win the Lost," 17.

"'Ye shall be witnesses unto me' (Acts 1:8). How many of us are willing to spend every bit of our nervous, mental, moral, and spiritual energy for Jesus Christ? That is what God means when He uses the word 'witnesses.' But it takes time, so be patient with yourself. Why has God left us on the earth? Is it simply to be saved and sanctified? No, it is to be at work in service to Him. Am I willing to be of no value to this age or this life except for one purpose and one alone—to be used to disciple men and women to the Lord Jesus Christ? My life of service to God is the way I say 'thank you' to Him for His inexpressibly wonderful salvation."[344]

246 Lights Shining Behind Me

C. H. Spurgeon was walking up Norwood Hill with a friend when he noted a lamplighter some distance ahead. Spurgeon watched the lamplighter until he had crossed over the top of the hill and faded out of sight. He then turned to his companion and said, "I should like to think that when I've gone over the brow of the hill, I shall leave lights shining behind me."[345]

History attests Spurgeon, in fact, did! I don't know about you, but Spurgeon's desire is mine. In my death, I want to leave "lights" (souls I won) shining behind me. How many "lights" do we presently have burning? Regardless of the number, it's not nearly enough!

247 Cartwright's Boldness in Witnessing

"Perhaps the most famous Peter Cartwright incident occurred as he was returning from a denominational convention in Baltimore. He arrived at an inn in the Cumberland Mountains near bedtime. A dance was in progress, and the music, laughter, and liquor flowed in abundance. The preacher took a seat in the corner and was approached by a ruddy young lady asking him to dance. Cartwright took her hand and walked with her to the middle of the dance floor.

"What happened next is one of the more remarkable stories in frontier evangelism. Stopping the music, Cartwright explained that he never did anything of importance without first praying over it. He dropped to his knees and began vigorously praying aloud. The girl struggled to free herself, but his grasp was firm. The fiddler ran from the room, but most people were too shocked to move. As Cartwright continued praying, the sound of weeping was soon heard. The girl dropped to her knees, and so did

---

[344] Chambers, *My Utmost*, February 15 entry.

[345] Morgan, R., *Preacher's SourceBook*, 2006, 315–316.

others. The dance became a preaching service, resulting in over thirty conversions and the establishing of a church."[346]

Just maybe we all need a good dose of Cartwright boldness to thwart the cowardice in the heart.

248 No Substitute for Absolute Obedience

Stephen Olford comments, "My very dear friend Dr. Alan Redpath has a motto that has hung in every one of his studies during his pastoral years: 'Beware of the Barrenness of a Busy Life.' George Goodman, that great Brethren Bible teacher, used to say, 'Beware, lest service sap spirituality.' If you were to ask me what the single most important word in the Christian vocabulary is—from the moment of your commitment to Christ initially in salvation to that moment of final redemption when Jesus comes back again, from Genesis to Revelation—I would say *obedience*. There is no substitute for absolute obedience. I heard Dr. William Fitch once say at the Mid-America Keswick Conference in Chicago, 'Any point of defective obedience constitutes total disobedience.'

"All across America today in evangelical circles among preachers, there's an attitude of 'do-it-yourself theology.' This means that your own brains will take you through, your own culture will take you through, your string of degrees will take you through, although God has condemned all these notions (Gal. 3:1–3)! That is no indictment upon hard work and hard study and hard application of truth, but our life is a miraculous life. I cannot by any means convert myself or by any means live by the power of an indwelling Christ in and of myself—since it's only Christ and Christ only who can do this in me. Having begun totally dependent on Christ, I must live my Christian life that way too."[347]

Absolute obedience to Christ necessitates the believer's engaging in witnessing (Acts 1:8). If one fails to obey here, such "constitutes total disobedience," according to William Fitch. Power for this task is derived from the Holy Spirit within the believer—not education, effort, or equipment.

249 Will You Delay?

C. H. Spurgeon, preaching on the subject *Harvest Men Wanted,* stated, "The idea of immediate need is contained in the figure, for the reaping of

---

[346] Ibid., 47.

[347] Ibid., 262.

the harvest is to a considerable extent with the farmer a matter of now or never. 'Ah,' says he, 'if I could postpone the harvest, if I could let it be gathered in by slow degrees, if we could work on till the harvest moon has gone and then through November and December till winter closes the year, then the scantiness of laborers would be a small evil; but there is a limited time in which the wheat can be safely housed, and it must be got in ere winter begins, or it is lost to us.'

"There is no time for us to waste in the salvation of the sons of men. They will not live for ever; yon grey head will not tarry till you have told him the Gospel if you postpone the good news for the next ten years. We speak of what we hope may be accomplished for our race in half a century, but this generation will be buried ere that time.

"You must reap your harvest at once, or it will be destroyed; it must be ingathered speedily, or it will perish. Today, today, today, the imperative necessities of manhood appeal to the benevolence of Christians. Today the sure destruction of the unbeliever speaks with pleading voice to the humanity of every quickened heart. 'We are perishing; will you let us perish? You can only help us by bringing us the Gospel now; will you delay?'"[348]

250   Is It Worth the Effort to Save Souls?

Oswald Sanders stated, "Upon our conception of the value of the object to be won will depend the strenuousness of our labors for their salvation. *Is it really worth inconveniencing ourselves and interfering with our own enjoyment to save souls?* we ask. Let us endeavor to arrive at some true estimate of the value of a soul.

"A man will work harder to recover diamonds than gravel. Why? Because they are of so much greater value. And so it is with the souls of men. Christ conceived the human soul to be of such transcendent value that He gladly exchanged the shining courts of Glory for a life of poverty, suffering, shame, and death, rather than that it should perish. He placed the world and all it could offer in the one scale and a human soul in the other and declared that the scale went down on the side of the soul."[349]

---

[348] Spurgeon, *Evangelism*, 57–58.

[349] Sanders, "Passion for People," accessed April 12, 2010.

SPURS TO SOUL WINNING

251 Tapping the Power Source

A company was building a bridge. As the construction men were drilling down to set a post to support the bridge, they ran into a sunken barge. They decided it had to be moved. So they tried everything they could to move it, but to no avail. They got cranes on barges and tried to lift it up, but that didn't work.

They had almost given up, when finally one fellow standing by observing the whole thing said, "If you will give me a contract, I'll move that thing in twenty-four hours."

They said, "All right. We want it moved." The contract for several thousand dollars was signed to move that barge.

He went to work. He had them bring in six barges. He hooked them all together. He put them over the top of the sunken barge, and he sent divers down. These divers took chains and hooked them onto the sunken barge. They secured it with many strong chains. Then, when it was all ready, he stood back and said, "Now, it's just a matter of time until it will be moved."

They asked, "What do you mean? What are you going to get in there to pull those six barges?"

He said, "We're not going to pull them; we're going to leave them there. The way I figure it, in a few hours the tide will be in. Then she'll come up."

They stood by and waited. Sure enough, the tide came, and those six barges began to pull. They creaked, groaned, cracked and popped; and the sunken barge came loose. He floated it out into the Atlantic, sunk it, collected his thousands of dollars and walked away.

What man could not do with all of his power, this one man did by harnessing the power of the Atlantic Ocean.

We have the power of God available in everything we do. What we can't do, God can do![350]

252 Why Christians Don't Tell

"Why is it that we do not yearn more over the perishing souls of men?" asked Spurgeon. "Is it not that we have but little grace? We are dwarfish Christians with little faith, little love, little care for the glory of God, and therefore with little concern for perishing sinners....

"Do you not think that men are careless about the souls of others because they have fallen into a *one-sided view of Gospel doctrines* and have turned the doctrines of grace into a couch for idleness to rest upon? 'God

---

[350] Hutson, "For Preachers," 3.

will save his own,' say they....Unquestionably the Lord will...but He will do this by the preaching or teaching of the word....

"In some professors, downright *worldliness* prevents their seeking the conversion of others. They are too fond of gain to care for saving souls, too busy about their farms to sow the seed of the kingdom, too much occupied with their shops to hold up the cross before the sinner's eye, too full of care to care for the salvation of the lost....

"With some, I fear that the cause of indifference is *want of faith*. They do not believe that God will bless their efforts, and therefore they make none....

"It is to be feared that with many church members, the reason of the absence of this passion is that they love ease and are worm-eaten with *indolence*. They say, 'Soul, take thine ease, eat, drink, and be merry; why trouble about others?' 'Send the multitude away,' said the disciples. They did not want to be worried with them....

"The secret of all is that the great majority of Christians are *out of sympathy with God* and out of communion with Christ. Is not this an evil? O eyes that never wept over dying men, do you expect to see the King in his beauty? O hearts that never throbbed with anxiety for those that are going down to the pit, do ye hope to leap for joy at the Master's coming? O lips that never speak for Jesus, how will ye answer to the searching questions of the last great day? I do beseech you, Christian people, if you have grown indifferent to the conversion of those around you, search out the secret reason, find what is the worm at the root of your piety, and in the name of Christ, seek to be delivered therefrom."[351]

253 Do Not Talk About It; Do It

"If we are what we profess to be, we are saved men, redeemed by the heart's blood of the Son of God. Do we not owe something to Christ for this? Shall we be easy till we have found many jewels for His crown? Can we be content while so many myriads are ignorant of Him or opposed to Him? If ye love Him, what will ye do for Him? Show Him proof of your love, and the best proof you can give is your own personal holiness and persevering effort to gather in His redeemed.

"Brother, sister, do something for Jesus. Do not talk about it; do it. Words are leaves; actions are fruits. Do something for Jesus; do something for Jesus today! Ere the sun goes down, think of some one action which may tend to the conversion of some one person, and do it with your might;

---

[351] Spurgeon, *Evangelism*, 211–212.

let the object of the effort be your child, your servant, your brother, your friend—but do make the effort today.

"Having done it today, do it tomorrow—and every day; and doing it in one way, do it another way; and doing it in one state of heart, do it in another. Let your joy enchant; let your sorrow arouse; let your hope attract; let your changeful moods help you to attack sinners from different quarters as your varying circumstances bring you into contact with differing persons. Be always awake. By all means save some."[352]

"It is of no use for any of you to try to be soul winners if you are not bearing fruit in your own lives. How can you serve the Lord with your lips if you do not serve Him with your lives? How can you preach His Gospel with your tongues, when with hands, feet and heart you are preaching the Devil's gospel and setting up an antichrist by practical unholiness?"[353]

254 No Other Message Saves

George W. Truett, for forty-seven years the great pastor of First Baptist Church, Dallas, Texas, proclaimed, "To be sure, 'other gospels' are abroad these latter days, but we shall unwaveringly hold to the one—'Christ and Him crucified.' And though many are seeking to be rid of the word 'crucified,' to us the great central fact of our redemption is that 'Christ bore our sins in His own body on the tree.' Salvation by His blood shall ever be our theme—we will know no other. We are not ignorant of the 'other gospels' that are now being offered as substitutes for the one....We know about them all, and we know that with all their keenness of speculation and polish of learning and profundity of philosophy, not one of them has ever regenerated a single soul.

"We are not of those who have concluded that the old Gospel of the cross is unsuited to the advanced thought and aesthetic taste of these cultural times. Not philosophy, nor culture, nor sociology, nor humanitarianism, in fullest possible measure, can save lost men. Underneath them all, the human heart will still sin on and sigh for Emmanuel's peace and pardon. The old, old story uttered by lips touched by a live coal from off God's altar and driven home to men's consciences with the voice of divine authority—this and this only can make the spiritual wilderness to blossom as the rose....

---

[352] Ibid., 214.

[353] Spurgeon, *Metropolitan Tabernacle Pulpit, 1876,* 255.

"This was the theme of Spurgeon for nearly forty years, and under his ministry, more than any other in his generation, lost men came flocking to God as doves to their windows....To *Paul,* the world was lost. On the brow of every unsaved man the awful judgment of God, 'condemned already,' was written in letters of Stygian blackness. This condemnation was not idle dream; but it was a present, awful reality, the contemplation of which burned in his bones like a fire and made him 'count not his life dear unto himself' if only he might preach unto a lost world the 'unsearchable riches of Christ.'"[354]

Despite the wind of doctrinal compromise that permeates America blown by charismatic preachers and teachers, we will not succumb. Despite the fact that such leaders gain a wide following due to men's "itching ears" for a "gospel" that suits their lifestyle, we will not give in. Despite the persecution and criticism received for standing firm upon the eternal truth of God's Word, refusing to adulterate it for the sake of increased membership of one or a thousand, we will remain relentless.

"Why such a stubborn, steadfast position," others may inquire. We answer with the apostle Paul, "I am not ashamed of the Gospel of Christ, for it is the power of God unto salvation to everyone that believeth" (Romans 1:16). No other "gospel" saves, outside the pure, untainted Gospel of Jesus Christ. So brazen up, stand erect with shoulders high, fearlessly look man in the eye, and lovingly declare, "You must be born again."

255 False Views about the Church's Purpose

"High time is it," states George W. Truett, "that the consciences of very many people were faithfully aroused as to the nature and meaning of Christ's churches in the world. False views abound on every side. A church of Christ is not an ark in which a few of the elect are to be happily housed in order that they may float around joyfully over the drowning world beneath them. Nor is it a ship, passage upon which will land us in the heavenly country. Nor is it an insurance company to which we may pay dues now and then, and thus certainly secure our dear selves against all loss. Nor is it a hospital for healing all manner of sickness. Nor is it a select social club with a toastmaster to call out such as shall provoke the building up of a mutual admiration society. Nor is it a debating society where more attention is to be given to the fine points of ecclesiasticism rather than to the consuming passion of Christianity. Nor is it a school where we may gather as students to be forever taught. Nor is it merely a place of worship where

---

[354] Truett, *We Would See Jesus,* 144–147.

we may give ourselves to song and praise and meditation about our heavenly inheritance.

"Christ's church is not any of these, nor all of them combined; but with my whole heart I declare that His church exists primarily to give the Gospel to all the world. This great motive is its native air, and any church that will persistently ignore this Heaven-appointed work does not have the moral right to the plat of ground on which the church building stands....Any other conception than that Christ's church is to be a soul-saving army is a caricature upon the churches of the New Testament....Any church that merely sits and sings 'Hold the Fort' will soon have no fort to hold."[355]

It is either evangelize or "fossilize." Don Wommack, I believe, stated that when the church fails to do evangelism, she becomes the only business to stay in business when it has gone out of business in a community.

256   A Matter of the Heart

In speaking to an associational evangelism gathering, I stated quite frankly that I was at wits' end as to how to motivate Christians to engage in soul winning. Despite parading all the noble reasons as to why the believer should—the command of Christ, the dire need of sinful humanity, the torment of Hell for the unbelieving, in gratitude to Christ for salvation, the blessing and benefit of winning souls, and the uncertainty of one's death— few seem to really "get it" and resolve to be a soul winner.

I now believe that the primary problem lies not with the "how to" or even the "why to," but with the "want to," which reveals a spiritual condition of either lostness or coldness. The unsaved or unsurrendered church member has not the firewood for soul winning, nor will he have it until the condition of the heart is first remedied. Regardless of the strong and consistent preaching of the need to witness, apart from the soul's being fertile to receive what is proclaimed, it will avail naught.

The matter of being unsaved. C. H. Spurgeon declared, "Fish will not be fishers."[356] I fear the reason why many "believers" neglect witnessing is due to a false hope of salvation. They yet are "fish" and need to be caught for Christ.

The matter of spiritual coldness. Praying Hyde stated, "Holiness precedes soul winning." In fact, without it, one will not choose to be a soul

---

[355] Ibid., 150.

[356] Spurgeon, *Sermons on Soul Winning*, 33.

winner, for sin stifles the desire to witness. It is the obedient, surrendered, holy heart that acts upon the call to go and tell.

Neglect of soul winning also is attributable to *the question of Lordship.* Herein lies the great deficiency of the church. Jesus is not Lord in the believer's life. Were Jesus truly Lord, the question of witnessing would be moot. Were Jesus truly Lord, one would dive into the lake of darkness, sink or swim, to rescue the spiritually drowning. It is attributable to neglect of sweet, sincere communion with Christ.

Sadly, the indictment handed down to the church at Ephesus is likewise extended to many in the church today: "Thou hast left thy first love" (Revelation 2:4)—'You don't love Christ with the same devotion and intensity as at the first.' Jesus said, "Because iniquity shall abound, the love of many shall wax cold." He does not say that "zeal shall wax cold," though it surely has; or that "doctrine shall grow unorthodox (more liberal)," though indeed it has; but that a love for Christ, His church, His people, His Book, His cause would wax cold.

Has your love for Jesus Christ waxed cold, cooled down from the burning inferno of past days? Apart from continual close communion with Christ and intimacy with Him, it is doubtful you will feel compelled to witness. Apart from striving to "love the Lord thy God with all thy heart, with all thy might, with all thy mind and with all thy strength," soul winning fires will not burn. The heart is too cold for it to do so. The absence of witnessing is a barometer that reveals the spiritual condition of the soul.

This then brings us to the bottom line of the heart preparation required to motivate soul winning. It is to say profoundly, as Andrew Murray put it, "O God, I accept Thy demands. I am Thine and all that I have. Absolute surrender is what my soul yields to Thee by divine grace."[357] It is to prostrate oneself before the Lord in humility, praying, "Search me, O God, and know my heart: try me, and know my thoughts: And see if there be any wicked way in me, and lead me in the way everlasting" (Psalm 139:23–24). It is to place the body with its members at His disposal to do with as He sees fit when He sees fit (Romans 12:1–2). It is total renunciation of self and its desires to put Him first (Matthew 6:33).

Watchman Nee declared, "[Winning souls] is something you cannot outgrow; it is a lifetime undertaking. We need to be joined to the Holy Spirit so that the living water may flow through us. But let me also say that the channel of life has two ends. One end is open toward the Holy Spirit, but the other end is open toward men. Beloved, there are two big days in the

---

[357] Murray, *Absolute Surrender*, 15.

life of a believer—the day on which he believes in the Lord, and every day after that when he leads someone to faith in Christ."[358]

257 Pilot Lights

Dr. Leo Eddleman has likened the soul winner to a "pilot light" on a gas stove. Its function is to start up a bigger flame. Spurgeon is known by many, but the layman who pointed his finger at him, saying, "Look to Jesus, young man," which led to his conversion, is unknown. He was just a "pilot light," but, oh, what a flame he kindled! Andrew is lesser known than his brother Simon Peter. But Andrew was Peter's "pilot light," thrusting him upward by bringing him to Christ. D. L. Moody was one of the world's most successful evangelists, but most do not know the name of the man who was the "pilot light" in his life, a Sunday school teacher named Kimball.[359]

Every Christian is God's "pilot light" which He desires to use to win souls and inflame souls to great heights spiritually. Sometimes the pilot light on a stove goes out, requiring relighting. Is your "pilot light" still burning?

258 Winning through Giving

Herschel Ford tells the story of some hunters in the mountains of the Northwest who got caught in a flash flood. One of the hunters was drowned. They desired to give him a Christian burial, but not one of them was a Christian. Not knowing what else to do, they decided just to cover the body and leave it there. Their guide, an Indian, said, "Is that the way that the white men bury their dead?"

One of the men replied, "No, but not one of us is a Christian, and we don't know what to say."

The Indian responded, "I am a Christian; permit me to perform the service." As he preached the funeral of this man, some of the hunters were saved on the spot.

One of these, upon arriving home, said, "Mother, as that Indian spoke, I gave my heart to the Lord."

---

[358] Morgan, R., *Preacher's SourceBook*, 2002, 40.

[359] Ford, *Christian Life*, 82.

"Thank God," said the mother. "This is the way the Lord has repaid me. Years ago I gave the first money to send missionaries to those Indians. Now you, my son, have been saved because of it."[360]

What a testimonial to the blessing of giving to missions! Sometimes, as in this case, the giving comes full circle back to bless personally the giver.

259 A Decaying Church

An artist was asked to paint a picture of what he conceived as a decaying church. People thought he would paint a tottering ruin, but instead he brushed onto the canvas a magnificent building. Upon peering into the open door of the church, one could see the richly carved pulpit, fine organ, and stained glass windows. Just inside the door was an offering box bearing a card that read, "For Foreign Missions." Over the slot on the box, the artist had painted cobwebs. The reason the church had decayed was that she had forgotten her primary purpose of being a missionary church.[361]

The Christian personally and the church corporately experience dry rot and decay when the primacy of evangelism is lost locally and globally. Budget allocation and emphasis placed on evangelism, both individually and as a church corporately, are the mirrors that reflect the true heart for lost souls.

Robertson McQuilkin stated, "No generation in two thousand years of church history has produced the task force necessary to reach the world. Is this because God has not called adequate numbers? Or is it because someone is not listening? The truth is, less than one percent of full-time Christian workers are engaged in evangelistic ministry among the unevangelized of the world. Is this the way the Commander-in-Chief would assign his troops? Or is someone not listening? With the need so vast and the laborers so few, why do we not go? Someone isn't listening!"[362]

260 Taking It to the Front Door

The April 23, 2010, newsletter from the First Baptist Church, Amarillo, Texas, reported that the church was going to visit 6,000 homes in Amarillo, distributing a multimedia CD containing testimonies, a gospel presentation, and a link where one can go to receive the New Testament in over 350

---

[360] Ibid., 18.

[361] Ford, *Salvation and Service*, 43.

[362] Morgan, R., *Stories, Illustrations*, 86.

languages. The CD, entitled *What's Missing?*, provides an answer to that very question.

What this fellowship is undertaking is the very heart of a New Testament church. By every scriptural and honorable means, the church must reach out to the unsaved, beginning in her "Jerusalem." The church of which you are a member may not be able to launch an outreach effort on the scale of that of First Baptist Church, Amarillo, but you can reach out on some scale. Be a catalyst in initiating such an evangelistic outreach in your church.

261 Indirect Advertising

Near the Kingsport Press in Tennessee, a southbound bus makes a routine stop for passengers to grab a bite to eat. One driver told the passengers, as the bus stopped at this locale, "Folks, we'll be stopping here for twenty minutes. This line makes it a strict policy never to recommend an eating place by name, but if anybody wants me while we're here, I'll be eating a wonderful T-bone steak and fresh fries at Toney's first class, spotlessly clean diner directly down the street."[363]

Indirect advertising can be extremely effective in communicating a message; therefore, believers should include it in their witnessing "tool bag." The believer engages in indirect advertising for Christ on the job, at school, in the home, and in the neighborhood when he manifests distinguishing traits like honesty, integrity, love, purity, and genuine concern for others that lead the unsaved to ask, "What makes you so different?"

Chester Swor tells the moving story of a deaf and dumb Christian man in Knoxville, Tennessee. This man loved Christ but was unable to speak of Christ to others. For years he rode the same streetcar to work, greeting the conductor with a smile as he put his fare in the box, sat down on the front seat, and began reading the Bible. As the Christian boarded the streetcar one morning after seven years, the conductor handed him a note which read, "Sir, I am not a Christian. But for seven years I have watched you, and I know that you have something that I need more than anything else in the world. Please turn this letter over and write on the back a time when you can meet me. You name the place and bring an interpreter with you to tell me how I can be saved." The deaf and dumb man met with the conductor, and he was saved.[364]

---

[363] Barnhouse, *Let Me Illustrate*, 348.

[364] Ford, *Sunday Morning*, 78–79.

This deaf and dumb man utilized "indirect advertisement" to win a soul to Christ.

262 Set Jesus Free to Tell

Carlisle Castle, Cumbria, is located less than ten miles from the Scottish border. Men imprisoned in its first floor dungeon would literally lick the walls for moisture to satisfy thirst ("the licking stones") and stay alive. Dungeons had slits in their walls that served as windows; an iron bar stretched from the top to bottom. In the window sills, one can see and feel the grooves worn into the stone by the fingers of the prisoners as they looked out toward the not-too-distant hills of Scotland. They so longed for Scotland that they literally pulled at the dungeon stones with their fingers, seeking to escape.[365]

"Christ in you, the hope of glory" (Colossians 1:27). Christ in you is straining to get out to touch the lives of others with the message of love and grace. Look upon the chambers of your heart. Do you not see the grooves worn into its stony surface by the fingers of Jesus seeking to be set free to tell the Gospel message? It's high time you opened the dungeon door that has held Him captive, allowing Him to flow through you the message of Calvary! In so doing, the truth of Galatians 2:20 will be manifest in your life: "I am crucified with Christ: nevertheless I live; yet not I, but Christ liveth in me."

263 Go and See That Man Tonight

Wayland Hoyt, while pastor in Brooklyn, was engaged in special meetings. One man who displayed some interest in Christ, a man for whom he had prayed, was in attendance one night. He felt inclined to speak with him about his soul but, due to fear, refrained. Arriving home late one night following the service, he was too nervous to sleep and began reading in the study. As he read, something seemed to whisper, *Go and see that man tonight.* But the preacher mentally replied, *It is after twelve o'clock. He and everyone else are in bed asleep.*

The impression grew stronger and was unshakeable. The preacher argued to the whisper, *It is snowing, and I am tired!* Finally he thought, *I have been working hard all day, and I don't want to go!* Despite the excuses for not going, the preacher finally yielded to the Holy Spirit's whisper and went.

---

[365] Barnhouse, *Let Me Illustrate*, 344.

Touching the man's doorbell, he thought, *What a fool I am to be ringing a man's bell at one o'clock in the morning. He will think I am insane.* The door instantly opened, and the man, fully clothed, said, "Come in, and God bless you. You are the man I have been waiting for all night. My wife and children and the servants are all asleep, but I could not sleep; I felt that I must find Jesus tonight."

Hoyt testified, "It was no trouble to show the man the way, for the Spirit who had guided me had also gone before me."[366]

The apostle Paul states, "As many as are led by the Spirit of God, they are the sons of God" (Romans 8:14). W. B. Riley stated, "He leads the yielded one, and His leadership insures success. It may take one by strange ways, and other men may question one's sanity at times; but, after all, the Spirit-led man is the only sane man. It was a strange thing for Phillip to leave the work in Samaria and go toward the south into a desert way; but it was Spirit-directed and, hence, sane. No man plays the fool who follows the leadings of the Holy Spirit, even though that take him against what he would commonly regard better judgment."[367]

264 The "Disruption Theory"

Ray Comfort cites an article where the author basically stated that the unsaved would be better off if we didn't try to witness to them until there's a disruption, like an illness, unemployment, shipwrecked marriage, a child in crisis, or a serious accident in their lives. Comfort comments, "Therein lies the tragic fruit of the methods of modern evangelism. It keeps quiet until there is a disruption....A friend told me that a Christian woman went into her house, closed the door, fell on the floor, and pleaded with God to forgive her. Her fiance's father had suddenly committed suicide. There were no warning signs. He wasn't saved, and she had never bothered to witness to him. A *disruption* never came. The "Disruption Theory" is about as credible as the theory of evolution."[368]

"Disruption" certainly opens the door to win a soul, but the soul winner must press forward with or without it.

---

[366] Hutson, *Preaching on Soul Winning*, 92–93.

[367] Ibid., 92–93.

[368] Comfort, *Way of the Master*, 253.

265 Sermons Are Not God's Primary Method of Reaching People

Charles Stanley wrote, "Sermons are not God's primary method of reaching people. People are His method of reaching people. What kind of people? Men and women whose lives and lifestyles have been deeply affected by the truths of Scripture, people who have discovered the Spirit-filled life. God is looking for imperfect men and women who have learned to walk in moment-by-moment dependence on the Holy Spirit; Christians who have come to terms with their inadequacies, fears, and failures; believers who have become discontent with 'surviving' and have taken time to investigate everything God has to offer in this life. God's method for reaching this generation is not preachers and sermons. It's Christians whose lifestyles are empowered and directed by the Holy Spirit. People are the key to reaching people!"[369]

266 The Story of John Pounds

"It was a terrible fall, and it sickened those who saw it. John Pounds, a tall, muscular teen laborer at the docks of Portsmouth, England, slipped and plunged from the top of a ship's mast, pitching headfirst into the bowels of the vessel. When fellow workers reached him, he was nothing but a mass of broken bones. For two years he lay in bed as his bones healed crookedly. His pain never ceased. Out of boredom, he began to read the Bible.

"At length, John crawled from bed hoping to find something he could do with his life. A shoemaker hired him; and day after day, John sat at his cobbler's bench, a Bible open on his lap. Soon he was born again.

"John ultimately gathered enough money to purchase his own little shoe shop, and one day he developed a pair of surgical boots for his crippled nephew Johnny, whom he had taken in. Soon John was making corrective shoes for other children, and his little cobbler's shop became a miniature children's hospital. As John's burden for children grew, he began receiving homeless ones, feeding them, teaching them to read, and telling them about the Lord. His shop became known as 'The Ragged School'; and John would limp around the waterfront, food in his pockets, looking for more children to tend.

"During his lifetime, John Pounds rescued five hundred children from despair and led every one of them to Christ. Moreover, his work became so famous that a 'Ragged School Movement' swept England, and a series of laws were passed to establish schools for poor children in John's honor.

---

[369] Lucado, *Life Lessons*, 22.

Boy's homes, girl's homes, day schools, and evening schools were started, along with Bible classes in which thousands heard the Gospel.

"When John collapsed and died on New Year's Day, 1839, while tending to a boy's ulcerated foot, he was buried in a churchyard on High Street. All England mourned, and a monument was erected over his grave, reading: 'Thou shalt be blessed, for they could not recompense thee.'"[370]

God is able to use adversity to put a man in a state of mind to be saved and to fulfill His plan. Undoubtedly John Pounds was grateful for the painful injury that ultimately placed him in the right place to become a Christian and to launch a ministry of rescue to children physically and spiritually. Joseph told his terrified and cowering brothers regarding his adversity, 'You meant it for evil, but God meant it for good.' In the midst of suffering, sickness, sorrow or grave difficulty, explore how it can be turned into a soul-winning opportunity.

267 The Power of God's Word to Save

"One of the most powerful personal evangelists of the nineteenth century was 'Uncle' John Vassar, who grew up in his family's brewery in Poughkeepsie, New York. Following his conversion to Christ, he abandoned beer making for soul winning, and on May 15, 1850, he was commissioned as an agent for the American Tract Society of New York. Vassar took off across the country, never resting in his mission of selling Christian literature and asking everyone he met about their relationship with Christ.

"On one occasion, while traveling in the West, he visited the home of a praying wife whose husband was an infidel. She begged for a Bible, and Vassar, giving her one, went his way. He had no sooner left, when the husband came home, saw the book and was enraged. Seizing the Bible with one hand and the ax with the other, he hurried to the woodpile, where he placed it on the chopping block and hacked it crosswise in two. Returning to the house, he threw half of the destroyed Bible at his wife, saying, 'As you claim a part of all the property around here, there is your share of this.' The other half he tossed into his tool shed.

"Months later, on a wet winter's day, the man wanted to get away from his Christian wife and retreated to his shed. The time passed slowly, and in boredom he looked around for something to read. Thumbing through the mutilated Bible, his attention was caught by the story of the prodigal son in Luke 15. He became absorbed in the parable, only to discover that its ending belonged to his wife's section. He crept into the house and secretly

---

[370] Morgan, R., *Stories, Illustrations*, 101–102.

searched for the bottom half of the book but was unable to find where his wife had hidden it. Finally he broke down, asked her for it, and read the story again and again. In the process, he came to the Heavenly Father like a penitent prodigal returning home."[371]

Never underestimate the power of God's Word! It is through the Word of God that the Holy Spirit convicts of sin, judgment, and righteousness. The Word of God is a hammer that can break the hardest heart (Jeremiah 23:29), a sword that can pierce the soul asunder (Hebrews 4:12), a fire that can purge the deepest sin (Jeremiah 23:29), and a light that can expose the deepest darkness (Psalms 119:130).

268   One Visit May Do It

C. E. Autrey stated, "It is possible for a life-changing decision to take place during one visit, and often it does."[372]

Expect God to work conviction that results in conversion in the first encounter with the prospect. Unknown to you, others may have sown and watered the gospel seed in a soul's heart, and God may have sent you to harvest the crop.

269   Church Planting Evangelism

Church planting is evangelism. A church planting expert states, "The idea is that planted churches reproduce themselves and make disciples by planting other churches. This is a process that will continue until the Savior returns. In fact, this is the true meaning behind the Great Commission."[373]

Wagner stated, "The single most effective evangelistic methodology under Heaven is planting new churches....Not to make an explicit connection between evangelism and the local church is a strategic blunder."[374]

New church plants experience greater growth on the whole than existing churches; the emphasis on outreach and soul winning propels them forward. Christian Schwarz, in *Natural Church Development,* cited his survey of 1,000 churches in 32 countries located in 6 continents and revealed that new

---

[371] Ibid., 149–150.

[372] Autrey, *Basic Evangelism*, 91.

[373] MacArthur, Mayhue, and Thomas, *Rediscovering*, 311–312.

[374] Ibid., 309.

churches of 100 were 16 times more effective in winning new converts to Christ than megachurches.[375]

Established churches probably spend 90 percent of their resources on ministering to the saved; new church works do the opposite. Kirk Hadaway discovered that not only do new church plants grow faster than established churches, but they impact the growth of our denomination as a whole. In fact, they make up one-fourth of the growth of the entire denomination.

The population in America is growing eight times faster than the current rate of new church plants. With 3,500 churches shutting their doors annually and only 1,250 new churches opening, the need exists for more congregations to establish new fellowships.[376]

Only 18 percent of Americans will attend a weekend service. America ranks third behind China and India in the number of unsaved people. America is the third largest nation in the world that stands in need of evangelization.[377]

The old saying "divide and conquer" certainly is valid with regard to reaching the masses of people; established churches need to found new churches with essential leadership. How many new church plants has your church established? Church plants are on the cutting edge of evangelism.

270   You Have What It Takes to Witness

"Notice that there is a great deal of Christian activity that goes on, presumably to be a witness, but it is motivated by far less than a sensitive understanding of what it actually means to be a witness. There are many people who feel, *I just couldn't witness because I don't have the boldness of other people.* Yet the Bible says nothing about being a witness on the grounds of some natural boldness we may have.

"The majority of us feel a certain degree of timidity. We don't want anyone to feel we are imposing ourselves, especially when it comes to spiritual matters. When the Lord said we will be His witnesses, He was not saying something that would be impractical for any of us. So there must be a way for this to happen for all of us, as opposed to its being something that only a handful of select personality types can do."[378]

---

[375] Unknown Author, "Why Church Planting?" accessed May 28, 2010.

[376] Brown, M., "Church Planting Myths," accessed April 26, 2010

[377] Unknown Author, "Church Planting," accessed April 29, 2010.

[378] Hayford, *Answering the Call*, 42.

The Lord would never command us to do something He knew we were ill equipped to do. In essence, in calling you to be His witness, He is declaring, "You have what it takes to witness for Me; now go and do it."

271 Adrian Rogers' First Soul-Winning Attempt

Adrian Rogers led hundreds of people to Christ, but he never ceased to cherish the memory of his first soul-winning attempt. As a sixteen-year-old attending a service in North Carolina, he was challenged by the sermon to be a soul winner. The preacher asked the congregation, "How many here will promise to be a soul winner? Who will promise to win a soul for God?"

Adrian, though a new Christian with little training in the Bible, raised his hand. Sometime later in West Palm Beach where he was raised, he walked into a store wearing Levi's but without a shirt. An old man with white whiskers confronted him pleading for money. The man admitted, "I've been an old fool. I live on a pension check. When I got my check this time, I cashed it; and a so-called friend of mine and I got drunk. I spent all my check on whiskey, and now I don't have any more money."

Adrian said, "Mister, if I had some money, I'd give it to you; but I don't."

But as Adrian started to walk away, the Lord spoke to his heart: *Adrian, speak to him about his soul.*

Adrian said, *God, I can't speak to him about his soul; I don't even have a shirt on!*

But, Adrian, the Lord seemed to say, *you promised.*

But, God, he's a man, and I'm a boy!

Adrian, you promised.

As Adrian turned back to the man, his heart was racing. But, mustering his courage, he said, "Mister, I don't have any money to give you, but I believe I have something better than money. Sir, are you a Christian?"

Tears suddenly streamed from the old fellow's eyes, and his chin started quivering. "No, son," he said, "I'm not a Christian."

"Sir, would you like to be?"

The man replied, "More than anything in this world. If only I knew how to be."

Then Adrian said, "I wish I had a Bible."

"I have one," replied the old man, and he reached into the lining of his old coat and pulled out a little New Testament. Adrian found John 3:16, read it out loud, and explained the verse as well as he could. "Well, what should I do?" said the old man when Adrian was finished.

"Well, I'm going to pray for you." And as Adrian began praying for the man, he too began crying. When he finished, he said, "Sir, you pray now and ask Him to save you." So the old man started to pray through his tears, and he asked Jesus to come into his heart, forgive his sin, and save his soul. When he finished his prayer, Adrian asked, "Well, did He do it?"

"I think He did," said the man.

Adrian thanked him, wished him well, and started to leave, but the old-timer called him back. "Young man, come back here," he said. "I'm an old man, and I have traveled through almost every state in this country, and you are the first person to ever speak with me about my soul. Thank you, young man; thank you." Adrian left the man rejoicing. That day, he discovered the ecstasy of soul winning.[379]

272 Do Whatever It Takes to Win One More Soul

William Barclay writes, "No business could exist on outworn methods—and yet the church tries to. Any business which had lost as many customers as the church has would have tried new ways long ago—but the church tends to resent all that is new.

"Once while on a world tour, Rudyard Kipling saw General Booth come aboard the ship on which he was traveling. He came aboard to the beating of tambourines, which Kipling's orthodox soul resented. Kipling got to know the General and told him how he disliked tambourines and all their kindred. Booth looked at him. 'Young man,' he said, 'if I thought I could win one more soul for Christ by standing on my head and beating a tambourine with my feet, I would learn how to do it.'"[380]

May all God's children be of the same resolve as Booth, to be adventurous in doing whatever is necessary to win one more soul.

273 The Man Who Cursed Moody

"Suppose," writes D. L. Moody, "each one of you now prayed, 'Give me some soul this week for my hire.' What would be the result? This room would not hold the multitude sending up shouts of praise to God and making Heaven glad....I remember a good many years ago, I resolved I wouldn't let a day pass without talking to someone about his soul's salvation. And it was in that school that God qualified me to speak the

---

[379] Morgan, R., *Real Stories*, 219–222.

[380] Barclay, *Daily Study Bible*, 68–69.

Gospel. If we [are] faithful over small things, God will promote us. If God says, 'Speak to that young man,' obey the word, and you will be given by-and-by plenty of souls.

"I went down past the corner of Clark and Lake Streets one day, and, fulfilling my vow, on seeing a man leaning up against a lamppost, I went up to him and said, 'Are you a Christian?' He damned me and cursed me and said to mind my own business. He knew me, but I didn't know him. He said to a friend of his that afternoon that he had never been so insulted in his life, and he told him to say to me that I was damning the cause I pretended to represent.

"Well, the friend came and delivered his message. 'Maybe I am doing more hurt than good,' I said. 'Maybe I am mistaken, and God hasn't shown me the right way.' That was the time I was sleeping and living in the Young Men's Christian Association rooms where I was then president, secretary, janitor, and everything else. Well, one night after midnight, I heard a knock at the door. There on the step leading into the street stood this stranger I had made so mad at the lamppost, and he said he wanted to talk to me about his soul's salvation.

"He said, 'Do you remember the man you met about three months ago at a lamppost, and how I cursed you? I have had no peace since that night; I couldn't sleep. Oh, tell me what to do to be saved.' And we just fell down on our knees, and I prayed, and that day he went to the noon prayer meeting and openly confessed the Savior. Soon after that he went to the war a Christian man. I do not know but he died on some southern battlefield or in a hospital, but I expect to see him in the kingdom of God. Oh, how often have I thanked God for that word to that dying sinner that He put into my mouth!"[381]

274 The Evening Opportunity to Witness

"In the evening of the day, opportunities are plentiful. Men return from their labor, and the zealous soul winner finds time to tell abroad the love of Jesus. Have I no evening work for Jesus? If I have not, let me no longer withhold my hand from a service which requires abundant labor. Sinners are perishing for lack of knowledge; he who loiters may find his skirts crimson with the blood of souls. Jesus gave both his hands to the nails; how can I keep back one of mine from his blessed work? Night and day he toiled and prayed for me; how can I give a single hour to the pampering of my flesh with luxurious ease? Up, idle heart; stretch out thy hand to work, or

---

[381] Rost, *Great Evangelical Teaching*, Chapter Seven: Part Three.

uplift it to pray. Heaven and Hell are in earnest; let me be so and this evening sow good seed for the Lord my God."[382]

275 "Now It's Too Late"

Watchman Nee tells the story of a missionary named Thomas Chalmers who was an overnight guest in a home where an agnostic also was staying. The two men spoke about world affairs before retiring to bed. Minutes later, the man was dead. As people gathered in the room of the deceased agnostic, Chalmers said, "Had I known that this would happen, I would not have spent the last two hours chatting about so many things. I would have pointed him to eternal things. But, alas, I have not used even five minutes to speak to him of the salvation of his soul....Now it is too late."[383]

Speak to people about soul matters as if they were sentenced to die when you finished. Never presume upon having another chance to talk to a person about his or her soul.

276 The Soul Winner in Prayer

"The soul winner must be a master of the art of prayer. You cannot bring souls to God if you go not to God yourself. You must get your battle-ax and your weapons of war from the armory of sacred communication with Christ. If you are much alone with Jesus, you will catch His Spirit; you will be fired with the flame that burned in His breast and consumed His life. You will weep with the tears that fell upon Jerusalem when He saw it perishing; and if you cannot speak so eloquently as He did, yet shall there be about what you say somewhat of the same power which in Him thrilled the hearts and awoke the consciences of men.

"My dear hearers, especially you members of the church, I am always so anxious, lest any of you should begin to lie upon your oars and take things easy in the matters of God's kingdom. There are some of you—I bless you, and I bless God at the remembrance of you—who are in season and out of season in earnest for winning souls, and you are the truly wise; but I fear there are others whose hands are slack, who are satisfied to let me preach but do not themselves preach, who take these seats and occupy these pews and hope the cause goes well, but that is all they do."[384]

---

[382] Spurgeon, *Morning and Evening*, September 20 entry.

[383] Morgan, R., *Preacher's SourceBook*, 2002, 40.

[384] Spurgeon, *Soul Winner*, 246–47. (Italics in original.)

John MacArthur stated, "The Bible, then, clearly expresses the appropriateness and propriety of praying for the lost....Evangelistic praying is the express teaching of I Timothy 2:1–8. These verses are polemical in nature; they confront a problem in the Ephesian church. Since Paul here commands prayer for the lost, we may conclude that such praying had slipped from the priority it should have been at Ephesus."[385]

Has it in your life?

277 They Called Him Madman

Spurgeon wrote a book entitled *Eccentric Preachers,* in which he described eleven peculiar ministers. Billy Bray, an alcoholic miner who got saved at age 29, was the final example included. "In an instant, the Lord made me so happy I cannot express what I felt," said Billy. "I shouted for joy. Everything looked new to me—the people, the fields, the cattle, the trees. I was like a man in a new world."

Billy joined the Methodists and set out immediately to win others. His bursting, driving energy made some people call him a madman. "But they meant 'glad man'!" said Billy.

He took Cornwall by storm. On meeting strangers, Billy would inquire about their souls, and he would shout "Glory!" whenever hearing of anyone's being saved. Sometimes he would pick people up and spin them around the room. "I can't help praising God," he said. "As I go along the street, I lift one foot, and it seems to say 'Glory!' I lift the other, and it seems to say, 'Amen!' And they keep on like that all the time I'm walking."

From age 29 to his death at 73, he danced and leaped and shouted his way through each day. He preached and built chapels and took orphans into his home. He fasted Saturday afternoon till Sunday night each week. When pressed to eat, he would say, "On Sunday, I get my breakfast and dinner from the King's table—two good meals too."

When his wife died, Billy jumped around the room in excitement, shouting, "Bless the Lord! My dear Joey is gone up with the bright ones! Glory! Glory! Glory!" And when his doctor told him he too was dying, he shouted, "Glory! Glory to God! I shall soon be in Heaven." Then lowering his voice, he added, "When I get up there, shall I give them your compliments, doctor, and tell them you will be coming, too?"

His dying word, as he fell asleep on May 25, 1868, was "Glory!"

---

[385] MacArthur, *Alone with God,* 161.

"It does not seem so very horrible after all," commented Spurgeon, "that a man should be eccentric."[386]

I don't know many Christians who wouldn't be greatly benefited by a good dose of the "religion" of Billy Bray!

278 No "Bone Fire" Until We Have a Bonfire

Vance Havner said that Jeremiah did not simply have something to say; he had to say something. In a sermon, Havner asked why Christians don't have a similar "bone fire." In Acts 19:19, he read about the Ephesians who, once converted, burned their sinful paraphernalia in a bonfire. Havner suggested that a believer can't have "bone fire" until he first has a bonfire.[387]

Stuff in your life—some good, some bad—smothers a "bone fire" to tell others of Christ. Not until these fire retardants are tossed into the "bonfire" of confession and repentance will the fire for lost souls burn intensely.

279 "Are You Willing for That Man to Be Saved?"

A revival broke out in the seminary, the schools, the hospital, and area churches in the China district where missionary C. L. Culpepper served. None were impacted perhaps more than Culpepper's friend Wiley B. Glass. This man in deep soul anguish said to Culpepper, "Charlie, pray for me!" The men knelt immediately to pray.

Culpepper states, "He was pale as death and kept groaning in his anxiety. I prayed with him and for him several times during that day and the next.

In the evening of the second day, he came running to me and threw his arms around me. "Charlie, it's gone!" he exclaimed.

I said, "What's gone?"

He replied, "That old root of bitterness." He told me that thirty years earlier, before he came to China, a man had insulted his wife. The insult had made him so angry that he felt he could kill the man if he ever saw him again. He realized a called servant of God should not feel that way, and it had bothered him for years. Finally, he just turned the man over to God.

When the Holy Spirit began working in his heart during that week, the question came, "Are you willing for that man to be saved?"

---

[386] Morgan, R., *Saints, Martyrs & Heroes*, May 24 entry.

[387] Morgan, R., *Preacher's SourceBook*, 2002, 240–241.

He answered, "Lord, I'm willing for You to save him; just keep him on the other side of Heaven!" Finally, he came to the place where he said, "Lord, if that man is alive, and if I can find him when I go on furlough, I will confess my hatred to him and do my best to win him to You." In reaching this decision, the joys of Heaven flooded his soul, and during the next few years he led hundreds to Christ.[388]

Is there anyone that you are unwilling to win to Christ due to a personal vendetta? God cannot use you mightily to win souls until you become as Glass and have your mind-set changed.

280 Soul Winners Will Shine Brightly throughout Eternity

"If you look at the sky tonight," writes Jon Courson, "you'll see stars shining with different intensities. Likewise, there will be different intensities in Heaven. Daniel 12 tells us that those who win souls shall shine as the stars forever. In other words, those who are serving the Lord now and making their lives count today will shine brightly throughout eternity. On the other hand, although those who give priority to their own bodies, possessions, interests, hobbies, careers, or agendas will be in Heaven if they believe in Jesus Christ, they will not shine with the same intensity. Make the Kingdom the priority and passion of your life, and I promise you, you'll not regret it."[389]

D. L. Moody, in a sermon on Daniel 12:3, said that all men like to shine, whether it is in the realm of politics, academics, athletics, or the armed services. "Yet there are very few who really shine in the world....But in the Kingdom of God, the very least and the weakest may shine if they will. Not only can one obtain the prize, but all may have it, if they will.

"It does not say in this passage that the statesmen are going to shine as the brightness of the firmament. It does not say that the nobility are going to shine. Earth's nobility are soon forgotten. John Bunyan, the Bedford tinker, has outlived the whole crowd of those who were the nobility in his day. They lived for self, and their memory is blotted out. He lived for God and for souls, and his name is as fragrant as ever it was.

"We are not told that the merchants are going to shine. Who can tell the name of any of the millionaires of Daniel's day? They were all buried in oblivion a few years after their death. Who were the mighty conquerors of that day? But few can tell. It is true that we hear of Nebuchadnezzar, but

---

[388] Morgan, R., *Book of Stories*, 70.

[389] Courson, *Application Commentary*, 1089.

probably we should not have known very much about him but for his relations to the Prophet Daniel. How different with this faithful prophet of the Lord! Twenty-five centuries have passed away, and his name shines on and on and on, brighter and brighter. And it is going to shine while the church of God exists."

Moody continues, "How empty and short-lived are the glory and the pride of the world! If we are wise, we will live for God and eternity; we will get outside of ourselves and will care nothing for the honor and glory of this world....If any man, woman or child, by a godly life and testimony, can win one soul to God, their life will not have been a failure. They will have outshone all the mighty men of their day because they will have set a stream in motion that will flow on and on forever and ever....So if you turn one to Christ, that one may turn a hundred. He may turn a thousand, and so the stream, small at the first, goes on broadening and deepening as it rolls toward eternity....Let us live for God, continually going forth to win souls."[390]

"They that be wise shall shine as the brightness of the firmament; and they that turn many to righteousness as the stars forever and ever" (Daniel 12:3).

281 Jump-Start to a Witness

A soul winner who had won many to Christ had a unique approach. Someone inquired why so many he spoke to received Christ. He said, "I only talk to people who are interested in spiritual things."

The inquirer asked, "Well, how do you know who is interested in spiritual things?"

The man said, "I ask them."

The inquirer said, "How do you ask them?"

The man said, "I say, 'Are you interested in spiritual things?'"[391]

This man won many souls using this method. Obviously the believer is to witness to people who are not interested in spiritual things in hope that they will become interested to the point of salvation, but this man's approach may be a good first step to soul winning.

---

[390] Hutson, *Preaching on Soul Winning*, 229–230; 234–235.

[391] Anders, *30 Days*, 197–198.

282 Getting Christians to Open Their Mouths

Every pastor faces the challenge of getting his people to open their mouths in the workhouse, schoolhouse, church house and clubhouse for Jesus. What motivations may be effective to assist him?

Exhortation. The minister should regularly preach on the Christian's duty to be a soul winner, ever flaming the fire in the soul for the lost. A fellow minister told me that he was personally motivated to witness through such sermons of other preachers.

Example. Preach it, and then practice it. "Do the work of an evangelist" (II Timothy 4:5). It is not of the flesh for us to tell the congregation, "Yesterday I visited with Jimmy Doolittle and won him to Christ." Let the people know of your evangelistic passion in action. Someone said that soul winning is more caught than taught.

Emphasis. Make soul winning a major emphasis of the church program—in the Sunday school, auxiliary missionary groups, children and student ministries, choir and praise teams. Make a big deal out of a member winning another to Christ privately and publicly. Keep witnessing front and center before the people.

Our big task today is to get the "church out of the church." The true purpose of every worship service is to get Christians ready to witness. Worship continues to be a form instead of a force—a form of escapism. Too many are seeking "sanctuary." We have produced congregations composed largely of dilettantes who follow Christ superficially or as a pastime."[392]

Education. Ease the fear of witnessing by providing simple training sessions.

Encouragement. Motivate, incite members to witness through providing inspirational meditations and incentives upon the subject, such as this book. As missionary moments are read in some churches, read a soul-winning story or challenge.

283 The One Thing That Only a Christian Can Do

William M. Jones stated, "What did you do today that only a Christian could do? There can be only one answer—'I witnessed to an unsaved person concerning Jesus.' You will never be unique as a Christian until you win someone to Jesus. Everything that you do as a Christian can be duplicated by the unsaved. You say, 'I gave money to the church'—unsaved people give to the church. You say, 'I try to live right'—the unsaved can say the same thing. You say, 'I believe in living by the Golden

---

[392] Martin, G., *Evangelistic Preaching*, 84.

Rule'—the unsaved can say the same. But when you engage in the business of witnessing for Jesus, you are doing something that no unsaved person can do."[393]

284 "I Don't Know; I Never Asked Her"

When Herschel Ford was in revival in Louisiana, in one of the services the pastor pointed out a man to him and said, "He is one of my most faithful deacons. His wife sings in the choir and is superintendent of the Junior Department of our Sunday school. They are the finest couple in the church." When he and the pastor accepted an invitation to eat in this couple's home, an employee of the couple prepared the meal and served it. Ford wanted to thank the lady for such a wonderful meal, but prior to going into the kitchen to do so, he asked the hostess what church the cook attended. She answered, "I do not know."

"Now, remember," Ford states, "that this lady sang in the choir, headed the Junior Department in Sunday school and was active in every phase of the church life." He asked a second question of the hostess: "Is your cook a Christian?"

Dropping her head, she replied, "I don't know; I have never asked her." In talking to the hostess, he learned the cook had been working in the home for three months.

"Now think of it," Ford said. "This woman was faithful and active in her church, but she had never been concerned about her servant's spiritual welfare, although they had been together every day for over three months."[394]

Incredible as it is, multitudes of Christians haven't the foggiest idea regarding the soul estate of employers, employees, teachers, professors, yard men, baby sitters, coaches, and housekeepers—people with whom they associate frequently. Make it your business to find out today.

285 Whether You Feel Like It or Not

"God has given every Christian a job, a responsibility, a command. You can obey God's command, or you can disobey it, but your orders are to witness. I say this because many Christians feel that soul winning is a leading, not a command. Occasionally someone asks me, 'But what if you don't feel led to witness?'

---

[393] Ibid., 86.

[394] Ford, *New Testament Texts*, 20-21.

"I always reply, 'Soul winning is not a leading; it is a command.' Suppose I said to my son, 'Go mow the lawn,' and my son smiled and said, 'I don't feel led to do that. But praise your name, Father; I love you!' I would look at my son and say, 'Did you understand what I told you to do?'

"'Yes, Sir.'

"'Well, then you go and mow that lawn!' If my son didn't mow the yard immediately, I assure you it would not be long until he would be in the lawn-mowing business—whether he felt led or not.

"Now Christians are to win souls, whether they feel like it or not. We are to do it because it is a clear command of Scripture. I have heard folks say, 'But I don't have the gift of soul winning,' as if soul winning were some special gift. A careful reading of I Corinthians 12 and Romans 12 will reveal that soul winning is not listed as a special gift. The truth of the matter is that soul winning is a command."[395]

286 A Solemn Question for the Minister

Writing to ministers, Horatius Bonar stated, "The question, therefore, which each of us has to answer to his own conscience is, 'Has it been the end of my ministry, has it been the desire of my heart to save the lost and guide the saved? Is this my aim in every sermon I preach, in every visit I pay? Is it under the influence of this feeling that I continually live and walk and speak? Is it for this I pray and toil and fast and weep? Is it for this I spend and am spent, counting it, next to the salvation of my own soul, my chiefest joy to be the instrument of saving others? Is it for this that I exist? To accomplish this, would I gladly die? Have I seen the pleasure of the Lord prospering in my hand? Have I seen souls converted under my ministry? Have God's people found refreshment from my lips and gone upon their way rejoicing, or have I seen no fruit of my labors and yet am content to remain unblessed? Am I satisfied to preach and yet not know of one saving impression made, one sinner awakened?'"[396]

C. H. Spurgeon, in his sermon "Am I Clear of His Blood," stated, "And what shall I say of the unfaithful preacher, the slumbering watchman of souls, the man who swore at God's altar that he was called of the Holy Ghost to preach the Word of God, the man upon whose lips men's ears waited with attention while he stood like a priest at God's altar to teach Israel God's law, the man who performed his duties half asleep in a dull and

---

[395] Hutson, "Winning Souls," 1.

[396] Bonar, *Words to Winners of Souls*, 4–5.

careless manner until men slept too and thought religion a dream?…What shall I say of the men who out of the pulpit have made a jest of the most solemn things, whose lives has been so devoid of holy passion and devout enthusiasm that men have thought truth to be fiction, religion a stage play, a prayer a nullity, the Spirit of God a phantom, and eternity a joke?

"If I must perish, let me suffer anyhow but not as a minister who has desecrated the pulpit by a slumbering style of ministry, by a want of passion for souls. God knoweth how ofttimes this body trembles with horror at the thought, lest the blood of souls should be required at my hands."[397]

May every preacher and layman know this same passion for ministry and lost souls.

287 The Cure for Being "On and Off" in Soul Winning

A pastor who was "on and off," "cold and hot" in soul winning told me he wanted to be consistent in the task. Every soul winner can identify with him, for all have been where he now is at one time or another. What enables consistency in witnessing?

Attitude. Fasten in the mind that soul winning is the most important thing one can do. Bailey Smith said, "The other things we have to do may be called important by those around us, but there is nothing on earth more important to do than to win a person to Jesus Christ."[398]

It is this attitude that led Spurgeon to push away from his books to lead a soul to Christ daily, that led R. G. Lee to lay aside the pressing matters of church care to win souls every day. The attitude displayed for soul winning will always be manifested in its altitude in one's life. A passionate mind-set for souls will lead to discipline in one's effort to reach them. It boils down to whether or not one thinks a lost soul is important enough to make seeking them a daily regimen.

Action. Do it—nothing spurs the desire to witness like leading a person to Christ. Plan it—at what time of day will you break away to specifically go soul winning? Goal it—determine to speak to at least one person about his or her soul daily.

Associate. Link up with a staff associate or layman to be a soul-winning partner. In witnessing, the wisdom of Solomon should be taken to heart: "Two people are better off than one, for they can help each other succeed." (Ecclesiastes 4:9 NLT).

---

[397] Spurgeon, *Metropolitan Tabernacle Pulpit, 1862,* 412.

[398] Smith, Bailey, *Real Evangelism,* 118.

Accountability. Hold yourself accountable regarding this delightful duty by reporting to a mentor or friend on a weekly basis. Additionally, I have found entering in my journal the number of souls I speak to daily keeps me accountable.

Ask. Pray for Holy Spirit empowerment to remain consistent in this greatest work on earth.

288 "I Just Needed Someone to Drag Me Out"

"I just needed someone to drag me out. All along I knew that my family and I needed to attend church and to know Christ as our Savior. During the last two years, I have thought often of our need of Christ, but I could not bring myself to start to church. I just needed someone to come along and drag me out." Such were the words of a man saved in a Sunday morning service. Soul winners had visited his family the day before, leading him, his wife, and two teen-aged children to Christ. He felt the need of Christ and the church, but had not the soul winners shown up at his door, such a decision would have been very unlikely. Multitudes around us identify with this man. Knowing what they need to do with Christ, they forever put it off. This is why every Christian must go and tell of Christ.[399]

289 Ordinary Laymen Can Reach People for Christ

One of Southern Baptists' greatest evangelism professors and leaders, C. E. Autrey, stated, "Individual evangelism can be done by any sincere person who has been saved and who loves lost souls. He may not at first know much about methods, but his earnestness will suffice until he has learned more through study and experience. It requires no extraordinary talents, nor does it require an extra amount of education. Ordinary laymen can do individual evangelism as effectively as anyone, if they exercise sane judgment and tact....

"The task is so urgent that we cannot wait until we have attained to start. A young lawyer pleads before the bar for the life of an innocent client and loses. His heart is crushed, and he is tempted to quit; but when he faces reality, he knows he cannot change his profession. He will work harder the next time. He must speak for those who do not know how to plead their own cases. The saved individual cannot wait until he has matured and become thoroughly taught. He must plead the cause of Christ the best he can in the courts of human hearts. He must help those who are not even

---

[399] Autrey, *You Can Win Souls*, 1.

aware of their doom. He must labor in ignorance, in tears, in earnestness, in willing eagerness for the souls of eternity-bound men."[400]

290 Stephen Olford Struggled with Soul Winning

"Does the subject of personal soul winning frighten you? If it does," states Stephen Olford, "you have my sympathy! I say that because I know from experience what you are passing through. There was a time in my life when even the thought of talking to people, publicly or privately, paralyzed me with fear. I was not only painfully shy by nature, but hopelessly indisposed to meeting new faces. Many a social occasion in our home was spoiled because of my unannounced disappearance!

"The fact that I was a committed Christian did not seem to make much difference. In one sense, it made me worse. As a saved person, I knew it was my duty to witness for my Lord and, when possible, to seek others for Him. But such a sense of duty only brought me into inner bondage.

"I have known what it is to screw up my courage and walk the entire length of a train, giving out gospel booklets to anyone who was courteous enough (and I often thought pitying enough) to take a copy. But was I ever glad when such a task was completed!...Then God graciously stepped in. He had permitted me to struggle on long enough to convince me that I could do nothing about it. I was shy, I was bound, and I was defeated. In a word, I was a failure.

"An old friend...crossed my path. In the course of the conversation, he drew my attention to an incident in the life of the saintly Oswald Chambers. A young Chambers was walking with a friend when a shepherd passed nearby. Chambers, walking away from his friend, confronted the shepherd, asking if all was well with his soul. Upon his return, Chambers was met with this solemn question: 'Tell me—did you get the permission of the Holy Ghost to speak to that man about his soul's welfare?'"

Olford said, "That story startled me into thinking. I began to see— slowly but clearly—that SOUL WINNING IS GOD'S WORK. From start to finish, He must plan and carry it through. My business is to be in line with His will. Winning men and women to the Lord Jesus Christ is not a matter of trial and error, but of being led by the Holy Spirit (Romans 8:14).[401]

---

[400] Ibid., 9–10.

[401] Olford, *Successful Soul Winning*, 15–16.

The Holy Spirit's business is to convict the world of sin, righteousness, and judgment to come, so be sure He intends on using YOU to be His conduit to convey the message of repentance and faith.

291 Two Embarrassing Questions

W. E. Sangster says, "The simplest way to embarrass a normal congregation is to ask them two ordinary questions: (1) When did you last lead someone to Christ? (2) When did you last *try?*"[402]

At the risk of embarrassing you, I address both questions to you. What are your answers? Being unsatisfied, unsettled and upset with the answers is potentially healthy, for hopefully it will spur a greater effort in soul winning.

292 If God Used Moody, He Can Use You

Moody is said to have won a million souls in his lifetime, but at the outset, he was more than likely less gifted than you in witnessing. Mr. Kimball, who led Moody to Christ and was his Sunday school teacher, stated: "I can truly say, and in saying it I magnify the infinite grace of God as bestowed upon him, that I have seen few persons whose minds were spiritually darker than was his when he came into my Sunday school class; and I think that the committee of the Mount Vernon Church seldom met an applicant for membership more unlikely ever to become a Christian of clear and decided views of Gospel truth, still less to fill any extended sphere of public usefulness."

A second Christian brother testified that Moody, when he began to publicly work for the saving of souls, had "little more than a half of a talent" of ability. This Christian went on to state that Moody so used that half talent that God added to it continually until he was endowed with ten talents to be "the mightiest among the mighty in the proclamation of the glad tidings of salvation by the gift of God."[403]

Certainly if God could use a man with a sixth-grade education, who butchered the King's English, and who at the first was turned down for church membership due to spiritual ignorance, to win souls, He will use anybody and everybody, which includes YOU.

---

[402] Rees, *Stir Up the Gift*, 106.

[403] Simmons, "D. L. Moody," accessed April 28, 2010.

293   A Golden Opportunity Missed

Tom Malone stated, "I had never met anybody who was a more wonderful soul winner than a deacon's wife whom I met—a mother with just as much to do as any other woman. She said, 'Brother Tom, we don't take a lot of pains with the home. A girl comes once a week to clean. That is about all it gets. I am on the go all the time.' She took me over to the telephone desk and showed me two or three notebooks of names and addresses with phone numbers. She said, 'I just work at it every day.'

"One day she went out and won five ladies to the Lord. Every time she won one, she called her pastor and said, 'Preacher, I have found another one; I want to bring him or her to your office.'

"Then, with big tears running down her face as she was driving along the street toward church, she told another preacher and me, 'Right there in that house I learned one of the most tragic lessons I have ever learned about soul winning. I was out one day going from house to house, witnessing to people. I had had a wonderful day. About three o'clock in the afternoon, I finished up in one house, and I decided to go home. I had been at it for hours, and I was tired. I think the Lord was saying to me, "Go on a little longer," but I decided to stop.'

"The next morning she started where she had left off. She knocked, and a little eight-year-old boy came to the door. She asked, 'Is your mother home?'

"The little boy said, 'No, Mamma is not home. She went to the hospital last night. Lady, are you a Christian? Do you know how to pray?' She said she was. The little boy said, 'Lady, if you know how to pray, will you come in and pray for my mamma? Last night my mamma took poison.'

"With a broken heart, she went into the room, got down on her knees and prayed with the little eight-year-old boy. She found out what hospital the lady was in, got in the car and drove as fast as she could go, praying every inch of the way, 'O God, give me another chance. Give me another chance.'

"When she got to the hospital, the woman was in a coma. This good Christian woman, this deacon's wife, this mother, this housekeeper, this woman who was as busy as any woman could be said she sat all afternoon by the bed and prayed, 'O God, if she ever opens her eyes one time, if You will ever give her mind back one moment, I want to win her. God, give me the soul of this woman.'

"Night came, and the sun went down. All night long she sat in that room; all one night she waited and begged God, but the woman never regained consciousness. She died, and as far as this woman knew, she is in

Hell today. That good woman who has won many people to Jesus said, 'I missed a golden moment when I could have won her to Christ.'"[404]

294 "Go" Is Still in There

A prominent pastor stated that he wished "Go" wasn't in the Great Commission, but since it is, he has no choice but to go. Great soul winners have attested that they don't like to go soul winning, but once they have begun, they enjoy it. So don't think yourself unspiritual if you don't want to "go"; just veto that attitude and go anyway. Not wanting to go is no sin; not going is!

Knowles Shaw, in 1865, wrote a challenge to the "goers."

Sowing in the morning,
Sowing seeds of kindness,
Sowing in the noontide
And the dewy eve;
Waiting for the harvest
And the time of reaping,
We shall come rejoicing,
Bringing in the sheaves.

Bringing in the sheaves,
Bringing in the sheaves,
We shall come rejoicing,
Bringing in the sheaves.

295 The Plumb Line Test

The Christian's doctrine and duty are subordinated to the plumb line of God's eternal Word (Amos 7:8). It's remarkable how far off center one can drift if he bases doctrine and duty upon tradition, conviction, denomination, and preachers, instead of this infallible plumb line.

Specifically apply this point to soul winning. Despite what God's Word states about soul winning's being every Christian's job, many think it's the task of ministers or for the specially gifted or evangelists, or that it refers to living by the Golden Rule or something that can be done by proxy, or that it's not a priority command. Put these views up against the true plumb line, the Bible, and one sees clearly how far off center they are. Will you take the plumb line test? Put your soul winning convictions and practice side by side

---

[404] Malone, "House to House Soul Winning," 13–14.

221

with God's Word (Matthew 28:18–20; Acts 1:8) and see where the "bubble" settles. If off center one iota, repent of former beliefs and practice, and commit yourself to the task of winning souls now.

296   Paul's Secret of Power

Hyman Appelman, in the sermon *Paul's Secret of Power,* stated, "With all of our organizations...with all of our busyness...with all of our evangelistic conferences...with all of our great churches of our orthodox fundamentalism, unless we have the power of God motivating us, inspiring us, impelling us, we are not going to get very far. Oh, we will accomplish some things; we will do some works—but the greatness of God's grace will not be ours to know. We are not going to do miraculous works, perform the impossible. Yet the promise of God is to us, as it has been to the children of God through the ages: 'Greater things than these shall ye do because I go to my Father.'"

In summation, Appelman declared, "Put all these things together now. Add a knowledge of the Scriptures to an exaltation of the Lord Jesus Christ, to an incessant Holy Spirit-led, Holy Spirit-inspired prayer life, to a crucifixion of self, to an intensity of concentration; frost it over with a blazing firmness of conviction in the hope of the soon coming of the Lord Jesus Christ. Brother, sister, you will, too, and so will I, count everything but refuse for the excellency of the knowledge of Christ Jesus.

"When we get to know Him as Paul knew Him, we too will spend and be spent in the one tremendous attack against sin and Satan, particularly in this matter of evangelism, every kind of evangelism—individual personal work, church evangelism, mass evangelism, whatever other program the Holy Spirit may lead us to engage in, in our day, in our time, in our circumstances....We can have [Paul's power] at the same price and on the same condition that Paul faced, that Paul paid, with which Paul complied."[405]

"Do you know, my friend," writes William E. Biederwolf, "there is a life that always honors God and always glorifies Christ, a life that will never bring us to a place of shame. It is the Spirit-filled life. Paul said, 'Be not drunk with wine...but be filled with the Spirit.' It is just as much of a command to 'be filled with the Spirit' as to 'be not drunk with wine.' And if you were to ask me what the filling of the Spirit means, I would say that, in a word, it is the yielding of myself so completely to the already indwelling Spirit of God that He may have His way, altogether, with me. It is this, and this only, that can cause us to walk and not stumble and in all things be

---

[405] Hutson, *Preaching on the Holy Spirit*, 96–97;108.

well-pleasing to Him. 'And grieve not the Holy Spirit of God, whereby ye are sealed unto the day of redemption.'"[406]

Curtis Hutson states that the filling of the Holy Spirit is based on three conditions. "The first is thirsting. The second condition is believing—believing that it is for you and you can be filled with the Holy Spirit. The third condition is asking. Luke 11:13 says, 'If ye then, being evil, know how to give good gifts unto your children: how much more shall your heavenly Father give the Holy Spirit to them that ask him?' Just keep on praying. Just keep on praying till light breaks through."[407]

297   Why God Used General William Booth

General William Booth met with Queen Victoria. The Queen said, "General Booth, you are not the most educated preacher in my realm, nor the most talented. You do not have the largest church. Why is it, then, that you are being used so mightily of God?"

Humbly, Booth replied, "Your Majesty, I guess it is because God has all there is of me."[408]

Regarding Charles Finney, George Clark said, "It was a mystery to me where he got his mighty power. It seemed to be always gushing up, always full. That mystery was solved when I read his memoirs. It was God in him that made him so great a blessing."[409]

Andrew Murray once asked a godly worker what he believed was the great need of the Church, and the message that ought to be preached. He answered, "Absolute surrender to God is the one thing."

Murray states, "The words struck me as never before. And that man began to tell how, in the workers with whom he had to deal, he finds that if they are sound on that point, even though they be backward, they are willing to be taught and helped, and they always improve; whereas, others who are not sound there very often go back and leave the work. The condition for obtaining God's full blessing is absolute surrender to Him."

Murray illustrates what is meant, "You know in daily life what absolute surrender is. You know that everything has to be given up to its special,

---

[406] Ibid., 1988. 194–195.

[407] Ibid., 228.

[408] Ibid., 98.

[409] Miller, B., *Charles Finney*, 129.

definite object and service. I have a pen in my pocket, and that pen is absolutely surrendered to the one work of writing; and that pen must be absolutely surrendered to my hand if I am to write properly with it. If another holds it partly, I cannot write properly....And now, do you expect that in your immortal being, in the divine nature that you have received by regeneration, God can work His work, every day and every hour, unless you are entirely given up to Him? God cannot."[410]

Every believer endeavoring by the Spirit to live a surrendered life will be a witness. You can't spell surrender without it. Are you practicing absolute surrender?

298 God Looking for a Man to Stand in the Gap

Will you be a "gap man" for God, interceding before His throne in behalf of lost souls? Andrew Murray presents a biblical case that every believer ought to be an intercessor. "There is a world with its perishing millions, with intercession as its only hope. So much love and work are comparatively vain, because there is so little intercession.

"There are millions living as if there had never been a Son of God to die for them. Every year, millions pass into the outer darkness without hope. Millions bear the Christian name, but the great majority of them live in utter ignorance or indifference....Churches and missions sacrificing life and labor with little result often lack the power of intercession. Souls, each one worth more than worlds—worth nothing less than the price paid for them in Christ's blood—are within reach of the power that can be won by intercession.

"We surely have no conception of the magnitude of the work to be done by God's intercessors, or we would cry to God above everything to give us the spirit of intercession....And we may praise God that in our days, too, there is an ever increasing number who begin to see and prove that in the church and mission, in all societies, large and small, intercession is the chief thing. They see that it is the power that moves God and opens Heaven. They are learning and long to learn better so that all may learn that in our work for souls, intercession must take the first place. Those who have received from Heaven, in the power of the Holy Spirit, what they are to communicate to others will be best able to do the Lord's work.

"Though God had His appointed servants in Israel—watchmen set by Himself to cry to Him day and night and give Him no rest—He often had to wonder and complain that there was no intercessor. He wondered why there

---

[410] Murray, *Absolute Surrender*, 7.

was no one who stirred himself up to take hold of His strength. And He still waits and wonders in our day that there are not more intercessors. He still wonders why all His children do not give themselves to this highest and holiest work and why many of them who do so do not engage in it more intensely and perseveringly.

"He wonders why ministers of His Gospel complain that their duties do not allow them to find time for this which He considers their first, highest, most delightful, and alone effective work. He wonders why His sons and daughters, who have forsaken home and friends for His sake, come so short in what He meant to be their abiding strength—receiving day by day all they need to impart to the nonbelievers. He wonders why multitudes of His children have little conception of what intercession is."[411]

"And I sought for a man...that should...stand in the gap before Me for the land, that I should not destroy it: but I found none" (Ezekiel 22:30). "I have set watchmen upon the walls, O Jerusalem, which shall never hold their peace day nor night: ye that make mention of the Lord, keep not silence, and give Him no rest...till He makes Jerusalem a praise in the earth" (Isaiah 62:6–7). In behalf of whom will you today passionately intercede before the throne of God?

299 Souls Are Dying

One lost sheep, the Shepherd sought me, leaving ninety-nine
Safe and shelter'd, but He yearned for this poor soul of mine.
Oh, He found me; then He laid me on His shoulders strong.
Now He grieves o'er all the straying, dying throng.

Souls are dying, millions dying, dying one by one—
Aliens, strangers, blinded, sinning, without Christ the Son.
Sons of Adam, born of woman, born with hearts of sin,
Only Jesus' blood can save them, trusting Him.

Once I had a friend and loved him, hoped to see him saved;
Waiting long, alas, I waited till he slipped away.
Death had claimed him, unforgiven, while I vainly sought
A convenient time to win him Christ had bought.

---

[411] Murray, *Ministry of Intercession*, 138–139;141–142.

Souls are dying; brother, do you care?
Souls undone, away from God—my brother, do you care?
Souls are dying; brother, do you care?
Souls are dying.[412]

Souls are dying. On the average, in excess of 200,000 people die every day, most of whom are unsaved. We must man the battle station, sound the alarm, and stymie opposition to tell the lost of Christ, because we *do* care about man's temporal and eternal estate!

300 A Worthy Hobby

A gospel tract won Carl Woodbury to Christ and influenced him afterward to be a tract evangelist. In fifty years of distributing tracts, he visited every state, every province in Canada, and forty-one countries sharing the Good News via the written page. Carl testifies, "My hobby has been to walk early in the morning every day for miles passing out tracts, then, knock on doors and win souls three to five hours."[413]

What an awesome hobby to embrace! What is your hobby?

301 The Five-Fold Call to Go

The Christian should engage in soul winning in response to five calls.

The Call from Above: Christ on His throne in Heaven calls the saved to be His witness. He declares, "Ye shall be witnesses unto me both in Jerusalem [home area] and in all Judea [state] and in Samaria [across America] and unto the uttermost part of the earth [everywhere else]" (Acts 1:8); "I have chosen you, that you should go and bring forth fruit" (John 15:16); and "Follow me and I will make you fishers of men" (Matthew 4:19). Total baptisms in the Southern Baptist Convention are the lowest since 1970, revealing the neglect of soul winning despite the Lord's crystal clear command *to go and tell.*

The Call from Around: Broken, bleeding, bound, and blind souls are crying out for help. Their body language and lifestyle are but a plea for you to tell them of Him who alone can make the eternal difference in their lives.

The Call from Within: In the heart of the saved is the voice of the Holy Spirit pleading with them, "Go and tell of Calvary's love and Jesus' desire

---

[412] Rice, *Heart-Warming Poems*, poem # 670.

[413] Woodbury, "Letters," 9.

to save from sin." Indeed, with Paul, the saint cries, "The love of Christ constraineth [me]" to go and tell. God plants within the soul of all He saves the desire to reproduce. In fact the person who has no desire to tell is not "born of Him" (Matthew 10:32–33). W. A. Criswell said, "The first impulse of a born-again Christian is to win somebody to Jesus. If we lose this drive, we are untrue to the Holy Spirit within us and we deny the great will of God for us."[414]

I can understand how a person may work hard at soul winning without ever winning a soul (though highly unlikely), but I will never understand how a person who claims to know Christ could never witness. It just doesn't mesh with what Scripture teaches. In the Bible, record after record is given about how those whom Jesus saved immediately began to go and tell. Among these were Philip, Andrew, and the woman at Jacob's Well. The saved cannot but speak out loud for their Savior. He places within the saved soul a "divine heartburn" for the lost. Do you hear this call from within the citadel of your own heart to go and tell?

The Call from Below: A call comes ringing loud and clear from the torment and darkness of Hell for the saved to be witnesses. Luke 16 gives the record of a man who died and went to Hell. In verses 27–28, the man cries from Hell to Abraham in Heaven, "I pray thee therefore, father, that thou wouldest send him to my father's house; for I have five brethren; that he may testify unto them, lest they also come into this place of torment." This man begged from Hell for someone on earth to warn his brothers, lest they die in their sin and end up there with him. Do you hear such pleas from Hell begging you to witness to a son, a daughter, a spouse, or a friend?

The Call from the Future: The certainty of death, yet its uncertainty as to when, where, or how, calls the believer to win others now, lest they meet death unprepared. The brevity of life and the ever decreasing opportunity for a man to be saved prompts the Christian to urgently engage in soul winning.

302 Letters from Heaven to the Unsaved

A new Christian testified that he had been saved by reading a copy of the Fifth Gospel. No, it wasn't Matthew, Mark, Luke, or John. It was the Gospel according to Mike the butcher. Mike's Christian life and testimony was used by God to save this man (II Corinthians 3:3).

How will most people be saved? Rarely will they do an investigative study regarding the birth, death, and resurrection of Jesus Christ; rather,

---

[414] Autrey, *You Can Win Souls*, 6.

they will do what this new convert did. They read God's Letter of Recommendation of Christians like Mike the butcher. This is what Paul is stating in II Corinthians 3:3 and 4:3. We are "letters" of Christ which men read every day showing God's redemptive work. "But if our Gospel be hid, it is hid to them that are lost." (II Corinthians 4:3).

Men read and admire the Gospel of Christ,
With its love so unfailing and true;
But what do they say, and what do they think
Of the Gospel according to you?

You are writing each day a letter to me;
Take care that the writing is true.
'Tis the only Gospel that some men will read—
That Gospel according to you.

You are writing a Gospel, a chapter each day,
By the deeds that you do and the words that you say.
Men read what you write, whether faithful or true.
Just what is the Gospel according to you? (Author Unknown)

What is the "Gospel according to YOU?" What kind of reference letter are you for Jesus? Does your life prove Christ's claim or deny it? When others "read" your letter, do they say "no thanks" regarding the Christian life or "what you have is what I really need? If Jesus could do that for you, I need Him to do the same for me?"

This letter is not written with "ink," Paul states, but upon the walls of our hearts. But what if it were? If God sent a letter to your friends and acquaintances seeking their salvation and included your life as His letter of recommendation, what would it include? Although it is wrong to do so, the lost, in large part, gauge the validity of the gospel message by the credentials of those who embrace it. Make your life a positive rather than a negative influence for the Gospel by living like a genuine believer.

303 Just Tell 'Em Your Story

Phillip's witness to Nathaniel well illustrates the type of witness the believer should share (John 1:45–49). Phillip found Nathaniel and said to him, "We have found Him." Note four things about this testimony.

It was a Spoken Testimony. He *said* to Phillip, "We have found him." It's important to live a Christlike life, but such does not exempt one from the responsibility of speaking the Gospel.

It was a Simple Testimony. A child could have understood. Be careful not to make complicated what God has made simple. Simply tell what He has done for you, as did Phillip.

It was a Sure Testimony. Phillip was most certain of the message from personal experience. He was saved and knew that what Christ did for him, He could do for Nathaniel. Are you sure of your salvation—as certain that Christ lives within you as Phillip was? Not until you are can you convincingly share your faith with others.

It was a Sufficient Testimony. Some witnesses may require more detail, but not this one. Phillip shared all that was needed.

As Phillip told Nathaniel, the saved are to tell others. Why?

The lost need it. Had Phillip not told Nathaniel, he may never have been saved. It is the same with your friends if you fail to go to tell. We may be someone's last roadblock on their way to havoc or Hell.

The Savior expects it. In Acts 1:8, Jesus gives us His valedictory message before leaving earth and says "Ye shall be witnesses unto me." Our Lord demands us to go and tell.

The apostles practiced it. Paul shared his testimony seven times in Acts and the epistles. Why so often? He knew the power of a personal testimony. Man cannot refute what you say has happened to you, so share your testimony boldly and often.

Calvary constrains it (II Corinthians 5:14–15, 20). In light of what Jesus did to save you, willingly endeavor to give all unto Him to win others. As Phillip found Nathaniel, go and find others to tell of Christ.

The Holy Spirit uses it. The Holy Spirit used Phillip's simple testimony to work conviction in the heart of Nathaniel that led to his conversion. Your testimony wrapped in love, biblical soundness, and concern will be empowered by the Holy Spirit.

The Christian can do it. Not all Christians can preach, teach, or sing, but all can tell their stories. Oh, that you and I may seek out the lost and tell them of Jesus, as did Phillip!

304 Are You Thirsty?

Jesus, in His agonizing death upon the Cross, uttered, "I thirst" (John 19:28). This was a physical thirst, but may it also have been a spiritual one? Might Jesus have been saying, as He shed His life blood that day for the souls of the world, "I thirst for every soul in Israel; I thirst for every soul in Africa; I thirst for every soul in America; I thirst for every soul in Indonesia; I thirst for every soul upon the face of the earth to be reconciled with God."

His life detailed such a thirst for lost humanity from the start to the finish. His whole purpose while here was to pursue the lost lovingly and compassionately so they might be saved. So, I have no problem spiritualizing this fifth saying on the Cross. It summed up His life's purpose.

Are you thirsty for souls, as Jesus was? Can you honestly state, "I thirst for Billy, Susan, Josh, Brandon, Erica to be saved?" If not, with open Bible upon bended knee, cry out to God to put the spiritual "salt lick" of Heaven to your lips to make you thirsty. Resolve to help satisfy Jesus' thirst by winning souls.

305 Characteristics of Highly Evangelistic Christians

Thom Rainer cites seven characteristics of highly evangelistic Christians. (1) They are people of prayer who realize it is God alone who can convict and convert. (2) They have a theology that compels them to evangelize—that Jesus is man's only way to God and escape from Hell and that man's need demands urgency in sharing the Gospel. (3) They spend time in the Scripture seeing the lostness of humanity and the love of God in Christ to save those who are lost. (4) They are compassionate toward the lost; their hearts break for those who are unsaved. (5) They love the communities in which they reside and seek to immerse them with the light of Christ. (6) They are intentional about evangelism, ever looking and praying for opportunities to share the Gospel. (7) They are accountable to someone for their evangelistic activities, realizing that many good activities can replace the best activities, if they are not careful. These believers make certain someone holds them accountable each week, either formally or informally, regarding their evangelistic endeavors.[415]

Based upon these seven characteristics, are you a highly evangelistic Christian? Don't you think you should be, based upon our Lord's Great Commission?

306 The Church Needs Revival

W. A. Criswell said, "That is revival; people baring their souls naked before the Lord: 'God, be good to me! In wrath, remember mercy! Forgive me! Help me, Lord, to do better; I can—with Thy grace, I shall!'

"This is revival; praying for the lost: 'See that man? I know him, and he's not a Christian. See this family? I know them; they're outside of the church. See this youngster? He's growing up as though he lived in a heathen land. See this child, untaught in the grace and mercy of Christ? God

---

[415] Rainer, "Seven Characteristics," accessed June 12, 2010.

help me as I encourage them to turn their faces Godward and their hearts Christward.'

"That is revival: the burden of souls upon our hearts."[416]

True revival brings renewed concern and commitment regarding the spiritual welfare of the lost multitudes. Pray for such a sweeping revival in the church locally and globally. John R. Rice said, "If we make small efforts to win souls, our love is small; if we make none, how can we say we love Him at all?"[417]

Spurgeon stated, "If there be any one point in which the Christian church ought to keep its fervor at a white heat, it is concerning missions. If there be anything about which we cannot tolerate lukewarmness, it is the matter of sending the Gospel to a dying world."[418]

307 Don't Give Up

•48% of salesman make one visit and quit
•25% make 2 visits and quit
•15% make 3 visits and quit
•12% keep going and do 80% of the business, while
•88% do only 20% of the business. Do not quit![419]

Soul winners are unlike door-to-door salesmen in many aspects, but similar in philosophy. Soul winners, like salesmen, realize the more doors knocked upon, the more presentations made, the more firm resolve displayed in seeking prospects, the greater the possibility of reaching people (for Christ).

Soul winning requires patience and persistence. The winning of some demands multiplied visits and relentless praying. Too many battles have been lost at the eleventh hour due to the soul winner's giving up. Elmer Towns declared, "Research tells us a person hears the gospel 3.4 times (the law of three hearings) before he accepts Christ. Usually they are stepping closer to salvation each time they hear the Gospel."[420]

---

[416] Criswell, "Day of Revival," accessed May 1, 2010.

[417] Wells and Ray, "One Step at a Time," accessed May 2, 2010.

[418] Spurgeon, "Sentence Sermons," accessed May 8, 2010.

[419] Wells and Ray, "One Step at a Time," accessed May 2, 2010.

[420] Towns, *Winning the Winnable*, 13.

This same research also revealed that it takes an average of 7.6 meaningful contacts by a church to get a prospect to visit. Paul mandates that the believer proclaim the Gospel "in season and out of season" (perennially), when it is convenient and inconvenient, when it is favorable or unfavorable to do so (II Timothy 4:2). Many would be Christians had that someone who had been sowing the seed in their hearts not quit! A soul is too valuable to give up on. God promises that His Word will not return unto Him void.

308 Not Unreachable—Simply Unreached

Many people in your city are not unreachable—simply unreached. Bill Bright, Campus Crusade founder, stated, "I am convinced that at least 25% of those in America who are not already Christians would accept Christ if properly approached." Knowing that one in four unreached persons will be receptive to Christ should add fuel to the fire of the soul winner.

Is there anything else that is better worth,
As along life's way we plod,
Than to find some wandering soul of earth
And bring him home to God?

I would rather find a soul that is lost
And bring him home again,
Than to own what all earth's acres cost
Or all the wealth of men.

Wouldn't I be glad when the day is done,
In breathing my latest breath,
To know some word of mine had won
And saved a soul from death?[421]

309 The Open Door to Share

"Withal praying also for us, that God would open unto us a door of utterance, to speak the mystery of Christ, for which I am also in bonds" (Colossians 4:3). The apostle Paul not only petitioned God for open doors to share the Gospel but asked the Colossians to do the same. These prayers were answered time and again as revealed in Scripture (I Corinthians 16:8–9; II Corinthians 2:12).

---

[421] Unknown Author, "Challenge of Evangelism," accessed April 21, 2010.

You and I need to pray likewise for ourselves and beg others to do the same in our behalf. "Lord, today please open the door of opportunity to speak to a soul about YOU"; "Lord, Jim needs You in his life, please open the door of opportunity to share the Gospel with him. I will be ready and walk into it for your name's sake."

310 Soul Winning Starts on the Floor

"The church has many organizers," says Leonard Ravenhill, "but few agonizers; many who pay, but few who pray; many resters, but few wrestlers; many who are enterprising, but few who are interceding. People who are not praying are playing. Two prerequisites of dynamic Christian living are vision and passion; both of these are generated by prayer.

"The ministry of preaching is open to a few. The ministry of praying is open to every child of God....Tithes may build the church, but tears will give it life. That is the difference between the modern church and the early church. Our emphasis is on paying; theirs was on praying. When we have paid, the place is taken. When they had prayed, the place was shaken (Acts 4:31). In the matter of effective praying, never have so many left so much to so few. Brethren, let us pray."[422]

Ron Dunn has said, "Prayer is not a substitute for work or merely preparation for work. It *is* work....Prayer is the secret weapon of the kingdom of God. It is like a missile that can be fired toward any spot on earth, travel undetected at the speed of thought, and hit its target every time....Satan has no defense against this weapon; he does not have an anti-prayer missile."[423]

Sidlow Baxter stated, "Men may spurn our appeals, reject our message, oppose our arguments,...but they are helpless against our prayers."[424]

L. R. Scarborough remarked, "A prayerless Christian is a powerless Christian, and a powerless Christian is never a soul-winning Christian. Prayer conditions power. Prayer makes possible power. And power is essential in winning men to Christ."[425]

God said, "Ask of me, and I shall give thee the heathen for thine inheritance" (Psalm 2:8). The winning of souls, according to this verse, is

---

[422] Hayes, *Fireseeds of Spiritual Awakening*, 86–87.

[423] Dunn, *Don't Just Stand There*, 17–20.

[424] Baxter, "Christian Prayer Quotes," accessed May 2, 2010.

[425] Scarborough, *Search for Souls*, 15.

linked to prayer. James stated, "Ye have not, because ye ask not" (James 4:2). The soul winner must claim souls on his knees before to them he urgently pleads.

311 Flying Rabbits, Swimming Eagles

Perhaps a big reason why you share the Gospel infrequently is due to comparison of ability with that of others more accomplished. Vance Havner stated that if there were an eleventh commandment, it would be, "Thou shalt not compare." I agree. All God's children are different, and it is in that difference that He wants to win the world.

Chuck Swindoll shared the following perspective. "Once upon a time, the animals decided they should do something meaningful to meet the problems of the new world, so they organized a school. They adopted an activity curriculum of running, climbing, swimming, and flying. To make it easier to administer the curriculum, all the animals took all the subjects.

"The duck was excellent at swimming; in fact, better than his instructor. But he made only passing grades in flying and was very poor at running. Since he was slow in running, he had to drop swimming and stay after school to practice running. This caused his web feet to be badly worn, so that he was only average in swimming. But average was quite acceptable, so nobody worried about that—except the duck.

"The rabbit started at the top of his class in running but developed a nervous twitch in his leg muscles because of so much make-up work in swimming.

"The squirrel was excellent in climbing, but he encountered constant frustration in flying class, because his teacher made him start from the ground up instead of from the treetop down. He developed charley horses from overexertion and so got only a C in climbing and a D in running.

"The eagle was a problem child and was severely disciplined for being a nonconformist. In climbing, he beat all the others to the top of the tree but insisted on using his way to get there....

"A duck is a duck—and only a duck. It is built to swim, not to run or fly, and certainly not to climb. A squirrel is a squirrel—and only that. To move it out of its forte, climbing, and then expect it to swim or fly will drive a squirrel nuts. Eagles are beautiful creatures in the air but not in a foot race. The rabbit will win every time, unless, of course, the eagle gets hungry.

"What is true of creatures in the forest is true of Christians in the family—both the family of believers and the family under your roof. God has not made us all the same. He never intended to. It was He who planned and designed the differences, unique capabilities, and variations....

"If God made you a duck saint, you're a duck, friend. Swim like mad, but don't get bent out of shape because you wobble when you run or flap instead of fly. Furthermore, if you're an eagle saint, stop expecting squirrel saints to soar or rabbit saints to build the same kind of nests you do....

"So relax. Enjoy your spiritual species. Cultivate your own capabilities, your own style. Appreciate the members of your family or your fellowship for who they are, even though their outlook or style may be miles different from yours. Rabbits don't fly. Eagles don't swim. Ducks look funny trying to climb. Squirrels don't have feathers. Stop comparing."[426]

I have been a soul winner for many years, yet I am not as successful as some others whom I admire. I never will be; in dispensing His Word to a lost world, I can only be who I am in Christ Jesus. The same is true for you.

312 Prayer Crossed the Ocean to Win a Soul

Read carefully the testimony of Wesley Duwell concerning the power of prayer to save. "Not only can prayer reach Heaven, but the arm of prayer can span the miles to any part of the world, and you in your place of intercession can touch someone who needs you, even thousands of miles away. This is not make-believe. It is spiritual reality.

"I shall never forget the two-week period in India many years ago when I felt a continuing burden to pray for our son. It came to a climax one Sunday afternoon when I was alone in the house, so lost in prayer for him that for a while I did not notice the passing of time or the existence of space. As I prayed on and on, suddenly it seemed that I was kneeling beside John with my hand on his shoulder, praying for him. I know not how long I prayed or what I said, but I know my arm of prayer had spanned the land and oceans for thousands of miles and my hand was on John's shoulder. It was so real as if I was by his side.

"Then assurance came, and I rose from my knees and later gave my Sunday evening message. Because of missionary responsibilities, I did not find opportunity to write John till after lunch the following afternoon. I went to my office and was sitting at my typewriter. 'Dear John,' I wrote, 'I don't know what this means to you, but I am sure it means something. For days I have been having a special prayer in concern for you, and yesterday afternoon as I was kneeling in our bedroom, it suddenly seemed I was kneeling by your side with my hand on your shoulder.' I was just ready to write the second paragraph when our doorbell rang. I went to the door and found a messenger from the telegraph office. He handed me a cablegram.

---

[426] Swindoll, *Standing Out*, 51–53.

"I stepped inside, closed the door, and opened the cable. It read: 'God is my Captain. Quiet but sure decision. Thanks for heritage, love and prayer. John.' I dropped on my knees as the tears coursed down my cheeks. God had permitted me to touch Heaven's throne with one hand and our son's shoulder with the other. After the necessary days had elapsed, John's letter had arrived. At the exact time when I was in prayer in Allahabad, India, John, kneeling alone in the darkness in the USA, had given his heart to the Lord."[427]

"Christ gives to you through prayer the keys to the salvation of more people in your circle of acquaintance and around the world than you realize. One day Christ will ask you what you did with the keys He held out for you. For how many people will you have unlocked Heaven's door? For how many will you have shut and locked the door of Satan's deceptions?...

"Prayers prayed in accordance with the will of God are never lost."[428]

313 Stir Them Up

Upon a park bench sat a Christian next to an unsaved seventy-eight-year-old man. The Christian, a stranger to the man, presented a witness. At the conclusion of the witness, the man said, "I have known for a long time that Christianity was the right thing. I only needed someone to stir me up."[429]

I often tell people I view my role in soul winning as that of a "soul stirrer-upper," someone who simply encourages one to do what he knows he should with Christ. To reach some unsaved ones, all that is necessary is to remind them of the need and urgency. Whom will you "stir up" unto consideration of salvation?

314 Conduit for God

Naaman, a leper, learned from a little girl who had been taken captive from Israel of a cure for his disease (II Kings 5:2–3). When Naaman shared this news with the king, he was immediately dispatched to Israel. You recall the story. It all ends on a triumphant note with Naaman being healed (v. 14). This healing was only possible because of a little girl in less than the best circumstances who allowed God to use her as a conduit to transmit His

---

[427] Duewel, *Touch the World*, 60–61.

[428] Ibid., 74–75; 223.

[429] Knight, *Illustrations for Today*, 315.

message. This is the task of every believer—to serve as God's conduit to the lost, communicating the source of salvation. Man's salvation hinges upon how good a conduit we are.

In 1930, at a London Arms Conference, King George V was about to give a speech that was to be carried around the world when it was discovered that a cable had accidentally been severed. Harold Vidian picked up one end of the cable in one hand and then the other end with his other hand, allowing the electrical current to flow through him. In doing this, he became a conduit through which the king's message was carried to the world. Christian's are to be the King's conduit through which His saving message is proclaimed to the entire world.[430]

315 Enlarge My Heart for the Lost

"There can be no substitutes for personal work," declared George W. Truett. "How shall we save our churches? My fellow Christians, there is one sure way, and that is that our churches be great life-saving stations to point lost sinners to Christ. The supreme indictment that you can bring against a church, if you are able in truth to bring it, is that such church lacks in passion and compassion for human souls. A church is nothing better than an ethical club if its sympathies for lost souls do not overflow and if it does not go to seek to point lost souls to the knowledge of Jesus....

"Do we love lost sinners? Do we care for the young men about us who are coasting the downward road? Do we care for the people whose toil is rigorous and whose lot in life is hard? Do we care for businessmen and professional men who are sidestepping with reference to the supreme things, namely, the things of God and the soul and eternity? Do we love these people well enough to go to them and earnestly and alone say to them: 'Is it well with your soul?'

"There is no power in human life like the power of love. The prayer that the psalmist of old prayed is the prayer that you and I ought to pray: 'Enlarge my heart.' He did not pray that his head might be enlarged. 'Enlarge my heart,' for out of the heart are the issues of life....

"Oh, do we care for the people around us who are lost? Do we really care? Shall I talk about responsibility? What shall I say about responsibility? Your responsibility and mine for these souls about us lost is a responsibility big enough to stagger God's archangel. You *are* your brother's keeper. What if you neglect him and he shall die in his sins? If you shall neglect him and he shall die in his sins when you might have won him, then

---

[430] Shivers, *Soulwinning 101*, 172.

it shall turn out that you are your brother's spiritual murderer. Men can be killed by neglect."[431]

"Do we believe that these men are lost and that these young people are lost? Do we believe it? Then, I pray you, even as I summon myself, let us go to them in the right spirit, pleading with God to teach us, to empower us, to enable us to plead that now, before the day is gone, they may repent of sin and be saved forever."[432]

Out of the believer's love for Christ is His command regarding soul winning birthed, bathed and behaved (II Corinthians 5:14).

316   Just Tell Them What He Did for You

George W. Truett states that there is nothing as powerful as one's personal testimony. "When Andrew found his Savior, he said: 'Brother, listen! I have found the Messiah. Let me tell you about Him.' And then, with words, that thrilled and burned, Andrew told his brother what he had tasted and seen and felt of—Jesus, the long-looked-for Messiah.

"My fellow Chris-tians, there is nothing else human quite so powerful as the power of an earnest personal testimony concerning Jesus' experience in your own life, as you tell somebody else what Jesus has been and consciously is to you yourself....There is no power like the power of personal testimony. You can tell that neighbor or friend how you heard Christ's voice and how you responded and what He said to you and what He did and what you have seen and experienced of His grace and love in your own little life. Tell that experience to somebody without delay."[433]

317   A Functioning Watch

A watchmaker told me that there were basically four things that caused a watch to malfunction: a cracked crystal, dirt, an imbalanced pendulum, and neglect of winding. A cracked crystal (duplicity of lifestyle), dirt (sin), an imbalanced pendulum (straying from the Bible), and neglect of winding (constant fellowship with Christ in the Word and prayer) likewise cause God's watchman to the world to malfunction.

---

[431] Truett, *Quest for Souls*, 67; 69–70;72.

[432] Ibid., 73.

[433] Ibid., 68–69.

Inconvenience, burnt toast, and perhaps missed opportunities arise when the watch malfunctions. But when God's watchman malfunctions, souls are led astray, hearts remain broken and hurting and, tragically far worse, die without Christ. All believers, as God's watchmen, must sound the alarm to the lost loudly, clearly, and constantly by staying in good repair spiritually.

318 General William Booth: A Vision of the Lost

"On one of my recent journeys, as I gazed from the coach window, I was led into a train of thought concerning the condition of the multitudes around me. They were living carelessly in the most open and shameless rebellion against God, without a thought for their eternal welfare. As I looked out of the window, I seemed to see them all—millions of people all around me given up to their drink and their pleasure, their dancing and their music, their business and their anxieties, their politics and their troubles; ignorant, willfully ignorant in many cases, and in other instances knowing all about the truth and not caring at all; but all of them, the whole mass of them, sweeping on and up in their blasphemies and devilries to the throne of God.

"While my mind was thus engaged, I had a vision. I saw a dark and stormy ocean. Over it the black clouds hung heavily; through them every now and then vivid lightening flashed and loud thunder rolled, while the winds moaned and the waves rose and foamed, towered and broke, only to rise and foam, tower and break again. In that ocean, I thought I saw myriads of poor human beings plunging and floating, shouting and shrieking, cursing and struggling and drowning; and as they cursed and screamed, they rose and shrieked again, and then some sank to rise no more.

"And I saw out of this dark angry ocean, a mighty rock that rose up with its summit towering high above the black clouds that overhung the stormy sea. And all around the base of this great rock, I saw a vast platform. Onto this platform, I saw with delight a number of the poor, struggling, drowning wretches continually climbing out of the angry ocean. And I saw that a few of those who were already safe on the platform were helping the poor creatures still in the angry waters to reach the place of safety.

"On looking more closely, I found a number of those who had been rescued industriously working and scheming by ladders, ropes, boats, and other means more effective to deliver the poor strugglers out of the sea. Here and there were some who actually jumped into the water, regardless of the consequences, in their passion to 'rescue the perishing.' And I hardly know which gladdened me the most—the sight of the poor drowning people climbing onto the rocks reaching a place of safety or the devotion and self-sacrifice of those whose whole being was wrapped up in the effort for their deliverance.

"As I looked on, I saw that the occupants of that platform were quite a mixed company. That is, they were divided into different sets or classes, and they occupied themselves with different pleasures and employments. But only a very few of them seemed to make it their business to get the people out of the sea. But what puzzled me most was the fact that, though all of them had been rescued at one time or another from the ocean, nearly everyone seemed to have forgotten all about it. Anyway, it seemed the memory of its darkness and danger no longer troubled them at all. And what seemed equally strange and perplexing to me was that these people did not even seem to have any care—that is, any agonizing care—about the poor perishing ones who were struggling and drowning right before their very eyes, many of whom were their own husbands and wives, brothers and sisters, and even their own children.

"Now this astonishing unconcern could not have been the result of ignorance or lack of knowledge, because they lived right there in full sight of it all and even talked about it sometimes. Many even went regularly to hear lectures and sermons in which the awful state of these poor drowning creatures was described.

"I have already said that the occupants of this platform were engaged in different pursuits and pastimes. Some of them were absorbed day and night in trading and business in order to make gain, storing up their savings in boxes, safes, and the like. Many spent their time in amusing themselves with growing flowers on the side of the rock, others in painting pieces of cloth or in playing music or in dressing themselves up in different styles and walking about to be admired. Some occupied themselves chiefly in eating and drinking; others were taken up with arguing about the poor drowning creatures that had already been rescued.

"But the thing to me that seemed the most amazing was that those on the platform to whom He called, who heard His voice and felt that they ought to obey it—at least they said they did—those who confessed to love Him much and were in full sympathy with Him in the task He had undertaken, who worshiped Him or who professed to do so, were so taken up with their trades and professions, their money saving and pleasures, their families and circles, their religions and arguments about it, and their preparation for going to the mainland, that they did not listen to the cry that came to them from this Wonderful Being who had Himself gone down into the sea. Anyway, if they heard it, they did not heed it. They did not care. And so the multitude went on right before them struggling and shrieking and drowning in the darkness.

"And then I saw something that seemed to me even stranger than anything that had gone on before in this strange vision. I saw that some of these people on the platform to whom this Wonderful Being had called, wanting them to come and help Him in His difficult task of saving these perishing creatures, were always praying and crying out to Him to come to them! Some wanted Him to come and stay with them and spend His time and strength in making them happier. Others wanted Him to come and take away various doubts and misgivings they had concerning the truth of some letters He had written them. Some wanted Him to come and make them feel more secure on the rock, so secure that they would be quite sure that they should never slip off again into the ocean. Numbers of others wanted Him to make them feel quite certain that they would really get off the rock and onto the mainland someday, because, as a matter of fact, it was well known that some had walked so carelessly as to lose their footing and had fallen back again into the stormy waters.

"So these people used to meet and get up as high on the rock as they could, and, looking towards the mainland (where they thought the Great Being was), they would cry out, 'Come to us! Come and help us!' And all the while He was down (by His Spirit) among the poor, struggling, drowning creatures in the angry deep with His arms around them trying to drag them out and looking up—oh, so longingly but all in vain—to those on the rock, crying to them with His voice all hoarse from calling, 'Come to Me! Come, and help Me!'

"And then I understood it all. It was plain enough. The sea was the ocean of life, the sea of real, actual human existence. That lightning was the gleaming of piercing truth coming from Jehovah's throne. That thunder was the distant echoing of the wrath of God. Those multitudes of people shrieking, struggling and agonizing in the stormy sea were the thousands and thousands of poor harlots and harlot makers; of drunkards and drunkard makers; of thieves, liars, blasphemers, and ungodly people of every kindred, tongue, and nation.

"Oh, what a black sea it was! And, oh, what multitudes of rich and poor, ignorant and educated were there. They were all so unalike in their outward circumstances and conditions, yet all alike in one thing—all sinners before God; all held by and holding onto some iniquity, fascinated by some idol, the slaves of some devilish lust, and ruled by the foul fiend from the bottomless pit! 'All alike in one thing?' No, all alike in two things, not only the same in their wickedness but, unless rescued, the same in their sinking, sinking—down, down, down—to the same terrible doom.

"That great sheltering rock represented Calvary, the place where Jesus had died for them. And the people on it were those who had been rescued. The way they used their energies, gifts, and time represented the occupations and amusements of those who professed to be saved from sin and Hell—followers of the Lord Jesus Christ. The handful of fierce, determined ones who were risking their own lives in saving the perishing were true

241

soldiers of the cross of Jesus. That Mighty Being who was calling to them from the midst of the angry waters was the Son of God, the same yesterday, today and forever, who is still struggling and interceding to save the dying multitudes about us from this terrible doom of damnation, and whose voice can be heard above the music, machinery, and noise of life, calling on the rescued to come and help Him save the world.

"My friends in Christ, you are rescued from the waters; you are on the rock; He is in the dark sea calling on you to come to Him and help Him. Will you go? Look for yourselves. The surging sea of life, crowded with perishing multitudes, rolls up to the very spot on which you stand.

"Leaving the vision, I now come to speak of the fact—a fact that is as real as the Bible, as real as the Christ who hung upon the cross, as real as the judgment day will be, and as real as the Heaven and Hell that will follow it. Look! Don't be deceived by appearances—men and things are not what they seem. All who are not on the rock are in the sea! Look at them from the standpoint of the Great White Throne, and what a sight you have! Jesus Christ, the Son of God, is, through His Spirit, in the midst of this dying multitude, struggling to save them. And He is calling on you to jump into the sea, to go right away to His side and help Him in the holy strife. Will you jump? That is, will you go to His feet and place yourself absolutely at His disposal?

"A young Christian once came to me and told me that for some time she had been giving the Lord her profession and prayers and money, but now she wanted to give Him her life. She wanted to go right into the fight. In other words, she wanted to go to His assistance in the sea. As when a man from the shore, seeing another struggling in the water, takes off those outer garments that would hinder his efforts and leaps to the rescue, so will you who still linger on the bank, thinking and singing and praying about the poor perishing souls, lay aside your shame, your pride, your cares about other people's opinions, your love of ease, and all the selfish loves that have kept you back for so long and rush to the rescue of this multitude of dying men and women?

"Does the surging sea look dark and dangerous? Unquestionably it is so. There is no doubt that the leap for you, as for everyone who takes it, means difficulty and scorn and suffering. For you it may mean more than this. It may mean death. He who beckons you from the sea, however, knows what it will mean—and knowing, He still calls to you and bids to you to come. You must do it! You cannot hold back. You have enjoyed yourself in Christianity long enough. You have had pleasant feelings, pleasant songs, pleasant meetings, pleasant prospects. There has been much of human happiness, much clapping of hands and shouting of praises—very much of Heaven on earth.

"You must do it. With the light that is now broken in upon your mind and the call that is now sounding in your ears and the beckoning hands that are now before your eyes, you have no alternative. To go down among the perishing crowds is your duty. Your happiness from now on will consist in sharing their misery, your ease in sharing their pain, your crown in helping them to bear their cross, and your Heaven in going into the very jaws of Hell to rescue them."[434]

319 A Vision of Lost Souls

Tom Malone said, "In that chapter (Acts 16), in verse 9, I read, 'And a vision appeared to Paul in the night; There stood a man of Macedonia, and prayed him, saying, Come over into Macedonia, and help us.' We need to see what Paul saw that night. When God brought a man to stand before Paul, he heard that night that man say, 'Come, help us.'

"That is a vision every Christian needs to see. We need to hear the cry of the lost souls of this world, still crying after two thousand years, 'Come, help us.' That is the cry of lost humanity. God give us a vision of lost souls!...Listen, Jesus saw the multitudes. He didn't see them as prospective votes. He didn't see them as statistics. He saw them as souls. Friends, the church of Jesus today needs to see a vision of lost souls.

"How many Christians today do you hear talking about missionary work? How many Christians today do you hear talking about visitation work? How many Christians today do you hear talking about revival? How many Christians do you hear today in the average church praising the Lord for souls that are being saved? The lack of all this is an indication that we need a vision of lost souls.

"We need a vision like Livingstone had when he went to that dark continent of Africa. In his day, some had never seen the face of a white man. They said, 'We never knew we were black, because we never had seen a man who was white until David Livingstone came.' All the years of his fruitful life, he walked among them. He braved the rigors of that land, the diseases that racked his body, the fever that almost killed him. He loved them to God until thousands were saved. They found him dead in the little pup tent. He had been kneeling at his cot, praying, 'O God, give me Africa!'—a prayer he always prayed. He died, literally, on his knees. They lifted his body and sent it back to England to be buried in Westminster Abbey. In the middle aisle where kings and important people of history are buried lies the body of David Livingstone. The natives said, 'His body belongs to England, but his heart belongs to Africa. Leave it here.' So his

---

[434] Booth, "Vision of the Lost," accessed May 6, 2010.

heart was taken from his body and buried in the soil of Africa. That was where his heart was."[435] I ask you this morning, where is your heart when it comes to the souls of men?

320 Remember William Carey

A true witness never gives up, never quits. William Carey preached, witnessed, and worked in India for seven long years without one convert. It is hard to imagine that someone serious about winning souls could go seven years without winning one person to Christ, yet it happened to Carey. I like this man's determination. He said, "I'll never give up until God gives me some souls of these Indian people." Do you love Jesus enough to knock on doors, pass out tracts, and pray for seven years, if necessary, without winning one person to Christ?[436]

The church needs preachers, missionaries and lay persons with the staunch disposition of a Carey who refuse to quit seeking souls despite periods of ineffectualness. In times of spiritual barrenness when actively seeking souls, remember William Carey!

C. H. Spurgeon, speaking to the Pastor's College at his church, said, "Our great object of glorifying God is, however, to be mainly achieved by the winning of souls. We *must* see souls born unto God. If we do not, our cry should be that of Rachel, 'Give me children, or I die.' If we do not win souls, we should mourn as the husbandman who sees no harvest, as the fisherman who returns to his cottage with an empty net, or as the huntsman who has in vain roamed over hill and dale. Ours should be Isaiah's language uttered with many a sigh and groan—'Who hath believed our report? and to whom is the arm of the Lord revealed?' The ambassadors of peace should not cease to weep bitterly until sinners weep for their sins."[437]

321 Five Hundred Dollars to Go Soul Winning

Were I to offer a reward of five hundred dollars to the first five people reading this who presented the Gospel to a lost person, inviting him to pray to receive Christ as Lord and Savior (whether he did or not) within the next five hours, would you be one of the many making a fast dash to do so? Whether or not you would, I am sure many would take me up on the offer,

---

[435] Malone, "Where There Is No Vision," accessed August 19, 2010.

[436] Malone, *With Jesus after Sinners*, 164.

[437] Spurgeon, *Lectures to My Students*, 337.

willing to do for money what they were not willing to do for love of God and man.

The apostle Paul would turn down my offer, stating, "Knowing therefore the terror of the Lord, we persuade men; but we are made manifest unto God; and I trust also are made manifest in your consciences....For the love of Christ constraineth us; because we thus judge, that if one died for all, then were all dead: And that he died for all, that they which live should not henceforth live unto themselves, but unto him which died for them, and rose again" (II Corinthians 5: 11, 14–15). If you will do for money, fame, or reputation what you will not do for love of Christ and the eternally lost, your motivations in soul winning are flawed and impure.

322 When to Start Witnessing

A Chinese pastor always told new converts about the need to witness as soon as possible. Hudson Taylor said this pastor asked a new believer, "Brother, how long have you been saved?"

The man replied, "Three months."

"And how many have you won to the Savior?"

The new convert responded, "Oh, I'm only a learner."

The Chinese pastor, shaking his head in disapproval, said, "Young man, the Lord doesn't expect you to be a full-fledged preacher, but He does expect you to be a faithful witness. Tell me, when does a candle begin to shine—when it's already half burned up?"

"No," said the convert, "as soon as it is lit."

The pastor then said, "That's right, so let your light shine right away."[438]

The woman at Jacob's Well went into the city testifying immediately when she had received Christ, and many believed as a result. The time to start witnessing is from the get-go.

323 When People Shut You Out

In times of a shut door in soul winning, what ought to be done? Edwin Markham, in his poem "Outwitted," offers excellent advice.

---

[438] Green, *Illustrations for Biblical Preaching*, 129.

He drew a circle that shut me out—
Heretic, rebel, a thing to flout.
But love and I had the wit to win;
We drew a circle that took him in.

This is literally what Jesus did in man's behalf. "He came unto His own, and His own received Him not" (John 1:11). He refused to give up on man, loving him all the way to the Cross and beyond, despite men's bitter reaction to His person and invitation of salvation. Dare we give up on someone simply because they think we are religious freaks or fanatics! As Markham suggests, certainly as Jesus did, simply keep enlarging the circumference of love around people who shut you out. Love will win in the end.

324 "Somebody Else" Will Talk to Them

I revised the anonymous poem "Somebody Else" to apply to soul winning.

There is a burdened young man named "Somebody Else";
There is no one he won't witness to.
He is busy from morning 'til way late at night
Talking to souls, substituting for you.

You're asked to talk to Jim or to Joan,
And what is the ready reply?
"Get somebody else; I'm too busy.
He can witness to them much better than I!"

There's so much to do in the harvest field,
So much and the workers so few;
And "somebody else" is weary and worn,
Just substituting for you!

So when you have the chance to share the faith,
Come back with this ready reply.
"Somebody else" cannot reach the dying lost alone;
Together we'll work, he and I.

Don't depend upon "Somebody Else" witnessing to the neighbor, work associate, teammate, classmate, or family member; do it yourself.

325 A Parade to Honor Firemen Who Saved Their Lives

Twelve thousand persons marched in a great parade in New York City. In the procession were three vans packed full of men, women, and children; in one was a judge of the Court of Appeals, and in the last one was a ragged street boy. Etched upon the sides of one of the cars was written, "These people have been saved from burning buildings by the New York firemen." Following the cars marched the men who saved them, wearing their medals.[439]

In the great parade that I envision taking place in Heaven, many saved from a burning Hell will march, followed by those who saved them wearing their medals. As a "fireman" of God, will you be included in this parade or simply stand as a spectator?

326 Arguments for Soul Winning

C. H. Spurgeon said, "Do you want arguments for soul winning? Look up to Heaven, and ask yourself how sinners can ever reach those harps of gold and learn their everlasting song unless they have someone to tell them of Jesus who is mighty to save. But the best argument of all is to be found in the wounds of Jesus. You want to honor Him, you desire to put many crowns upon His head, and this you can best do by winning souls for Him. These are the spoils that He covets; these are the trophies for which He fights; these are the jewels that shall be His best adornment."[440]

I need no other argument; I need no other plea.
It is enough that Jesus died to set man free
And that He wants to win them through me.

327 Souls, Souls, Souls

"A man may be a successful physician," states William Evans, "without having love for his patients, he may be a successful lawyer without having love for his clients, he may be a successful merchant without having love for his patrons, but no man can be a successful coworker with God without having love for souls and a longing desire to see them saved....The secret of success is here. Christ had a burning love for souls. Listen to Him as He

---

[439] Unknown Author, "Salvation Sermon Illustrations," accessed April 14, 2010.

[440] Spurgeon, "Spurgeon Quotes on Evangelism," accessed May 8, 2010.

stands on the mount overlooking the Holy City and says, 'O Jerusalem, Jerusalem, thou that killest the prophets, and stonest them which are sent unto thee, how often would I have gathered thy children together, even as a hen gathereth her chickens under her wings, and ye would not!' (Matt. 23:37). 'And when he was come near, he beheld the city, and wept over it' (Luke 19:41).

"Have you ever wept over souls? 'No,' you say, 'I have never felt the burden of souls heavy enough for that; how may I feel the weight of souls?' Consider the value of a soul—what it cost; what a sacrifice was made to redeem it; its capabilities; its eternal destiny to glory or despair; that you are in a very real sense your brother's keeper—and then ask God to make you feel the mighty importance of trying to rescue some perishing soul as a brand plucked from the burning.

"When John Knox, in the enclosure behind his house, pierced the stillness of the night with the thrice-repeated, intense appeal: 'Give me Scotland, or I die!' that eager, yearning, well-nigh broken heart got its Scotland. When Brainerd went to sleep thinking of souls and dreaming dreams of them and, waking, still thought and prayed for them, souls became his. 'Tell me,' says Maclaren, 'the depth of a Christian man's compassion, and I will tell you the measure of his usefulness. The wealth of Egypt's harvest is proportioned to the depth of the Nile's overflow.' Christ, the model Christian worker, is portrayed as 'moved with compassion,' as though a great surging tide flowed over His heart when He saw the multitudes standing before Him in their want.

"The power of these great religious leaders of all time lay deeper than their mighty intellects—it lay in their love for souls. 'Souls, souls, souls! I yearn for souls.' This is the cry of the Savior—and to save souls He died upon the cross and remains until eternity their Intercessor. 'Souls, souls, souls!' This is the cry of Satan—and to obtain them he scatters gold to tempt them, multiplies their wants and pleasures, and gives them praise that only infatuates. 'Souls, souls, souls!' This must be our one cry and passion, Christian worker; and for the sake of one soul, we must be willing to spend and be spent."[441]

328 John Dillinger: The Rest of the Story

Evangelist Rex Humbard was speaking at Cadle Tabernacle in Indianapolis in the 1940s when, following a service, a lady shared a story with him about her brother John who had been released from reform school. She told Humbard that he really made an effort to straighten his life out. Attending

---

[441] Evans, "Personal Worker," accessed May 8, 2010.

church one Sunday morning, he felt led to respond to the minister's altar call. He walked the aisle and knelt along with others at the altar. "But nobody," she said, "went to pray with John." The saints of the church well knew who he was and that he was no good. In leaving church that Sunday, he told his sister, "I'll never go to church again as long as I live."

"And," she states, "he never did."[442]

John Dillinger was so close to the new birth and a new life, but due to the failure of a Christian to deal with him, he became a most-wanted criminal for the FBI. Don't check soul winning at the entry door of the church, but constantly be on the lookout while in worship and fellowship for seeking hearts to introduce to Christ. Soul winning opportunities must be seized within the walls of the church as well as without.

329 Calloused and Guilt-Free

In researching the numerous resources for this present book, I came across one author who suggested that he who does not win souls shouldn't feel guilty. This smacks the Bible square in the face, for Scripture teaches that disobedience should lead to repentance. If one feels no guilt about disobeying God's command to witness, there certainly will be no godly sorrow unto repentance expressed. So, yes, if you are not seeking to introduce others to Jesus Christ, you ought to feel guilty—guilty enough to repent and be obedient.

Calloused hearts created from deafness to repeated appeals from the Word and pulpit to witness are another symptom seen in the church. It's not that the command is no longer being shouted from Heaven's throne, but, due to spiritual hardness, it is no longer heard. This is why many believers listen to moving missionary, evangelistic sermons about sharing the Good News without feeling the slightest twinge of personal responsibility.

Lead me to some soul today;
Oh, teach me, Lord, just what to say.
Friends of mine are lost in sin
And cannot find their way.

---

[442] Unknown Author, "Editorials & Letters," June 25.

Few there are who seem to care,
And few there are who pray.
Melt my heart and fill my life;
Give me one soul today.
—Will H. Houghton

330   One in Four Churches Baptizing No One

In 2008, 24.7 percent of SBC churches baptized no one. "More and more churches," states Richard Harris, "are baptizing nobody. When one in four churches are baptizing nobody, they can't really be serious about fulfilling the Great Commission." A recent NAMB study reported 61.6 percent of SBC churches baptized five persons or fewer last year, and 78.6 percent baptized 10 or fewer. The report further stated that only 21.4 percent of SBC churches are baptizing 11 or more annually. In 2009 only 201 churches baptized 100 or more.[443]

Youth baptism is in decline. In the early 1970s, youth baptisms in our churches reached an all time high of close to 138,000. Thirty-five years later, despite increased numbers of trained youth workers, youth baptisms have declined to about 81,000. In 2007, more than 20,000 churches did not baptize one teenager in the SBC.[444]

With roughly 50,000 churches and church-type missions, the SBC is baptizing fewer than she did with many fewer churches in 1950. These statistics ought to crush every believer's heart and lead to renewed efforts in soul winning. Oswald J. Sanders gives great advice to every church: "The church that does not evangelize will fossilize."[445]

Sanders quotes Watts as saying, "Go into the public assembly with a design to strike and persuade some souls there into repentance and salvation. Go to open blind eyes, to unstop deaf ears, to make the lame walk, to make the foolish wise, to raise those that are dead in trespasses and sins to a heavenly and divine life, and to bring guilty rebels to return to the love and obedience of their Maker by Christ Jesus, the great Reconciler, that they may be pardoned and saved. Go to diffuse the savor of Christ and His

---

[443] Noah, "President Search," accessed May 9, 2010.

[444] Ledbetter, "Better Equipped," January 29, 2007.

[445] Sanders, "Daily Christian Quote," accessed June 9, 2010.

Gospel through a whole assembly and to allure souls to partake of His grace and glory."[446]

Many churches simply swap saints, not save souls. Church switchers are primarily the ones who visit churches, while the unchurched and unsaved stay home. "So," states Ed Stetzer, director of LifeWay Research, "if you build your outreach on recruiting and reaching church visitors, you will often build a church on church switchers.

Attractional evangelism, the focus of reaching people with great programs, has become less and less effective, as fewer of the unchurched are willing to visit a church. Certainly the Christian must keep inviting the lost to attend church, but obviously this will not be the method by which the masses will be reached. Stetzer states that the church must "move from an attractional 'come and see' ministry to an incarnational 'go and tell' ministry, joining Jesus in the harvest field."[447]

331 Soulwinophobia

C. E. Autrey stated, "Many who feel that they cannot visit and fear to try turn out to be the most effective visitors once they have gotten into it."[448] Roland Q. Leavell said, "Fear is a stifling, stultifying, scourging thing for soul winners."[449]

Paul declared, "For God gave us not a spirit of fearfulness; but of power and love and discipline. Be not ashamed therefore of the testimony of our Lord" (II Timothy 1:7 ASV). The Lord's command not to fear is the most repeated command in Scripture. The saturation of the heart and mind with the "fear not" promises of God will incite holy boldness in the soul winner. Personalize these promises, using them as prayers and claiming deliverance from hindering fear (Deuteronomy 31:6, 8; Joshua 8:1; Isaiah 41:10; Hebrews 13:5–6).

332 "Orders Remained Unchanged"

Cliff Barrows, in a message delivered at the dedication of the COSBE Hall of Faith, closed his remarks with a story. He said, "I'm reminded of the

---

[446] Smith, Oswald, *Revival We Need*, Chapter 2.

[447] Kelly, "Evangelism Must Begin," accessed April 22, 2010.

[448] Autrey, *Basic Evangelism*, 80.

[449] Leavell, *Evangelism*, 162.

changing of the guard at the Tomb of the Unknown Soldier in Arlington, Virginia. Every hour on the hour, one group replaces the next one. Only three words are spoken every hour, twenty-four hours a day. Three words are said as one departing group leaves and the other takes their place; here they are: 'Orders remain unchanged.'

"The Church has been given our orders. They are simple. 'Go ye into all the world, and preach the gospel to every creature,' and, 'Lo, I am with you alway, even unto the end of the world.'"[450] No theologian, minister, or religious leader has discretionary power to change the orders. "Orders remain unchanged!"

The Duke of Wellington was once present where a party of Christian men was discussing the possibility of success in missionary effort among the heathen. Appeal was made to the duke to say whether, in his judgment, such efforts were likely to prove a success commensurate to the cost. The old soldier replied: "Gentlemen, what are your marching orders? Success is not the question for you to discuss. If I read your orders aright, they run thus: 'Go ye into all the world, and preach the gospel to every creature.' Gentlemen, obey your marching orders."[451]

The old soldier is right. The Commander-in-Chief has clearly sounded the marching orders; we have no option but to obey.

333 Pray Specifically for the Salvation of Others

C. H. Spurgeon remarked, "There is a general kind of praying which fails for lack of precision. It is as if a regiment of soldiers should all fire off their guns anywhere. Possibly somebody would be killed, but the majority of the enemy would be missed."[452]

David Jeremiah expanded Spurgeon's comment and stated, "How often have we prayed something like, 'O Lord, be with cousin Billy now in a special way'? Have we stopped to consider what it is we're requesting?

"Imagine that you are a parent who is preparing to leave his children with a babysitter. Would you dream of saying, 'O Betsy, I ask you now that you would be with my children in a special way?' No way. You would say, 'Betsy, the kids need to be in bed by 9 p.m. They can have one snack before their baths, and please make sure they finish their homework. You can

---

[450] Ball, "Voice of the Evangelist," 45.

[451] White, *Gospel Workers*, 115.

[452] Spurgeon, "Prayer and Intercession Quotes," accessed May 19, 2010.

reach us at this number if there's any problem. Any questions before we go?' We are very specific with our requests and instructions for our babysitters. We want them to know specifics. It should be no different with prayer."[453]

Specifically pray in this manner regarding the unsaved. "O Lord, I pray for Brandon that his eyes may be open to see personal sin and need of salvation. Tear down the strongholds of evil companionship, pride, and rebellion, that the Gospel may gain entrance into the citadel of his soul. Prepare him for my witness; orchestrate every detail surrounding his life, that I may share the Gospel in power without interruption. Jesus, You died upon the cross for Brandon, and now I claim him for You. I plead Thy precious blood upon his life. Save him for Thy name's sake, I beg. In Jesus' name, amen."

334 He Uses Nothings

Bishop Montgomery stated, "The humble man of God has a curious sense of powerlessness. I have often thought God looked all the world over to find a man weak enough to do the work."

J. G. Gregory said, "Mark the fact that the Lord uses instruments that are remarkable for their weakness."

Paul declared, "But God hath chosen…things which are not, to bring to nought things that are: that no flesh should glory in his presence" (I Corinthians 1:27–29).

We start as nothings, and we should, if we have wisely obeyed God with our substance, leave nothing. J. N. Darby, founder of the Brethren movement, said, "Oh, the joy of having nothing and being nothing, seeing nothing but a living Christ in Glory, and being careful for nothing but His interest down here."

Martin Luther said, "It is the nature of God to make something out of nothing; therefore, when anyone is nothing, God may yet make something of him. Whom God chooses to make wise, He first makes a fool; whom He chooses to make strong, He first renders weak. He delivers to death the man whom He means to quicken; He depresses to Hell whomsoever He intends to call to Heaven."[454]

Adolph Saphir wrote, "We are nothing unless we abide in God; we can do nothing apart from Christ. We know and admit this as a doctrine, but to

---

[453] Jeremiah, "Prayer and Intercession Quotes," accessed May 19, 2010.

[454] Harvey and Harvey, *Royal Insignia*, 142–144.

realize it as a fact, painful and humbling experience is often needed. But in this lowest humiliation is our true and highest exaltation. God takes all things from us that we may turn again to Him as our sure portion; He makes us feel our weakness, our poverty, our ignorance, in order that we may return to Him."[455]

The secret of soul winning is to know that God uses nobodies to win somebodies. This is good news for us all. God takes our inabilities, weaknesses, and imperfections, once laid upon the altar, and turns them into a mighty dynamo to reach the lost.

335 For Heaven's Sake, Don't Let Them Go to Hell

Robert M. M'Cheyne, the Scottish preacher, in a sermon entitled *Future Punishment Eternal,* shared reasons why Christians speak to the unsaved about Hell: because of its reality; love for sinners; to be free from blood-guiltiness. In conclusion of this great message, M'Cheyne said, "Dear brothers and sisters, all this Hell that I have described is what you and I deserved. We were over the lake of fire, but it was from this that Jesus saved us; He was in prison for you and me; He drank every drop out of the cup of God's wrath for you and me; He died, the Just for the unjust.

"O beloved, how should we prize, love, and adore Jesus for what he hath done for us! Oh, we will never, never know, till safe across Jordan, how our Hell has been suffered for us, how our iniquity has been pardoned. But, O beloved, think of Hell. Have you no unconverted friends who are treasuring up wrath against the day of wrath? Oh, have you no prayerless parents, no sister nor brother? Oh, have you no compassion for them, no mercy's voice to warn them?"[456]

The fact of the reality of a literal Hell, personal salvation, Christ's love for sinners and yours for Him, and divine accountability should incite you to warn and win as many as possible to "snatch them as brands from the burning."

---

[455] Ibid., 112.

[456] M'Cheyne, *Sermons,* 167–168; 172–173.

336 "Too Big for God to Use Me"

G. Fred Bergin was director of the Müller Orphan Homes in Bristol. One of his last messages was, "Tell my younger brethren that they may be too big for God to use them, but they cannot be too small."[457]

"Too big for God to use me!" O Lord, forgive my sin,
And let the pride that hinders be taken from within.
So much of self in service the blessing cannot come,
And thus the work is useless which I had thought well done.

"Too big for God to use me!" This is the reason why
Poor longing souls are famished to come and go and die!
O God my Savior, help me, in deep humility,
To make a full surrender henceforth to own but Thee.

"Too big for God to use me!" But if I am possessed
With unction through His Spirit, then shall my work be blessed.
I'll count myself as nothing, seek Christ to magnify,
And use my gifts in service my Lord to glorify.[458]

This was the attitude of Paul, resolving to be nothing, that God could be everything. "Yea doubtless, and I count all things but loss for the excellency of the knowledge of Christ Jesus my Lord: for whom I have suffered the loss of all things, and do count them but dung, that I may win Christ" (Philippians 3:8). May it likewise be yours.

337 Rescue the Perishing

"You can't save a man by telling him of his sins," Fanny Crosby used to say. "He knows them already. Tell him there is pardon and love waiting for him." Rev. S. Trevena Jackson gives the account of the writing of "Rescue the Perishing" as he received it from the lips of Fanny Crosby.

"It was written in the year 1869, when I was forty-nine years old. Many of my hymns were written after experiences in New York mission work. This one was thus written. I was addressing a large company of working men one hot summer evening, when the thought kept forcing itself on my mind that some mother's boy must be rescued that night or not at all. So I

---

[457] Harvey and Harvey, *Royal Insignia*, 105.

[458] Ibid., 105

made a pressing plea that, if there was a boy present who had wandered from his mother's home and teaching, he would come to me at the close of the service.

"A young man of eighteen came forward and said, 'Did you mean me? I promised my mother to meet her in Heaven, but as I am now living, that will be impossible.' We prayed for him, and he finally arose with a new light in his eyes and exclaimed in triumph, 'Now I can meet my mother in Heaven, for I have found God!'

"A few days before, Mr. Doane, the musical composer, had sent me the subject 'Rescue the Perishing,' and while I sat there that evening, the line came to me, 'Rescue the Perishing, care for the dying.' I could think of nothing else that night. When I arrived home, I went to work on the hymn at once, and before I retired, it was ready for the melody. The next day my song was written out and forwarded to Mr. Doane, who wrote the beautiful and touching music as it now stands to my hymn."[459]

Rescue the perishing; care for the dying;
    Snatch them in pity from sin and the grave.
Weep o'er the erring one; lift up the fallen;
    Tell them of Jesus, the mighty to save.

Fanny Crosby, though blind, was a soul winner. Are you?

338   Dim Lights in a Dark World

"On a dark and stormy night, with waves piling up like mountains on Lake Erie, a boat rocked and plunged near the Cleveland harbor. "Are we on course?" asked the captain, seeing only one beacon from the lighthouse.

"Quite sure, Sir," replied the officer at the helm.

"Where are the lower lights?"

"Gone out, Sir."

"Can we make the harbor?"

"We must—or perish!" came the reply. With a steady hand and a stalwart heart, the officer headed the ship toward the land. But, in the darkness, he missed the channel, and the vessel was dashed to pieces on the

---

[459] Ninde, "Christian Biography Resources," accessed May 10, 2010.

rocks. Many lives were lost in a watery grave. This incident moved Philip P. Bliss to write the familiar hymn, "Let the Lower Lights Be Burning."[460]

Paul said, "And even if our gospel is veiled, it is veiled to those who are perishing. The god of this age has blinded the minds of unbelievers, so that they cannot see the light of the gospel of the glory of Christ, who is the image of God" (II Cor. 4:3–4 NIV). Don't let sin dim or veil your light (Matthew 5:16), lest the lost perish in spiritual darkness.

339 "Mr. Gorbachev, Tear Down This Wall"

On June 12, 1987, President Ronald Reagan appealed to Soviet Union General Secretary Mikhail Gorbachev to "tear down this wall." I make this appeal, regarding the wall separating you from the unsaved. "Tear down this wall." Whatever its makeup (apathy, fear, pride, race), it must come down to facilitate connection with the lost, introducing them to Jesus Christ.

God has just the right dynamite to tear it down. It is the dynamite of the Holy Spirit. "For the weapons of our warfare are not carnal, but mighty through God to the pulling down of strong holds; Casting down imaginations, and every high thing that exalteth itself against the knowledge of God, and bringing into captivity every thought to the obedience of Christ" (II Corinthians 10:4–5).

> A wall of my own making stands between the lost and me,
>   Preventing my witnessing to them in perilous need.
>   "Tear down this wall!" I hear Christ plead,
> "To open the channel for the unsaved to hear of Me."

340 Their Salvation Is in God's Hands

A prominent theologian and evangelist heard a preacher tell missionaries in Japan, "Don't worry about people going to Hell because you didn't get the Gospel to them or if you had no soul winning power. Their salvation is in God's hands, not in yours."[461]

I'm sure that kind of teaching didn't incite soul winning among the missionaries! After all, if God is going to save the lost regardless of our witness, why go? If such were the case, He never would have extended the Great Commission (Matthew 28:18–20) mandating the believer to go and

---

[460] Green, *Illustrations for Biblical Preaching*, 401.

[461] Rice, *Predestined to Hell? No!*, 7.

tell all people in every nation the message of salvation, nor clearly stated that Jesus was the only door to salvation (John 10:9) and that the condition for salvation was repentance and faith (Acts 20:21). The preacher was wrong. Christians are to be concerned about people who are going to Hell and exhaust their best effort to win them.

341   A Red-Hot Ball Rolling over the Earth That Is Unstoppable

D. L. Moody stated, "I don't know any work so blessed in Chicago as the going out into the billiard saloons and preaching the Gospel there. If they will not come to church, go down where they are, in the name of our God, and you will reach them. If you say, 'Oh, they will put you out,' I say, 'No, I have never been turned out of a saloon in my life.'

"Go down in a saloon where there are thirty or forty men playing and ask them if they don't want a little singing. They say, 'Yes, we don't mind your singing.'

"'Well, what will you have?' And perhaps they ask you to sing a comic song. 'But we don't know any. We don't know how to sing comic songs. Wouldn't you like to have us sing the "Star Spangled Banner" or "My Country, 'Tis of Thee."' And so you sing 'My Country, 'Tis of Thee,' and they stop playing cards.

"'Now, boys, wouldn't you like to have us sing a hymn our mothers taught us when we were boys?' And then you can sing, 'There Is a Fountain Filled with Blood' or give out 'Rock of Ages, Cleft for Me,' and it won't be long before the hats will be coming off, and they will remember how their mothers sang that to them once when they were in bed. The tears will begin to run down their cheeks, and it won't be long before they will want you to read a few verses out of the Bible. Then they will ask you to pray with them, and you will be having a prayer meeting there before you know it.

"We took sixteen out of a saloon in that way one night, and nine of them went into the inquiry room. What we need in Boston is to go out and get these men. If men will not come out to hear the glorious Gospel of the Son of God, let us take and carry it into these attic homes and saloons. Thank God!

"Boston is going to be visited. Let every man, woman and child help us a little, and we pray that as they go into these attics and these households, the Holy Spirit may help them to present Christ in all His glory and loveliness. Let all take hold and help, and then religion will be like a red-hot ball rolling over the earth, and nothing can stand against it. The churches can be crowded full and the masses reached, if we go about it in the Spirit of the Master."[462]

You have to be awestruck at the passion of Moody for souls. If people didn't come to hear him preach, he went to preach to them. May that same soul-fire possess us and incite our taking the Gospel to wherever the lost are found.

342 Sow the Seed; God Will Take Care of the Results

John Phillips, in his commentary on Psalm 126:5–6, states: "First comes the sowing, 'bearing precious seed.' There is power in a seed. There is life in a seed. There is life in a seed that can crack concrete. There is power in the Word of God, power to overcome all opposition. We must go out and plant it. We must spread the Word. We must broadcast the Gospel. But what if people do not receive it? That is not our concern. That is God's concern....

"Recently, I was staying in the home of a farmer. He told me how he was saved. He had been a bitter, hard-drinking, foul-mouthed sinner. He couldn't understand what people saw in church. It made no sense to him to sit and listen to a preacher when he could be out fishing. His wife kept on urging him, and one Sunday he went with her to church. He forced himself into collar and tie and Sunday suit and sat awkward and unhappy through the sermon. But something that was said convicted him. He went home knowing he was a lost sinner.

"The next morning he had his breakfast and prepared to go out. He had his foot poised over the threshold of his house, when a voice said to him, *If you go out in your sins and have an accident, you'll be in Hell.* He moved his foot back, went into the living room, lit a cigarette, and thought it over. He decided he was imagining things.

"He finished his smoke and headed for the door. As soon as he reached the threshold, the same voice said, *If you go out in your sins and have an accident, you'll be in Hell.* He went back into the house, went upstairs, knelt by his bed, and said, "God, I don't want to go to Hell. Please save me, for Jesus' sake. Amen." Then and there he was saved, and his life was transformed. His foul mouth was cleansed. His cigarettes went into the fire. He began to lead others to Christ. We sow the seed. God takes care of the results."[463]

---

[462] Moody D. L., *To All People*, 168.

[463] Phillips, *Exploring Psalms*, 59–60.

SPURS TO SOUL WINNING

343 Spiritual Battles Won on the Doorstep

Barry Goldwater years ago declared, "The political battles of this generation will be won on the doorstep." Likewise, this is where spiritual battles for man's soul will be won. The Mormons and Jehovah's Witnesses realize this truth and are harvesting on the doorsteps of homes in your community. According to the "Moody Monthly" of November, 1987, these are engaged in the right method but possess the wrong message. In America, Jehovah's Witnesses spend an average of 3,518 hours witnessing for each convert baptized. Witnesses typically spend 60–100 hours monthly evangelizing.[464]

Certainly if adherents to a false doctrine will go to this extent to win a convert, how much farther should the Christian go to win a soul? How much time do you spend weekly witnessing to the lost?

344 Aquarium Keepers

Vance Havner said churches have become aquarium keepers when we are to be fishers of men. We like living in the aquarium. It is climate controlled and user friendly. It is an environment with virtually no risk of rejection or persecution, made up of people that look like us, dress like us, and talk like us. The aquarium is a place of feasting and fellowship among fellow fish with those handpicked to join us. And, yes, it is a place of protection, for its walls separate us from the undesirables outside. By the way, fish normally don't jump into an aquarium.

Fishing in open water is another matter. You really don't know fully what to expect. There is the uncertainty as to whether you will get a reception by the fish and what type fish you will catch—and don't forget the smell! Yet Jesus said, "Follow me and I will make you fishers of men" (Matthew 4:19). It's time to get out of the aquarium to do some serious fishing in the local community pond. Our aquariums are shrinking. Unless we go, this trend will continue to escalate.

345 Counting Fish

D. L. Moody, upon being asked how many souls he had won to Christ, answered, "I don't keep the Lamb's book of life."[465]

No pastor, evangelist, missionary, or layman does. The best man can do is count those who make professions of faith. To number souls won to

---

[464] Unknown Author, "Jehovah's Witnesses," accessed June 1, 2010.

[465] Cook, "Effective Soul Winner," assessed September 22, 2010.

elevate self, achieve the praise of man, or for bragging rights is of the flesh and must be renounced.

I concur with Warren Wiersbe, who said, "There is no place for competition in the work of God, unless we are competing against sin and Satan. When we see words like 'best,' 'fastest growing,' 'biggest,' and 'finest' applied to Christian ministries, we wonder who's getting the glory. This does not mean that it is wrong to keep records. Charles Haddon Spurgeon used to say, 'Those who criticize statistics usually have none to report.' But we must be careful that we are not making others look bad just to make ourselves look good. And we should be able to look at the achievements and blessings of others as if they were our own (Romans 12:10)."[466]

Counting souls won can be advantageous if the flesh is divorced from it. It is good for accountability. It is often shocking for the believer to suddenly discover the weeks or months that have passed without winning a soul. Maintaining a soul-winning record will enable this truth to be known sooner rather than later. It encourages the saint. Broadcasting the number of souls won reminds saints that God is still in the soul-saving business, spurring them forward to witness expectantly. It magnifies God. Sharing life-changing conversion statistics and testimonials brings praise to God.

346 Get Them Signed Up; Then Follow Up

Discipleship training is not optional but imperative to the conservation of new believers. E. J. Daniels states that while pastors (and I add laymen) may be good spiritual obstetricians, they are often poor pediatricians. The soul winner must allow God to use him in both the birthing and cultivating processes.

L. R. Scarborough wrote, "The evangelism that stops at conversion and public profession is lopsided, wasteful, and incomplete. It should go on to teach, to train, and to develop and utilize the talents and powers of the new convert. This educational phase of evangelism is transcendently important." He continued, "Modern evangelism finds here its greatest leakage and waste."[467]

George Sweazey stated, "The second half of evangelism is less exciting than the first. Getting decisions is thrilling. It is like a game that can be scored. The results come rapidly, but bringing those decisions to fulfillment

---

[466] Wiersbe, *Be Free*, 145.

[467] Scarborough, *With Christ*, 107–108.

in an established Christian life is not very dramatic. It takes months instead of minutes."[468]

The soul winner's priority is to reach unsaved men with the Gospel. Follow-up is crucial, but do not regard the chance that it may not be possible as justification for not winning a soul. Don't get the cart before the horse. Win the soul and then do whatever you can about discipleship training. Ultimately, trust God to continue His grace work in the souls saved.

347 The Soul Winner's Six Mighty Motivations

Adrian Rogers counts the Apostle Paul to be the mightiest soul winner of all times. Using II Corinthians 5, he cites what motivated him to be such a great soul winner.

"People asked Paul, 'Why do you work so hard?' And here is his answer.

"The Soul Winner's Compulsion. Paul had a compelling motive that drove him (II Corinthians 5:9). He is simply saying, 'I want to be acceptable to God. I want Him to be pleased with me.' If you're not endeavoring to bring souls to Christ, you are not acceptable to God. I don't care how much money you may give, how faithfully you may attend church, or how faithfully you may live. If you are not endeavoring to bring souls to Jesus Christ, you are not acceptable or pleasing to Him.

"The Soul Winner's Compensation. He was also motivated by future rewards (v. 10). One of these days, our lives will be reviewed before the Lord, and our works will be tested by fire (I Corinthians 3:11–15). It will be a time of reward for some but a time of regret for others. If you're a soul winner, your life will be gold, silver, and precious stones; and you will receive a crown. If you're not, it will be wood, hay, and stubble; and your works will be destroyed.

"The Soul Winner's Conviction. Paul was a soul winner because he knew what it meant for a soul to die unredeemed and go to Hell (v. 11). There is a place of everlasting fire that the Bible calls Hell. But when you lead a soul to Jesus Christ, no longer are they facing an eternity in Hell or the terror of the Lord.

"The Soul Winner's Compassion. Paul was also motivated by an overwhelming compassion that caused some to say he was not mentally stable—that he was 'beside himself' (vv. 13–14). He was driven by the love of Christ that was shown to him. And that love caused him to love others. How can we say we love Jesus and not be concerned for souls He died for?

---

[468] Sweazey, *Effective Evangelism*, 216.

"The Soul Winner's Confidence. Here's his confidence—'if I lead a soul to Christ, he will be a new creature' (v. 16-17). He will become brand new in the Lord Jesus Christ.

The Soul Winner's Commission. And, finally, Paul was motivated by his calling—his commission (v. 18). We too have been called to the ministry of reconciliation. We have been appointed; and if we're not interested in winning souls, we are guilty of treason against Heaven's King. To refuse is not only to be ineffective; it is to be in revolt.

"Do you want to win souls for Christ? What's stopping you? Would you say, 'Lord, with Your help, I will endeavor to win at least one soul for You this year'?"[469]

348 Billy Graham's Focus on Witnessing

Billy Graham was focused on sharing the Gospel in every venue. He always would find a way to do it. The A. Larry Ross firm handled Graham's media and public relations for more than twenty-three years. Ross says, "One of the distinctives of Mr. Graham's ministry has been his ability to make positive points for the Gospel in any situation. You can ask Billy Graham how he gets his suits dry-cleaned on the road, and he'll turn it into a Gospel witness.

"I cut my teeth in the corporate world before I worked with Mr. Graham," says Ross, "and I set up numerous media interviews. Almost always before a TV interview, they do a microphone check, and they ask the interviewee to say something—anything—so they can adjust the audio settings. Often a corporate executive, for that check, will count to ten, say their ABCs, or recite what he had for breakfast. Mr. Graham would always quote John 3:16—'For God so loved the world that he gave his only begotten Son, that whosoever believeth in him should not perish but have everlasting life.' When I asked Mr. Graham why he does that, he replied, 'Because that way, if I am not able to communicate the Gospel clearly during the interview, at least the cameraman will have heard it.'"[470]

Be clever and witty in presenting the Gospel, in even the most unusual places and circumstances. The Gospel is so powerful that even the smallest of its portions can penetrate darkness.

---

[469] Rogers, "Six Mighty Motivations," accessed March 11, 2011.

[470] Myra and Shelley, "Sound Check," accessed May 11, 2010.

SPURS TO SOUL WINNING

349 Firemen Who Don't Fight Fires

A red 1950 fire truck serves the United Nations. This truck has low mileage mostly accumulated in test runs through an underground garage. Though equipped to fight fires, it never has had a major fire alarm.[471]

Many Christians are like this fire truck. They are equipped with all the necessary fire-fighting and life-saving equipment; they are trained and tested but never fight a fire. Content with polishing the fire equipment and routinely having fire drills, they never fight fires seeking to make soul rescues.

"Suppose that, by some painful operation," says C. H. Spurgeon, "you could have your right arm made a little longer. I do not suppose you would care to undergo the operation. But, if you foresaw that by undergoing the pain you would be enabled to reach and save drowning men who otherwise would sink before your eyes, I think you would willingly bear the agony and pay a heavy fee to the surgeon to be thus qualified for the rescue of your fellowmen.

"Realize, then, that to acquire soul-winning power, you will have to go through fire and water, through doubt and despair, through mental torment and soul distress. It will not be the same with all of you, or perhaps with any two of you, but according to the work allotted you will be your preparation. You must go into the fire if you are to pull others out of it, and you will have to dive into the floods if you are to draw others out of the water. You cannot work a fire escape without feeling the scorch of the blaze or man a lifeboat without being covered with the waves. If Joseph were to keep his brothers alive, he himself had to go down into Egypt. If Moses were to lead the people through the wilderness, he must first spend forty years there with his flock."[472]

350 So You Think You Have Endured Enough!

Prior to throwing a self-pity party over the hardship endured for missionary or soul-winning service, consider the grave difficulties that confronted David Brainerd, the first missionary to the American Indians.

David Brainerd's diary entry April 17, 1743, remarks, "It seemed to me I should never have success among the Indians. My soul was weary of my

---

[471] Tan, *A Treasury of Illustrations,* #1692.

[472] Spurgeon, *Soul Winner,* 177–178.

life; I longed for death beyond measure."[473] He felt his prospects for winning souls were "dark as midnight."

May 18, 1743, Brainerd wrote: "My circumstances are such that I have no comfort of any kind but what I have in God. I live in the most lonesome wilderness, have but one single person to converse with that can speak English. Most of the talk I hear is either Highland Scotch or Indian. I have no fellow Christian to whom I might unbosom myself or lay open my conversation about heavenly things and join in social prayer. I live poorly with regard to the comforts of life. Most of my diet consists of boiled corn, hasty pudding, etc. I lodge on a bundle of straw, my labor is hard and extremely difficult, and I have little appearance of success to comfort me."[474]

At the end of July, 1745, things really began to change with the conversion of an Indian landowner named Moses Tautomy. August 16, 1745, Brainerd wrote, "I never saw the work of God appear so independent of means as at this time. I discoursed to the people and spoke what, I suppose, had a proper tendency to promote convictions. But God's manner of working upon them appeared so entirely supernatural and above means that I could scarce believe He used me as an instrument or what I spake as means of carrying on His work....God appeared to work entirely alone, and I saw no room to attribute any of this work to any created arm."[475]

In reading Brainerd's memoirs, one may count him to be a failure, but he was far from it. Few men have exhibited the perseverance in work and passion for souls as he. In his five years of missionary service, he won at least 150 Indians to Christ—a huge victory, especially in that day. Additionally, due to Jonathan Edwards' publishing of the diary of Brainerd's struggles and achievements, scores have been called out into missionary service and encouraged to win souls at all costs. Brainerd died on the mission field at age 29. Remember David Brainerd in times of hardship and discouragement in seeking souls, and be uplifted to press forward.

351 Don't Neglect the Children

"Three Visalia children are lucky to be alive, in large part thanks to the heroic efforts of two neighbors. The pair helped save the three young children from a burning house Wednesday night. It started around seven at a home in Central Visalia. Ediberto Cervantes was working on his car when

---

[473] Edwards, *Life and Diary of David Brainerd*, 119.

[474] Ibid., 124.

[475] Ibid., 224.

the fire erupted next door. He was able to run to the home, despite the flames, and help the mother of five save three small children who were in the home."[476]

We all rejoice in the success of this daring rescue. But how about children who need to be rescued from a burning Hell? Christians should be at least just as eager to save them as this man was to save the neighbor's children. Spurgeon, in *Come Ye Children*, stated, "As soon as a child is capable of being lost, it is capable of being saved. As soon as a child can sin, that child can, if God's grace assist it, believe and receive the Word of God....Believe that children can be saved just as much as yourselves. I do most firmly believe in the salvation of children. When you see the young heart brought to the Savior, do not stand by and speak harshly, mistrusting everything."[477]

Effective witnessing to children hinges upon confidence (they can be saved); communication (clarity of need and the way to be saved); conciseness and conservation (once they are saved). Children are at the ripe time in life to hear and receive the Gospel (Ecclesiastes 12:1).

352 The Real Heroes Are on the Ground

During World War II, it took forty men on the ground to keep one pilot in the air. Sometimes I think we fail to remember that it takes saints "on the ground" to keep evangelists and missionaries on the field. Embrace those who are winning souls with continuous prayers, encouragement, and monetary support. These servants well know that without your backing their "plane" would never get off the ground, hindering God's mission from being accomplished. Support of soul winners is an indirect but definite way to win souls. It is my conviction that the believer who enables another to win souls at home or on the mission field is credited in Heaven along with that servant for all the souls he reaches for Christ.

353 Silence Is Golden

Silence certainly is golden in times of soul winning when the Holy Spirit clearly forbids the soul winner to share a witness. It is for a divine purpose. Brother Andrew, God's smuggler, shares about a girl who became a Christian because he didn't share the Gospel with her when he had the perfect opportunity. This Spirit-led unwillingness on his part seized this

---

[476] Unknown Author, "Children Saved," accessed May 11, 2010.

[477] Spurgeon, *Come Ye Children,* 101, 103.

266

girl's heart with fear, causing her to think she was moving past the hope of salvation and prompting a decision of salvation. Scripture teaches that the Lord ordereth the steps of a good man (Psalms 37:23), and I add that his tongue is ordered also. The soul winner must "walk in the Spirit" in order "to be led by the Spirit" in witnessing encounters (Galatians 5:25; Romans 8:14).

354 Saved by a Letter

A moving story is told in Graham Twelftree's *Drive the Point Home*. A young man, Jimmy Lee Davis, was sentenced to death row for rape and murder. Even his mother wrote to the state governor, "Don't reprieve him. What he has done is so bad I want my boy to die." A news magazine from America carried the headline: "'I Want My Son to Die,' Says Mother."

A young Pentecostal man in Melbourne, Australia, read the story. He was moved to write to Jimmy and tell him that Jesus loved him. To his amazement, he got a letter back saying, "It's the most wonderful letter I have ever had in my life. I do wish I could meet you. I just wish I could know Jesus in my life like you do. I've made such a mess of it. You have given me hope."

The young man felt that God wanted him to go to America and visit Jimmy. After praying and sharing the idea with friends, he raised the money and went. By a series of coincidences, he got permission to go into death row twice a week for four hours a visit for two months. He took his guitar, and they sang choruses, told jokes, and laughed—and he led Jimmy to Jesus. His last visit was to Jimmy's baptism. For two years, Jimmy's faith grew. In one of his letters, he wrote, "There is one thing I'm not going to do. I'm not going to dishonor the Gospel by using my conversion to escape the death penalty."

Then one day the young man in Melbourne got a ring from his wife. "Can you come home at once? Jimmy's just got permission to ring us from prison; he's being executed tonight." He tore home and got through to the prison two hours before Jimmy was due in the gas chamber. But he just broke down and cried on the phone. However, Jimmy, at the other end, said, "I love you, man. Thank you for all that you have done for me. I've got to go now. Goodbye. Be seeing you." And Jimmy hung up.[478]

Due to distance or verbal difficulty in witnessing to someone, the writing of an evangelistic letter or card is a tool to use. Roland Q. Leavell wrote, "A postage stamp is a mighty ally in soul winning. In a letter, one

---

[478] Tripp, "Stories of Faith," accessed May 11, 2010.

can write smoothly and succinctly the essential things of salvation which the unsaved man should believe and accept."[479]

C. H. Spurgeon said, "Paper and ink are never better used than in soul winning."[480] Henry Clay Trumbull was won by a letter.

355   The Power of the Pen

Billy Graham stated that part of the neglect of soul winning is attributable to so little writing on the subject. Graham cited that he had only a handful of books in his library on soul winning.[481]

When I was checking resources for this present writing, I found that the local Christian bookstore carried seven or eight volumes on evangelism, and only one volume dealing strictly with soul winning! I also discovered in a major Christian university library, though numerous volumes on the subject were found, most dated back 50 to 100 years. Authors, I challenge you to write on soul winning. The church sorely needs such books to regain focus and instruction regarding her primary business.

Don't dismiss the power of the pen. D. M. Patton wrote, "Christian literature never tires, never grows disheartened, never flinches, and never shows cowardice. It is never tempted to compromise; it travels cheaply and requires no hired hall; it works long after we are dead."

Oswald Smith wrote, "What was it that gave us the Reformation? You say it was Martin Luther's preaching. I do not believe that it was. Martin Luther wrote nearly one hundred books and circulated them throughout Western Europe, and as a result of the writings of Martin Luther, there came the Reformation. Where would you have been today if it had not been for the Reformation? I believe that the greatest miracle of our day and generation is the increasing literacy around the world. Three million people learn to read every seven days."[482]

I can testify of the power of the pen in the hand of men like A. W. Tozer, C. E. Autrey, John Bisagno, Andrew Murray, Oswald Smith, C. H. Spurgeon, George Sweazey, C. E. Matthews, L. R. Scarborough, and Roland Leavell in my life. Though long dead, these men and others like

---

[479] Leavell, *Winning Others*, 94.

[480] Spurgeon, *Sermons on Soul Winning*, 19.

[481] Olford, *Successful Soul Winning*, Foreword.

[482] Panton, "Printed Page," 8.

them have impacted my life beyond description with their writings. I am indebted for their discipline to write, especially in a time when doing so was no easy chore. I do give hearty thanks to these men, for through them, my spiritual life has been deeply enriched and my abilities to minister sharpened. I cut my teeth in evangelism studying *Basic Evangelism* by C. E. Autrey and *The Power of Positive Evangelism* by John Bisagno.

D. L. Moody said, "Think of Paul up yonder. People are going up every day and every hour, men and women brought to Christ through his writings. He set streams in motion that have flowed on for more than a thousand years. I can imagine people going up to him and saying, 'Paul, thank you for writing that letter to the Ephesians; I found Christ in that.' 'Paul, thank you for writing that epistle to the Corinthians.' 'Paul, I found Christ in that epistle to the Philippians.' 'Thank you, Paul, for that epistle to the Galatians; I found Christ in that.' When Paul was in prison, he didn't fold his hands and sit down in idleness! No, he began to write. And his epistles have come down through the ages and brought thousands upon thousands to a knowledge of Christ crucified."[483]

The passion of every Christian author is, or should be (certainly is mine), that their writings bear spiritual fruit in decisions of salvation, surrender, sacrifice, and service, as did Paul's. This is the ultimate reward I, as an author, desire.

So why write? Write you must, if the Holy Spirit presses a burden upon your heart which He wants to become a book. The Holy Ghost thrusts a person into writing! Write to enlarge the coast of your influence for the Kingdom regarding a specific matter. The silent page will bear the author's witness in pulpits, villages, cities, countries, schools, colleges, and seminaries where physically he will never be invited.

Write to impact lives for time and eternity for the Lord. Men and women have been saved by means of a book, preachers have been encouraged and enabled for ministry through a book, students have been called into ministry as a result of a book, and saints have been strengthened spiritually due to a choice book. Write to leave a message for future generations. Write, and in so doing, extend your ministry beyond this life. Books are like streams that flow long after we are dead and gone, carried by the current of the Spirit impacting lives.

Never underestimate the temporal and future value of a book in the hands of an Almighty God. If He but chooses (even in the absence of eloquence and perfect literary style), the Holy Spirit may blow His breath upon its sails, enabling its far and wide circulation to His glory and honor.

---

[483] Moody D. L., "Paul, I Found Christ," 18.

Pray for better books to be written and for their profitability to the cause of Christ.

356 Plow, Plant, Pluck

Witnessing is not soul winning, but it certainly opens the door to soul winning. Not every person confronted is ready for a soul winning presentation; they stand in need of a witness first. A witness is the plowing of the hard soil in the soul with the gospel plow, a task that may be tedious and lengthy. A witness is the planting and watering of the precious seed in the soul. Soul winning is the plucking of the fruit produced by the plowing, planting, and watering. This is why Paul said, "Who then is Paul, and who is Apollos, but ministers by whom ye believed, even as the Lord gave to every man? I have planted, Apollos watered; but God gave the increase. So then neither is he that planteth any thing, neither he that watereth; but God that giveth the increase. Now he that planteth and he that watereth are one: and every man shall receive his own reward according to his own labour. For we are labourers together with God: ye are God's husbandry, ye are God's building" (I Corinthians 3:5–9).

Don't discount the immense value of the plowing stage, the planting stage, and the watering stage of witnessing. They are part and parcel of the teamwork God has devised to win souls. As believers, we lock arms together in the harvest field.

357 Watch for God at Work and Join Him

Henry Blackaby, in the classic book *Experiencing God,* told the students at his church, "According to these passages (Romans 3:10–11; John 6:44), people do not seek God on their own initiative. People don't ask questions about spiritual matters unless God is at work in their lives. When you see someone seeking God or asking questions about Christianity, you are witnessing God at work. That is something that only God does in people's lives."[484]

"That Sunday, I told the students, 'If during the course of your day attending class, someone starts asking you spiritual questions, whatever else you planned to do, don't do it. Cancel what you had planned and spend time with that individual to discover what God is doing.' That week our students went onto campus, watching to see where God was at work so they could join Him."[485]

---

[484] Blackaby, *Experiencing God*, 69.

[485] Ibid., 70.

A female student testified that a girl she had attended class with for two years approached her wanting to talk. Remembering what Blackaby had told them, she immediately changed plans and skipped class to talk with her. The girl told her that 13 girls had been studying the Bible, but none of them were a Christian, and they wanted someone to start a Bible study with them. As a result of this one encounter, three Bible studies were started in the girls' dorm and two in the boys' dorm. Over the following years, hundreds of students were saved as a result of this church's student ministry. "Right now, God is working all around you."[486]

Keep watching for Him at work, and immediately stop what you are doing and join Him. Watch for God at work among fellow employees, at school among classmates, at home among family members, and in the locker room among teammates. When people talk of spiritual matters, God is at work!

Some years ago I had witnessed to an employee at a Waffle House and believed God was at work in his life. As distinctly as if it was only yesterday, I remember seeing him later walking on the highway, and I passed him by due to a dentist appointment I had just enough time to make. I never saw that man again. I was wrong to pass up that opportunity, and should that man die lost, his blood will be on my hands. God has never let me escape the memory of that day, and it serves to remind me of the need to strike while the iron is hot.

G. Campbell Morgan offers great advice for every believer, especially the soul-winning kind. "I never begin my work in the morning without thinking that perhaps He may interrupt my work and begin His own."[487]

358 Our Duty to Those at the Top

L. R. Scarborough, in writing of *Our Duty to Men at the Top,* makes this observation. "This case of personal evangelism in which Jesus sought to win, and probably did win, this big moralist (Nicodemus), the man in high position, ought to be a strong, burning lesson and message to preachers and soul winners everywhere. It does not take much courage for us to go into the downtown missions, the jails, the shops, the factories, and the hospitals to speak about Christ and salvation to the men and women who are down and out or who are helpless behind prison bars or on beds of disease or are men of the commoner walks of life; but it does take courage to approach

---

[486] Ibid., 70.

[487] Tan, *7700 Illustrations*, 1586–1587.

men high in the social, political, commercial, professional, and official world.

"There are many thousands of them who are high in position and in popularity but lost just the same, and they are neglected. When we see them, we talk about something else. We are afraid to boldly tell them of their sins and of their destiny in Hell without Christ. We are afraid of offending them. This case of Nicodemus is a great lesson to all of us who meet our friends in the upper walks of life....I have made up my mind not to neglect the sinners who are up and out as well as those who are down and out."[488]

Many times in soul winning, believers are happy in fishing for the "fish" easiest to catch. I challenge you to tackle "fish" that are presumed to be more difficult to reel in for Jesus—the boss, the supervisor, the coach, the teacher, the politician, the banker. These people have the same problem (sin and separation from God) as everyone else, although they may mask it better. They need what Jesus Christ alone can provide. Brazen up and speak to them.

359   Saved through a Sound Check

C. H. Spurgeon tested the acoustics of the Crystal Palace in London by citing "Behold the Lamb of God, which taketh away the sin of the world" (John 1:29). Unknown to him, a workman was working high up in the dome. The workman did not know that Spurgeon was speaking on the platform. The message of God's great love for the world thundered from the great platform below upward to the lone man's ears and heart, smiting him immediately with deep conviction of sin. This man left his tools, went to his room, and gave his heart to Christ. Feeling a call to preach, he surrendered and proclaimed the Gospel to the lost for a quarter of a century.[489]

The simple reciting of John 1:29 was all it took to win that man. Why are we so determined to complicate what God made simple? You may not have much when it comes to soul-winning ability, but it doesn't take much to win souls. Spurgeon concluded from the above experience, "How well it is to utter great texts, even when we are not preaching, for they are arrows from the quiver of God and will not fly abroad in vain."[490]

---

[488] Scarborough, *How Jesus Won Men*, 68–69.

[489] Ibid., 15.

[490] Hayden, *Unforgettable Spurgeon*, 208.

360 Tongue-Tied Saints

"Sometimes Christians," says J. Vernon McGee, "are very reluctant to witness. We are all tongue-tied at times, but we ought not to be."[491]

Never be ashamed of Christ, in the daylight or twilight, in the bliss of life or throes of death, in the solitude or multitude. Boldly bear His name and cause to one and all without intimidation or hesitation. Review how tradition suggests the disciples died for not being ashamed of Christ, and be challenged never to cower down.

Peter was crucified upside-down.
Andrew was crucified.
James, son of Zebedee, was killed by a sword.
John, brother of James, died of old age.
Philip was crucified.
Bartholomew was crucified.
Thomas was killed by a spear.
Matthew was killed by a sword.
James, son of Alphaeus, was crucified.
Thaddaeus was killed by arrows.
Simon the Zealot was crucified.
Paul was beheaded by Nero.

A Christian who was to work at a lumber camp was advised by another not to let the lumberjacks know he was a Christian or else he would be scorned. When the Christian returned home, the friend inquired, "Well, how did you get along with the lumberjacks?"

The man replied, "All right. They didn't find out."[492]

"For I am not ashamed of the gospel of Christ: for it is the power of God unto salvation" (Romans 1:16).

361 Unknown Fruit

One day as he was walking in a street in the city of Lausanne, Felix Neff, the Swiss reformer, saw at a distance a man whom he took for one of his friends. He ran behind him, tapped him on the shoulder before looking him in the face, and asked him, "What is the state of your soul, my friend?" The stranger turned. Neff perceived his error, apologized, and went his way.

---

[491] McGee, *Thru the Bible*, II Timothy 1:12.

[492] Hallock, *Evangelistic Cyclopedia*, 37.

Some three or four years afterward, a man came to him, indebted for a great kindness. Neff did not recognize him and begged him to explain. The stranger replied, "Have you forgotten an unknown person whose shoulder you touched in the street in Lausanne, asking him, 'What is the state of your soul?' It was I. Your question led me to serious reflection. Now I find it is well with my soul."[493]

Neff learned of the powerful impact of his simple words to the mistaken stranger. You and I may not, at least not until our arrival in Heaven. The power of gospel words shot as burning arrows to the heart of men does its convicting and converting work often without our knowledge; therefore, keep shooting gospel arrows, for you never know when such a word will turn the course of a man.

362 "Saved and Saving"

The famous evangelist D. L. Moody said, "I thought it was the finest thing I had ever seen, at the time, and I bought it. It was the picture of a man floundering in the water and clinging with both hands to the Cross of Refuge. But afterward I saw another picture which spoiled this one for me entirely—it was so much lovelier. It was a picture of a person coming out of the dark waters with one arm clinging to the Cross, but with the other she was lifting someone else out of the waves."[494]

Gerard Hallock comments on Moody's statement. "Yes, 'saved' is good, but we all will agree that 'saved and saving' is a far better and nobler picture of the Christian life. Saved and saving—keeping a firm hold upon the cross ourselves, but striving ever to lift other souls from the dark billows of sin that beat on the dangerous coast of eternity! Poor, weak, and feeble men and women that we are, God will use us if we are willing....To be sure, we cannot convert men, but telling them the Gospel and persuading them to accept it is our work. Conversion is God's work, but if we do ours, God will do His."[495]

Today, with one hand securely clinging to the Cross, use the other to reach down to save the drowning.

---

[493] Stevens, "National Magazine," 224.

[494] Tan, *A Treasury of Illustrations,* #5871.

[495] Hallock, *Evangelistic Cyclopedia,* 164–165.

363 Your Brother Is Down There

Years ago in Victoria Park on the east side of London, as construction was taking place for a new drain, a collapse took place, burying men beneath tons of dirt. People gathered around to view what had taken place. One man standing near the brink of the cave-in watching the rescue attempt unfold was touched on the shoulder by a woman who said, "Bill, your brother is down there." You should have witnessed the change in this man. Off came his coat, and into the trench he jumped, working as hard as ten men.[496]

Among the multitudes buried beneath the burden and penalty of sin (the lost) is your brother or your sister or your son or your daughter! Stop being a spectator, fling off your coat, and jump into the trench to rescue them before they perish. If I knew that my brother was lost, I would work as Bill—ten times as hard as other Christians—to win him to faith.

364 The Eightieth Time Did It

J. H. Jowett tells the account of a man who worked in their Institute during the day, only to spend his evenings in the gap between God and sinners. This soul winner had his eyes fixed on the saving of a man whom Jowett called "a perfect beast—devil-ridden, lust-ridden, battered, bruised, altogether in bondage." Night by night, effort was made to rescue this man from sin. Finally, this soul winner brought news to Jowett exclaiming, "Mr. Jowett, the eightieth time did it."

Jowett remarks, "Eighty nights, seventy-nine failures—the eightieth time he got the man to the Institute. By the mercy of man, he led him to the mercy of God, and tonight, while I speak, he is at home in Christ."[497]

How convicting is this story! Most try to win a man once or twice and give up—certainly not eighty times! We would do well to learn a lesson in perseverance in soul winning from Jowett's employee. All are prone to give up too easily in winning a soul.

365 "I Couldn't Leave Him, Could I?"

In the flood of 1919 in Corpus Christi, Texas, Esther Fuller, seventeen years of age, battled the swelling waters, holding onto her eleven-year-old

---

[496] Ibid., 30–31.

[497] Ibid., 88.

unconscious brother for five hours. Recounting the event, Esther said, "I couldn't leave him, could I?"[498]

Every Christian should possess this attitude regarding those drowning in sin: "I couldn't leave him, could I?" Exhausting labor is required in soul winning, but Christ will provide the strength equal to the task. God forbid we walk away from one drowning in sin, leaving him to die! Always carry and be ready to use the "lifeline" to save perishing men.

366 A Human Ladder Rescue

A parsonage burned in Epworth, England, and all appeared to have been saved, when the minister noticed one of his children at a window crying to for help. Immediately, men made a human ladder, one standing upon the shoulders of the next, until the window was reached and the boy was saved. Who was that young boy? John Wesley, the great Methodist evangelist. Ponder it—a human ladder to save a Wesley, whom God used mightily for the advancement of the Gospel. In all probability, the people who formed the human ladder told with joy for years to follow how they saved him.[499]

Soul winning may be likened to the rescue of men entrapped in a burning building on a high floor that requires a human ladder. One person's reach is not high enough. However, the reach of several working together may be. What a joy to jointly rescue a damned soul! And who but knows it may be a Wesley who will shake a continent for God?

367 Leave Her and Live, or Die with Her

At Myrtle Beach, South Carolina, when I was a college student, I saw two teenagers drowning, probably forty yards from me in the ocean. I immediately made a rescue attempt, first by helping the boy (who was closest to me) recover, and then I assisted the girl. I found her most difficult to help. Struggling, she kept trying to lock arms around my neck, which would have drowned us both had she succeeded. Fighting the ocean current and her was a grave challenge. I recall clearly thinking that I had a choice to make—leave her and live or die with her. Fortunately, I was wrong in the assumption that these were my only two choices. I chose to save her or die trying, and by God's grace, I did save her. As I reached the shore, life guards arrived to help.

---

[498] Ibid., 95.

[499] Ibid., 111.

Isn't it odd how a person resolves to give his life to save a complete stranger without forethought? This same resolve must be exhibited toward strangers about us who are drowning in the ocean of depravity, depression, and destruction, to save them without consideration of cost or sacrifice. Don't attempt a soul rescue for praise or glory but because it is the right and noble thing to do. This young lady, still unknown to me, did not once express gratitude for what I did, nor did she need to. Knowing she was saved is enough.

368   Follow-Up or Foul-Up

Claude King cites, "There may be multiple reasons that we are failing to assimilate new Christians for active participation in the body of Christ. Here are a few thoughts:

"1. They need to be helped at the very foundational aspects of Christian living: how to pray, how to win victory over sin, how to hear God speak through His Word, etc.

"2. They need to get plugged in to a small group where they can experience the full benefits of belonging to a body that knows, loves, and cares for one another.

"3. They need to be encouraged very early on to understand that the call to follow Christ is a call to active duty, and then they need help to find their place to serve the Lord through the body. Far too many have joined the Christian Reserve Corps (reserve me a place in Heaven and don't ask me to do anything until then). God's Spirit flows through those who are actively serving Him.

"4. They need to be helped to experience a deep and abiding love for Christ, the wounded Savior, so they will choose to obey His commands.

"5. They need to be set free from the love for the world and the things of the world that may choke out their first love for Christ. I'm sure there are many more."[500]

Paul instructs older women in the church to mentor the young women in regard to seven matters (Titus 2:2–5). The older men in the church have an equal responsibility to mentor the young men. Be a Barnabas and "adopt" the new convert. The Apostle Paul would not have become what he was for God had it not been for Barnabas in his early life. Barnabas took Paul under his wings while he was just a babe in Christ and developed him in the things of Christ.

---

[500] King. Personal Correspondence. May 12, 2010.

Of this, Luke wrote, "But Barnabas took him [Paul] and brought him to the apostles, and declared unto them how he had seen the Lord in the way, and that he had spoken to him, and how he had preached boldly at Damascus in the name of Jesus" (Acts 9:27). The words "took him" literally mean that Barnabas physically held on to Paul to help him.

It is important that all new converts have a Barnabas to "hold on" to them by supplying love, guidance and protection from spiritual harm. Wiersbe wrote, "The term 'disciples' was the most popular name for the early believers. Being a disciple meant more than being a convert or a church member. 'Apprentice' might be an equivalent term. A disciple attached himself to a teacher, identified with him, learned from him, and lived with him. He learned, not simply by listening, but also by doing."[501]

The failure of the spiritually mature to coach (be a Barnabas to) new believers (and preacher boys) is the great weakness of the modern church movement.

369   Enemies of the Soul Winner

"We have constant need of watchfulness, lest we grow cold. A garden uncultivated runs into weeds. A body unfed tends toward death. A vessel not propelled is sure to drift. A fire not increasing is going out. There are so many currents to carry the Christian back that only constant effort can keep him advancing."[502]

"The captain of a ship sailing from Cuba in a storm thought he had gone sixty miles, but when the clouds disappeared, he discovered he had lost thirty miles. The undercurrent had taken the ship back. The Christian like-wise is apt to drift by undercurrents. Continuously we must take our bearings."[503]

The undercurrents of business, pleasure, disappointment, biblical untruth and cold formality in Christian devotion and duty gradually but surely will extinguish the soul-winning fire. Paul told young Timothy (all believers) to keep fanning the flame, lest the undercurrents (enemies of soul winning) shipwreck his vessel (II Timothy 1:6). 'Take heed lest you fall' (I Corinthians 10:12).

---

[501] Wiersbe, *Bible Expository Commentary*, Matthew 28:20.

[502] Hallock, *Evangelistic Cyclopedia*, 211.

[503] Ibid., 211.

Billy Sunday provides a resolute challenge to the Christian: "Let's quit fiddling with religion and do something to bring the world to Christ."[504]

370 You Know You Are a Soul Winner When...

You know you are a Soul Winner when:

You win souls whether anyone knows you do or not
You win souls whether others do or not
You win souls out of delight instead of duty
You win souls to save them from condemnation, not in competition
You win souls for Christ's glorification, not reputation or gratification
You will talk to anybody, anywhere, anytime about being saved
You get up in the morning praying for opportunities to win souls
You possess a harvest mind, ever looking for the chance to win souls
You regularly pray for lost souls to be saved
You win souls for love of Christ, not the commendation of the pastor
Your day is incomplete without talking to a person about Christ

Pursue the heart of a soul winner. Work at it. Cultivate it. Soul winning is absolutely the greatest work on earth. The great preacher Lyman Beecher was asked, "Mr. Beecher, what do you consider the greatest thing a human being can do or be?"

Without hesitation, the famous pulpiteer replied, "The greatest thing is not that one should be a scientist, important as that is; nor that one should be a statesman, vastly important as that is; nor even that one should be a theologian, immeasurably important as that is. But the greatest thing of all is for one human being to bring another human being to Christ."[505]

C. H. Spurgeon stated, "Every Christian is either a missionary or an imposter."[506]

371 Nothing Substitutes for Winning Souls

C. H. Spurgeon states, "Now take note; if you or I or any or all of us will have spent our lives merely in amusing or educating or moralizing men, when we come to give in our account at the last great Day, we will be in a very sorry condition. We shall have but a very sorry record to render.

---

[504] Ellis, *"Billy" Sunday*, 61.

[505] Wiersbe, *World Evangelism*, 21.

[506] Clark, "New England Baptist," accessed May 14, 2010.

Of what avail will it be to a man to be educated when he comes to be damned? Of what service will it be to him to have been amused when the trumpet sounds, heaven and earth are shaking, and the pit opens wide her jaws of fire and swallows up the soul unsaved? Of what avail will it have been even to have moralized a man, if still he is on the left hand of the Judge and if 'Depart from me, ye cursed' (Matthew 25:41) will still be his portion? Blood red with the murder of men's souls will be the skirts of professing Christians, unless the end and aim of all their work has been to 'save some.'"[507]

A man fell in a pit and couldn't get out (Psalm 40:2).

A *subjective* person came along and said, "I feel for you down there!"

An *objective* person came along and said, "It's logical that someone would fall down there."

A *Christian Scientist* came by and said, "You only think you are in the pit."

A *pharisee* said, "Only bad people would fall in a pit. You deserve your pit."

A *mathematician* calculated how he fell in the pit.

A *news reporter* wanted the exclusive story on his pit.

Confucius said, "If you would have listened to me, you would not have fallen into that pit."

Buddha said, "Your pit is only a state of mind."

A *realist* said, "That's a pit."

A *scientist* calculated the pressure necessary (lbs./sq. in.) to get him out of the pit.

A *geologist* told him to appreciate the rock strata in the pit.

An *evolutionist* said, "You are a rejected mutant destined to be removed from the evolutionary cycle." In other words, "He is going to die in the pit, so he can't produce any pit-falling offspring."

The *county inspector* asked if he had a permit to dig the pit.

A *professor* gave him a lecture on the elementary principles of the pit.

An *evasive* person came along and avoided the subject of pits all together.

A *self-pitying* person came along and said, "You haven't seen anything until you've seen my pit.

---

[507] Spurgeon, *Soul Winner*, 242–243.

A *soul winner,* seeing the man, told him about Jesus, who alone could deliver him from the pit. The man was saved, and now this man spends his time helping others out of their own pits (soul winning).[508]

Christ has delivered you from a horrible pit of darkness, depravity, despair, and eternal separation from God (Psalm 40:1–3). As someone told you about Jesus who would grant a miraculous rescue from the pit, tell others.

372 What's Wrong with This Picture?

R. A. Torrey recounts this story. "A blind woman came to my office in Chicago and said, 'You don't think my blindness will keep me from doing Christian work, do you?'

"I replied, 'On the contrary, it might be a great help. A great many people, seeing your blindness, will come and sit down with you; then you can talk with them about the Saviour.'

"'That is not what I mean. When a woman can talk to five or six hundred, she doesn't want to spend time talking to one.'

"I answered, 'Your Master could talk to five thousand at once, for we have it on record; but He didn't think it beneath His dignity to talk to one at a time.'"[509]

This blind woman's attitude is symptomatic of many in the church (preacher and layman). Waiting to speak to the large gatherings, they walk past needy sinners. They will in a heartbeat, perhaps, stand to testify for Christ in the church, prison, rescue mission, or crusade but count it too mean a task to speak to the lone sinner. What's wrong with this picture?

373 The Biggest Blunder in Soul Winning

"The best way to learn how to do it," says R. A. Torrey, "is to do it. 'He that goeth forth and weepeth, bearing precious seed, shall doubtless come again with rejoicing, bringing his sheaves with him.' If, however, you make a stupid blunder the first time, go at it again. But if you never start until you are sure you will not make a blunder, you will make the biggest blunder of your life. Get alone with God first and see if you are right with Him. Put

---

[508] Unknown Author, "The Pit," accessed May, 14, 2010.

[509] Torrey, "Importance of Soul Winning," accessed May 15, 2010.

away every known sin out of your life, surrender absolutely to God, ask for the fullness of the Holy Spirit, and then pitch in."[510]

374 The Form of the Cup Doesn't Matter

Alexander Maclaren wrote, "If we are true to our Lord, we shall feel that we cannot but speak up and out for Him, and that all the more where His name is unloved and unhonored. He has left His good fame very much in our hands, and the very same impulse that hurries words to our lips when we hear the name of an absent friend calumniated should make us speak for Him. He is doubtfully a loyal subject who, if he lives among rebels, is afraid to show his colors. He is already a coward and is on the way to being a traitor.

"Our Master has made us His witnesses. He has placed in our hands, as a sacred deposit, the honor of His name. He has entrusted to us, as His most select sign of confidence, the carrying out of the purposes for which on earth His blood was shed and on which in Heaven His heart is set. How can we be loyal to Him if we are not forced by a mighty constraint to respond to His great tokens of trust in us, and if we know nothing of that spirit which said, 'Necessity is laid upon me; yea, woe is unto me, if I preach not the gospel!' (I Corinthians 9:16)? I do not say that a man cannot be a Christian unless he knows and obeys this impulse. But at least we may safely say that he is a very weak and imperfect Christian who does not.

"'They *spake.*' It was no set address, no formal utterance, but familiar, natural talk to ones and twos as opportunity offered. The form was so simple that we may say there was none. What we want is that Christian people should speak anyhow. What does the shape of the cup matter? What does it matter whether it be gold or clay? The main thing is that it shall bear the water of life to some thirsty lip.

"All Christians have...to tell the Good News. Their task is to carry a message. No refinement of words is needed for that; arguments are not needed. They have to tell it simply and faithfully, as one who cares to respect what he has had given to him. They have to tell it confidently, as having proved it true. They have to tell it beseechingly, as loving the souls to whom they bring it. Surely we all can do that, if we ourselves are living on Christ and have drunk into His Spirit. Let His mighty salvation, experienced by yourselves, be the substance of your message; and let the

---

[510] Ibid., accessed May 15, 2010.

form of it be guided by the old words, 'And the spirit of the Lord will come upon thee…that thou do as occasion serve thee' (I Samuel 10:6–7)."[511]

375   Preaching Failed, but Personal Contact Succeeded

Billy Graham stated that "God has a lot of preachers but few soul winners."[512] Pastors, descend the pulpit platform and engage in one-to-one soul confrontation with the congregation and those in the community.

A prominent pastor of years ago said, "I laid my hands upon the shoulder of a noble specimen of young manhood and asked him if he was a Christian. I had not seen him to know him or to separate him from the crowd before that moment. He replied, with an evident desire to detain me, 'No sir; I have heard you preach every Sunday for seven years without exception, but I am not a Christian yet.' He is now one of the most faithful members of the church. What seven years of preaching had failed to do, five minutes of heart contact and personal relation accomplished."[513]

"Mr. Moody, what is the way to reach the masses with the Gospel?"

"Go for them," he would reply.[514]

376   Got Your Ticket

George Sherwood Eddy tells of a predicament he was placed in by a rule of the Chinese of Canton, which required a ticket in order to gain admittance into a Christian service. "The ticket in this instance was not a piece of cardboard, but a person prepared to receive the message of Christianity. I pushed my way through the crowd and presented myself at the door. The usher stopped me and asked if my ticket was with me. 'Ticket?' I asked in surprise. 'Why I am the speaker.'

"'We know you are the speaker, Mr. Eddy, but the rule is no one is to be admitted without a ticket, and we can make no exception in your case.' Mr. Eddy was puzzled at the first but then decided to meet the condition. He

---

[511] Wiersbe, *World Evangelism*, 44; 46.

[512] Olford, *Secret of Soulwinning*, Foreword.

[513] Hallock, *Evangelistic Cyclopedia*, 214.

[514] Ibid., 215.

sought out Sun Yat Sen, the first President of the China Republic, to be his ticket. In the service, Eddy delivered an evangelistic message.[515]

What if the church you attend required such a "ticket" for admittance this Sunday? Would you be granted entrance? What a worthy challenge the Chinese of Canton present to the Christians in their land and ours! Rule or no rule, God help us as His children to bring a "ticket" to church and revival.

377   A Little Push Saved Her

In an evening service, a lady for whom a minister had been praying regarding salvation was in attendance. The minister preached earnestly, seeking to reach her. Following the sermon, he asked all interested in knowing Christ to meet him in the inquiry room. As he approached the room, he noticed this very young woman hesitating at the door. He spoke a simple word of encouragement to her as he passed, placed his hand gently on her arm, and gave the slightest suggestion of a push toward the door. She made the decision to come in. Later this woman testified it was that little push that prompted her to be saved.[516]

Many of the unsaved are hesitating at the "door" of salvation and with a light, gentle push will enter. Speak words of encouragement to those who you know are tottering near salvation to enter the "door" to be saved before it is eternally too late. "A word fitly spoken is like apples of gold in pictures of silver" (Proverbs 25:11). "A word spoken in due season, how good is it!" (Proverbs 15:23). Almost saved is not saved. Not far from the Kingdom is not the same as being *in* the Kingdom. He whose soul is aroused to be saved must be persuaded to do so without delay.

378   Saved by a Scrap of Paper

A soldier, while on sentry duty, found a piece of paper on which was written the hymn, "We're traveling home to Heaven above; will you go? Will you go?" This soldier had been contemplating a decision for Christ but was hesitating. The words of this hymn were the final straw to lead him to decide for Christ. Under the hymn, he inscribed, "By the grace of God, I'll go. John Waught, Company Y, U.S. Volunteers. June 26, 1863." He

---

[515] Ibid., 215–216.

[516] Ibid., 225.

announced this decision for Christ at the next chaplain's meeting with the troops.[517]

There is no length to which God will not go to save a soul, even to the extent of using a stanza of a hymn on a scrap of paper or merging your life with the unsaved at a choice moment. Certainly if God can orchestrate the use of a scrap of paper in the saving of a soldier's soul, He can also do so with you.

379 Don't Win the World and Let Your Own Boy Go to Hell

The great eloquent preacher R. G. Lee told the story of a boy dying in a hospital. Family members encircled his bed with tears streaming silently down their cheeks. The boy seemingly was asleep, but he roused himself, calling for his father. He looked up into his father's face, saying, "Father, I understand that I'm not going to live long."

The father, with tears, answered, "Son, that's true. As far as the medical men can tell us, life is not long."

The son then said, "If that be true, Dad, I have one last request."

His father promptly responded, "Son, anything, anything! Just name it."

He replied, "Daddy, when I die, I'd like to be buried down behind the house by the lot gate."

His father said, "Son, that's a rather strange request. I don't know why you want this, but if that is what you want, that is what will be done. But why?"

"Because, Daddy," the boy responded, "I know that every morning when you go to the field to work, you go through that lot gate. When you come home every day at noon for dinner, you come back through that lot gate. You go after dinner, back out into the field to do your work, and you come in the same gate late in the afternoon. Every time you pass through that gate, I want you to look over there and say to yourself, *There lie the bones of a son of mine in Hell today who never heard his daddy pray.*

Soul winning begins in the home. The wife of a famous evangelist stated that he won the world to Christ but let his own son die and go to Hell. Start in your *Jerusalem* (family) in winning souls before going into *Judea.*

---

[517] Ibid., 343.

SPURS TO SOUL WINNING

380 Don't Give Up, Back Up, Shut Up, or Let Up

How long should you seek the salvation of the lost? The answer is clearly illustrated in the parable of the lost coin, lost sheep, and lost son (Luke 15). The shepherd sought the lost sheep "until" it was rescued; the woman searched her house "until" the silver was recovered; the father looked for his son "until" he returned. I believe these stories combine to make the striking point that the Christian must not give up, back up, shut up, or let up in the quest to win the lost.

381 Fall In Anywhere and Start Soul Winning

A soldier strayed from his troop and finally joined the ranks of another army regiment. Immediately, he asked an officer, "What can I do?"

"Fall in anywhere," the officer replied. "There's good fighting all along the line." Good advice for believers with regard to soul winning. Fall in anywhere, for within and without the walls of the church there are plenty of souls to win.

Commenting on I Samuel 13:20, the British pastor C. H. Spurgeon stated, "We are engaged in a great war with the Philistines of evil. Every weapon within our reach must be used. Preaching, teaching, praying, giving—all must be brought into action; and talents which have been thought too mean for service must now be employed. Each moment of time, in season or out of season; each fragment of ability, educated or untutored; each opportunity, favorable or unfavorable must be used, for our foes are many and our force but slender."[518]

Don't wait for an assignment; fall in anywhere and start winning souls. The Commander-in-Chief is sounding the alarm for the soldiers in His army who are AWOL or deserters or inactive to immediately return to the battle of snatching men as a brand from the burning.

382 Soul-Winning Checklist

Getting ready to go soul winning check-off list:

_ Confessed up:	Clean and holy
_ Prayed up:	Covered with divine protection and power
_ Stirred up:	Broken and compassionate for the lost
_ Lifted up:	With expectation and excitement
_ Brazened up:	Boldness to share
_ Filled up:	Domination by the Holy Spirit

---

[518] Spurgeon, *Morning and Evening*, March 2, morning entry.

_ Yielded up:	To the guidance of the Spirit
_ Loaded up:	With gospel tracts and Bible in hand
_ Pumped up:	Ready and eager to go and tell

Now you are ready to lift the *Savior up* before men. Jesus promised, "And I, if I be lifted up from the earth, will draw all men unto me" (John 12:32).

383 Turn Setbacks into Witnessing Opportunities

Adrian Despres' truck broke down on the road, but instead of whining, he was excited, figuring a tow-truck driver somewhere needed Christ. It ended up that he got to share Christ with ten mechanics at a garage. A man was listening to Despres' experience on a CD, and he asked God to break his car down so he could have a similar opportunity to share. Despres states that the man's car began "rumbling and lost the ability to accelerate on the highway," necessitating him to stop at a mechanic shop. At this shop, he shared the Gospel with three mechanics![519]

Look at apparent setbacks and inconveniences as opportunities to share Christ which would not have been possible without them.

384 The Dragnet, When Full, Will Be Pulled Up

The two main forms of fishing in Jesus' day were with a casting net and with a dragnet. The first was thrown from the bank into the waters, and the second was cast down into the waters from a boat. Jesus used the dragnet type of fishing in a parable to convey a lesson about what the Kingdom of God is like (Matthew 13:47). A dragnet was a great, square net with cords at each corner, weighted so that in the water it stood upright. From their boat, fishermen would thrust this net into the water. As they moved forward, it would form a great cone, catching all manner of fish in its path.

The church is God's dragnet for the catching of as many fish (souls) as possible. This dragnet is outstretched from one end of the world to the other, being pulled toward the end of the age and the judgment. This dragnet is indiscriminate with regard to the manner of fish caught; all souls are sought for Christ. Tares will unavoidably become mingled with the wheat in the dragnet. At the climax of the age ("when it was full"), there will be a separation of the tares from the wheat; the tares will be cast into the lake of fire, and the wheat will be ushered into the eternal presence of God (Matthew 13:48–50).

---

[519] Despres, "Shandon on Mission," 1.

Only God knows when the net will become full and man's opportunity to be saved forever shut. Believers must work zealously and rapidly to get as many as possible in the "dragnet" with them prior to its being "drawn" from the earth.

385 By All Means Save Some

"If we are the Lord's," says Francis Dixon, "then the one great business of your life and mine should be the salvation of souls. This was the master passion in our Savior's life (Luke 19:10; John 9:4; I Timothy 1:15)....Every soul we touch is to be regarded as a potential Christian....It will mean being on the watch for souls all the time. In the home, in business, while traveling, in our letter writing, on holiday—at all times and in every circumstance, we must be ready to present the claims of Christ to those who need Him....We are to adopt every means available to secure the salvation of souls....

"What means should we adopt? The most important thing is that we should be at the disposal of the Holy Spirit. He will lead us as to the methods to adopt in soul winning. He will certainly lay upon us a burden of prayer (Romans 10:1), and He will direct us to the needy souls whom He has prepared to receive our testimony (Acts 8:26, 29–30). He may lead us to speak or to use carefully chosen tracts or portions of Scripture; He will enable us to steer our conversations into the right channels so that we may speak of our Lord....

"The most any servant can do is to save some....But God's plan is that we should all have the joy of saving at least some precious souls (II Corinthians 1:14; I Thessalonians 2:19)."[520]

Don't allow Satan to talk you out of sharing Jesus with the lost by saying they are unwilling to hear. That is just not the truth. A LifeWay Research survey of 1,400 people revealed that 78 percent of the unsaved would be willing to listen to a Christian share with them about Jesus.[521]

Lord, lay some soul upon my heart
And love that soul through me;
And may I bravely do my part
To win that soul for Thee.

---

[520] Dixon, "Growing," accessed May 12, 2010.

[521] Bouknight, "Lost and Found Collection," May 30, 2010.

386 Don't Obscure the Passion

John MacArthur states, "Every Christian is to have a passion for the lost. However, the busyness of our schedules and the mind-set of our culture can obscure that passion. Richard Baxter said, 'Time must be redeemed from worldly business and commodity when matters of greater weight and commodity do require it. Trades and plow and profit must stand by when God calls us (by necessity or otherwise) to greater things. Martha should not so much as trouble herself in providing meat for Christ and His followers to eat when Christ is offering her food for her soul, and she should with Mary have been hearing at his feet....Time must be redeemed from smaller duties, which in their season must be done, as being no duties when they hinder greater duty which should then take place.' Take time to reevaluate your priorities and schedules to keep that passion from being obscured."[522]

Guard against allowing mundane things of life to swallow your passion for souls.

387 You Don't Have to Go Empty-Handed

The psalmist gives the soul winner a promise: "They that sow in tears shall reap in joy. He that goeth forth and weepeth, bearing precious seed, shall doubtless come again with rejoicing, bringing his sheaves with him" (Psalms 126:5–6). Junior Hill pleads, "Dear Christian, you don't have to go empty-handed. You don't have to stand before Him without one single soul. The God of Heaven has given you this unfailing formula for victory over barrenness, and, praise His holy name, it works for everyone."[523]

388 The Essential Trio

R. A. Torrey declares, "There are three things, and only three, that are absolutely essential to spiritual health and growth. These three things are constant Bible study, constant prayer, and constant effort for the salvation of others. Where these three things are, there will be spiritual health, spiritual growth, spiritual strength. When any one of these things are lacking, there will be spiritual deterioration, spiritual disease, spiritual weakness, spiritual death.

"If you lack Bible study but take time for prayer and effort for the salvation of others, you will fail, for your prayer will be unintelligent and your effort without result. If, on the other hand, you have Bible study and

---

[522] MacArthur, "Passion for the Lost," accessed June 8, 2011.

[523] Smith, Jack, *Motivational Sermons*, 103.

effort for the salvation of others but omit prayer, there will be spiritual death, for your Bible study will be without spiritual discernment and your effort without power. And again, if there is Bible study and prayer and you neglect effort for the salvation of others, there will be failure, deterioration, spiritual weakness. "But if you have all three together, constant Bible study, constant prayer, and constant effort for the salvation of other men, everything will prosper. You will know God better and the truth more fully every day of your life, and you will have success in your efforts to glorify God by saving others." Torrey went on to say, "[W]ithout constant soul winning, your Bible study and prayer will come to nothing. You cannot be effective, unless you are a soul winner."[524]

389 Are You a Friend of Jesus?

"Every man and woman here who calls himself a Christian and is not winning others to Christ is disobedient to Jesus Christ. It is serious in war to be disobedient to your commanding officer, and it is serious business for a Christian to be disobedient to Jesus Christ. Jesus says, 'Ye are my friends, if ye do whatsoever I command you.'

"One evening I was told that a minister's son was to be present in my congregation and that, though he professed to be a Christian, he did not work much at it....At the close of the service, I hurried to the door by which he would leave and shook hands with different ones as they passed out. When he came, I took his hand and said: 'Good evening! I am glad to see you. Are you a friend of Jesus?'

"'Yes,' he answered heartily, 'I consider myself a friend of Jesus.'

"'Jesus says,' I replied, "Ye are my friends, if ye do whatsoever I command you."'

"His eyes fell. 'If those are the conditions, I guess I am not.' I put that same question to you. Are you a friend of Jesus? Are you doing whatsoever He commands you? Are you winning souls as He commands? If I should ask every friend of Jesus to rise, could you conscientiously get up?"[525]

390 Soul Winning *Is* New Testament

The Bible makes it clear that soul winning is to be pivotal in the church and life of the believer.

---

[524] Torrey, "Soul Winning," 844.

[525] Ibid., 845.

S   The passion of Jesus (Luke 19:10)
O   The product of compassion (Matthew 9: 36–37)
U   The precept of the Great Commission (Matthew 28: 19–20)
L   The practice of the early churches (I Thessalonians 1:8; Acts 5:42)
W   The plan for reaching people (Luke 14: 23)
I   The pattern for disciples (Acts 1:8)
N   The proof of love for Christ (John 14:15)
N   The path to church growth (Acts 2:47; 5:14)
I   The price of fruit bearing (John 15:16)
N   The procedure authorized (Mark 6:7–12)
G   The profit of the perishing (Matthew 10:6–7; John 3:16)

"Pure religion and undefiled before God and the Father is this, To visit…" (James 1:27).

391 Who Would Have Figured—Saved by Smoking the Bible

Jacob Koshy's goal in life was to be financially successful. His drug smuggling international network and gambling landed him in a Singapore prison. He was a smoker, and smoking was not allowed in the prison, so he rolled smuggled tobacco in the pages of a Gideon Bible. He fell asleep smoking, only to awaken with a scrap of charred paper in his hand. He read: "Saul, Saul, why do you persecute Me? (NIV)."

Jacob asked for another Bible to read the story of Saul's conversion, after which he received Christ into his life. He testified to fellow inmates of his conversion. Upon release, he became a missionary in the Far East. He tells everyone, "Who would have believed that I could find the truth by smoking the Word of God?"[526]

Don't put God in a box with regard to the means He may use to win a soul. Who would have figured that God would use a scrap of charred Scripture to win Koshy! Stay alert and open-minded as to the means He may want you to use to win a soul.

392 Three Minutes to Win a Soul

A minister in England applied to serve as an army chaplain. In an effort to test him to ascertain his qualification for such service, the Chaplain General, with his watch in hand, said, "All right, just imagine that I am a soldier dying on the battlefield. I have only three minutes to live. Can you tell me how to be saved?"

---

[526] Morgan, R., *Book of Stories*, 148.

The preacher squandered the first two minutes, floundering around the matter. At that point the Chaplain General said, "I have one minute left. What have you to say to me?" Sadly, all the minister could do was pull out his prayer book. The Chaplain General said, "No, that won't help in an hour like that."[527]

Confronted with a real situation like that of this man, could you tell the dying soldier how to be saved in three minutes? Do you know clearly the message of salvation that a lost and dying world needs so desperately to hear? I've got my stopwatch out—ready, set, go.

393 Charlotte Elliott's Conversion

Charlotte Elliott was visiting some friends in West London, where she met a minister named César Malan, who at supper told her that he hoped she was a Christian. Charlotte took great offense in what he said. The preacher apologized and told her he hoped one day she would become a worker for Christ. The Lord orchestrated a meeting between these two again three weeks later at a friend's home. Charlotte told Malan that she had been trying to find the Savior ever since he last spoke to her and wanted him to tell her how she might be saved. He told her, "Just come to him as you are."[528] This she did and was gloriously saved. Twelve years later, Charlotte Elliott wrote the beloved hymn *Just As I Am*.

God put Charlotte Elliott in the path of a man He knew would share a witness. Grateful the church is for César Malan, who not once, but twice shared Christ with Charlotte, leading her to Christ. It was a divinely orchestrated encounter, unexpected by either person. You and I never know when God will divinely orchestrate such an encounter regarding us; therefore, we must ever be alert redeeming the opportunity, as did Malan. Had Malan hesitated or delayed in sharing with Charlotte Elliott, she never would have experienced the lyrics of the song *Just As I Am*, and, therefore, she would never have written them. Can God trust you to share the faith enough to merge your life with a Charlotte Elliott?

394 Care for Souls

Many are the reasons why we should care for the souls of men. Porter Bales suggests five.

---

[527] Ford, *Sunday Evening*, 93–94.

[528] Sankey, *My Life*, 208.

531 Motivations for Winning Souls

1. The Kingdom workers have come from homes where a sympathetic interest in and a sincere care for their souls were manifested. A study of the biographies of one hundred twenty-eight missionaries some years ago revealed the fact that one hundred twenty-one came from homes that were deeply and manifestly religious—homes that magnified Christ, were loyal to the program of the church, faithful in the work of our Lord, and reverent in spirit; homes where it was easy in youth to find God.

2. A second reason for caring for the souls of men is that many men are anxious and will respond to the proper interest in their souls. Down deep in the hearts of all men, there is a heart hunger for God. They may try to hide it and suppress it and conceal it, they may try to cover it with all sorts of excuses, but it is there....They care for their souls, because they know that life is uncertain.

3. Another reason is because of the reality of God's saving grace. Christ Jesus, God's only begotten and beloved Son, can change the hearts of men. He saves with an everlasting salvation. He turns men about and starts them on the road to right living.

4. Again, we should have a care for the souls of men because of the impressions made on us in early youth by those who have asked about our souls. These are the impressions that last down through life's long day. These are the ones that are imperishable. These are they that never fade away. Some of you can feel yet the hand that rested on your head and hear yet the appealing voice that spoke about your soul long years ago. The one supreme care of every child of God should be an interest—an abiding, everlasting interest, a heart-hungering interest, a soul-longing interest—in the spiritual welfare of man.

5. We should care for the souls of men because Jesus Christ and Him crucified is the world's only hope. The world is sick and feverish and restless and tossing....The supreme need of the world is Jesus. He will cure every ill of every individual, of every home, of every community anywhere. He will cool the fever of the restless world, soothe its nerves, bring order out of chaos and peace to a troubled soul. He and He alone is the remedy for the world's ills."[529]

395 Don't Despair over Handling Excuses

Nearly every book on soul winning I have researched deals with the myriads of excuses the unsaved will throw up in the soul winner's face as to why they cannot or will not be saved. It is so easy for the believer to look at

---

[529] Bales, *Revival Sermons*, 172.

these and at once decide there is no way he possibly can learn enough to handle them, causing him to quit soul winning before he begins. Don't despair. In more than forty years of soul winning, I have never heard most of them, and probably the authors who detail them haven't either. Instead of focusing on a sinner's possible excuses for not being saved, hone in on biblical texts that may be used to awaken and convict. Often the sinner's excuses melt away under the devouring fire of the Word, becoming non-issues.

396 One Thousand Christians Failed to Tell Him

A pastor entered a large department store, going directly to the office. Finding the owner, he said, "Mr. T—, I have talked with you on many subjects, but never have I engaged in conversation with you on the subject of my chief business in the world. Would you give me a few minutes?" The owner consented. As the pastor drew his New Testament from his pocket, he said, "My business is to show men CHRIST, and I have neglected you."

In a short time, the man said through his tears, "Pastor, I am seventy-six years of age. I was born in this city. I have been in contact with more than five hundred ministers since I came into this business, and with many times five hundred church officials; but you are the only man who has ever yet spoken to me about my soul."[530]

Your town, school or community multiplies that story many times. With whom have you neglected to share Christ? When was the last time you sought to win a person to Christ?

397 "Go into the Street Which Is Called Straight"

The Christian certainly can be given direct orders from the Lord regarding a soul assignment. Ananias was, for the Lord said to him, "Go into the street which is called Straight, and inquire in the house of Judas for one called Saul, of Tarsus" (Acts 9:11). Ananias was on both speaking and listening terms with God, making this assignment possible. We must be equally so, lest a divine appointment be missed. Ananias had reason to avoid the encounter with Saul, for it was this man who beat up on Christians (Acts 9:13–14), and he told God so! But God replied, "Go thy way" (Acts 9:15); my paraphrase: "Ananias, I know what I am doing; now go and talk to him."

---

[530] Riley, *New Testament Soul-Winners*, 11.

Like Ananias, we don't get to pick and choose every person we confront with the Gospel; many are handpicked by God. The believer has no discretionary power to change or alter these divine appointments, regardless of that person's background or lifestyle. He is simply to "Go..." Is your walk with Christ intimate enough that His voice may be heard regarding soul winning assignments? Ananias was used to give sight to a blind man, to lead Saul to Christ, which, no doubt, was the high-water mark of his soul winning encounters. To what spiritually blind person will God lead you so that they may see?

398 One Never Knows the Impact of a Soul Won

One never knows in the winning of a soul what impact the person will have for Christ. Ananias won Paul, and Paul immediately became a great force for the cause of the Gospel through missionary journeys and personal soul winning. Phillip won the eunuch, and it is believed he was the vehicle for the Gospel's entrance into Africa. Paul and Silas won the jailer, and his entire family and all his servants were saved. Jesus won the woman at Jacob's Well, and a large part of a city believed due to her testimony.

A Sunday school teacher won a shoe clerk, and that shoe clerk (D. L. Moody) shook two continents for God. César Malan won a stranger named Charlotte Elliott to Christ, and her music has touched millions for Christ. A counselor, J. D. Prevatte, won a teenage boy to Christ in a Mordecai Ham crusade, and that boy (Billy Graham) impacted the world for Christ in the twentieth century like none other.

A peddler sold a gospel tract entitled *The Bruised Reed* to a young boy, and it led to his conversion. That young boy was Richard Baxter, whose writings roused, among scores and hundreds of others, the soul of Philip Doddridge....Doddridge's book *Rise and Progress of Religion* was the means of saving William Wilberforce. William Wilberforce's book *Practical Christianity* brought Legh Richmond to Christ. Legh Richmond's book *Dairyman's Daughter* won many to Christ (over 1,500 at one count).[531]

You never know the impact of the soul won to Christ. The next person you win to Christ will perhaps be the next Billy Graham or Lottie Moon or Billy Sunday to shake a nation, yea, the world, for God. Isn't soul winning so exciting!

---

[531] Bland, *Soul Winning*, 126.

SPURS TO SOUL WINNING

399 How Soul Winning Is Best Done

John R. Rice states, "The New Testament type of Christianity has been so perverted and misshapen that now people generally consider Christian work to be primarily done in a church house, in formal services, conducted by preachers. The simple truth is that in New Testament times there were no church houses (not a single one mentioned in the New Testament). The public meetings were informal and more or less incidental to the main work of carrying the Gospel all over town, yes, all over the world, speaking to individuals....

"The right kind of gospel preaching sends Christians out to win souls and bombards the hearts of sinners. It dynamites the hard ground and arouses the conscience and makes a climate for personal soul winning. And the personal soul winning is best done, always, where there is plain Bible preaching, evangelistic preaching. No man who is against mass evangelism is ever a very good personal soul winner, and the greatest soul winners have been the best advocates of mass evangelism. Who ever did better personal soul winning work than D. L. Moody and R. A. Torrey? And who ever developed personal soul winners like these great evangelists and other evangelists?

"In an evangelistic ministry of nearly forty years, and having seen tens of thousands of people come to Christ, I can say that personal contact, personal invitation, had a part in winning nine out of ten of all those I have seen come to Christ. The best gospel preaching and the best personal soul winning effort go together."[532]

400 We Took It to the Streets

It was on a Saturday evening that a team of students was sent from the CSU campus to minister at the Salvation Army chapel in Charleston, South Carolina. No one showed up except the team. I suggested to the rest of the team that we walk down into the neighborhood and conduct an open air meeting. The singer attracted a crowd. Billy Cashion shared a personal testimony, and I preached. At the conclusion of the invitation, thirty professions of faith had been made. All on the team well realized this was a "God thing" in changing the venue of ministry that resulted in this glorious harvest.

Don't stubbornly be set on doing ministry in the traditional way. Watch for the promptings of the Holy Spirit to engage the lost in manners that to many are "outside the box." Dare to be different for the sake of souls. Had

---

[532] Rice, "Personal Soulwinning," accessed May 17, 2010.

the team that Saturday, seeing the chapel door locked, simply returned to campus, we would have missed God's divine assignment. Cultivate sensitivity to the leadership of the Holy Spirit in soul winning.

401 The Conversion of a Soul Would Be Greater

"What is it to save a soul from death? Can anyone accurately give the product of that sum, the meaning of that quantity? The distinctions of this world and its almost superhuman achievements are not to be compared with it.

"Could we rise to the possession of a princely fortune and have ducal honors shed upon us and have the million looking up and admiring our elevation— *the conversion of a soul would be greater than that.* Could we indefinitely augment the empire of science and incalculably enrich the treasures of art—*the conversion of a soul would be greater than that.* Could we build and munificently endow a hospital of palatial grandeur and proportion—*the conversion of a soul would be greater than that.* Could we heal all manner of disease, and were we to go through the length and breadth of this western continent giving strength to the infirm, eyesight to the blind, hearing to the deaf, soundness to the lame, health to the sick; could we thus fill thousands of suffering homes with joy and roll down the valleys, over the hills, and across the plains of this fair land one loud and gathering song of thanksgiving and love; could we do all this—*the conversion of a soul would be an achievement infinitely loftier!*"[533]

402 Open My Eyes That I May See Others

Paul states that a voice said to him, "I have appeared unto thee for this purpose to make thee a minister and a witness…to open their eyes and to turn them from darkness to light, from the power of Satan unto God, that they may receive forgiveness of sins."

"Do you think that Christ has opened our eyes for a lesser purpose than that for which He opened the eyes of Paul? If we are not witnessing and turning men from darkness to light, where is the trouble? What is the reason? Just this—we are afflicted with spiritual blindness; for if we saw men and women as they really are, we could not rest day or night till we had done all we could to better their condition. The people having the largest spiritual vision are the ones doing the greatest work for Christ. Our eyes are opened that we may see not alone for ourselves, but for others,

---

[533] Bland, *Soul Winning*, 127–128.

therefore let this be our constant prayer, 'Open Thou my eyes that I may see others, and seeing, help them.'"[534]

Oswald Sanders observed, "Eyes that look are common; eyes that see are rare."[535]

403   God Uses Ordinary People

God uses ordinary people in extraordinary ways to accomplish extraordinary things. He specializes in using the "weak" and those of little ability (I Corinthians 1:27). God used a 17-year-old boy, Joseph, to save his family, Israel; a Jewish Queen, Esther, to save the Jews from a holocaust; a shepherd boy, David, to defeat Goliath; a fisherman, Peter, to win 3,000 on the day of Pentecost; a little boy with a sack lunch to feed over 5,000 people; a man with a rod to deliver Israel from bondage; and a widow with two mites.

D. L. Moody said, "God had no children too weak, but a great many too strong to make use of. God stands in no need of our strength or wisdom, but of our ignorance, of our weakness; let us but give these to Him, and He can make use of us in winning souls. Speaking of this, Paul counts up five things (I Cor. 1:27–29) that God makes use of—the weak things, the foolish things, the base things, the despised things, and the things which are not. He does this so that no flesh might glory in his sight—all five being just such as we should despise. He can and will use us."[536]

In understanding this truth, one understands Bill Stafford when he states, "Jesus loved me enough to keep me weak."[537]

404   IF

J. Wilbur Chapman declared:

"If to be a Christian is worthwhile, then the most ordinary interest in those with whom we come in contact would prompt us to speak to them of Christ.

---

[534] Unknown Author, "Spiritual Blindness," accessed May 17, 2010.

[535] Sanders, "Daily Christian Quote," accessed June 9, 2010.

[536] Moody D. L., "Qualifications for Soul Winning," accessed May 18, 2010.

[537] Stafford, Bailey Smith Real Evangelism Conference, March 1, 2006.

"If the New Testament be true—and we know that it is—who has given us the right to place the responsibility for soul winning on other shoulders than our own?

"If they who reject Christ are in danger, is it not strange that we, who are so sympathetic when the difficulties are physical or temporal, should apparently be so devoid of interest as to allow our friends and neighbors and kindred to come into our lives and pass out again without a word of invitation to accept Christ, to say nothing of sounding a note of warning because of their peril?

"If today is the day of salvation, if tomorrow may never come, and if life is equally uncertain, how can we eat, drink and be merry when those who live with us, work with us, walk with us, and love us are unprepared for eternity because they are unprepared for time?

"If Jesus called his disciples to be fishers of men, who gave us the right to be satisfied with making fishing tackle or pointing the way to the fishing banks instead of going ourselves to cast out the net until it be filled?

"If Jesus himself went seeking the lost, if Paul the Apostle was in agony because his kinsmen, according to the flesh, knew not Christ, why should we not consider it worthwhile to go out after the lost until they are found?

"If I am to stand at the judgment seat of Christ to render an account for the deeds done in the body, what shall I say to Him if my children are missing, if my friends are not saved, or if my employer or employee should miss the way because I have been faithless?

"If I wish to be approved at the last, then let me remember that no intellectual superiority, no eloquence in preaching, no absorption in business, no shrinking temperament, or no spirit of timidity can take the place of or be an excuse for my not making an honest, sincere, prayerful effort to win others to Christ."[538]

405 Get Them to Think about That

A Christian went to a judge in Georgia and said: "Judge, I hear that you and your wife are to separate."

He was highly indignant and said: "Sir, that is an insult. No two people in this world have loved each other more devotedly. Separate! Nothing could separate us."

His friend said: "But, Judge, your wife is a Christian. She is far from well, and the doctor tells me that she cannot live long; and you are not a

---

[538] Chapman, "You Want to Be a Soul Winner," accessed May 20, 2010.

Christian. Your wife will go straight to God. You are turning your back on Him."

The old judge stood with tears running down his cheeks and lips trembling as he said, "My God! I never thought of that."[539]

It's the Christian's job to get people to think about "that"—eternity and the continuation or not of relationships with family and friends who are saved. As with the judge, most people are too occupied with the temporal to ponder the eternal; but once induced to do so, they may be awakened to their need of Christ.

406   Take a Knee

Leonard Ravenhill shares how the Lord impresses on the heart of believers to pray for others. "One day I was at a conference with Dr. V. Raymond Edman of Wheaton College, one of the greatest Christian educators in this country. He told us of an experience he had while he was in Ecuador as a missionary. He hadn't been there long before he was sick and dying. He was so near death that they had already dug his grave. He had great beads of sweat on his brow, and there was a death rattle in his throat. But suddenly, he sat straight up in bed and said to his wife, 'Bring me my clothes!' Nobody knew what had happened.

"Many years later, he was retelling the story in Boston. Afterward, a little old lady with a small, dog-eared, beaten-up book approached him and asked, 'What day did you say you were dying? What time was it in Ecuador? What time would it be in Boston?' When he answered her, her wrinkled face lit up. Pointing to her book, she said, 'There it is, you see? At 2 a.m., God said to get up and pray—the Devil's trying to kill Raymond Edman in Ecuador.' And she'd gotten up and prayed."[540]

Most surely if the Lord would impress a woman to arise to pray for a missionary in the early morning, He desires to move hearts to be sensitive to His promptings to pray for the unsaved. Stay alert to Holy Spirit impresssions to go to your knees in behalf of a lost soul. It may not be clear at the moment the reason for the burden to pray, but in time it will become manifest.

---

[539] Chapman, "Eternity," accessed May 20, 2010.

[540] Ravenhill, "Prayer," accessed May 21, 2010.

407   Practical Things Everybody Can Do

(1)   Fill your pocket, purse, or briefcase with tracts for ready distribution.

(2)   Acquire evangelistic books like Lee Strobel's *The Case for Christ* to give out.

(3)   Get some Christian DVDs like *Lay It Down* (students); *Homerun for Rusty* (children); *The Crossing* (adults) to distribute.

(4)   Write a letter; send a greeting card expressing the passion of Christ for that person to be saved.

(5)   Place evangelistic recordings of sermons in restaurants frequented by truckers and tourists.

(6)   Invite a person to a revival or evangelistic meeting.

(7)   On airplanes, buses, or trains, share Christ with the person seated next to you.

D. L. Moody, the greatest soul winner of his day, engaged in soul winning regularly on the streetcars. On one occasion, Moody asked a man on a Detroit streetcar, "Are you a Christian?"

The man replied, "No, sir; but I wish I were." Moody won him to Jesus then and there. All believers should make this a like practice of life, though the mode of transportation is different.

(8)   Pray specifically (by name) for the lost.

408   It's a Matter of Irrepressible Want-To

A man in Texas who could not read refused to believe he couldn't win souls. He filled his pocket full of gospel tracts and started hitchhiking. Each time someone offered him a ride, he would ask that they would read one of the tracts to him. He then would share what Jesus had done for him, seeking to win them to Christ. Once the witness was complete, he would get out and start hitchhiking in the opposite direction doing the same thing. In the first year, this man had won 168 people to Christ, choosing to use his weakness (inability to read) to the glory of God instead of as an excuse for doing nothing. He wasn't an evangelist, theologian, or pastor, but he loved Jesus and wanted others to know Him![541]

Whatever you may count as a weakness that hinders soul winning can be transformed into a strength if yielded to Christ. In college, I met a man who was unable to carry on a conversation without serious stuttering;

---

[541] Carr, "Traits of a Successful Soul Winner," accessed May 21, 2010.

however, in times of testifying for Christ, he spoke clearly. He refused to allow the weakness to keep him quiet about Christ. This the Lord honored with special grace to testify. "But God hath chosen the foolish things of the world to confound the wise; and God hath chosen the weak things of the world to confound the things which are mighty; And base things of the world, and things which are despised, hath God chosen, yea, and things which are not, to bring to naught things that are" (I Corinthians 1:27–28).

409 My Personal Responsibility to God

"Every personal worker," declares William Evans, "ought to read often the third and thirty-third chapters of Ezekiel. Possibly no part of the whole Bible sets forth the responsibility of one man for another as do these chapters. It may not be our responsibility to bring every individual to Christ, but it is our responsibility to see that Christ is brought to every individual. Every man may not want Christ; but Christ wants every man, and it is our business to let every man know that Christ wants him. God has appointed me 'my brother's keeper,' whether I will it or not. 'When I say unto the wicked, O wicked man, thou shalt surely die; if thou dost not speak to warn the wicked from his way, that wicked man shall die in his iniquity; but his blood will I require at thine hand. Nevertheless, if thou warn the wicked of his way to turn from it; if he do not turn from his way, he shall die in his iniquity; but thou hast delivered thy soul' (Ezek. 33:8–9).

"Daniel Webster was once asked what was the most solemn thought he had ever entertained. In reply, he said, 'My personal responsibility to God.' Can there be any more solemn thought than this for a Christian worker?"[542]

"No matter how faithfully you attend church," states Adrian Rogers, "how generously you give, how circumspectly you walk, how eloquently you teach, or how beautifully you sing, if you are not endeavoring to bring people to Jesus Christ, you are not right with God."[543]

"The personal worker must be an opportunist; he must believe in opportunism. The buying up of opportunities for Christ is not to be understood as an effort to save hours which we might be tempted to waste from idleness, but the effort to so control our time that we shall not allow any selfish motive, any cowardly timidity, to stand in the way of our doing good. The Christian worker must emulate the merchant who is quick to seize every bargain that is passing before him. As he buys up goods, so we

---

[542] Evans, "Elements of Success," accessed May 22, 2010.

[543] Rogers, *Adrianisms*, 176.

must buy up opportunities for doing good, and especially those opportunties which are afforded us of speaking to men about their souls."[544]

410 "Where Fell It?"

Students attending Elijah's School of the Prophets, while working in the field, lost the axe head from the axe. The work was halted (for it could not continue until the axe head was found), and Elijah was informed. Elijah frankly asked, "Where fell it?" (II Kings 6:5–6). Sadly many Christians are doing the work of soul winning with a lost "axe head"; the power of the Holy Spirit is absent. This accounts for much labor but little fruit or cessation of labor altogether. How might the lost axe head be recovered?

Realize its absence. The road to recovery of divine power begins with awareness it is missing. Many are like those of Hosea's day, 'Worshiping foreign gods has sapped their strength, but they don't even know it. Their hair is gray, but they don't realize they're old and weak' (Hosea 7:9 NLT). Face the fact honestly that you have become a dry shadow of the former self that was overflowing with Holy Spirit power.

Recognize its cause. "Where fell it?" Return to the place where the power was lost. Was it in neglect of the prayer closet or intake of the Word or worship with the saints, or was it an impure act or some other form of disobedience? It is expedient that you acknowledge the place in the "water" where it fell, that it may be restored.

Restore its use. Don't keep swinging the axe without the axe head, for such is futile. Get the power back. How?

1. Acknowledge to God the attitude or action that quenched or grieved the Holy Spirit and prompted His withdrawal of power.

2. Confess it as sin.

3. Turn away from the grievous act.

4. Ask the Holy Spirit to infill you with His presence and power for the sake of God's glory and that of lost souls.

The students found the lost axe head and reattached it to the axe, and the work resumed successfully. Do the same, and the results will be the same.

411 Ignorant of the Power Available

A slow-witted farmer purchased a chain saw after being told that it was guaranteed to cut down forty trees a day. After a week, he returned the

---

[544] Evans, "Instructions," accessed May 22, 2010.

chain saw to the store. The salesman inquired as to the problem, and the farmer replied, "I have been working my head off, and I ain't able ta bring down more than five trees a day." With a frown, the salesman looked at the chain saw and then pulled its starter cord. As it roared to life, the farmer jumped back and exclaimed, "What's that?"

Often believers have the right tool (the Bible, gospel tracts) coupled with the right desire and discipline to win souls but remain barren for failure to "pull the starter cord" allowing the Holy Spirit to empower them. "But ye shall receive power, after that the Holy Ghost is come upon you: and ye shall be witnesses unto me both in Jerusalem, and in all Judaea, and in Samaria, and unto the uttermost part of the earth" (Acts 1:8). The prerequisite to soul winning is the anointing of power by the Holy Spirit. The Holy Spirit waits to spring up wells of enablement and empowerment in your life, granting you the ability to "cut down forty trees a day." Hudson Taylor once stated, "We have given too much attention to methods and to machinery and to resources, and too little to the Source of Power, the filling with the Holy Ghost."[545]

412 Life's Time Clock Is Running Out to Win Souls

Here is a time clock, a mathematical parallel of the seventy-year life-span with a day, from 6 a.m. until midnight. Though we are not promised to live to the age expectancy or beyond, this life clock gives a visual aid to help us see how much time has elapsed in life and the potential time that remains to invest in the winning of souls.

—If you are 15, it's 9:51 a.m.
—If you are 20, it's 11:08 a.m.
—If you are 25, it's 12:25 p.m.
—If you are 30, it's 1:42 p.m.
—If you are 35, it's 2:59 p.m.
—If you are 40, it's 4:16 p.m.
—If you are 45, it's 5:33 p.m.
—If you are 50, it's 6:50 p.m.
—If you are 55, it's 8:08 p.m.
—If you are 60, it's 9:25 p.m.
—If you are 70, it's approaching midnight!

What time is it by this time clock for you? The later the time, the more certainly it should incite a greater effort in evangelism. Paul gives excellent advice, "This is all the more urgent, for you know how late it is; time is

---

[545] Taylor, "Rope Holder Quotes," accessed May 25, 2010.

running out. Wake up, for our salvation is nearer now than when we first believed" (Romans 13:11 NLT).

413 No Mistake As Bad As Not Making the Effort

"One thing I know, that, whereas I was blind, now I see" (John 9:25).

"It is our expression of conviction," Charles Trumbull said, "as to what Jesus has done for us and as to what He will do for others—that is the only message which will win men to Him. What mistakes shall we fear in this work? Only one. And that is not the mistake of doing the thing in a bungling way or an awkward way or even in a way that may actually antagonize. To be sure, a study of principles will help us to avoid such mistakes, but we need not fear those mistakes as we must fear one, the greatest and only real mistake in the work—and that is the mistake of keeping still."[546]

"I saw that it was better to make a mistake in one's first effort at personal religious conversation and correct that mistake afterward than not to make any effort. There can be no mistake so bad in working for an individual soul for Christ as the fatal mistake of not making any honest endeavor. How many persons refrain from doing anything, lest they should possibly do the wrong thing just now! Not doing is the worst of doing.

"The Christian witness should seize openings when they come; but, more than that, he may need to *make* them. The real question is not, "Is this the best time for a personal word for Christ?"; it is, "Am I willing to improve this time for Christ and for a precious soul whether it is the best time or not?" If the Christian waits until the sinner gives sign of a desire for help or until the Christian thinks that a loving word to the sinner will be most timely, he is not likely to begin at all. The only safe rule for his guidance—if indeed a Christian needs a specific rule as a guide—is to speak lovingly of Christ and of Christ's love for the individual whenever one has an opportunity of choosing his subject of conversation in an interview with an individual who may be in special need, yet who has given no special indication of it."[547]

414 Things That Shut the Door in Soul Winning

Opportunity to win souls may shut without warning, spurring wise use of time, talent and treasure now. What might shut this door?

---

[546] Trumbull, *Taking Men Alive*, 21.

[547] Trumbull, Pioneer Personal Worker," accessed May 23, 2010.

SPURS TO SOUL WINNING

Disease or injury can shut the door. Illnesses or injuries that force confinement in a hospital, nursing home or one's own home can shut this door, or at least greatly limit the degree to which it is open. You may be in excellent health presently and free to travel and see whomever you desire to see. This can suddenly change in a flash!

Frailty of body can shut the door. Few, if any, will be like Moses in old age, of whom Scripture states, "And Moses was an hundred and twenty years old when he died: his eye was not dim, nor his natural force (*vigor*) abated" (Deuteronomy 34:7). Face it; the body is decaying, sapping strength and stability in the process and gradually shutting the door of soul winning possibility. While the mind is sharp, the eyesight is not dim, hearing is not impeded, and energy is not abated, engage in winning the lost.

Death shuts the door. "It is appointed unto men once to die" (Hebrews 9:27). At death, the door to soul winning will be forever shut. Soul winning is a work one can do on earth which he cannot do upon the streets in Heaven. At death, it's too late to be concerned about a child, parent, grandchild, sibling, or friend. Now is the time while life fills your body to boldly tell them of Jesus. All are only a heartbeat away from eternity and not guaranteed another hour of life.

The Second Coming of Christ. "It will happen in a moment, in the blink of an eye, when the last trumpet is blown. For when the trumpet sounds, those who have died will be raised to live forever. And we who are living will also be transformed. For our dying bodies must be transformed into bodies that will never die; our mortal bodies must be transformed into immortal bodies" (I Corinthians 15:52–53 NLT). The arrival of Christ can happen "in a moment," bringing to a climax the opportunity for the believer to win souls. Prophecy certainly indicates His coming is upon us, even at the door; therefore, believers must zealously redeem the time that remains in evangelistic outreach (Mark 13:29).

415 "Witness to This Man"

Former professional baseball player Terry Coomer missed an opportunity to share Christ with a doctor who gave him a physical examination. Coomer states that while he was seated in the examining room, "Immediately, the Holy Spirit started speaking to me about witnessing to Dr. Short. We had had conversations in the past, and he thought it was cool that I was a professional baseball player. What a great opportunity to tell him about what God had done in my life. Normally, when a doctor comes in, he is less than personal and has to get on to the next patient—short, sweet (not always), direct, and to the point.

"Dr. Short walked in and immediately said, 'Wow, I like your shirt.' I had a silk shirt on. Most ball players spent a lot of money on clothes, and I did too. He asked me where I got the shirt and how much it cost. I was a young Christian, and all the time the Holy Spirit was saying, *Witness to this man.*

"Dr. Short left the room to get some sample medicine for me....While he was gone, I had a conversation with God. I spoke out loud and argued with God. Have you ever done anything like that? I said, 'Lord he won't listen to me; he is a doctor.' God said, *Tell him about Me.* I said, 'Lord, I will leave him a tract here on this table, and he will read it.' I failed to witness because of fear....I failed that day at the task that is so important to the heart of God. I brushed it off and went on. After all, I was on my way to be a preacher.

"About a month later, I was in Chattanooga, Tennessee, starting my education....My mother called me, and we talked for about thirty minutes on the phone. At the end of the conversation, almost as an afterthought, she said, 'By the way, I do not know if you know this or not, but your doctor, Dr. Short, was killed last Friday night in a car accident. He was driving his Corvette late at night at a high rate of speed and missed a curve.'

"Immediately, the Holy Spirit spoke to my heart. I got off the phone immediately and went to the bedroom and asked God to forgive me for my failure to witness....I wept that night over my disobedience and my sin and the soul of the man with whom God had put me in the position to talk. I promised God that I would always take the opportunity and listen to Him in these matters from that day forward. You know, I hope Dr. Short read that tract I left, but I doubt he did."[548]

When will saints learn that the impressions of the Holy Spirit are not to be taken lightly? There is rhyme and reason to His prompting to speak to the "Dr. Shorts" in our pathway. Heed it.

416 Getting Used to Being Saved

Spurgeon writes, "Believer, do you recollect the day when your fetters fell off? Do you remember the place where Jesus met you and said, 'I have loved thee with an everlasting love; I have blotted out as a cloud thy transgressions, and as a thick cloud thy sins; they shall not be mentioned against thee any more forever.' Oh, what a sweet season is that when Jesus takes away the pain of sin!

"When the Lord first pardoned my sin, I was so joyous that I could scarce refrain from dancing. I thought on my road home from the house where I had been set at liberty that I must tell the stones in the street the

---

[548] Coomer, "Failing to Witness," accessed May 24, 2010.

story of my deliverance. So full was my soul of joy, that I wanted to tell every snowflake that was falling from heaven of the wondrous love of Jesus who had blotted out the sins of one of the chief of rebels."[549]

Certainly all the redeemed testify of similar experiences. What happened to the indescribable burden to tell "the stones in the street" and "every snowflake that was falling from heaven of the wondrous love of Jesus"? Have we gotten used to being saved? Or have we forgotten what He did for us on that glorious day? Or have we simply let being a Christian become old hat?

The saddest verse in Scripture pertaining to the Christian is perhaps Revelation 2:4: "Yet I hold this against you: You have forsaken your first love" (NIV). Too many Christians have allowed their love for Christ to become lukewarm and their walk to stale. If you are in this group, Jesus admon-ishes, "Return unto your first love"—like it was at the first. First love is a love that is so full of devotion to Christ that one, in fact, *will* tell the stones in the street and the snowflakes that fall of Jesus!

417 Waiting for a Sign to Witness

Norman Cates shared the humorous story of a guy who prayed this prayer every morning: "Lord, if you want me to witness to someone today, please give me a sign to show me who it is." One day he found himself on a bus, when a big, burly man sat next to him. The bus was nearly empty, but this guy sat next to our praying friend. The timid Christian anxiously waited for his stop so he could exit the bus. Before he could get very nervous about the man next to him, the big guy burst into tears and began to weep. He then cried out with a loud voice, "I need to be saved. I'm a lost sinner, and I need the Lord. Won't somebody tell me how to be saved?" He turned to the Christian and pleaded, "Can you show me how to be saved?" The believer immediately bowed his head and prayed, *Lord, is this a sign?*[550]

Many believers are like this timid Christian. They fail to recognize the numerous "signs" to witness. Stay alert as you move through life today for "signs" that you should share.

418 Keep Your Axe Sharp

There was a rookie lumberjack who was determined to beat his company's average of cutting down fifteen trees a day. On the first day, he cut

---

[549] Spurgeon, *Morning and Evening*, February 1 entry.

[550] Cates, "So Much Work," accessed April 24, 2010.

down ten trees and counted it a grand start. On the second day, he managed to cut only ten trees again, showing no progress toward his goal. On day three, he cut down seven trees. On day four, he doubled his effort to reach his goal but surprisingly only felled five trees.

Every day, the number of trees he cut down grew fewer and fewer, despite his hard work in swinging the axe. At the end of two weeks of felling fewer and fewer trees each day, he approached a veteran lumberjack, asking, "I don't understand what's going on. I work hard every day, swinging my axe from dawn to dusk, but I keep doing worse and worse. What can I be doing wrong?"

"Young fella," the old man replied after a long pause, "I can see them calluses on your hands and bigger muscles in your arms to prove you been swingin' your axe. But let me ask you somethin'. When was the last time you sharpened your axe?"

The reason many believers' tiresome labor seeking to win souls avails little is due to an unsharpened spiritual axe. It's time to stop swinging so laboriously and to sharpen the dull axe through prayer, intake of the Word, and obedience. Allow them to do the task.

419 Why Are So Many Yet Unreached?

Robertson McQuilkin, in *The Great Commission: A Biblical Basis for World Evangelism,* relates a story that took place while he was teaching students. Half of the world's population, McQuilkin told them, had not heard the Gospel, nor could they hear it, due to the lack of a witnessing church in their midst.

"How come?" a voice rang from the back of the auditorium.

"How come what?" McQuilkin asked.

"With so many lost people, how come so few are going?"

"That is a good question," McQuilkin responded. "In fact, I know Someone who asks that question every day."

"Who's that?" asked the student from the back of the auditorium. McQuilkin lifted his eyes, gesturing upward. A silence settled over the classroom.

McQuilkin provides five answers to the question: "How come?"

1. Heart Trouble. We do not care about the lost. We are preoccupied with our own interests and needs.

2. Eye Trouble. We do not have a vision. We do not see the people from God's perspective.

3. Head Trouble. We think there must be another way.

309

4. Knee Trouble. We treat praying as a nonessential in life. Studies show that many spend as little as four minutes a day in prayer.

5. Ear Trouble. Someone is not listening to the call. God is calling, but people are not listening.[551] "And how can they believe in him if they have never heard about him? And how can they hear about him unless someone tells them?" (Romans 10:14 NLT).

"How come?" Sometimes it is due to the lack of an example in pastoral leadership. Calvin Ratz asserts, regarding the pastor, "To some degree, the shepherd looks after the sheep, while the sheep give birth to the lambs. But then again, if evangelism isn't happening in our lives, it probably won't happen much in the church....It's been said, 'A student learns what his teacher knows, but a disciple becomes what his master is.' My people will not become what I say they should be; they'll become what they see is important in my life. And that's true with evangelism. People want to be led, to be inspired, to be challenged. Pastors who lead their churches into evangelism do it primarily by example, by modeling, by making evangelism a priority."[552]

420 "I Could Not Get Anyone to Help Me Harvest the Field"

A terrible storm ruined a fine crop of grain. Crops on other farms had been gathered before the storm struck. The owner of the field sadly stood in silence, looking at his ruined harvest. A stranger walking along the road came up to the farmer and said, "It is a really sad sight, isn't it?"

The farmer replied, "You would really think it was a sad sight if it were your field. I could not get anyone to help me harvest the field."[553]

Instantly upon reading this story, the mind turns to Christ's effort in recruiting laborers for the field of the world. The field is ripe unto harvest, the storm of condemnation is about to descend, yet few have responded to His appeal to assist in the harvest. Sorrow of sorrows will be Christ's proclamation at the judgment regarding the reason no more were saved than actually were. "I could not get anyone to help Me harvest the field." Are you willing to help Jesus harvest His field?

---

[551] Unknown Author, "Sowing and Reaping," accessed May 24, 2010.

[552] Ratz, "Pastor's Role," accessed June 19, 2010.

[553] Unknown Author, "Sowing and Reaping," accessed May 24, 2010.

421   The Lost Matter to God

The lost sheep knew it was lost but didn't know the way back home. The lost coin was lost but didn't realize it. The prodigal son realized he was lost but also knew the way home (Luke 15).

"Bill Hybels in *Becoming a Contagious Christian* suggests that Jesus told these three stories in rapid succession to make an impression on His listeners. This is the only time that Jesus told three parables in a row. He wanted to make sure that everyone understood what and who really matters to God. In each story great value was attached to what was missing. The lost sheep mattered to the shepherd. The lost coin was of great value to the woman. The wayward son mattered to the father. All Heaven rejoices when the lost are found. The lost matter to God!"[554] And therefore they ought to matter to us!

Ralph Neighbour estimates that the average church spends 300 hours annually equipping members for service within the church walls and less than twelve hours equipping them to witness outside the church.[555] No wonder the harvest field is lacking for trained and willing laborers! What the church prioritizes sets the agenda for her members. What do the budget allocation for evangelistic training and outreach and the time actually invested in soul winning training in your church reveal about its passion for the lost? Is it saying to the Lord and the lost world what it should? In and through our priorities, are we saying "The lost matter to us"?

422   Jesus' View of Soul Winning

"Jesus was a great believer in carrying the Gospel to men one by one, face to face, in personal approach. Jesus Himself was the Great Shepherd of souls; and, as the Shepherd, He set the example for all pastors in soul winning. He put the pastor in the churches as God's big man, His key man in soul winning. The pastor ought to love it, believe in it, study it, prepare for it, practice it, preach it, and major in it.

"Jesus was a great believer in utilizing the men and women in the ranks of His disciples for soul winning. He used more than apostles. He used the seventy, who, as far as we know, were laymen. The example of Christ in the matter of picking up souls wherever He found them is a great encouragement to all those who would testify for Christ by the waysides, roadsides, seasides—everywhere.

---

[554] Ibid., accessed May 24, 2010.

[555] Ibid., accessed May 25, 2010.

"Jesus believed in soul winning in season and out of season. It was the master passion of His life, the primal task of his ministry. He believed in it everywhere. In these and in other ways, Christ and the example He gave through His ministry show us today the importance, the necessity, and the call to a life of evangelism."[556]

423 Let's Do It

Paul did not merely talk about soul winning; he did it! Sermons, songs and studies on soul winning are a dime a dozen. The church needs men and women who actually do as Paul did and knock on doors seeking the lost. Billy Graham stated, "There are many preachers but few soul winners."[557] John Bunyan said, "The heart of Christianity is in the practice part."

D. L. Moody was attending a conference on soul winning, when he decided to walk outside to the street and actually witness to the unsaved. He practiced soul winning while those in the church proclaimed it. In his church in Chicago, he had written above each exit, "You are now entering the mission field of the world—go soul winning." May these words be inscribed above the doors of every Sunday school, worship center and saint's home door. W. A. Criswell said, "We are found to find others, we are won to win others, we are told to tell others, and we are saved to save others." As you leave home today you are entering the mission field of the world; go soul winning.

424 Don't Give Up

John MacArthur stated, "Don't give up on those who mock Christ when you share your faith. God is able to turn their hearts to saving faith in the most surprising ways."[558]

Who of Paul's day would ever have thought that he of all people would get saved? But he did. G. S. Dobbins writes, "Are we not prone to give up too easily? A successful insurance agent says that he sometimes makes as many as forty to fifty contacts before he at length sells his prospect a policy. Wise business and professional men cultivate good will as they look many years ahead to future business."[559]

---

[556] Scarborough, *How Jesus Won Men*, 209–211.

[557] Olford, *Secret of Soulwinning*, Foreword.

[558] MacArthur, *Follow Me*, 65.

[559] Dobbins, *Winning Witness*, 86.

C. H. Spurgeon wrote, "I sometimes hear of persons getting very angry after a good sermon, and I say to myself, *I am not sorry for it.* Sometimes when we are fishing, the fish gets the hook into his mouth. He pulls hard at the line. If he were dead, he would not; but he is a live fish, worth the getting. Though he runs for a while with the hook in his jaws, He cannot escape. His very wriggling and his anger show that he has got the hook and the hook has got him. Have the landing-net ready; we shall land him by and by. Give him more line, let him spend his strength, and then we will land him; and he shall belong to Christ forever."[560]

I can yet hear my father's instruction about fishing: "Hook him first, Son. Give him some line. Keep tension on the line. Don't let him get away. Let him run awhile. Now pull him in." That's great advice for catching men. Keep reeling off line to the sinner; if he is hooked, he cannot get away.

425   Do You Really Believe That Men without
Christ Are Going to Hell?

Billy Sunday was asked what the secret of his success was in reaching souls. It is said that he walked over to a window, looked upon the masses of people on the street, and declared, "They are going to Hell! They are going to Hell! They are going to Hell!" He went on to say, "If there is a secret to my winning so many souls, it is because I really believe that men without Christ are going to Hell."[561] The soul winner must have a deep conviction that men without Christ are indeed going to Hell if he is to seek their rescue.

426   Take What Jesus Said Literally

C. H. Spurgeon declared to his preacher boys attending his college, "'Go ye into the highways and hedges and compel them to come in'— although it constitutes part of a parable, it is worthy to be taken very literally; and in so doing, its meaning will be best carried out. We should actually go into the streets and lanes and highways, for there are lurkers in the hedges, tramps on the highway, streetwalkers and lane haunters whom we shall never reach unless we pursue them into their own domains. Sportsmen must not stop at home and wait for the birds to come and be shot

---

[560] Walden, *Sword Scrapbook*, 77.

[561] Murphrey, *Drawing the Net*, 47.

at; neither must fisherman throw their nets inside their boats and hope to take many fish."[562]

A Voice from Hell

You lived next door to me for years;
We shared our dreams, our joys and tears.
A friend to me you were indeed,
A friend who helped me when in need.
My faith in you was strong and sure.
We had such trust as should endure.
No "words" between us could impose;
Our friends were like—and so, our foes.

What sadness, then, my friend, to find
That, after all, you weren't so kind.
The day my life on earth did end,
I found you weren't a faithful friend.
For all those years we spent on earth,
You never talked of second birth.
You never spoke of my lost soul
And of the Christ Who'd make me whole.

I'm lost today eternally
And tell you now my earnest plea.
You cannot do a thing for me—
No words today my bonds will free.
But do not err, my friend, again;
Do all you can for souls of men.
Plead now with them quite earnestly,
Lest they be cast in Hell with me!
—Author unknown

427 Paul's Great Object

"Paul's great object," states C. H. Spurgeon, "was not merely to instruct and to improve, but to save. Anything short of this would have disappointed him. He would have men renewed in heart, forgiven, sanctified—in fact, saved. Have our Christian labors been aimed at anything below this great point? Then let us amend our ways, for of what avail will it be at the

---

[562] Spurgeon, *Lectures to My Students*, 256.

last great day to have taught and moralized men, if they appear before God unsaved?...

"His prayers were importunate, and his labors incessant. To save souls was his consuming passion, his ambition, his calling. He became a servant to all men, toiling for his race, feeling a woe within him if he preached not the Gospel. He laid aside his preferences to prevent prejudice. He submitted his will in things indifferent, and if men would but receive the Gospel, he raised no questions about forms or ceremonies. The Gospel was the one all-important business with him. If he might save some, he would be content. This was the crown for which he strove, the sole and sufficient reward of all his labors and self-denials.

Dear reader, have you and I lived to win souls at this noble rate? Are we possessed with the same all-absorbing desire? If not, why not? Jesus died for sinners. Cannot we live for them? Where is our tenderness? Where our love to Christ, if we seek not his honor in the salvation of men? Oh, that the Lord would saturate us through and through with an undying zeal for the souls of men."[563]

428 Global Intercession

William Carey, father of modern missions, had an enormous burden for the lost, even as a youth. Working in a cobbler's shop, he would save discarded bits and pieces of shoe leather to craft a makeshift globe. In ink, he sketched the outlines of the continents and countries. It is said that Carey's tears of intercession for the lost in the world literally blurred the outlines of the nations formed on the globe. Ultimately, Carey became a missionary to India, giving his life to win the unreached to Christ. "He that goeth forth and weepeth, bearing precious seed, shall doubtless come again with rejoicing, bringing his sheaves with him" (Psalms 126:6).

The believer's intercession for the unsaved is not wasted or squandered time. It is the exact opposite. Prayer always precedes soul winning. Like Carey, get a globe and begin praying for the lost people of the world. Additionally, pray for laborers for global missions. G. Campbell Morgan asserted that, "The Holy Spirit is waiting in the far-distant places of the earth for the voice of anointed men to preach, in order that through that instrumentality He may carry on His work of convicting of sin, and of righteousness, and of judgment."[564]

---

[563] C. H. Spurgeon, Morning and Evening. December 7, Evening.

[564] Morgan, G., *Spirit of God*, 164.

"I ask you, fellow Christian, to face with me this pertinent question: Does God's Spirit ever win souls independently of us Christians? No more than we Christians will ever be able to win souls independently of Him. Carey is correct in insisting that the Great Commission Christ gave to the apostles is obligatory on all succeeding ministers. Every Christian has an inescapable responsibility regarding global missions. Paul asserts, 'We are laborers together with God' (I Corinthians 3:9)."[565]

429 Helping People Avoid Hell

"Today…people will go to Heaven, and people will go to Hell. The percentage of people going to Heaven and the percentage of people going to Hell today is determined by how well you did your job yesterday. If you remember Heaven today, it will help someone avoid Hell tomorrow."[566]

"That I might by all means save some" (I Corinthians 9:22). Don't lock yourself in a box utilizing only one or two methods of outreach. "By all means" save some! Utilize T-shirts. Brazil's soccer team, in winning the 2002 World Cup, took off their jerseys to reveal a T-shirt that gave a brief statement to the world about Jesus! Utilize tracts. Utilize "?" buttons worn upon the lapel that prompt others to inquire of its meaning (to ask if they have considered life's greatest question: "If they should die today, where would they go?"). Utilize Christian movies and books. Resources are many and effective, empowered by the Holy Spirit to open doors for the purpose of winning souls. And they are fun to use.

430 Be Yourself in Soul Winning

Reinhard Bonnke, in *Time Is Running Out,* says, "The means must match the moment. People talk about jumping at the opportunity, but I think Paul kept jumping until opportunity came. The best methods are when we each do what we do best, using our own specific methods and not imitating others." He also stated, "The Gospel is you and me telling the story of Christ, whatever the chosen means of transmission." Stephen Olford wrote, "It must be recognized that no rigid rule can be laid down for personal soul winning or, indeed, for any other form of Christian service. God is sovereign in His work and never deals with any two people in exactly the same way."[567]

---

[565] Surgener, *Lost!*, 93.

[566] Unknown Author, "Sowing and Reaping," accessed May 25, 2010.

[567] Olford, *Secret of Soulwinning*, 57.

Methods of soul winning must never override the soul winner's message nor hinder his effort in winning souls. In soul winning, there are no sure-fire methods. The soul winner must take his cue from the Holy Spirit as to which method to use if he is to be productive. C. H. Spurgeon said, "We cannot make the fish bite, but we can do our best to draw them near to the killing bait of the Word of God; and once they are there, we will watch and pray till they are fully taken."[568]

Methods in soul winning are not "the law of the Medes and Persians." It is the message that is unchangeable. The believer must be open to changing the method (never the message) of outreach from one generation to the next, yea, even from one person to the next, that more may be won.

431 It's Too Important Not to Share

The Mercedes Benz Company had a television commercial which showed a Mercedes Benz automobile colliding with a cement wall, demonstrating the energy-absorbing car body of the automobile. In the commercial, it was asked why the company did not patent the car body design to prevent it from being copied by other automobile companies. The company spokesman said, "Because some things in life are too important not to share." The wonderful transformation that Christ has wrought in the believer's life is too important not to share!

432 So Little Time

So little time! The harvest will be over—
Our reaping done, we reapers taken home,
Report our work to Jesus, Lord of Harvest,
And hope He'll smile and that He'll say, "Well done!"

How many times I should have strongly pleaded;
How often did I feel to strictly warn?
The Spirit moved, oh, had I pled for Jesus!
The grain is fallen, lost ones not reborn.

Despite the heat, the ceaseless toil, the hardship,
The broken heart o'er those we cannot win,
Misunderstood, because we're oft peculiar—
Still no regrets we'll have but for our sin.

---

[568] Spurgeon, *Only a Prayer Meeting*, 160.

A day of pleasure or a feast of friendship,
A house or car, or garments fair, or fame
Will all be trash when souls are brought to Heaven,
And then how sad to face the slackers' blame!

The harvest white with reapers few is wasting,
And many souls will die and never know
The love of Christ, the joy of sins forgiven.
Oh, let us weep and love and pray and go!

Today we reap or miss our golden harvest!
Today is given us lost souls to win.
Oh, then to save some dear ones from the burning,
Today we'll go to bring some sinner in.
— John R. Rice[569]

433   Boresome Duty or Blessed Delight?

A. W. Tozer commented, "The testimony of the true follower of Christ might be something like this: 'The world's pleasures and the world's treasures henceforth have no appeal for me. I reckon myself crucified to the world and the world crucified to me. But the multitudes that were so dear to Christ shall not be less dear to me. If I cannot prevent their moral suicide, I shall at least baptize them with my human tears. I want no blessing that I cannot share. I seek no spirituality that I must win at the cost of forgetting that men and women are lost and without hope. If, in spite of all I can do, they will sin against the light and bring upon themselves the displeasure of a holy God, then I must not let them go their sad way unwept. I scorn happiness that I must purchase with ignorance. I reject a Heaven I must enter by shutting my eyes to the sufferings of my fellowmen. I choose a broken heart rather than any happiness that ignores the tragedy of human life and human death.

"'Though I, through the grace of God in Christ, no longer lie under Adam's sin, I would still feel a bond of compassion for all of Adam's tragic race, and I am determined that I shall go down to the grave [and] up into God's Heaven mourning for the lost and perishing.'"[570]

---

[569] Rice and Martin, *Songs and Hymns,* #409.

[570] MacArthur, "Passion for the Lost," accessed June 8, 2011.

R. G. Lee said, " Look on soul winning as a business, not an incidental matter; as work, not play; as time well spent, not wasted; as a privilege, not a boresome duty."[571]

George W. Truett preached, "If one is born again, that one is concerned that somebody else may be saved. 'If any man have not the spirit of Christ, he is none of His.' And the spirit of Christ is the spirit of compassionate anxiety that lost people may be saved."[572]

Dr. Sharp of Charles Street Church, Boston, before his death, said, "I would rather have one young man come to my grave and affirm, 'The man who sleeps there arrested me in the course of sin and led me to Christ,' than to have the most magnificent obelisk that ever marked the place of mortal remains."[573]

434 The Empty Chair

Place an empty chair in the Sunday school classroom, worship center and student room to remind yourself of the importance of outreach. Determine to invite someone unsaved to fill that chair. Upon having that chair filled, set another empty chair out to challenge yourself and your group in the matter of outreach. The empty chair will serve as a constant reminder of the unsaved that stand in need of Jesus and of our role in bringing them to Him.

Gather them in, for there yet is room
At the feast that the King has spread.
Oh, gather them in; let His house be filled
And the hungry and poor be fed.

Gather them in, for there yet is room;
But our hearts, how they throb with pain
To think of the many who slight the call
That may never be heard again.

---

[571] Murphrey, *Drawing the Net*, 16.

[572] Truett, *Quest for Souls*, 60.

[573] Hutson, *Preaching on Soul Winning*, 89.

Gather them in, for there yet is room;
'Tis a message from God above.
Oh, gather them into the fold of grace
And the arms of the Savior's love.

Out in the highway, out in the byway,
Out in the dark paths of sin,
Go forth, go forth with a loving heart
And gather the wand'rers in![574]

435   A Risk-Taking Flavor in Life

John Piper declared, "My desire...is that your life and ministry have a radical flavor, a risk-taking flavor, a gutsy, countercultural wartime flavor that makes the average prosperous Americans in your church feel uncomfortable; a strange mixture of tenderness and toughness that keeps worldly people a little bit off balance; a pervasive summons to something... hazardous...a saltiness and brightness...like...Jesus. Salt and light are a joyful embrace of suffering."[575]

John the Baptist took a risk in decrying King Herod's sin; Paul took a risk in returning to Lystra to preach after being stoned by its citizens; Daniel took a risk in praying as was his custom, despite the King's edict that prohibited praying to any god but him; Queen Esther took a risk in approaching the King without having been called in behalf of the Jewish people; Gideon took a risk in going to war with a small army against the Midianites; Paul again took a risk in witnessing to King Agrippa. Why shouldn't you take a risk in sharing the faith? Muse over the statement of Piper and turn it back to God in a prayer.

436   To What Length Will You Go to Win a Soul?

A student in Edinburgh University who was a good athlete was ruining his life in drunken orgies nightly. A convert of Henry Drummond, desiring to see this student saved, asked permission to house with him. For six months, the Christian put up with the uncleanness and coarseness of his roommate, sat up for him nights, and gave him the ministry of Christian friendship. In the end, he won him to Christ. This drunken medical student,

---

[574] Crosby, "Gather Them In," accessed April 14, 2011.

[575] Piper, "Risk-Taking Adventure!" accessed May 26, 2010.

now a new man in Christ, became one of Drummond's best workers in the university and later went to South Africa.[576]

Think of it—a life with promise but destined for ruination and Hell altered, because someone cared enough to intervene in a drastic manner. Undoubtedly this Christian saw this drunken medical student not as he was, but as what he would be if he were born again. To what length will you go to win a soul to Christ—how far is far enough before backing off? If you asked Jesus this question, His response would be, "I will go as far as necessary, even to the cross, to save a soul."

437 Billy Sunday's Power for Soul Winning

When preaching, Billy Sunday always laid his sermon notes upon a Bible opened to the text of Isaiah 61:1, which reads: "The Spirit of the Lord is upon me; because the Lord hath anointed me to preach good tidings unto the meek; He hath sent me to bind up the broken-hearted, to proclaim liberty to the captives, and the opening of the prisons to them that are bound."

"Many people wanted to possess the Bible Mr. Sunday had used during a campaign. When he granted the request, it would be found that these pages in the book of Isaiah were almost worn out."[577]

"What experience with God did Billy Sunday have that made him always open the Bible to that one verse of Scripture? What holy vow, what compact with God moved this mighty soul winner so that always, when he preached the Gospel, his Bible lay open on the pulpit to these words: 'The Spirit of the Lord God is upon me; because the Lord hath anointed me to preach...'?

"Surely Mr. Sunday knew beyond a shadow of doubt that the Spirit of the Lord was upon him. And he surely knew that he was anointed to preach. I have no doubt he treasured, beyond any other knowledge, the knowledge that his power was the power of God and that he dare not trifle with it. Knowing that he had a holy anointing, he pleased God instead of men; he preached without any compromise; he preached in a way that offended, that cut, that burned, and that assaulted and captured the castles of men's hearts for Christ.

"If Billy Sunday had told me with his own voice, looking me in the face, that he knew he had a definite enduement of power from God for soul

---

[576] Tan, *A Treasury of Illustrations,* #5880.

[577] Rodeheaver, *Twenty Years with Billy Sunday*, 10.

winning and that it was a holy trust with which he dared not trifle but must keep its conditions always in mind, it would not be more certain in my mind than it is....But he was filled with the Holy Ghost and knew it and claimed this as his treasure above all treasure, his one indispensable equipment for soul winning. That we certainly know, by his own emphasis on the power of the Holy Spirit in his preaching and by the fact that he always opened his Bible to this one text in Isaiah 61:1 before preaching the Gospel.

"Other people may not have known where Billy Sunday got his power, but he knew; he knew! And he reminded himself of the one source from which he could have blessing and power every time he ever preached! And we are justified in supposing that every time Billy Sunday opened his Bible to Isaiah 61:1 and laid it on the pulpit before him before beginning his sermon, he made a fresh covenant with God, relying upon the power of the Holy Spirit for that sermon and humbly beseeching God for His blessing. A definite enduement of power from on high is the only possible explanation of Billy Sunday's ministry."[578]

The Holy Spirit who infilled Sunday and empowered his soul winning stands ready to do the same for every believer who submissively yields to His control.

438 Time Is Running Out for 232,876 People Every Day

"If 232,876 people die every day (on average), then how many people die per second? Well, 232,876 divided by 24 hours=9,703 people who die every hour. Then 9,703 divided by 60 minutes=161 people who die every minute. And 161 divided by 60 seconds=2.6 (we'll say 2) people who die every second. Can you imagine this? Two people die in this world every second of every minute of every hour of every day of every week of every month of every year! It adds up to 85,000,000 people a year. Let's assume that I'm right concerning the percentages in saying that only one percent of the population is truly born-again. This means that 2,328 people enter into Heaven each and every day. Sadly, 230,548 people plunge into hellfire each and every day."[579]

We are in a race against death in reaching the lost. Each moment delayed or squandered in sharing Christ may close the door to salvation for eternity for a lost soul. An inscription upon one's watch with the words, "2 per second" would serve as a noble reminder of the cost of delay in witnessing.

---

[578] Rice, "Great Soul Winners," 18.

[579] Stewart, "Billions of People," accessed May 26, 2010.

439 Instantly Go

Paul Rader, an evangelist, had urged a New York banker numerous times to be saved, but without success. One day Rader discerned that the Lord immediately wanted him to share once again with this man. He boarded a train and as quickly as possible made his way to the bank where the man was employed. The banker said, "Rader, I'm glad to see you! I wrote a telegram begging you to come but later changed my mind and didn't send it."

"That's all right," said the evangelist. "Your message came through anyhow by way of Heaven." The banker, under deep conviction of sin, received Christ as Savior and Lord within the hour. Suddenly, he gave a strange gasp and fell into Rader's arms—dead![580]

When you feel the urging of the Holy Spirit to speak to a soul, do so with all haste, as did Rader. Delay on Rader's part would have been tragic.

440 Questions to Ask Ourselves

"I die daily," says I Corinthians 15:31. "We must be ready and willing to pay that ultimate cost, but we should not miss the more applicable usage for our lives. We are to die to ourselves and our control of our privacy and schedules and become available to share by life and action what Christ means to us and can mean to others. The dynamic power of the Holy Spirit will be given in constant flow as long as we are engaged in communicating.

"We are to be conduits or channels, not reservoirs or holding tanks. A flowing river purifies itself; a swamp has inlets but no outflow. The Dead Sea is used often as an example. Fish can live only around the closest reaches of the inflow from the Jordan. But since there is no outflow to the sea, they would die a few yards away. Our lives become dull and dreary as Christians if all we do is take in inspiration from study of the Bible, worship and preaching, and an endless round of classes taught by stirring teachers where application is not mandated. The Holy Spirit's power is given for witness!

"Here are some good questions to ask ourselves and others in preparation for our first Pentecost or for a flow of its continuing power. Who has the Lord put on our agenda to love and introduce to Him? Who now is alive forever because we cared about him or her and were used as the Lord's spiritual obstetricians? Who in our lives may have missed both the abundant and eternal life because of our silence? Are we willing to be made willing for the basic, undeniable calling of every Christian? The

---

[580] Tan, *A Treasury of Illustrations,* #5888.

Lord's power will not be squandered on us for long if we refuse to be channels of His grace as witnesses."[581]

441 The Climbing Wall

I had asked to be the first to try out our new climbing wall at Camp Longridge, despite my acrophobia. As I viewed the three-story climb, I frankly entertained mixed emotions, but I was determined to make the effort. I would be in a safety harness with a rope extending to two staff members whose task was to insure my safety should I miss my footing and fall. As the moment approached to ascend the wall, one of our staff said, "Frank, if you make it to the top, it will be a motivation to me to do it." Without knowing how far I might be able to ascend, I was determined to give it my best effort. As I scaled the wall, encouragement came from below, and, to my amazement, I made it to the top!

Initially in soul winning, one faces a similar challenge. It's not acrophobia, but "soulwinningphobia." Just as I could have chosen not to take the risk, remaining on the ground in my comfort zone, so you may do with regard to sharing the faith; but if you do so, you will never know the joy of the "climb" or whether or not you have the ability to do it. I really had no idea if I could succeed in climbing the wall, but in faith I proceeded with the encouragement and support of others. You may feel this same way in regard to soul winning, but with an experienced soul winner's help, encouragement, and support, at least give it a good try. Do so, and you may be amazed that you actually can do this!

Jason, the staffer at the climbing wall to whom I referred above, did climb the wall to the top. Your soul winning "climb" will motivate the Jasons around you to share Jesus; after all, "if Frank can do it, so can I."

442 Do You Care Enough to Inquire?

Charlie Thompson was one of the first people I met upon arrival in St. George, South Carolina, to begin a student pastorate during my sophomore year in college. In a barber shop, he asked me point blank if I was saved! I soon learned that this was the reputation of "Amen Charlie," as he was affectionately known. Charlie toted his huge Bible and gospel tracts all over town, telling people of Christ without intimidation or fear. Some counted him strange, but I thought of him as a real champion for God.

---

[581] Ogilvie, *Preacher's Commentary,* 39–40.

To my knowledge, St. George has not had a man like "Amen Charlie" to bless her with such soul winning zeal since his departure. It is better to be counted strange for speaking of Christ to one and all like Charlie than to sit idly by, allowing souls to die and go to Hell. Yes, I do remember "Amen Charlie" vividly, for in my lifespan of sixty-two years, he is one of the three who ever cared enough for my soul to inquire about my salvation.

443 What Influences People to Be Saved?

What influences people to be saved?

Advertisement	2%
Organized visitation	6%
Contact by Pastor	6%
Friends and Relatives	86%[582]

J. Wilbur Chapman said that the New Testament records the healing by Jesus of forty people with the identical sickness. Thirty-six of these forty people either were taken to Jesus by friends or had friends who brought Jesus to them. In only a few cases out of the forty did the sickly get to Jesus without assistance.[583]

What is the point? Far more will come to Christ if a friend brings them than if they are left to themselves. The best thing a friend can do for another friend is to bring him to Jesus. The first person I ever won to Christ was my best friend while yet in high school. Talk to that friend today about Christ; they will listen.

444 That I Might by All Means Save Some

C. H. Spurgeon says, "Just be men among men, keeping yourselves clear of all their faults and vices but mingling with them in perfect love and sympathy and feeling that you would do anything in your power to bring them to Christ, so that you might even say with the apostle Paul, 'Though I be free from all men, yet have I made myself servant unto all, that I might gain the more. And unto the Jews I became as a Jew, that I might gain the Jews; to them that are under the law, as under the law, that I might gain them that are under the law; to them that are without law, as without law (being not without law to God, but under the law to Christ), that I might gain them that are without law. To the weak became I as weak, that I might

---

[582] Towns, *Winning the Winnable*, 6.

[583] Tan, *7700 Illustrations*, #7383.

gain the weak: I am made all things to all men that I might by all means save some.'"[584]

"You need a compassion for souls," Hyman Appelman states, "that makes you willing to mark their way to the cross with your heart's blood, a compassion for souls that puts you in such torture, in such agony, in such anguish for those who are on the road to Hell that you say to God, 'Anything, any cost, any amount, any prayers, any sacrifice, anything, Lord, only give me those souls.'"[585]

445 The Best Soul-Winning Training School

"General Booth of the Salvation Army was speaking to a graduating class in the Army's training school. These young people had been there several years, learning how to work for God and win souls. The general said, 'Young men, if I could have had my way, I would never have had you here for these years of training. But I would have put you in Hell for twenty-four hours. I would have allowed you to feel the pains and pangs of the damned, to hear the weeping and wailing and gnashing of teeth. I would have caused you to see how they suffer forever. Then I would have sent you out into the world to warn men to flee from the wrath to come.' General Booth was right. If we really knew what Hell was like, nothing could stop us from urging men to come to Christ."[586]

446 If I Love People, I Will Warn Them

"Suppose that a train carrying 500 passengers was coming down the track and that you and I were 20 miles ahead of the train. And suppose we found that a trestle over a mighty river had fallen in. As I think of the train that is approaching, I say, 'I must warn them and save their lives.' But you say, 'I wouldn't do that; it might scare the passengers. Some of them would faint. Be nice to them and don't disturb them.' So the train rushes on to tragedy, and the passengers are killed.

"Have I done the right thing? Have I been prompted by love? No. If I loved people, I would warn them. And if I love lost souls, I must hold up my Bible and say, 'This is God's Word. It tells us that there is a Hell for

---

[584] Spurgeon, *Soul Winner,* 57–58.

[585] Smith, Shelton L., *Preaching on Revival,* 87.

[586] Ford, *Heaven, Hell and the Judgment,* 68–69.

those who reject Christ. Come to him and be saved from such an awful fate.'"[587]

447 He That Winneth Souls Is Wise

"The text does not say, 'He that winneth sovereigns is wise,' though no doubt he thinks himself wise; and, perhaps, in a certain grovelling sense, in these days of competition, he must be so. But such wisdom is of the earth and ends with the earth, and there is another world where the currencies of Europe will not be accepted nor their past possession be any sign of wealth or wisdom.

"Solomon, in the text before us, awards no crown for wisdom to crafty statesmen or even to the ablest of rulers. He issues no diplomas even to philosophers, poets, or men of wit; he crowns with laurel only those who win souls. He does not declare that he who preaches is necessarily wise; and, alas! there are multitudes who preach and gain much applause and eminence who win no souls and who shall find it go hard with them at the last, because, in all probability, they have run, and the Master has never sent them. Solomon does not say that he who talks about winning souls is wise, since to lay down rules for others is a very simple thing, but to carry them out oneself is far more difficult. He who actually, really, and truly turns men from the error of their ways to God, and so is made the means of saving them from going down to Hell, is a wise man."[588]

448 He Won All His Neighbors on the Street

"Henry Bilbrey became a Christian...at thirty-seven years of age. After Christ came into his life, his whole personality changed. Prior to this, he had lived more or less as an introvert, indifferent to people. After becoming a Christian, he led seventeen of his neighbors and friends to Christ, in addition to being responsible for four others who joined the church by letter. He was a shift worker at the Victor Chemical Company and used every available moment—beginning sometimes as early as six in the morning and continuing until late at night—to witness to others of the saving power of Christ in his life.

"The life of Henry Bilbrey as a Christian was pressed into just five and one-half months of service, but it is a glorious example of what the soul winner with a passion for the lost can do. At his funeral service, two men he

---

[587] Ibid., 71.

[588] Spurgeon, *Soul Winner*, 217–218.

had been seeking to win made their public profession of Christ. The following Sunday, two others came. Henry Bilbrey literally won his whole street to the Lord! After his death, the work went on. Within a month, a total of more than thirty people came into the church as a result of his influence. Two notebooks were found containing the names of thirty-six prospects with whom he had already visited and prayed. The neighbors and friends who came to Christ through his efforts agreed that they would like to carry on this work with the thirty-six prospects he left behind, and they added more of their own."[589]

Bilbrey won more to Jesus in those few months than ninety-five percent of believers do in a lifetime. May God inflame our hearts for souls as Henry Bilbrey's was.

449 The Matchless Soul Winner

Jesus is the matchless Soul Winner. We can learn from His example and be fueled with His burning passion for the damned. Jesus began His work as an Evangelist by winning Andrew and sending him out as a soul winner. Next, He won Phillip and dispatched him to win Nathaniel. Following that, Jesus, for three years, in sermon, personal encounters and Bible teaching, dealt with lost men. He witnessed to the likes of Nicodemus, Zacchaeus, Bartimaeus, the woman at the well, the Pharisees, publicans, priests, soldiers, children, and even kings.

Day and night, His heart burned for the lost. He witnessed to all classes of people. He refused to let racial or cultural barriers impede His witness. He refused to let man or schedule or opposition douse that burning flame for the lost. Scripture records nineteen personal soul winning encounters of Jesus. He didn't just tell us to do it; He did it! He met the lost where they were. According to J. K. Johnston, the Gospels record 132 contacts that Jesus had with people. Six were in the Temple, four were in the synagogues, and 122 were out with the people in the mainstream of life.[590]

To have a passion for souls like Jesus, you must do four things that He did.

You must see as Jesus saw. What did Jesus see? "When He saw the multitude, He was moved with compassion on them, because they fainted, and were scattered abroad, as sheep having no shepherd" (Matthew 9:36). What do you see when you look at athletes, bankers, waitresses, waiters,

---

[589] Washburn, *Outreach for the Unreached*, 143–144.

[590] Johnston, *Why Christians Sin*, 142.

and mechanics? Do you see just people, or do you see souls for which Jesus died? We should look at sinners through the lenses of Christ our Savior and be inflamed with a burden for them, as He manifested.

You must feel as Jesus felt. As Jesus looked upon the multitude, He was moved with compassion (v. 36). If we are going to impact our world, change our schools, and win our friends and acquaintances, we must not only see as Jesus saw, but we must also feel as Jesus felt for the lost. A famous surgeon was asked, "Do you fear a day when your hands will no longer be able to operate?"

He replied, "No, I fear the day when my heart no longer feels the suffering of those on whom I operate." Fear the day when your heart becomes calloused and indifferent to those dying and going to Hell around you.

You must pray as Jesus prayed. No doubt, if we see as Jesus saw and feel as He felt for the lost, we will pray as He prayed for them (v. 38). We are to pray for the lost and also for the willingness of saints to share Jesus with them.

Finally, *you must do as Jesus did.* He planned to win souls. He never lost sight of His goal to bring people face to face with their sin and need of God. You must plan to win souls. You must be intentional.

450   Never Told Hitler of Jesus

On January 25, 1934, the courageous pastor Martin Niemoller, with other pastors, met with Hitler regarding the church's place in Germany. But when he made a suggestion, Hitler snapped, "I'll take care of the Third Reich; you just worry about your sermons!" In a speech in the 1960s, Niemoller stated with great regret that on that occasion, when other pastors and he spent time face to face with Hitler, not once did they mention the name of Jesus, and that this failure had been a recurring nightmare of his.[591] What if they had witnessed and Hitler had been converted? After all, no man is beyond the grasp of God's mercy and grace.

Can you empathize with Niemoller? Have you failed to mention the name of Jesus while in the presence of enemies of the church or political leaders due to their status? Determine to redeem such opportunities as they unfold in the future. No man is any more important than another with regard to salvation, but the conversion of some will bear greater impact for the Kingdom of God.

---

[591] Bouknight, "Lost and Found Collection," May 30, 2010.

451   The Longest Bridge

China's Weinan Weihe Grand Bridge is the longest bridge in the world in use as of this writing (49.5 miles). The longest spiritual bridge for the vast majority of Christians to span is the two to three feet between their friends and themselves in the sharing of Christ. Determine today to cross this bridge with the saving message of the Cross. Friends are waiting.

452   United Flight 175's Last Seconds

"One of the victims on the United Airlines plane that hit the WTC South Tower was Al Marchand. Al's wife, Rebecca, believes that it was part of God's plan for them. Four years earlier, neither of them knew Christ as their Savior. But through the witness of the hired cleaners at the bar where Al worked, both of them became Christians. It was a total change, and Al would often go share his faith in Christ with his old buddies from the bar where he used to be a bartender. Eventually, Al decided to start another career as a flight attendant. He felt that it would be an opportunity to be a witness for Christ. Al told Rebecca, 'What if there is a time when a flight is going down? What if I am the only one who can share the Gospel?'

"A month before Al was killed on 9-11, he flew home on standby next to a nervous passenger named Linda Links. Following 9-11, Linda recalled her conversation with Al. He had said, 'I became a flight attendant so if a plane went down, I could have 30–40 seconds to speak the Gospel to people so they could receive Christ.' Rebecca is certain that the passengers on United Flight 175 heard the Gospel before they crashed into the WTC, because her husband, Al, had a passion to share the love of Christ with others. Maybe that's why it isn't surprising that Rebecca got to share this whole story during an interview with Tom Brokaw on NBC's *Today Show*. Plus, over 100 people became Christians at Al's memorial service!"[592]

On September 11, 2001, Al Marchand had the opportunity he had previously envisioned, to tell panic-stricken passengers who were about to die how they might know Christ. Only Heaven will reveal the number of people who, in those 30–40 seconds or so, heard and heeded. Who knows but that it was for this hour that he was brought into the Kingdom! Marchand lived in anticipation of such a moment and was ready to redeem the opportunity. How about you? Are you living in expectation of the opportunity on the job, at school, or in the neighborhood to tell others of Christ?

---

[592] Emmert, "Keep Your Eyes on the Prize," August 18, 2004.

453 Save Everyone but Him

Apparently, the elder brother in the parable of the Prodigal Son did not want his wayward brother "saved"; if he did, he surely didn't show it (Luke 15:28). He was upset about the return of his brother and the party that was thrown in his honor. Do you identify with him in wanting to see most people saved, but not everyone? After all, who desires the salvation of people who persecute, ostracize, injure, defraud, and shun them? For one, Jesus does! In His torture and grave suffering upon the Cross, He cried, "Father, forgive them; for they know not what they do." Walk in His steps and delete no one from your list to invite to Christ, regardless of their crime against Heaven, others, or yourself.

John Stott wrote that Jesus "had the temerity to sweep away centuries of inherited traditions ('the traditions of the elders') in order that God's Word might again be seen and obeyed. He was also very daring in his breaches of social convention. He insisted on caring for those sections of the community who were normally despised. He spoke to women in public, which, in his day, was not done. He invited children to come to him, although, in Roman society, unwanted children were commonly 'exposed' or dumped, and His own disciples took it for granted that He would not want to be bothered with them. He allowed prostitutes to touch him (Pharisees recoiled from them in horror) and Himself actually touched an untouchable leper (Pharisees threw stones at them to make them keep their distance). In these and other ways, Jesus refused to be bound by human custom; His mind and conscience were bound by God's Word alone."[593]

454 "It's a Big Ocean to Be Lost In"

Nine hundred miles out to sea, an ocean liner sighted a small sloop flying a Turkish flag, a distress signal, and other flags asking for its position at sea. The small vessel had become lost due to a faulty chronometer or immature navigation. The ocean liner, for nearly an hour, circled the boat, providing its crew with correct latitude and longitude. Among the curious passengers on the liner watching all this transpire was a twelve-year-old boy who remarked, "It's a big ocean to be lost in."[594]

It's a big world to be lost in. Like the Turkish small sloop, multitudes of people are lost, needing a Christian to encircle them, sharing directions on how they may be found. It's a big world to be lost in; therefore, believers must ever keep on the lookout and be prepared to make a rescue.

---

[593] Stott, *Balanced Christianity*, 29.

[594] Blair, "It Is a Big Ocean," accessed May 31, 2010.

455 Don't Change the Telegram

Imagine that a World War II Western Union clerk received a telegraph informing parents of their son's death on the battle field. Out of compassion, the clerk changes the message to read, "Dear Mom and Dad, I am well and miss you much. I will be home soon. Jim." The altered message would certainly make them feel better, but when they finally learn the truth, they will wish they had received it instead of the "compassionate lie."

Christians who sugarcoat the truth about a man's sin against God and its tragic eternal consequences do him no favor. In Hell, the lost will wish they had been told the staunch, unadulterated truth rather than the "compassionate lie," and they will question why you didn't tell that to them. In soul winning, compassionately and urgently tell the whole truth and nothing but the truth. Don't water it down, for an adulterated gospel is not a saving gospel.

456 Soul Winning Is a Win-Win Task—Never Win-Fail

No person is a failure who attempts to win souls, regardless of the outcome of such efforts. If you are faithful to sow the seed, the Lord counts you successful. Soul winning is a win-win task, never win-fail. D. L. Moody exclaimed that it's better to tell others about Jesus in a faltering way than never to tell them at all.

457 "Fore; Fore!"

According to the September 18, 2002, edition of "The State," James Tomkins claimed that fellow golfer George Long failed to warn him with the traditional "fore" when Long hit a wayward shot that hit Tomkins in the right eye, knocking him out of a golf cart. Long testified in court that he did yell out a warning. The jury returned a verdict of not guilty.

The soul winner must be careful to shout out warning to the sinner of the judgment that will be his lot if he continues to live in defiance of God's law. This shout of "fore" must not be whispered so as not to disturb or scare sinners, but blasted to gain their attention and alert them of the urgency of salvation. At the Judgment Bar of God, it will be sad for some believers to hear the Lord declare, "You gave a warning to John and Susan, but it was so low key that they didn't hear or believe it; and now their blood will I require at thy hand." Don't fail to yell, "Fore; fore!" to those traveling the broad road to Hell today.

458 "I Have Forgotten My Message"

A magazine carried a cartoon during the 1960 Olympics, depicting a marathon runner rushing into the palace of a king. Fatigue and anguish were written all over his face. As he fell before the king, he was shown looking up to him, saying, "I have forgotten my message."

I fear many believers, when they go soul winning, have forgotten their primary message. I fear many preachers have likewise strayed from it. The message the King of Kings has charged the believer to tell to the eternally damned is not one dealing with baptism, church membership, tithing, doing right, religious reform or "quitting your meanness," but, "Ye must be born again" (John 3:7). Paul Little stated that the soul winner's message must include and evolve around five truths: (1) Jesus Christ, who He is; (2) Jesus' diagnosis of human nature; (3) the fact and meaning of the crucifixion of Jesus Christ; (4) the fact and meaning of the resurrection of Jesus Christ; and (5) the how of becoming a Christian.[595]

Using these five truths as a guide, review your past witnessing encounters to see how much on target you were or were not. Satan doesn't care one iota how much the believer engages in soul winning, as long as he fails to share the Gospel, which alone has the power to save. As you go soul winning, don't forget the pivotal message for going!

459 What Christians Are Supposed to Do

An employee at a dentist's office took to heart what I had told her the night before on soul winning and confronted a pastor (patient) at work. The pastor had been a regular client of the dentist for several years, and yet, never once had he said a word to her about Jesus. Upon inquiring as to the reason why he had not, lame excuses were made. She, in response, said, "I thought that was what Christians were supposed to do." I'm sure the pastor became speechless and greatly embarrassed. How about you? Can a nurse, dental hygienist, doctor, mechanic, yard boy, barber, beautician, or store clerk say of you what was said of this pastor?

460 Get Interested in the Whole Man

W. E. Biederwolf stated, "Men need to be constrained to come to God. It was for this purpose that we ourselves were saved, that we might be of service in bringing others to Christ. We could do this service, if we went about it in the right way. It can be done by

(1) Getting interested in the whole man. There's more to a man than his soul, and we ought to be concerned about the man in his entirety;

(2) Giving a cordial welcome to the stranger in the house of God;

---

[595] Little, *Give Away Your Faith*, 57–58.

(3) A cheerful Christian disposition;

(4) An earnest, consistent Christian life."[596]

461 Why Get Involved in Evangelism?

Joseph Aldrich said, "You don't get involved in evangelism because you feel guilty. You don't get involved in evangelism because it's your duty. You don't get involved in evangelism because someone makes an emotional appeal, complete with sobering charts and grim statistics. Do you know why you get involved in evangelism? You get involved, because Jesus is a pearl so precious that a man would sell everything he owned in order to get it. You get involved in evangelism, because Jesus stretched out his arms in love on the Cross to draw to Himself His lost sons and daughters. You get involved, because Jesus is the King of kings and Lord of lords, the Rose of Sharon, the Lamb of God, the Prince of Peace, and our great treasure. My friend, once you fall in love with this Jesus, you will do everything in your power to introduce others to Him."[597]

462 Don't Greet Anyone on the Road

In dispatching the seventy to witness, Jesus instructed, "Don't take any money with you, nor a traveler's bag, nor an extra pair of sandals. And don't stop to greet anyone on the road" (Luke 10:4 NLT). The mission was top priority, and they must not become distracted from its completion. The believer has received the same mandate. He must not "greet anyone on the road" that would interrupt the winning of souls, nor become entangled with the cares of this world that would deter the work. Soul winning must be kept a priority.

As a child, I was in a lake where salt was mined, when I unexpectedly stepped into a pit and began to drown. My cries for help were drowned by the roar of a motor boat pulling a skier. Though help literally was only feet away, I nearly drowned, because people were focused on the entertainment of the skier. Spiritually, this is often repeated. With people drowning in the lake of sin crying out for rescue, their cry is drowned by the Christian's focus on entertainment in and outside of the church. Thankfully, one person heard my cry for help and saved me in the last moment. Determine not to let the cries of the dying lost go unheard due to pleasure or entertainments, but do as my mother did and make the saving rescue.

---

[596] Hallock, *Evangelistic Cyclopedia*, 153.

[597] Aldrich, *Gentle Persuasion*, 236–237.

463 Keys to Decisions That Stick

In excess of eighty per cent of those who are saved and remain members of a local church are won by a friend. In excess of seventy per cent who profess Christ and drop out of church are "won" by a stranger. Seventy per cent of those who stay in church were introduced to Christ by someone who engaged in the nonmanipulative approach, while almost ninety per cent who "drop out" were won to Christ by someone who engaged in the manipulative approach. In excess of ninety per cent of the new converts who remain in the church following conversion testify of their dissatisfaction with their nonreligious lifestyle prior to being told of Christ. In contrast, in excess of seventy-five per cent of those who "drop out" of church following conversion expressed no real dissatisfaction in their lifestyle prior to being introduced to Christ.[598]

What a mirror these statistics are to help us see the reason for the huge fall-out rate among new converts in the church! I glean from this study that evangelism is most productive when friends share with friends, when the soul winner does not try to manipulate a decision for Christ, and when the new convert was deeply distressed over his lifestyle apart from Christ. Doubtfully will any man be saved apart from dissatisfaction and distress in life due to sin against God. C. H. Spurgeon remarks, "No man will ever put on the robe of Christ's righteousness until he is stripped of his fig leaves, nor will he wash in the fount of mercy till he perceives his filthiness. Therefore, my brethren, we must not cease to declare the Law, its demands, its threatenings, and the sinner's multiplied breaches of it."[599]

464 A Torn-Up Tract Reassembled Saved Him

T. J. Bach, a great missionary statesman, was saved through the reading of a gospel tract. Upon receiving the tract from a stranger on a street in Chicago, he immediately tore it into pieces and threw it to the pavement. The stranger began to weep. Strangely touched, Bach picked up the various pieces of the tract and placed them in his pocket. In his room, he reassembled the tract, read it, and received Christ. The Lord used the tract for sure to save Bach, but had it not been for the broken heart of the stranger that arrested Bach in his tracks, the tract would never have been retrieved to be read.[600]

---

[598] Ibid., 98–99.

[599] Comfort, *Evidence Bible*, 411.

[600] Aldrich, *Gentle Persuasion*, 95.

Fill your pockets with tracts and hit the streets distributing them compassionately. Don't underestimate the power God invests in a tract delivered to the lost by a broken heart. It is unknown if the stranger who handed Bach the tract ever learned of his decision. Let this encourage you to continue tract distribution though it appears futile.

465 What It Means to Have a Burden for Souls

Bailey Smith writes, "As difficult as that burden for the world without Christ is, we must not allow it to escape us. When it leaves, we might sigh a sigh of personal relief, but at that moment, our life will lose its zeal and contagious enthusiasm for a disciplined life of service.

"Having the burden does not mean that we will constantly feel weighed down, worried, haggard, and joyless. It does mean that we, like our Lord, will have a daily sense of genuine interest in confronting the lost with God's eternal hope. It means that we will have ever before us the vision of the lostness of men apart from Jesus, willing to be used of the Holy Spirit in loving, caring, and sharing....

"Win Arn is right. 'To grow in Christlikeness means to share His burden for the salvation of the world.' That, indeed, is the Christian life at its best and deepest. We all must get a new urgency about rescuing every person who is lost, knowing that they are only one heartbeat from Hell. Keep the burden and be a blessing."[601]

466 You Can't Take the Gospel to the Wrong Address

Following a message on soul winning I delivered in a church, a lady with resolve to become a soul winner asked, "To whom am I to talk?" In one word, I responded, "Everyone." In soul winning, confront all—religious and nonreligious—for the lost are in both camps. As someone said, "You can't take the Gospel to the wrong address."

467 The Pilot's Last Chance

Over the table of parachute makers was written: "Make sure it's good; it constitutes a pilot's last hope." This statement can be adapted for soul winners as follows: "Make each presentation the best possible; it's the person's last chance." Don't rush the presentation to get to the next house or shop. Take the necessary time to rightly share the *who, what, why, how,* and *when* of salvation.

---

[601] Smith, Bailey, *Real Evangelism*, 40.

My wife, Mary, and I were staying at a hotel, when the fire and voice alarm sounded for evacuation. I was satisfied that it was a false alarm and, therefore, did not evacuate. Later when I was asked the reason for such a determination, I responded that had the fire alarm been real, it would have sounded continuously, not for the brief moments it did. I think the unsaved take our "fire alarms" lightly because of the lack of intensity and persistence exhibited. Not until the lost trapped in the burning building of condemnation realize our warning is not a "false alarm" will they exit, yielding their souls to Christ.

468   You Have to Begin to Ever End

Lewis Carroll, in *Alice in Wonderland,* wrote: "The Mock Turtle, in a deep hollow tone, said, 'Sit down, and don't speak a word 'til I've finished.' So they sat down, and nobody spoke for some minutes. Alice thought to herself, *I don't see how he can ever finish if he doesn't begin."* You can never finish, if you fail to start.[602]

Soul winning has to have a beginning point, or else one simply hears and learns about doing it. Let today be that starting point!

469   "Doctor, What Is Your Name?"

A soldier was wounded in Williamsburg. An artery of his arm was severed by shell fragment, and death was imminent unless treatment was administered. He saw a surgeon passing at a distance and called to him for help. The doctor dismounted and rendered the necessary treatment to save the soldier's life. As the doctor was leaving, the soldier said, "Doctor, what is your name?"

"Oh! no matter about that," was the reply.

"But, doctor, I want to tell my wife and children who it was that saved me!"[603]

Just so, when Jesus comes to our rescue, healing our hurts, forgiving our sin, saving our dying souls, turning our world inside out for the better, we are constrained to tell others "who it was that saved me." It makes no sense that one who has been saved from hell on earth and a literal Hell hereafter does not want to tell others of His Savior.

---

[602] Aldrich, *Gentle Persuasion*, 183.

[603] Ibid., 152.

SPURS TO SOUL WINNING

470 We Will Find a Way to Speak for Jesus

A King in Lydia had a son who was unable to speak who dwelt with him in the palace. A battle ensued between the Persians and the Lydians, and Croesus was overthrown. A soldier was about to slay the unhappy monarch, who was unknown to him to be a king, before the eyes of his son. In that moment horror, fear and love did what medical science could not do. "Spare him; he is the king!" the boy cried. His determined effort to save his father had burst the string that had tied his tongue. If we were as anxious to snatch others from eternal death as this poor prince was to save his father, we should find that we too could speak; we should no longer be silent.[604]

471 Come!

In the deserts, when caravans need water, they send a wave of several riders separated by a short distance to search. Upon the first rider's discovery of water, he shouts aloud, "Come!" The next one repeats the word, "Come!" So the shout is passed on to another, until the whole desert echoes with the word, "Come!"[605]

This beautifully depicts the task of the saved. We who have discovered the wellspring of "living water" are to shout "Come!" throughout our ranks, so the spiritually thirsty about us may know where to drink. Imagine the evangelization that would occur if all the redeemed would shout "Come!" until the whole world echoes with it. This will never happen until YOU shout it!

472 The Last Call

To everything there comes a "last." Athletes are familiar with the saying: "Casey at the Bat"—score tied, bases full, two outs. Folks attending auctions are familiar with the auctioneer's warning: "Going once; going twice; gone." Shoppers are familiar with the promotion which states: "Better hurry. This offers ends at midnight tonight." And all have heard of the urgent "blue-light special" with warnings that these deals will not last long.

The Bible likewise thunders with the warning of the "last call." There will be a "last call" for man to be saved, a "last call" for the saint to repent and be restored spiritually, a "last call" to vocational ministry, and a "last call" to engage in soul winning. The common denominator linking these "last calls" is that their time of occurrence is unknown. Perhaps today you

---

[604] Hallock, *Evangelistic Cyclopedia*, 120–121.

[605] Ibid., 46.

will be issuing God's "last call" to salvation to a lost soul or be receiving your "last call" to win a soul.

473 Laity Soul Winning Enables the Pastor

J. Wilbur Chapman remarked, "Mr. Moody used to say that it was far better to set ten men to work than for one to attempt to do the work of ten men. No greater blessing could come to the church than that the members should be inspired to enter upon some special service. Each pastor would be more effective if he could know that his people were actively aroused to the duty of personal evangelism and were engaged in direct effort to reclaim the lapsed church members and to win the unsaved to Christ."[606]

I read an account of one church member who assured his pastor that every Sunday he would be responsible for having at least one soul walk the aisle during the invitation. May God increase his number in the church! Can your pastor count on you to win souls?

474 A Fourteen-Year-Old Boy Won Them

A fourteen-year-old boy from a missionary school went into a village temple and noted an old man passing from idol to idol praying and offering incense sticks. The boy, with tears flowing down his cheeks, approached the man, saying, "Would you mind a boy speaking to you? I am young; you are old." The elder man was not offended and allowed the boy to share the message of God's love.

In response to the boy's words, the man said, "Boy, I have never heard such words before." He invited the boy to go home with him to share the story of God's love with his wife. He and his wife were led to the Savior by the teenage boy.[607]

Age is not a factor in soul winning. The young can win souls as much as the old. As a child or teenager, are you actively engaged in winning your friends to Christ?

475 Use What's in Your Sack

The little boy only had five loaves and two fishes in his sack, but that was all that was needed for Jesus to feed five thousand. Five stones were all David had in his sack, but they were sufficient to fell a giant. You have in

---

[606] Ibid., 217.

[607] Ibid., 31.

your sack things that God will transform into tools to reach the lost if yielded unto Him.

What's in your sack? Is it the ability to repair things, bake cakes, fix vehicles, teach, speak publicly, speak multiple languages, play a musical instrument, sing? God wants to use these abilities to serve as bridges for the entrance of the Gospel into the hearts of the unsaved. Piggyback such rendering of hospitality or help to others with verbally sharing Christ. Use what's in your sack.

476 Hunting for Souls Now

Kim, a native African, hunted tigers for years. One day he heard the Gospel and was saved. Later a missionary met him on a trail and inquired what he was carrying in his bag. "Ammunition," he replied and opened it for the missionary.

Seeing only a New Testament and a hymnal, the missionary said, "You can't hunt tigers with those things."

"That's right," said Kim, "but I'm hunting for souls now!"[608]

From the moment of conversion, the Christian ought to be "hunting for souls now!" Are you?

477 Never Grow Satisfied with Empty Nets and Useless Hooks

W. B. Riley stated, "The man who is satisfied in soul winning is stultified in spiritual interest."[609] How can the soul winner ever be satisfied with either his labor or fruit when so many need to be rescued from the grip of sin and Satan? Paul certainly wasn't satisfied with his soul winning effort, for he cried, "I say the truth in Christ, I lie not, my conscience also bearing me witness in the Holy Ghost, That I have great heaviness and continual sorrow in my heart. For I could wish that myself were accursed from Christ for my brethren, my kinsmen according to the flesh" (Romans 9:1–3). The soul winner should rejoice much in the work of soul winning but never grow satisfied and complacent with empty nets and useless hooks.

478 It's Not Too Soon to Tell

"Philip had only just found the Lord himself, and at once he set out to seek Nathanael. He certainly lost no time, but why should he lose any time?

---

[608] Knight, *Knight's Illustrations*, 315.

[609] Hutson, *Preaching on Soul Winning*, 97.

He had made a tremendous discovery. How long should he have waited before sharing his discovery with someone else? Philip had the prime qualification for being a soul winner—he knew the Lord personally; and if you know the Lord as your personal Savior, you are at once qualified to begin this work of soul winning. The best preparation for this is a heart full of love for the Lord Himself, so do not imagine that you are too young a Christian or do not have the necessary gifts to tell someone what you know of the Lord and to commend Him to them—and the best time is to start now!"[610]

479 Be Always Ready

En route to speak in a church, I stopped at a McDonald's. Parked in a shaded area in the back of the parking lot, I was suddenly confronted by a man who said, "Can you tell me about God?" Immediately, I got out of my car and shared the Gospel with him. He was for real. Seldom have I had such an experience when someone approached me inquiring of God. Realizing that such a confrontation is a possibility, the believer should always have his "gun" loaded and be ready to share the Gospel at the spur of the moment. Is yours loaded?

Luke 15 records the "Lost and Found Collection" of Jesus, regarding the lost sheep, coin, and son. The emphasis of this trilogy is Heaven's focus on the salvation of the lost and God's joy when one is saved. The entire trilogy pulsates with God's love for the lost and His desire for them to be found. Since this is the heart of God for the lost, should it not also be ours? The "found" ones diligently are to seek the "lost" ones until they are rescued; then it's party time in Heaven and among saints on earth, for "a sinner has come home."

Randolph, with gas can in hand, was walking along the side of the road; his truck was out of fuel. I stopped my car, offering him a ride to the nearest gas station. En route, I spoke to him of Christ, to which he responded, "He's been knocking on my door a lot lately, and I think it's time to listen." Randolph did listen this time and was gloriously saved. At that very moment, his life moved from the "lost" to the "found" column in God's record book, and rejoicing broke out among the inhabitants of Heaven. Many "Randolphs" in the "lost" column await a believer to introduce them to Christ that they may move to the "found" column.

---

[610] Dixon, "Ten New Testament Soul Winners," accessed June 11, 2010.

SPURS TO SOUL WINNING

480 Start Out Like You Can Hold Out

Years ago, when I was a young evangelist, I was staying in a home during a revival. Regarding what she was prepared to do for me during the stay, the hostess, right out of the chute, said, "I'm going to start out like I can hold out." This is great advice for the novice soul winner: "Start out like you can hold out." Initially accepting too many assignments, placing upon yourself too many goals regarding tracts distributed, souls won, contacts made (worthy as these desires are) will serve to overload and weigh you down. Remember that soul winning is to be more delight than duty, desire than discipline, and that it is a lifelong effort. Gradually increase soul winning commitments instead of heaping them all on the plate at the same time.

481 Temptations of the Soul Winner

Criticism. Face it—some people will not appreciate your soul winning efforts and methods. D. L. Moody, when criticized for his method of evangelism, replied, "I agree with you. I don't like the way I do it either. Tell me, how do you do it?"

The woman replied, "I don't do it."

Moody retorted, "Then I like my way of doing it better than your way of not doing it."[611] That's a good answer, for most opposition to evangelism will arise from believers who are not doing it.

Complacency. The tendency in soul winning is to become content with the routine, though few fish are being caught. Cast out into deeper waters, let down your net where fish are known to exist, change fishing poles and lures, but never be satisfied with empty buckets at the end of the day.

Conniving. In times of barrenness, don't revert to the flesh to manufacture decisions. The conniving of some soul winners to get a decision is self-centered and utterly detestable. If the Holy Spirit does not convict man of sin and the need of salvation, certainly nothing in your bag of tricks can!

Counting. Spurgeon said, "No fisherman can live on catching and counting. It is a very deceptive thing for a man to sustain his faith upon the success of his labors."[612]

"I am weary of this public bragging," continued Spurgeon, "this counting of unhatched chickens, this exhibition of doubtful spoils. Lay

---

[611] Hodgin, *1001 Humorous Illustrations,* 330.

[612] Spurgeon, "Breakfast with Jesus," accessed March 13, 2010.

aside such numberings of the people, such idle pretense of certifying in half a minute that which will need the testing of a lifetime. Hope for the best, but in your highest excitements, be reasonable."[613] It is not wrong to count and credit souls won to God if the purpose is indeed to glorify Him, but when the motive is of the flesh, it must be despised.

Comparing. Don't compare how God uses you in soul winning with another, for it may lead to either a spirit of prideful arrogance or discouraging inadequacy. It is healthy to watch soul winners at work so you can be instructed and sharpened for the task, but never for comparison. Not all of God's fishermen are gifted or equipped equally.

Carelessness. Stay cautious. Don't allow yourself to be alone in a private place with a member of the opposite sex in presenting a witness. Stronger giants than you have fallen into sexual sin simply due to carelessness.

Coldness. Soul winning begins and continues in devotion at the Savior's feet. Don't shortchange private communion with Christ in Word and prayer, ever going deeper with Him, lest spiritual shipwreck occur. Keep your heart "hot."

L. R. Scarborough cites how the soul winner may have victory in temptation. "When Jesus Christ faced the Devil in these three soul-testing temptations, His answers were positive, with conviction, and in the same line in which we can answer. His reply each time to the Devil was scriptural. It is necessary for us, as Jesus was, to be armed with the truth hidden away in our hearts, that we may have the wherewithal to answer every fiery temptation of the evil one."[614]

482   Jesus Gave His Best Effort to Win Her

Jesus gave His best effort in witnessing to the woman at Jacob's Well (John 4:22–23). He did not save His best witness for someone more promising or affluent but spoke to this woman's heart as if she were the only lost person in the world. The soul winner must give his best effort in reaching every sinner.

On Sunday morning, January 6, 1850, a young boy by the name of Charles Spurgeon was one of only fifteen present for worship at a Primitive Methodist Chapel. The speaker, a layman, preached the best he could, urging Spurgeon specifically to "look unto Christ." Spurgeon responded to

---

[613] Smith, Bailey, *Real Evangelism*, 126.

[614] Shivers, *Soul Winning 101*, 139.

that call and was gloriously converted.[615] One can only wonder how different Spurgeon's life may have been had this layman not done his best, despite the few that were gathered that morning.

483   What the Marigold Teaches about Soul Winning

If you can talk a person into being "saved," somebody else can talk him out of it. A little boy inquired, "Why is it that when I open a marigold, it dies; but when God opens one, it lives." The reply came, "Because when God opens a marigold, He opens it from the inside out." The soul winner must never forget the lesson of the marigold as he seeks to "open man's heart" for salvation.

Lewis Drummond stated, "Any form of evangelism that resorts to the manipulation of people, regardless of the motive, is unworthy of the Gospel. Even more tragically, such a use of evangelism can lead unsuspecting and honest inquirers into a shallow understanding that falls short of a genuine experience of salvation. Scriptural evangelism demands that the evangelist fill the presentation of the Gospel with solid theological content. That price must be paid if God's approval of the work is to be expected, for people are rarely if ever genuinely converted by psychological maneuvering, persuasive oratory, or emotional stories devoid of the impact of the Holy Spirit. For the sake of those whom we would reach for Christ, authentic theology and evangelism must not be separated. We must avoid superficial 'believism.' People deserve to hear the full truth of Jesus Christ and salvation."[616]

484   "Spiritual Manslaughter"

Monroe Parker told a story he called "Spiritual Manslaughter." "I was in a revival in Detroit, and a man asked me to go to the county prison and talk with a relative of his who was sentenced for manslaughter. I went down to the prison and led the man to Christ....That man was in prison three years for manslaughter, not first-degree murder. He had been left in charge of a railroad gate. He failed to put the gate down when a train was coming. A car ran onto the track, and a man was killed. So this prisoner was doing time for dereliction of his duty.

---

[615] Hayden, *Unforgettable Spurgeon*, 15.

[616] Drummond, *Reaching Generation Next*, 100–101.

"I left prison that day asking this question, 'Lord, is it true that if I fail to put down the gate of warning and people run past me into Hell, I become guilty of spiritual manslaughter?'"[617]

God answers that question in Ezekiel 3:18 and 33:8, clearly stating "Yes, you are guilty of it."

485 Draw the Net

The purpose in soul winning is to win souls; it's senseless to present the Gospel and not "draw the net." Soul winners must invite people to repent of their sin and in faith embrace Christ at the end of their presentation of the gospel message. When I spoke on soul winning in Monroe, North Carolina, the pastor responded to the invitation to be a better soul winner. Sharing a meal shortly afterward, he said that his "soul winning" efforts fell short of asking the trigger question. In essence, he simply was presenting a witness.

Share the gospel presentation and always ask a trigger question in conclusion, like, "What would you like to do with Jesus in response to what I have just shared?"; "Can I pray with you about receiving Christ into your life?" Failure to "draw the net" will never win a soul.

486 Remember the Chariots of Fire

Recall the story of the prophet Elisha in Dothan under siege by the Syrian army (II Kings 6:8–18)? Elijah awoke early one morning, only to see the city surrounded by chariots, horses, and a host of enemy Syrian troops. Elisha's servant, seeing all this, said, "Alas, master, how shall we do?"

Elisha responded, "Fear not: for they that be with us are more than they that be with them." The prophet then prayed for God to open the servant's eyes that he might see the grand host of chariots of fire upon the mountain that surrounded them.

Out there in the trenches, knocking on doors, handing out tracts, and presenting the Gospel at times becomes a scary thing with regard to whom you see and where you see them. In such a time, remember the *Chariots of Fire*. There is no need to fear or panic, for God has encompassed your every side with a heavenly host providing protection. You may need to pause and pray, requesting God to open your eyes to "see them," but they are there, regardless. In warring for souls, God backs the soul winner up to the hilt! You can take that to the bank.

---

[617] Smith, Shelton, "Soul Winning," 4A.

SPURS TO SOUL WINNING

487 The Holy Spirit's Promise to the Soul Winner

L. R. Scarborough wrote that the Holy Spirit has promised to go before us (Isaiah 45:2), behind us (Isaiah 58:8), beneath us (Deuteronomy 33:27), with us (Matthew 28:20), within us (John 14:17), upon us (Acts 1:8), and all around us (Matthew 3:11). He has promised to hold us with the right hand of his righteousness (Isaiah 41:10) and never to let us fall (John 10:27–28; Jude 24).[618] With Him as our constant Companion, success is assured in the labor of winning souls.

488 The "Choicy" Unsaved

Some people, like Naaman, will be "choicy" regarding the means of their salvation. A woman complained about the life preservers to the captain of a vessel. "Just look at them," she said.

"What's the matter with them?" inquired the captain.

"Matter with them?" the woman replied. "Don't you see that they are dirty? If a woman with a nice summer dress on had to put one of those things over it, it would never be fit to wear again!" That may be humorous, but it is sadly true spiritually. The task of the soul winner is to make plain that man has a choice about salvation, but not as to its means (John 14:6).

489 A Serious Handicap to Soul Winning

Leonard Sanderson wrote, "One of our most serious handicaps in bringing others into the Kingdom is the dearth of knowledge of the great fundamental doctrines of the Kingdom on the part of those who are supposed to represent it....The ambassador [soul winner] must know the power of his kingdom.

"It is inconceivable that an ambassador would be unfamiliar with his country's power potential, militarily and politically. The Christian ambassador must know experientially the power of Christ to make one a new creation and to guard and keep him in life and eternity. A Christian will be a poor witness, for example, if he does not know how God answers prayer. He likewise must be familiar with God's judgment and the eternal danger of ignoring God's proffered salvation."[619]

The lack of spiritual knowledge in the church pressed me to write *Christian Basics 101* to enhance biblical knowledge and comprehension.

---

[618] Scarborough, *With Christ*, 36.

[619] Bisagno, Chafin, and Freeman, *How to Win Them*, 122.

490 "The One Thing Needful"

Marshall Craig was asked why he was always in a hurry, rushing here and there. "One reason is the urgency of the work to be done," he answered. Leonard Sanderson states, "Spirit-born believers, who comprise churches of Christ, have the most urgent mission in the world. We must not allow ourselves to be forever involved in the parasitic entanglements of small things and secondary issues that sap our strength and occupy so much of our time. We must devote ourselves, under the power of the Spirit, to 'the one thing needful,' always careful that our practice matches our preaching."[620]

Noncombatant British fifers and drummers played an important role in the eighteenth-century military in sounding signals to the troops regarding battle commands. It is interesting to note that, though these signaled the command for battle, they were noncombatant. Their type is still around in the church—those who signal the order to battle (pursuit of souls for Christ) without engaging in the pursuit.

491 Harvest Time Is Now or Never

Jesus said to His disciples, "Do you not say, there are yet four months, then comes the harvest? I tell you, lift up your eyes, and see how the fields are already white for harvest" (John 4:35).

"Everybody knows that there are seasons of the year when the farmer lives a reasonably relaxed life, but it is not at harvest time. All his investment of time and money for the whole year is at stake. It is now or never. All hands must be busy almost around the clock. Meals are eaten on the run. Nearly all social life is canceled. Even the family receives little attention. Young people must sometimes miss some school work. Workers may be brought in from outside.

"This is the emphasis of Jesus in stressing soul winning....When we set aside time for witnessing, let us observe it with complete dedication. It may be a day each week the year round. It may be a week of evangelistic emphasis. It may be church visitation night. Remember, harvest time is now or never. It is easier to do any other kind of visitation than evangelistic visitation. This is true for pastors and others.

"They tell us it is more difficult to win others now. This is perhaps true, but it has never been easy in my lifetime. The harvest problem is basically a labor problem. People can still be brought to Jesus. They still need Jesus. Jesus still saves. He still commands us to go. He still promises power. We have no alternative but to obey or disobey. Those who persist in sowing,

---

[620] Ibid., 129.

cultivating, and watering continue to bring in the harvest. Let us be dedicated fishermen."[621]

492 The Showcase of the Heart

Somebody asked Billy Graham, "Can a man be a Christian and contain Christ—bottle him up in his heart?"

Graham replied, "No, we have to share Him."[622]

Soul winning is a divine imperative and, therefore, is not optional.

Give us a watchword for the hour,
A thrilling word, a word of power,
A battle cry, a flaming breath
That calls to conquest or to death,
A word to rouse the church from rest,
To heed the Master's strong request.
The call is given, "Ye hosts, arise!"
Our watchword is evangelize!

The glad evangel now proclaim
Through all the earth in Jesus' name;
This word is ringing through the skies:
Evangelize! Evangelize!
To dying men, a fallen race,
Make known the gift of gospel grace;
The world that now in darkness lies,
Evangelize! Evangelize![623]

Leonard Ravenhill states that the tongue showcases what's in the heart. He said, "Our words reflect what's in our hearts. If a man loves sports, he talks sports. If he loves money, he talks money. If he loves art, he talks art. I marvel at the slackness of speech among Christians and at how often preachers are guilty of gross exaggerations in their reports about their meetings and at how carelessly they slander others.

---

[621] Ibid., 131–132.

[622] Ibid., 103.

[623] Smith, Oswald J., "Evangelize! Evangelize!" accessed May 4, 2010.

"I was at a ministers' conference some years ago, and we drove back and forth in packed buses all week between the hotel and the conference center. But never once among all those ministers was the conversation about God or holiness or the coming of Jesus. It was sports or golf handicaps or how big their Sunday school was. It was just senseless chatter even among preachers. But preachers aren't the only ones guilty of conversation which is unprofitable and unedifying."[624]

What's in the heart will flow through the lips. How much are your lips telling of Jesus and the cross?

493   The Sin of the Desert

Jay Strack, in his nine trips to the Holy Land, used the same Bedouin tour guide, unto whom he witnessed each time. The final time he talked with him, the guide inquired as to why he was so persistent in sharing his faith. Strack explained that he was a friend for whom he cared deeply and that he just had to share the way of salvation. The guide looked at him, saying, "I understand now. You do not want to commit the sin of the desert." Not knowing what that meant, he asked the guide to explain. Strack learned that to the Bedouins, who are a nomadic people, the ultimate sin of the desert is…knowing where water is but refusing to tell.[625]

The sin of the desert is the greatest sin of this church age. People all around us are dying for lack of 'water'; knowing where water is, Christians simply fail to tell. This is inexcusable. This is detestable. Go and tell a thirsty soul where the fountain of living water flows today.

494   God Prepares the Lost Soul for the Soul Winner

Keith Parks, while President of the Foreign Mission Board of the Southern Baptist Convention, said, "As far as I know, we are never told in Scriptures that we should prepare the hearts of people. That's God's business. What we are told is to be busy ourselves at sowing and reaping." Paul Powell adds, "It's God's business to prepare the hearts of people, and He is always doing that. He furrows the hearts of men through scores of circumstances to prepare them to receive the Gospel."[626]

---

[624] Ravenhill, "Taming of the Tongue," accessed June 9, 2010.

[625] Powell, *Special Sermons for Special Days*, 87.

[626] Ibid., 95.

Underline this truth in soul winning. God prepares the soul; Christians sow and reap.

495 "The Consequences of Delay Justify Great Risk"

It was June 6, 1944. Allied forces were poised for Operation Overlord, the cross-channel attack from England to France. It would be D-Day, the invasion of Normandy. If this operation was successful, it would usher in the beginning of the end of WWII. The invasion was scheduled for June 5, but inclement weather forced delay for twenty-four hours.

General Eisenhower asked the meteorologist, J. M. Staggs, for a weather update. Stagg replied, "A fresh weather front provides hope of improved conditions the following day. We will have a corridor of about thirty-six hours where the ceiling will be 3,000 feet. If we wait beyond that, it will be at least a month before the weather will allow us to go."

Eisenhower asked the assembled commanders how they viewed the weather's impact on the invasion. But ultimately, he had to make the decision to go or not. After they voiced positions on the matter, he sat in silence for thirty, maybe forty, seconds. Looking up, he voiced to the commanders, "The consequences of delay justify great risk. We'll go."[627]

Paul Powell, commenting on this historic event, wrote regarding soul winning, "Our decision to go affects more than the outcome of a war in time. It affects the souls of men for eternity. We are sowing and reaping for everlasting life. How many hours do we have before the ceiling falls? I do not know, but it's getting awfully dark outside. God knows we have had enough time already. The time has come for us to say, 'The consequences of delay justify great risk. We'll go.'"[628]

496 We've Got to Get the Message Out

A man asked for money for food from another man standing on a street corner. The man replied, "I won't give you money, because I don't know how you would spend it, but I will buy you the meal."

The beggar said, "No. I'm busy and you're busy. Just give me the money, and I will go my way, and you go yours."

To this the first man answered, "No, come with me, and I'll buy you a meal." Finally the beggar agreed to those terms and ate like he was half-

---

[627] Ibid., 95–96.

[628] Ibid., 96.

starved. Following the meal, the man who bought the meal asked the beggar, "Tell me, what were you going to do with the money? You weren't going to spend it on food, were you?"

The beggar replied, "No, I was not. I'll tell you what I was going to do with it. You see, sir, I'm a Communist. Two blocks down the street, we have a print shop. We have type all set up, but we couldn't get paper, because we ran out of money. Three of my comrades and I vowed we would go without eating for four days and use the money for our meals to buy paper. You see, sir, we have to get the message out."[629]

The Christian must be consumed with the importance of "getting the message out" with this same devotion.

497 "It's Death or Deep Water"

S. D. Gordon stated, "Long years ago, in the days before steam navigation, an ocean vessel came from a long voyage, sailed up St. George's Channel, and headed for Liverpool. When the pilot was taken on board, he cried abruptly to the captain, 'What do you mean? You've let her drift off toward the Welsh coast, toward the shallows. Muster the crew.' The crew was quickly mustered. The pilot told of the danger in a few short words and then said sharply, 'Boys, it's death or deep water; hoist the mainsail.' And only by dint of hardest work was the ship saved.

"If I could get the ear of the church today, I would, as a great kindness to it, cry out with all the earnestness of soul I could command, 'It's death or deep water—deep water in the holy service of changing the world, or death from foundering.'"[630]

Awaken, thou man of God who is asleep in Zion while the battle rages in the field. Launch out into the deep.

498 "Hey, Mister, Lift Me Up So I Can See"

R. G. Lee, watching a parade in Memphis, Tennessee, saw a little, dirty, raggedly dressed boy trying to get around some adults so he could stand in front and see the parade. Finally, only one tall man obstructed his passage. He was blocked on both sides of the man, unable to move forward. Desperately he reached up and tugged on the man's coattail. The man looked around but didn't see the boy. The tug came again, with more

---

[629] Bisagno, Chafin, and Freeman, *How to Win Them*, 45–46.

[630] Gordon, *What It Will Take*, 155.

insistence. This time the man saw the dirty little boy. The boy, with a smile bright as a new silver dollar, said, "Hey, mister, lift me up so I can see!"

Lost, dirty, raggedly dressed boys and girls (and others) are saying to Christians, "If you've got anything that'll help, lift us up; help us to see."[631]

499 All This, and Heaven Too!

"If we are to win people to Jesus Christ, then it must be to Jesus Christ that we win them—not to a short-lived surrender or less-than-for-life commitment. Saving faith in Jesus involves the mind, heart, and will in unconditional surrender and absolute obedience to him....It may be trite to repeat it, but it is nevertheless still true that evangelism is incomplete until the evangelized becomes an evangelist. If one's faith in Christ is so weak as to not be shared, there is sincere cause for careful scrutiny as to the validity of that kind of faith. *Saving faith is always sharing faith.*"[632]

Wayne Ward wrote, "We are in the miracle business! We marvel at doctors who can take one heart and put it in another person. I'll admit that's wonderful. But do you know something? Every time you go down on your knees with a lost soul and see one born again...you have seen a greater miracle. You have seen a person turned inside-out-reborn. The final 'wind-up' of that miracle will be that day when all the reborn come forth unto life *eternal*. Not just a work for this earth—*all this, and Heaven too!* Can you be content to go your way and fail to tell men and women, boys and girls, about this wonderful *new* life in Christ?"[633]

500 Do You Value Souls?

Do you value souls? "Oh, that men and women may become impressed with the fact that we are in dead earnest! Bishop Phillips Brooks quoted a man who said to a preacher, 'I am not really convinced by what you say. I am not sure but what I could answer every argument you have presented. But one thing puzzles me and makes me feel that there is power in your message. I cannot understand why you go to so much trouble and why you labor with me in this way, as if you cared for my soul!' That is it! Many a skeptic has been won to Christ, not so much by argument as by realizing that the preacher believed what he said.

---

[631] Bisagno, Chafin, and Freeman, *How to Win Them*, 91–92.

[632] Ibid., 144.

[633] Ibid., 158.

"A Jewish millionaire went to the Royal Opera House, London, to hear D. L. Moody. One of his friends said to him, 'You don't believe what he preaches, do you?'

"And the reply was to the point, 'No, I don't; but he does. And that is why I go to hear that man.'"[634]

501 Turn the Radio Up

Years ago an old time preacher named N. D. Brewer would tell listeners to his gospel radio show to roll down their car windows and turn the radio up so the Gospel could impact those in listening range. I for one did as he suggested. There is no telling how many over the years were impacted by Brewer's music and message in this manner.

I have added to Brewer's suggestion. I open my car door and turn on and turn up gospel music at the conclusion of my daily run at the park. All who walk the trail by my car hear about Jesus. Why not share the Gospel in similar ways? The Gospel is powerful by whatever means it is delivered.

502 Wrap Them in Hot Tears

At a Keswick Conference years ago, the person to close out the session was unable to speak, so the floor was opened to testimonies. People stood one after the other, testifying to the wonderful grace of God. The last to rise was a preacher in his seventies.

"Brother Moderator and you other brethren," the man said, "I thought for a while I would not say a word, but I can't keep from it. I want to tell you what the Lord has done for me....You know my wife and I were married when I was twenty-four and she was just twenty-two. For a long time the Lord withheld the blessing of a child. Then a boy came, a bonnie boy, a beautiful boy, a blessed boy. We loved him, worshiped him, adored him, maybe too much....

"When he got to be four, he became ill of a nameless sickness that no doctor could diagnose. Our family physician called in some of the mightiest specialists in the country, but nothing could be done. The boy lay stretched out in bed, a wasting skeleton." He went on to say that the church he pastored took up a generous offering for his son and told him to take a leave of absence to seek out further medical help. "For eight long months," he stated, "we traveled up and down the continent trying to find a cure, but to no avail. We came back and put that little tiny skeleton to bed to die.

---

[634] Cook, "Effective Soul Winner," assessed September 22, 2010.

"One day the doctor walked into my study to say, 'Brother Pastor, come with me into the lad's room. He is dying.' I stood there holding the hand of my wife. What could I do?" Soon the child was pronounced dead.

"I turned to my wife, 'Wife, light the oven. Get all the blankets and comforters you have. Heat them and bring them here.' I opened my coat and my shirt and tore my undershirt down. I picked up that little cooling body and pressed it against my hot, sweating body. My wife wrapped a heated blanket around us. It was almost impossible to stand it, but, gritting my teeth, I took it. When that one cooled off, my wife put another one about us. When that one cooled off, she put on still another one, and on and on and on. We kept it up for nine hours."

Lifting his hands to God, he said with a voice hoarse with emotion, "My boy has been preaching the Gospel for seventeen years."[635]

Oh, that the Christian would take the spiritually dead to his burning heart, warming them to life in Christ Jesus. Oh, that Christians might wrap the unsaved with their hot tears, fervent prayer, and compassionate concern, until they are born again. Let others, if they choose, give up on one "dead," but not you.

503   The Soul Winner's Correspondence School

"Perhaps you say," Charles T. Cook states, "'If I am going to do this, it is going to involve much time and labor.' Well, my friends, what else do you expect? If you are going to enter trade or industry, if you are going to be a lawyer, a medical man, an army officer, or a nurse, in order to become proficient, you have to study hard. You have to live laborious days and pass the most severe examinations and gain a diploma before you even begin your career.

"As I said at the beginning, there is no higher or more important vocation upon earth than to be a soul winner. Do you imagine that to save a soul from eternal death is one of the unskilled occupations? Thank God, He can and He does use the humblest and the least-instructed believer. The Lord will make you a soul winner from the beginning, if all your heart goes out in desire for the salvation of men and women. But the more you understand the significance of your work, the more you will come to realize that a man who is going to become skilled in the winning of souls is the man who must give diligence to the task and attention to methods by which the Lord can make him more helpful to those in need.

---

[635] Smith, Shelton, *Preaching on Revival*, 89–90.

"Beware of the man who comes to you and says, 'Never mind about such things. After all, the apostles were untrained men.' I do not believe that a greater untruth has ever been uttered than that. The apostles attended the finest theological college the world has ever known. For three years they had personal instruction in the things of God by none other than the infallible Son of God Himself. There never was such a college as that in Galilee, when Peter, James, and John and the others followed the Lord.

"In the New Testament, we have recorded for us the lessons that those men were taught, so that as we read the Gospels and ponder the things our Lord said to His disciples and the object lessons He gave them in the miracles, we, too, are attending the Bible school of Christ. And when we read Paul's thirteen epistles, we join the Apostle Paul's correspondence school. Yes, we have the same curriculum as the men our Lord commissioned at the first to go into all the world and preach the Gospel to every creature.

"Though some here may not have opportunity to attend a Bible school, you have the Word of God in your hand, and you have the Spirit, who gave the Word, as the interpreter. Even though you have no other help, yet with the Word itself and prayer and dependence upon the Holy Spirit, you can become wise in the things of Christ....Now, my brother, my sister, remember that you can be as effective a soul winner where God has placed you as the man who is used by Him to bring about hundreds and thousands of public decisions. Whatever our gifts and whatever our opportunities, we can all have an equal measure, if we will, of the passion for souls. And our special God-given work can be as truly directed to a soul-winning end as that of any other."[636]

504 The Law of the Magnifying Glass

"You can take a magnifying glass and place it in between the sun and a piece of paper. The lens will draw several light rays to focus at a common point. Move it back and forth to get it properly focused until a tiny image of the sun is thrown on the paper. In a few moments, heat will ignite the paper, and it will burst into flames.

"It is the same with your life. Move in between the Son and a lost world. Then move your life back and forth until it is in proper focus, until a tiny image of the Son is projected through you to a point in this world. In time, the result is powerful and combustive!

---

[636] Cook, "Effective Soul Winner," assessed September 22, 2010.

SPURS TO SOUL WINNING

"The focus of your life depends upon closeness to the lost. One other thing about that magnifying glass—the magnifying power of its lens depends on its focal length. The focal length is the distance from the lens to the object. The average focal length of a magnifying glass is about ten inches. Mark it down. Your life will never have much influence on those you know from afar. You will never be an effective witness if you keep everyone at arm's length. You must get close to people—about ten inches close! You must really get next to people for an effective witness. This will necessitate some buttonholing, some very personal confrontations. You must verbally speak to people. Share with them face to face!…You must so relate your life to Him that He might reflect His life through you to a point in this godless world. But the focus of your life also depends upon your closeness to people. Remember, proper focal length is ten inches—you must witness face to face!…This activity is usually referred to as personal soul winning.

"How can you claim to live in the Promised Land, if the activity of your life is not centered in witnessing? Everybody living in God's country will be concerned with witnessing of him. They will have tried and failed, struggled and cried, trusted and won through until their lives begin to affect others! Richard Hogue…aptly put it: 'Witnessing will become your lifestyle.' The person who is filled and controlled by the Holy Spirit will 'witness as naturally as he puts on his pants in the morning…as naturally as a radio commentator gives the news…as naturally as a football player dons a helmet.' God will cease to fill any life that closes itself off from the world."[637]

505 "John, Don't Go!"

A shipwreck occurred on the New England coast. As the lifeboat arrived at the shore, someone in the crowd cried out, "Were all the men rescued?"

The captain replied, "All but one man. He was late getting off. The ship was about to go down, and the lifeboat was full, so we had to leave him. One man is still out there somewhere, hanging on a bit of wreckage."

John Holden, in hearing this news, determined to try to save the man. He took off his clothes and got in the lifeboat with the captain, as his mother cried, "John, don't go! John, don't go!"

As John Holden and the captain rowed the lifeboat toward the wrecked vessel, cries from John's mother were heard, saying, "Your dad, four years ago, was drowned in the sea. Your brother went to sea a year ago, and we

---

[637] Mahoney, *Journey into Fullness*, 140–142.

haven't heard from him since. Don't go, John!" Nevertheless, John pressed ahead through the storm-tossed sea to rescue the man. In time, the lifeboat approached the shore with three men. It is said that John Holden, in standing up, heard a voice from the shore ask, "Did you get the man?"

Holden responded, "We got the man. And tell Mother it is Will."[638]

How different this remarkable story would have ended had the mother persuaded her son not to go; how different it would have ended had John not been willing to risk his life to save another. You see, Will was her other son, and he would have perished!

Don't discourage others from making soul rescue attempts locally or globally out of fear for their well-being. Trust God to protect them. Refuse to be persuaded by family or friends not to save all you can, by every means you can, wherever you can, regardless of cost or consequence. You just never know who you might save!

506   Get the Lost to Jesus by All Means

C. H. Spurgeon, commenting on Mark 2:4, states, "Faith is full of inventions. The house was full, a crowd blocked up the door, but faith found a way of getting at the Lord and placing the palsied man before him. If we cannot get sinners where Jesus is by ordinary methods, we must use extraordinary ones. It seems, according to Luke 5:19, that a tiling had to be removed, which would make dust and cause a measure of danger to those below; but where the case is very urgent, we must not mind running some risks and shocking some proprieties. Jesus was there to heal; and, therefore, fall what might, faith ventured all so that her poor paralyzed charge might have his sins forgiven. Oh, that we had more daring faith among us! Cannot we, dear reader, seek it this morning for ourselves and for our fellow workers; and will we not try today to perform some gallant act for the love of souls and the glory of the Lord?

"The world is constantly inventing; genius serves all the purposes of human desire. Cannot faith invent too and reach by some new means the outcasts who lie perishing around us? It was the presence of Jesus which excited victorious courage in the four bearers of the palsied man. Is not the Lord among us now? Have we seen His face for ourselves this morning? Have we felt His healing power in our own souls? If so, then through door, through window, or through roof, let us, breaking through all impediments, labor to bring poor souls to Jesus. All means are good and decorous when faith and love are truly set on winning souls. If hunger for bread can break

---

[638] Malone, *Tom Malone Preaches on Salvation*, 78–79.

through stone walls, surely hunger for souls is not to be hindered in its efforts. O Lord, make us quick to suggest methods of reaching Thy poor sin-sick ones, and bold to carry them out at all hazards."[639]

507   Keep the Motive Pure

Charles T. Cook, speaking at Moody's Founders Week Conference in London, England, in 1937, states, "If we are to be effective soul winners, we must have a pure and unselfish motive. We must be 'approved unto God.' That is one of the picturesque expressions of the New Testament. It means being subjected to drastic tests.

"I found an illustration of that in Saturday's *Daily News*. Here is a picture of a worker in a foundry taking molten steel from the furnace. From there it goes to the laboratory, where it is subjected to the close scrutiny of metallurgical experts. The fire will try every man's work. Study—give diligence, says Paul, to be approved unto God—to be bright metal cleansed from every bit of dross, effective for its purpose. Oh, let us beware, lest there is any alloy mixed with our motive! Beware of trying to gain a reputetion for yourselves as a soul winner, instead of seeking the glory of Christ."[640]

508   It's Worth Being Laughed At

A well-dressed lady was observed passing out gospel tracts to tramps and others who were the down and out of society. The response was mixed. Some tore the tracts up, others laughed in scorn, and some accepted them. Knowing she was the wealthiest person in the city, someone asked her, "How can you do this? You could be enjoying all that money has to offer."

"In her quiet manner, the lady responded, "I find that about one out of fifty to whom I give a tract becomes a Christian. It is worth being laughed at forty-nine times to lead one soul to Christ."[641]

How far will you go to win a soul to Christ? Will you endure the lost laughing at you in scorn forty-nine times to win one of them ultimately to Christ? Fear of criticism or rejection keeps many Christians sidelined from taking the Gospel to the lost. Get over it. Brazen up and pay the price to win souls to Christ.

---

[639] Spurgeon, *Morning and Evening*, Morning, September 7.

[640] Cook, "Effective Soul Winner," assessed September 22, 2010.

[641] Unknown Author, "Price and Reward," accessed September 7, 2010.

509 Give Me One Soul Today

Will H. Houghton echoes the heart of the true soul winner.

"Lead me to some soul today;
Oh, teach me, Lord, just what to say.
Friends of mine are lost in sin
and cannot find their way.
Few there are who seem to care,
And few there are who pray.
Melt my heart and fill my life;
Give me one soul today."[642]

510 "Saved Alone"

The great Chicago fire in 1871 left three hundred dead and one hundred thousand homeless. A friend of D. L. Moody, Horatio Gates Spafford, assisted the homeless, grief-stricken, and needy for two years. Spafford and his family then decided join the Moody team on one of their evangelistic crusades in Europe. Horatio Spafford was delayed departing with his wife and four daughters on the ship *Ville du Havre* due to business. He would meet up with them later on the other side of the Atlantic. Their ship collided with the English sailing ship the *Loch Earn* and sunk within twenty minutes. Spafford's wife, Anna, survived. Upon reaching Europe, she sent him a message that consisted of two words: "Saved Alone."

The Spafford's decided to enter missionary service in a distant land, giving their fortune to win the lost. It was their determination that when they reached Heaven to give their report, it would not be "Saved Alone." May you and I so live that likewise, when our report is so given to the Lord, it will not be "Saved Alone."

511 What Attracted You to Christ?

In a questionnaire submitted to members of All Souls congregation, John Stott asked these two questions. "What first attracted you to Christ and the Gospel?" and "What mainly or finally brought you to Christ?" In excess of half of the congregation stated it was something they had seen personally fleshed out in Christian people—their parents, pastors, teachers, colleagues or friends.

---

[642] Houghton, "Lead Me to Some Soul Today," accessed April 14, 2011.

One respondent said that these "had something in their lives which I lacked but desperately longed for." Several others said it was "their eternal joy and inward peace." Stott further stated, "To a student nurse it was 'the genuine and open friendship' offered by Christians; to an Oxford undergraduate studying law, their 'sheer exuberance'; to a police constable, the 'clear aim, purpose and idealism which Christian life offered' as seen in Christians; to a secretary in the BBC, 'the reality of the warmth and inner resources which I observed in Christians'; and to a house surgeon, 'the knowledge of Christ's working in another person's life.'"[643]

Christians ought to so live that their very lives are soul winning tools in the hand of the Holy Spirit. Sad but so true is the saying, "Your life speaks so loudly, I cannot hear what you speak."

512 A Young Boy Won Him

A godless sea captain who became critically ill at sea, fearing he was soon to die, inquired if anyone on the ship had a Bible or could tell him how to prepare to meet God. A boy known for always reading the Bible was brought to the captain. The captain said to him, "Son, can you help the old captain to find something in the Bible that will help him to die and meet God?" The young boy read Isaiah 53:5 to the man. The captain responded, "Son, I don't understand how somebody could die for others, as that Scripture says."

"Captain," the boy said, "if you'll just repeat the words after me, I think I can help you understand." The boy substituted two or three words from the Scripture as he read verse 6, and the captain repeated what he said. It went like this: "All we like sheep have gone astray and…turned everyone to his own way, and the Lord hath laid upon Him (Christ) MY iniquities…the chastisement of MY peace was upon Him, and with His stripes I am healed."

With trembling voice, the captain said, "Son, I think I get it now. He was wounded for *my* transgressions, he was bruised for *my* iniquities, he was wounded for *my* sins, and, because of this fact, I can be saved."[644]

This young boy's witness to the captain was simple, short, but sufficient to bring the captain to Christ. In soul winning, don't complicate the simple; don't get bogged down with a lot of nonessentials. Certainly you can use the approach of this young boy to win many to Christ.

---

[643] Stott, *Guilty Silence,* 71.

[644] Daniels, *Why Jesus Wept,* 62–63.

513 The Miracle of Making Fish into Fishers

"We are like the fishes, making sin to be our element," states C. H. Spurgeon, "as they live in the sea. And the good Lord comes, and with the gospel net He takes us, and He delivers us from the life and love of sin. But He has not wrought for us all that He can do, nor all that we should wish Him to do, when He has done this; for it is another and a higher miracle to make us who were fish to become fishers, to make the saved ones saviors, to make the convert into a converter, the receiver of the Gospel into an imparter of that same Gospel to other people.

"I think I may say to every person whom I am addressing, if you are yourself saved, the work is but half done until you are employed to bring others to Christ. You are as yet but half formed in the image of your Lord. You have not attained to the full development of the Christ-life in you unless you have commenced in some feeble way to tell others of the grace of God; and I trust that you will find no rest to the sole of your foot till you have been the means of leading many to that blessed Savior who is your confidence and your hope.

"Let us ask Him to give us grace to go afishing, and so to cast our nets that we may take a great multitude of fishes. Oh, that the Holy Ghost may raise up from among us some master fishers, who shall sail their boats in many a sea, and surround great shoals of fish!"[645]

"Because that for his name's sake they went forth" (III John 7). Let's go forth winning the lost "for His name's sake."

514 A Dry-As-Dust Presentation of the Gospel to the Hellbound

John R. Rice, in speaking upon the text Psalm 126:5–6, states, "My teacher in Southwestern Seminary, Dr. L. R. Scarborough, used to say, 'No sowing, no reaping; and no weeping, no rejoicing.' One reason the joy, the lilt of blessing and praise, is gone from so many of our hearts is that we do not have the preparation, the groundwork that brings the joy. If we do not go out weeping and do not have a burden for souls, we do not see souls saved. It is one of the great essentials; in fact, it is the second one named here. If you are going to be a soul winner, then you are going to have to care about it.

"After all, I think that should be obvious. How could God see fit to bless anybody who would go through the forms and ceremonies of soul-winning work, who would be in any wise preaching or singing the Gospel or testifying, but who did not have a sincere, fundamental longing to see the

---

[645] Spurgeon, *Soul Winner,* 260–261.

will of God done?…How can the Holy Spirit put His blessing and seal on a dry-as-dust presentation of the truth?

"If there be one thing that is absolutely essential to any preaching or teaching or soul-winning effort, it is a sincerity of soul with compassion and burden of heart about getting people saved.…There is a fundamental insincerity to the professing Christian who has no burden for souls. How unnatural in a spiritual sense it is; how abnormal in a spiritual sense it is for a Christian not to have a deep burden for souls to be kept out of Hell."[646]

Rice concludes the sermon in saying, "God, give us a broken heart! Why don't you say today, 'O God, take away this coldness, this hypocrisy, this insincerity! O God, give me a compassion like Jesus had'? Remember, David said, 'A broken and contrite heart, O God, thou will not despise' (Psalm 51:17)."[647]

515 The Mail Must Go Through

George Sweeting tells the story of John Currier in his book, *The No-Guilt Guide for Witnessing.* In 1949, Currier was found guilty of murder and sentenced to life in prison. He was transferred to a work farm in Nashville, Tennessee. Twenty years later, Currier's sentence was changed to time served, and a letter notifying him of his freedom was mailed. Sadly the letter was lost in the mail, and he remained a prisoner another ten years until the mistake was caught. Sweeting finished the story with a question: "Would it matter to you if someone sent you an important message—the most important in your life—and year after year the urgent message was never delivered?"[648]

God has sent a letter stamped "Special Delivery" to the world in which He proclaims freedom to the captive in Satan's prison camp through the Cross of His only son, Jesus Christ. Are you failing to deliver it, causing friends, family members and acquaintances prolonged captivity to the cruel captor Satan? If you were yet lost, would it matter to you if God's letter of love was never delivered? Determine to do all you can to make sure the message from the King gets delivered without delay, for every day is filled with heartache and havoc while one is shackled to sin.

---

[646] Rice, "Broken Heart in Soul Winning," 1, 12.

[647] Ibid., 15.

[648] Sweeting, "Our Daily Bread," November 6.

516 The Soul Winner's Book

Dr. R. A. Torrey said, "There are four reasons why every Christian worker should know his Bible: first, to show men their need of a Savior; second, to show them that Jesus is the Savior they need; third, to show them how to make this Savior their Savior; and, finally, to deal with specific difficulties that stand in the way of their accepting Christ."

Knowledge of the Bible, in addition to its profit in introducing a lost soul to Christ, instills confidence and boldness to win souls. Master the Word, let it master you, and then it, through you, will bring others to the Master. Give the unsaved the Word, not simply your comment upon it. Henry Moorhouse said to D. L. Moody, "You are making a mistake in giving people your own words. Give them the Word of God, and you will learn the secret of power." Robert Murray M'Cheyne similarly stated, "It is not our comments upon the Word that bring life; it is the Word itself."[649]

Go soul winning with the "Sword" polished and sharp, knowledgeable of how to use it, and souls will be won to Christ.

517 First Is to Win the Person to Yourself

Charles Trumbull in *Taking Men Alive* stated, "If we would take a man alive for Christ, we must first of all know something, be it ever so little, about that man and his present interests. Our knowledge may be gained in ten seconds; again, it may take ten months to gain. But we can never have this needed knowledge of the man as a first step toward winning the man himself, unless we devote our whole energy, for the time being, to knowing the man. Therefore it is that he must fill our whole horizon as we prepare to come into close quarters with him. We must be thinking not about others, but about this other—just this one in the whole universe.

"This is the simple secret of tact—that mysterious power which a few favored ones seem to possess and which is regretfully supposed to be beyond one's reach, if one does not happen to have the 'gift'. But tact is simply touch—a touch on the right spot rather than the wrong, a touch which will win another rather than antagonize him, a touch in keeping with rather than opposed to his present interests. And it is impossible to touch one at a point that will interest him unless we know something of what his interests are. The art of taking men alive calls for tact at the very beginning, which means, first of all, studying your man.

"This concentrating all our attention on the individual at the outset so that we may know what interests him is to enable us to put forward some-

---

[649] Cook, "Effective Soul Winner," assessed September 22, 2010.

thing that shall attract and hold his attention. In fishing, the attractive thing thus put forward by the fisherman is called bait. And bait is a prime essential in the man-fishing to which Christ called His disciples, and in which He promised to train them to expertness. For let us bear in mind that we are in the business of winning men to Christ. We cannot win by antagonizing. And we must win by drawing men to us as a first step in drawing them to Christ."[650]

518 How Is It?

How is it, when we ponder man's sin that breeds hurt, havoc, and hell; when we think of the love, forgiveness, peace, and restoration God offers;

How is it, when we contrast Heaven with Hell;

How is it, in personally experiencing the joy of His salvation, the weight of sin lifted, and newness of life;

How is it, upon remembering the price Christ paid for man's reconciliation with God—the rejection, the scourging, the mocking, the anguish, the unimaginable pain that was induced by the nails piercing His hands and feet, the sword to His side, and the crown of thorns upon His brow;

How is it, in knowing that it is Christ's passion for all to be saved; that He has given instruction for believers to aggressively seek to win the lost;

How is it, in knowing that as believers we have the cure to man's malady of sin—the remedy to his sorrow, hopelessness, failure, doubt, depression, alienation to God;

How is it, when we as the redeemed have found the door that leads to God and eternal bliss, while multitudes spiritually blind yet are seeking it;

How is it, that we as the saved do not value a soul as Christ; that concern for the unsaved is minimal; that we do not eagerly, anxiously, compassionately, tearfully, consistently rush to the perishing ones, telling of Jesus the mighty to save;

How is it, that when seventy per cent of USA residents have no meaningful church relationship,[651] and the North American continent is the only continent on earth where Christianity is declining,[652] evangelical believers yet "sleep"?

---

[650] Trumbull, *Taking Men Alive,* 73–75.

[651] Logan, "Church Planting," accessed May 28, 2010.

[652] Barna, "Church Planting," accessed May 28, 2010.

I ask you, *How is it?* It just doesn't figure, does it?

519 Go and Grow, or Stay and Decay

Evangelist Freddie Gage tells of his experience regarding two churches he visited back to back. The first church was dying; the other was thriving. The first church had a large sign in its yard that read, "All Welcome; Come on In." The second church had a sign, but it was on the inside, visible only as members departed the church. This sign read, "You are now entering the mission field of the world; go soul winning." Christians are not to sit back in their padded pews waiting for the unsaved to come in, but passionately go after them. It's time for the church to leave the building and go soul winning. The church that goes grows; the church that stays decays.

520 Will the Church Just Sing Louder?

"I lived in Germany during the Nazi Holocaust. I considered myself a Christian. We heard stories of what was happening to Jews, but we tried to distance ourselves from it, because what could we do to stop it? A railroad track ran behind our small church, and each Sunday morning, we could hear the whistle in the distance and then the wheels coming over the tracks. We became disturbed when we heard the cries coming from the train as it passed by. We realized that it was carrying Jews like cattle in the cars.

"Week after week, the whistle would blow. We dreaded to hear the sound of those wheels, because we knew that we would hear the cries of the Jews en route to a death camp. Their screams tormented us. We knew the time the train was coming, and when we heard the whistle blow, we began singing hymns. By the time the train came past our church, we were singing at the top of our voices. If we heard the screams, we sang more loudly, and soon we heard them no more. Although years have passed, I still hear the train whistle in my sleep. God forgive me, forgive all of us who called ourselves Christians and yet did nothing to intervene."[653]

Are you going to just keep singing louder while souls all about you die and go to Hell? God forgive you, me, and others for not doing more to intervene in their behalf. Even church things can wrongly be used to distract from hearing the cries of the eternally lost among us. Stop singing for a moment; sit in silence and hear the cries rise up from the lost.

---

[653] Lutzer, *When a Nation Forgets God*, 21–22.

SPURS TO SOUL WINNING

521 "I Thank You, John; I Thank You, John."

John A. Broadus was saved as a young man, and the next day, he approached a schoolmate, Sandy Jones, and said, "I wish you would be a Christian. Won't you?"

Sandy said, "I don't know. Perhaps I will." Shortly Sandy was saved in church; he walked across the building to John Broadus, held out his hand, and said, "I thank you, John; I thank you, John."

Dr. Broadus later left that small town, but nearly every summer he would return for a visit. Without fail, an awkward, red-haired old farmer would approach him, stick out his hand, and say, "Howdy, John. I will never forget you, John."

On his deathbed, John Broadus said to family members gathered about, "I rather think the sweetest sound to my ears in Heaven, next to the welcome of Him whom having not seen, I have tried to love and serve, will be the welcome of Sandy Jones, as he will thrust out that great hand of his and say, 'Howdy, John. Thank you, John; thank you, John.'"[654]

Can you expect such a greeting in Heaven from one you won to Christ?

522 The Church at Work, School and Play

A mechanic was driving a visiting minister from his hometown to another city. En route, the mechanic said, as they passed a huge factory, "Do you see that red brick building over there behind the gray stone one? I work on the second floor on the south side. There are seventy-four of us in that department, and as far as I know, I am the only one in the crowd who ever goes to church or tries to live a Christian life. Sometimes I have to remind myself that, as far as that department is concerned, I am all there is of the Christian church. If I don't do good work, then the church has failed, as far as those men are concerned. If I can't be relied upon, then the church is undependable. If I am careless, then some poor unfortunate soul may have to pay for the church's carelessness. It is pretty serious business being the church in the midst of seventy-four other people."[655]

It is serious business for you to be the church at work, school, or play. How good a job are you doing as the church in pointing your "congregation" to Jesus Christ? How many have you personally introduced to the Savior?

---

[654] Moody, W. R., *Record of Christian Work,* 603.

[655] Peters, *Bible Illustrations*, 303.

523 The Mighty Magnet

Declared C. H. Spurgeon: "What drew you to Christ but Christ? What draws you to Him now but His own blessed self? If you have been drawn to religion by anything else, you will soon be drawn away from it; but Jesus has held you and will hold you even to the end. Why, then, doubt His power to draw others? Go with the name of Jesus to those who have hitherto been stubborn and see if it does not draw them.

"No sort of man is beyond this drawing power. Old and young, rich and poor, ignorant and leaned, depraved or amiable—all men shall feel the attractive force. Jesus is the one magnet. Let us not think of any other. Music will not draw to Jesus; neither will eloquence, logic, ceremonial, or noise. Jesus Himself must draw men to Himself; and Jesus is quite equal to the work in every case. Be not tempted by the quackeries of the day, but as workers for the Lord, work in His own way and draw with the Lord's own cords. Draw *to* Christ and draw *by* Christ, for then Christ will draw by you."[656]

In soul winning, it is an imperative to implement the precept of John 12:32, if the promise of the same text is to be realized.

524 It Took Seven Years

A businessman en route to prayer meeting noted a man looking in the door of the church. Upon the businessman's invitation, the man joined him in the service and was gloriously saved. Afterward, this man told the businessman, "I lived in the city for seven years before I met you. No one had ever asked me to go to church. I wasn't here three days before the grocer, the dairy man, the insurance man, and the politician called on me. You are the first one to invite me to church."[657]

Who in your community or workplace has waited seven years for you to invite them to church, or better, to introduce them to Jesus Christ?

525 The Soul Winner Came Too Late

A Baptist missionary far up the Amazon River was overheard by an elderly man telling children the message of Christ. Upon the dismissal of the children, this aged man approached the missionary with this question: "May I ask, Madam, if this interesting and intriguing story is true?"

---

[656] Spurgeon, *Faith's Checkbook,* 286.

[657] Ibid., 306–307.

"Of course," the missionary replied, "it is the Word of God."

Doubting the truthfulness of what the missionary said, he responded, "This is the first time in my life that I have ever heard that one must give his life to Jesus to have forgiveness of sin and to have life with God forever." Then, with a note of certitude, he said, "This story cannot be true, or else someone would have come before now to tell it. I am an old man. My parents lived their lives and died without ever having heard this message. It cannot be true, or someone would have come sooner." The missionary's attempt to convince him it was indeed true did not avail. The old man soon turned and walked back into the dark jungle, repeating as he walked, "It cannot be true; it cannot be true, or someone would have come sooner."[658]

Is this what your neighbors, friends, classmates, and/or fellow workers are saying? I'm pretty sure that all these are wondering, if it is true, why you haven't bothered to tell them!

526 Switching the Tags

A gang of thieves broke into a jewelry store and pulled a major prank. They switched the price tags of the jewelry. This switch went unnoticed by the owner, and the next day people were spending huge amounts of money to buy cheap junk, while others were paying a couple of dollars for incredibly expensive jewels. As I see it, someone has switched the "tags" in the church to the end that Christians are focusing on the wrong things—the lesser of importance is taking priority over the greater (soul winning).

527 Never Quit in Passing Out Tracts

A Christian handed a man a gospel tract while traveling aboard a ship. The man, courteous in receiving it, said to the Christian, "I haven't much faith in that kind of work."

The tract distributor replied, "It was through a gospel tract given to me twenty years ago that I was converted." Further discussion revealed that it was that man that had given him the tract that led to his conversion!

The former tract distributor, in discouragement, ceased his tract distribution due to seeing so few results; but, upon hearing this testimony, he declared, "By the grace of God, I shall start again."[659] Don't allow

---

[658] Ibid., 301.

[659] Ibid., 300.

visible results to discourage or dishearten sowing of the gospel seed through tract distribution or any other means. God promises that His Word will not return unto Him void.

528 "Preaches As If He Was A-Dying to Have You Saved"

An elderly Scotswoman was asked her opinion of the preaching of Robert Murray M'Cheyne. She hesitated a moment and then said, "He preaches as if he was a-dying to have you saved."[660] Do you possess this same spirit in talking to men about the paramount need of their souls?

J. Wilbur Chapman stated, "I have many times wondered if we have to a sufficient degree a wooing note in our preaching."[661] I think not at large. But neither do we have to a sufficient degree a wooing note in our soul winning efforts. Pursue and then manifest the spirit of M'Cheyne, whether in preaching or personal soul winning, and great will be the outcome.

529 You Sat Where the Lost Now Sit

A minister witnessed to a man awaiting execution, but without success. En route home, he met up with one of the elders of the church and asked him to visit the man. Following the visit, the elder reported back to the pastor that the man had gotten saved. The pastor wanted to know why he failed and the elder succeeded in winning the man to Christ. He found the answer in the remark the criminal made following his conversion. "When the minister spoke to me, it seemed like one standing far above me; but when the good man came in and sat down by my side and classed himself with me, I could not stand it any longer."[662]

Remember in soul winning that you once sat where the lost now sit, and exhibit empathy and compassion. It is far more effective to sit with them than to stand above them. Never fail to remember that as the lost now are, you once were.

530 Everyone Was Saved in the Town

Ray Sharpe asked Rev. Willis, a man saved during the Welsh Revival as a youth, at what point did people in his town stop getting saved during that

---

[660] Chapman, *Another Mile*, 102.

[661] Ibid., 102.

[662] Peters, *Bible Illustrations*, 239.

great revival. He answered, "It didn't stop until the last person in town became a Christian."[663] Can you imagine such a scene—everybody in town being saved! I say, "Do it again, Lord; do it again!" Are you praying and working toward reaching your entire town for Christ? The Christian must never be content with soul winning success as long as one remains lost.

531 Please Get My Mother In

A well-known preacher was getting ready for bed one night, when he heard a knock at the front door. Upon answering it, he found a little girl dressed in rags. As he stood looking into her thin, haggard little face, she said, "Are you the preacher?"

"Yes, I am," he replied.

"Well, won't you come down and get my mother in?" she asked.

The preacher answered, "My dear, it is hardly proper for me to come and get your mother in. If she is drunk, you should get a policeman."

"Oh, sir," she quickly replied, "you don't understand! My mother isn't drunk; she's at home dying, and she's afraid to die. She wants to go to Heaven but doesn't know how. I told her I would find a preacher to get her in. Come quick, sir; she's dying!" The preacher could not resist the appeal of the little girl, so he promised her he would come as soon as he was dressed.

The little girl led him into the slum district to an old house, up a rickety stairway, along a dark hall, and finally to a dismal room. There the dying woman lay in the corner. "I've got the preacher for you, Mother. He wasn't ready to come at first, but he's here. You just tell him what you want, and do what he tells you, and he'll get you in!"

Too weary to sit up, the poor woman raised her feeble voice and asked, "Can you do anything for a sinner like me? My life has been lived in sin, and now that I'm dying, I feel that I'm going to Hell. But I don't want to go there; I want to go to Heaven. What can I do now?"

Looking at her sin-weary face, the preacher thought, *What can I tell her? I have been preaching salvation by reformation, but this poor soul has gone too far to reform. I have been preaching salvation by character, but she hasn't any. I know what to do. I'll tell her what my mother used to tell me as a boy. She's dying, and it can't hurt her, even if it doesn't do her any good.* Bending down beside her, the preacher began, "My dear woman, God is very gracious and kind; and in His Book, the Bible, He says, 'God so

---

[663] Sharpe, "Change the World," accessed November 3, 2010.

loved the world, that He gave his only begotten Son, that whosoever believeth in Him should not perish, but have everlasting life.'"

"Oh," exclaimed the dying woman, "does it say that in the Bible? My! That ought to get me in. But, sir, my sins; my sins!"

He was amazed at the way the verses came back to him. "My dear woman," he continued, "the Bible says that 'the blood of Jesus Christ His Son cleanseth us from all sin.'"

"All sin, did you say?" she asked earnestly. "Does it really say ALL sin? That ought to get me in."

"Yes," he replied, kneeling down beside her. "It says all sin. God's Book also says, 'This is a faithful saying and worthy of all acceptation, that Christ Jesus came into the world to save sinners; of whom I am chief.'"

"Well," she said, "if the chief got in, I can come. Pray for me, sir!"

The preacher bent down and prayed with the poor woman. Just as she was, she came to Jesus, who never turned anyone away, and she "got in." "And in the process," added the preacher, "while she was getting in, I myself got in. We two sinners, the preacher and that poor woman, entered salvation's door together that night."[664]

Praise the Lord the preacher was willing to go without delay, or else the lady would have died without Christ. Never delay the prompting of the Spirit or the call of another to introduce someone to Christ; strike while the iron is hot and the door is yet open.

By the way, are *you* in?

---

[664] Unknown Author, "Please Get My Mother In," accessed November 3, 2010.

Bibliography

Ackland, Donald F. *Joy in Church Membership.* Nashville: Convention Press, 1955.

Aldrich, Joseph C. *Gentle Persuasion.* Portland: Multnomah, 1988.

Allen, Kerry James. *Exploring the Mind and Heart of the Prince of Preachers.* Oswego, IL: Fox River Press, 2005.

Anders, Max E. *30 Days to Understanding the Christian Life in 15 Minutes a Day.* Nashville: Thomas Nelson, 1998.

Andross, Matilda. *Prevailing Prayer.* www.path2prayer.com/article.php?id=206.

Appelman, Hyman J. *The Savior's Invitation and Other Evangelistic Sermons.* Grand Rapids: Baker Book House, 1981.

Atkinson, Bruce. "General William Booth." www.revivaltimes.org/index.php?aid=621.

Autrey, C. E. *Basic Evangelism.* Grand Rapids: Zondervan, 1968.

———. *You Can Win Souls.* Nashville: Broadman Press, 1961.

Bales, Porter M. *Revival Sermons.* Nashville: Broadman Press, 1938.

Ball, David, ed. "The Voice of the Evangelist." Spring, 2009.

Barlow, Fred. "Evangelist John R. Rice: Giant of Evangelism." www.soulwinning.info/gs/john_rice/giant.htm.

———. *Profiles in Evangelism.* Murfreesboro, TN: Sword of the Lord Publishers, 1976.

———."Travail for Souls." Sword of the Lord, October 8, 2004.

Barclay, William. *The Daily Study Bible Series,* Rev. ed.: The Gospel of Luke. Philadelphia: The Westminster Press, 2000.

Barna, George. "Church Planting." www.thecrossingchurch.org/about-us/church-planting.

———. *Revolution.* Carol Stream, IL: Tyndale House, 2006.

Barnhouse, Donald Grey. *Let Me Illustrate.* Grand Rapids: Fleming H. Revell, 1967.

Baxter, J. Sidlow. "Christian Prayer Quotes." www.christian-prayer-quotes.christian-attorney.net.

Berg, David B. "There Is No Limit." www.deeptruths.com/treasures/no_limit.html.

Bisagno, John. *Letters to Timothy.* Nashville: Broadman and Holman Publishers, 2001.

Bisagno, John, Kenneth Chafin, and C. Wade Freeman. *How to Win Them.* Nashville: Broadman, 1970.

Blackaby, Henry. *Experiencing God.* Nashville: Broadman and Holman, 2008.

Blackwood, Andrew. *Evangelical Sermons of Our Day.* New York: Harper and Brothers, 1959.

Blair, Brett. "It Is a Big Ocean." jmm.aaa.net.au/articles/20170.htm.

Bland, H. F. *Soul Winning: A Course of Four Lectures.* Toronto: William Briggs, 1883.

Bonar, Horatius. *Words to Winners of Souls.* Phillipsburg, NJ: P & R Publishing, 1995.

Booth, William. "A Vision of the Lost." whatsaiththescripture.com/Stories/A.Vision.of.the.Lost.html

———. "Missions Slogans and Notables Quotes from Missionaries." http://home.snu.edu/~hculbert/slogans.htm.

Bouknight, Bill. "The Lost and Found Collection." Sermon delivered at Shandon Baptist Church, Columbia, SC.

Bright, Bill, ed. *Ten Basic Christian Steps to Maturity: Teacher's Manual.* Arrowhead Springs and Bernardino, CA: Campus Crusade for Christ, International, 1965.

Bronson, Michael. "How Many People Die on an Average Day?" biblehelp.org/dieday.htm.

Brown, Alistair. "The Call of God." www.cmalliance.org/serve/call-of-god.

Brown, Michael. "Church Planting Myths." www.docstoc.com/docs/29374478/Barriers-to-Church-Planting.

Bibliography

Carr, Alan. "The Traits of a Successful Soul Winner." www.sermonnotebook.org/new testament/john1_35-42.htm.

Carre, E. G. *Praying Hyde: Apostle of Prayer.* Alachua, FL: Bridge-Logos, 1982.

Cates, Norman. "So Much Work, So Little Help." www.free-sermons.org/sermons/SO-MUCH-13178.

Chadwick, Samuel. "Practical Pastoral Methods for Bringing in Outsiders." http://www.path2prayer.com/article.php?id=924.

Chambers, Oswald. *My Utmost for His Highest.* Grand Rapids: Discovery House Publishers, 1992.

Chapman, J. Wilbur. *"And Peter."* Chicago: Fleming H. Revell, 1896.

———. *Another Mile and Other Addresses.* New York: Fleming H. Revell Company, 1908.

———. "Eternity." Classic Sermon Library, www.newsforchristians.com/chapman/jwc_001.html.

———. "So, You Want to Be a Soul Winner." www.expositoryechoes.org/matthew4-19.htm.

Clark, Allyson. "New England Baptists Highlight Missions." www.bpnews.net/bpnews.asp?id=31800.

Clephane, Elizabeth. "The Ninety and Nine." www.cyberhymnal.org/htm/n/i/90_and_9.htm.

Coleman, Robert E. *The Master Plan of Evangelism.* Old Tappan, NJ: Fleming H. Revell Company, 1988.

Comfort, Ray. *The Evidence Bible.* Gainesville, FL: Bridge-Logos, 2002.

———. *The Way of the Master.* Alachua, Florida: Bridge-Logos, 2006.

Cook, Charles T. "The Effective Soul Winner." www.soulwinning.info/articles/effective.htm.

Coomer, Terry L. "Failing to Witness." www.greatpreachers.org/witness.html.

Courson, Jon. *Jon Courson's Application Commentary.* Nashville: Thomas Nelson, 2003.

Criswell, W. A. "The Day of Revival." wacriswell.org/Search/videotrans.cfm/sermon/243.cfm.

———. "The Story of Four Lepers." wacriswell.org/PrintTranscript.cfm/SID/1867.cfm.

Crosby, Fanny. "Gather Them In." www.cyberhymnal.org/htm/g/a/t/gatherti.htm.

Curry, Erin. "Collection Captures Eddie Martin's Innovative Soul-Winning Methods." www.bpnews.net/bpnews.asp?id=15248.

Daniels, E. J. *Dim Lights in a Dark World.* Orlando: Daniels Publishers, 1971.

———. *Fervent, Soul-Stirring Sermons.* Orlando: Daniels Publishers, 1974.

———. *Why Jesus Wept and Other Sermons.* Orlando: Daniels Publishers, 1975.

DC Talk. *Jesus Freaks.* Minneapolis: Bethany House Publishers, 2002.

Despres, Adrian. Shandon on Mission (newsletter), May/June, 2010.

Dixon, Francis. "Growing in the Christian Life." wordsoflife.co.uk/BibleStudy/Growing/Growing9.htm.

———. "Getting a Passion for Souls." wordsoflife.co.uk/BibleStudy/Series25/Study3.htm.

———. "Ten New Testament Soul Winners." wordsoflife.co.uk/BibleStudy/Series15/Study3.htm.

———. "The King's Business Requireth Haste." Bournemouth, England: Lansdowne Bible School and Postal Fellowship.

Dobbins, G. S. *A Winning Witness.* Nashville: The Sunday School Board of the Southern Baptist Convention, 1938.

Dorsett, Lyle W. *The Life of D. L. Moody: A Passion for Souls.* Chicago: Moody Press, 1997.

Bibliography

Douglas, J. D. ed. *The Work of an Evangelist.* Minneapolis: World Wide Publications, 1984.

Downey, Murray. *The Art of Soulwinning.* Grand Rapids: Baker Book House, 1976.

Draper, James T. "Jimmy Draper Urges Baptists to 'Grasp Opportunity.'" www.gofbw.com/news.asp?ID=2991.

Draper, James T. ed. *Preaching with Passion.* Nashville: Broadman and Holman, 2004.

Drummond, Lewis. *Reaching Generation Next.* Grand Rapids: Baker Books, 2002.

Drummond, Lewis and Betty. *The Spiritual Woman.* Grand Rapids: Kregel Publications, 1999.

Duewel, Wesley L. "Ablaze with a Passion for Souls." Herald of His Coming, August, 2003.

————. *Touch the World through Prayer."* Grand Rapids: Zondervan, 1986.

Dunn, Ron. *Don't Just Stand There, Pray Something.* San Bernardino, CA: Here's Life Publishers, 1991.

Edwards, Jonathan. christianquotes.org/tag/cat/10/10. 21 June, 2010.

————. *The Life and Diary of David Brainerd.* Grand Rapids: Baker Book House, 1989.

————. *The Life of David Brainerd.* Grand Rapids: Baker Book House, 1978.

Elliot, Elisabeth. *Through Gates of Splendor.* Wheaton, IL: Tyndale House Publishers, 1981.

Ellis, William T. *"Billy" Sunday: The Man and His Message.* Philadelphia: The John C. Winston Company, 1914.

Emmert, Byron. "Keep Your Eyes on the Prize." www.yfc.org/columns/devos2006.php?DevoID=144.

Evans, William. "Elements of Success in Personal Soulwinning." www.wholesomewords.org/etexts/evans/evansoul2.html.

———. "Instructions to the Soul Winner."
www.wholesomewords.org/etexts/evans/evansoul2.html.

———. "The Personal Worker Himself—His Qualifications."
www.wholesomewords.org/etexts/evans/evansoul3.html.

Exum, Baxter T. "Soul Winning."
fourlakescoc.org/Sermons/websermonupdates/1034web.pdf.

Fabarez, Michael. *Preaching That Changes Lives.* Nashville: Thomas Nelson, 2002.

Fay, William. *Share Jesus without Fear.* Nashville: Broadman and Holman, 1999.

Finney, Charles. *Revivals of Religion.* New York: Leavitt, Lord and Company, 1835.

Ford, Herschel. *Simple Sermons for Special Days and Occasions.* Grand Rapids: Zondervan Publishing House, 1967.

———. *Simple Sermons for Sunday Evening.* Grand Rapids: Zondervan Publishing House, 1968.

———. *Simple Sermons for Sunday Morning.* Grand Rapids: Zondervan Publishing House, 1968.

———. *Simple Sermons on Heaven, Hell and the Judgment.* Grand Rapids: Zondervan, 1969.

———. *Simple Sermons on New Testament Texts.* Grand Rapids: Baker Publishing, 1985.

———. *Simple Sermons on Salvation and Service.* Grand Rapids: Zondervan, 1966.

———. *Simple Sermons on the Christian Life.* Grand Rapids: Zondervan, 1962.

Fordham, Keith. Personal correspondence.

Fuchida, Mitsuo. "From Pearl Harbor to Calvary."
www.biblebelievers.com/fuchida1.html.

Goll, James W. "Crisis Intervention through Intercession."
www.prayerstorm.com/images/pdf/crisis_10_07.pdf.

Bibliography

Gordon, S. D. *What It Will Take to Change the World.* Grand Rapids: Baker, 1979.

Green, Michael P. ed. *Illustrations for Biblical Preaching.* Grand Rapids: Baker Book House, 1982.

Hallock, G. B. F. *The Evangelistic Cyclopedia.* New York: George H. Doran Company, 1922.

Harrison, E. M. *How to Win Souls.* Wheaton, IL: Van Kampen Press, 1952.

Harvey, Edwin & Lillian. Comp. *Royal Insignia.* Shoals, IN: Old Path Tracts Society, 1992.

Havergal, Frances. "A Worker's Prayer." www.wholesomewords.org/biography/bhavergal5.html.

Hawkins, O. S. *Drawing the Net.* Dallas: Annuity Board of the Southern Baptist Convention, 2002.

Hayden, Eric. *The Unforgettable Spurgeon.* Greenville, SC: Emerald House Group, 1997.

Hayes, Dan. *Fireseeds of Spiritual Awakening, Rev. ed.* Dickinson, ND: Dickinson Press, 1995.

Hayford, J. W. ed. *Answering the Call to Evangelism : Spreading the Good News to Everyone. Spirit-Filled Life Kingdom Dynamics Study Guides (42).* Nashville: Thomas Nelson, 1997.

Henry, Matthew. *Matthew Henry Commentary on the Whole Bible.* Grand Rapids: Fleming H. Revell, 1983.

Hill, Junior. Personal Correspondence.

Hobbs, Herschel, comp. Ronald K. Brown. *My Favorite Illustrations.* Nashville: Broadman Press, 1990.

Hodgin, Michael. *1001 Humorous Illustrations for Public Speaking.* Grand Rapids: Zondervan, 1994.

Houghton, Will H. "Lead Me to Some Soul Today." hymntime.com/tch/htm/l/e/a/leadmsst.htm.

House, Polly. "2,000 and Counting: Soul Winner Still Going Strong." www.baptistcourier.com/1926.article.

Hunter, George III. *How to Reach Secular People.* Nashville: Abingdon Press, 1992.

Hutson, Curtis. "For Preachers." Murfreesboro, TN: Sword of the Lord, February 4, 2011.

————. ed. *Great Preaching on Hell.* Murfreesboro, TN: Sword of the Lord Publishers, 1989.

————. ed. *Great Preaching on Soul Winning.* Murfreesboro, TN: Sword of the Lord Publishers, 1989.

————. ed. *Great Preaching on the Holy Spirit.* Murfreesboro, TN: Sword of the Lord Publishers, 1988.

————. *Salvation Crystal Clear II.* Murfreesboro, TN: Sword of the Lord Publishers, 1991.

————. "Soul Winning: Every Christian's Job." www.swordofthelord.com/onlinesermons/Soulwinning.htm.

————. "Winning Souls and Getting Them Down the Aisle." Murfreesboro, TN: Sword of the Lord Publishers, 1978.

Jenkens, Millard. *Brands from the Burning.* Nashville: Broadman Press, 1955.

Jeremiah, David. "Prayer and Intercession Quotes." www.tentmaker.org/Quotes/prayerquotes.htm.

Johnston, J. Kirk. *Why Christians Sin.* Grand Rapids: Discovery House, 1992.

Jowett, John H. *Brooks by the Traveller's Way.* New York: A. C. Armstrong and Son, 1902.

————. *The Passion for Souls.* New York: Fleming H. Revell, 1905.

Kelly, Mark. "Evangelism Must Begin Beyond the Sanctuary." http://www.transworldnews.com/NewsStory.aspx?id=44244&cat=15.

Kemp, Joseph W. *The Soulwinner and Soulwinning.* New York: George H. Doran Company, 1916.

King, Claude. Personal Correspondence.

Bibliography

Knight, Walter B. *Knight's Illustrations for Today*. Chicago: Moody, 1970.

―――. *Knight's Master Book of New Illustrations*. Grand Rapids: William B. Erdmans, 1956.

Laidlaw, Robert A. "The Sinfulness of Prayerlessness." Herald of His Coming, August, 2003.

Larson, Craig Brian. Ed. Illustrations for Preaching and Teaching from Leadership Journal. Grand Rapids: Baker Books, 1993.

Leavell, Roland Q. *Evangelism: Christ's Imperative Commission*. Nashville: Broadman Press, 1951.

―――. *Winning Others to Christ*. Nashville: The Sunday School Board of the Southern Baptist Convention, 1936.

Ledbetter, Tammi Reed. "Better Equipped Than Ever but Less Effective." http://texanonline.org/default.asp?action=article&aid=4937.

Lee, Robert G. *From Feet to Fathoms*. Orlando: Christ for the World Publishers, 1981.

―――. "Is Hell a Myth?" www.newsforchristians.com/clser1/lee-rg006.html.

―――. *Seven Swords: And Other Messages*. Grand Rapids: Zondervan, 1958.

―――. *Seven Swords: And Other Messages*. Orlando: Christ for the World Publishers, 1981.

Lincoln, Dick. "The Chief Mission of the Church." Columbia, SC: Shandon Baptist Church, June 27, 2010.

Little, Paul. *His Guide to Evangelism*. Downers Grove, IL: InterVarsity Press, 1977.

―――. *How to Give Away Your Faith*. Downers Grove, IL: InterVarsity Press, 1973.

―――. *Know What You Believe*. Downers Grove, IL: InterVarsity Press, 2003.

Logan, Robert E. "Church Planting—The Most Successful Form of Church Growth." enrichmentjournal.ag.org/200004/012_most_successful.cfm.

Lucado, Max. *Life Lessons from the Word of God: Book of Acts.* Waco, TX: Word Publishing, 1997.

Luther, Charles C. "Must I Go and Empty-Handed?" www.cyberhymnal.org/htm/m/u/mustigoa.htm.

Lutzer, Erwin. *When a Nation Forgets God.* Chicago: Moody Publishing, 2010.

M'Cheyne, Robert Murray. *Sermons of Robert Murray M'Cheyne.* Carlisle, PA: The Banner of Truth Trust, 2000.

Mabie, Henry C. *Method in Soul Winning on Home and Foreign Fields.* New York: Fleming H. Revell Company, 1906.

MacArthur, John. *Alone with God.* Wheaton, IL: Victor Books, 1995.

———. *Follow Me.* Nashville: Countryman, 2004.

———. *John MacArthur's Bible Studies: Making Disciples.* Chicago: Moody, 1991.

———. "A Passion for the Lost." www.gty.org/Resources/Print/Study Guide Chapter/90-6.

MacArthur, John F., Jr., Richard Mayhue, Robert L. Thomas. *Rediscovering Pastoral Ministry: Shaping Contemporary Ministry with Biblical Mandates.* Dallas: Word Publishing, 1995.

Mahoney, James. *Journey into Fullness.* Nashville: Broadman Press, 1974.

Malone, Tom. *Dr. Tom Malone Preaches on Salvation.* Murfreesboro, TN: Sword of the Lord Publishers, 1995.

———. "House-to-House Soul Winning, God's Way." Murfreesboro, TN: Sword of the Lord Publishers, 1962.

———. "Where There Is No Vision the People Perish." www.soulwinning.info/sermons/dr_malone/no_vision.htm.

———. *With Jesus after Sinners.* Murfreesboro, TN: Sword of the Lord Publishers, 1991.

Martin, Gerald, ed. *Great Southern Baptist Evangelistic Preaching.* Grand Rapids: Zondervan, 1969.

Bibliography

Martin, Roger. *R. A. Torrey: Apostle of Certainty.* Murfreesboro, TN: Sword of the Lord Publishers, 2000.

Matthews, C. E. *Every Christian's Job.* Nashville: Broadman Press, 1951.

McComas, Kenny. "Win the Lost at Any Cost." Murfreesboro, TN: Sword of the Lord, December 1, 2006.

McGee, J. Vernon. *Thru the Bible Commentary (elec. ed.).* Nashville: Thomas Nelson, 1990.

McKay, Charles L. *The Call of the Harvest.* Nashville: Convention Press, 1956.

Miller, Basil. *Charles Finney.* Minneapolis: Dimension Books, 1941.

———. *George Müller: Man of Faith and Miracles.* Minneapolis: Bethany Fellowship, 1941.

Miller, Herb. www.fumcokmulgee.org/newsletter/01-23-06.pdf.

Moody, D. L. *To All People.* New York: E. B. Treat, 1877.

———. "Inspiring Quotes to Live By." www.soulwinning.info/gs/quotes.htm.

———. "Paul, I Found Christ Through Your Writings." Murfreesboro, TN: Sword of the Lord, August 7, 2009.

———. "The Hardest People to Reach." Murfreesboro, TN: Sword of the Lord, April 16, 2010.

———. "The Qualifications for Soul Winning." www.biblebelievers.com/moody_sermons/m1.html.

Moody, W. R., Ed. *Record of Christian Work, Vol. 23.* East Northfield, MA: Record of Christian Work, Co., 1904.

Morgan, G. Campbell, *The Spirit of God.* New York: Fleming H. Revell Company, 1900.

Morgan, Robert J. *Nelson's Annual Preacher's SourceBook.* Nashville: Thomas Nelson, 2002.

———. *Nelson's Annual Preacher's SourceBook.* Nashville: Thomas Nelson, 2006.

———. *Nelson's Complete Book of Stories, Illustrations, and Quotes (electronic ed.)*. Nashville: Thomas Nelson, 2000.

———. *On This Day: 365 Amazing and Inspiring Stories about Saints, Martyrs & Heroes (elect. ed.)*. Nashville: Thomas Nelson Publishers, 2000.

———. *Real Stories for the Soul* (electronic ed.). Nashville: Thomas Nelson, 2000.

Murphrey, Buddy. *Drawing the Net*. Self-published, 1969.

Murray, Andrew. *Absolute Surrender*. Springdale, PA: Whitaker House, 1981.

———. *God's Best Secrets*. Grand Rapids: Kregel Publishers, 1993.

———. *The Ministry of Intercession*. Springdale, PA: Whitaker House, 1982.

Myra, Harold and Marshall Shelley. "Sound Check Demonstrates Billy Graham's Purpose." www.preachingtoday.com/search/?query=Sound+Check+Demonstrates +Billy+Graham%E2%80%99s+Purpose&searcharea=illustrations&type =&x=0&y=0.

Ninde, Edward S. "Christian Biography Resources." www.wholesomewords.org/biography/bcrosby4.html.

Noah, Mickey. "Trustees: NAMB President Search to Gear Up, Chairman Reports." www.gofbw.com/news.asp?ID=11397.

Ogilvie, L. J. and L. J. Ogilvie. *The Preacher's Commentary Series, vol. 28*. Nashville: Thomas Nelson Inc., 1983.

Olford, Stephen. *Successful Soul Winning*. Edinbugh: Marshall, Morgan and Scott, 1958.

———. *The Secret of Soul Winning*. Nashville: Broadman and Holman, 2007.

Ormer, William. *The Practical Works of the Rev. Richard Baxter*. London: James Duncan, 1830.

Bibliography

Orr, Bob. "Will You Rescue Me?" drboborr.blogspot.com/2010/10/will-you-rescue-me.html.

Osterbind, Scott. "Forgiven." www.interlinc-online.com.

Palau, Luis. "Telling Others the Gospel, Even When It's Difficult." www.christianity.com/Christian%20Foundations/Becoming%20a%20Christian/1172292/.

———. "The Unfinished Task of Declaring His Glory." www.urbana.org/articles/the-unfinished-task-of-declaring-his-glory-1976.

Panton, D. M. "The Printed Page." Murfreesboro, TN: Sword of the Lord, August 7, 2009.

Peskoller, Markus. "Servant Magazine." London Telegraph.

Peters, Ruth. Comp. *Bible Illustrations, Book One.* Chattanooga: AMG Publishers, 1995

Phillips, John. *Exploring Psalms Vol. 5.* Neptune, NJ: Loizeaux Brothers, 1988.

Pierson, A. T. *Evangelistic Work in Principle and Practice.* New York: The Baker and Taylor Company, 1887.

Pink, Arthur. *The Holy Spirit.* La Vergne, TN: Lightning Source, 2002.

Piper, John. "Risk-Taking Adventure." witnessingencouragement.wordpress.com/2009/07.

Powell, Paul W. *Special Sermons for Special Days.* Dallas: Annuity Board of the Southern Baptist Convention, 1993.

Rainer, Thom. "Seven Characteristics of Highly Evangelistic Christians." www.joyouslife.us.

Ratz, Calvin, "The Pastor's Role." http://www.ctlibrary.com/lebooks/masteringministry/masteringoutreach/mstmin10-2.html.

Ravenhill, Leonard. "Billy Nicholson—The Irish Whitefield." www.ravenhill.org/nicholson.htm.

———. "Prayer." www.ravenhill.org/prayer.htm.

———. "The Taming of the Tongue." www.ravenhill.org/tongue.htm.

Rees, Paul S. *Stir Up the Gift.* Grand Rapids: Zondervan, 1952.

Reid, Alvin I. "Get Real." www.baptistfire.com.

———. *Radically Unchurched.* Grand Rapids: Kregel, 2002.

Rice, John R. *742 Heartwarming Poems.* Murfreesboro, TN: Sword of the Lord Publishers, 1982.

———. "How Great Soul Winners Were Filled with the Holy Spirit." Murfreesboro, TN: Sword of the Lord Publishers, 1949.

———. *How to Make a Grand Success of the Christian Life.* Murfreesboro, TN: Sword of the Lord Publishers, 1975.

———. "Personal Soul Winning." www.soulwinning.info/books/john_rice/ps/toc.htm.

———. "Predestined to Hell? No!" Murfreesboro, TN: Sword of the Lord Publishers, 1958.

———. "The Broken Heart in Soul Winning." The Sword of the Lord, September 17, 2010.

———. *The Golden Path to Successful Personal Soul Winning.* Murfreesboro, TN: Sword of the Lord Publishers, 1961.

———. *The Soul Winner's Fire.* Murfreesboro, TN: Sword of the Lord Publishers, 1941.

Rice, John R. and Joy Martin. Comp. *Soul Stirring Songs and Hymns.* Murfreesboro, TN: Sword of the Lord Publishers, 1972.

Riley, W. B. *Seven New Testament Soul Winners.* Grand Rapids: Wm. B. Eerdmans Publishing Co., 1939.

Rodeheaver, Homer. *Twenty Years with Billy Sunday.* Nashville: Cokesbury Press, 1936.

Rogers, Adrian. *Adrianisms: The Wit and Wisdom of Adrian Rogers.* Memphis: Love Worth Finding Ministries, 2006.

———. "The Master Soul Winner." www.sermonsearch.com/content.aspx?id=14606.

Bibliography

———. "The Sin of Silence."
www.sermonsearch.com/content.aspx?id=14419.

———. "The Soul Winner's Six Mighty Motivations."
www.lwf.org/site/News2?page=NewsArticle&id=11087&news_iv_ctrl
=1261.

———. "Witnessing at Work." www.oneplace.com/ministries/love-worth-
finding/read/articles/witnessing-at-work-8555.html.

Roloff, Lester. "Family Altar News," Volume 29, Number 4, 2009.

Rost, Stephen. *Heritage of Great Evangelical Teaching.* Nashville: Thomas
Nelson, 1997.

Rumble, Dale. *Behold the Harvest.* Shippensburg, PA: Destiny Image
Publishers, 1998.

Sanders, J. Oswald. "Daily Christian Quote."
dailychristianquote.com/quotessa-so.html.

———. "Passion for People."
www.heartofgod.com/Frontlines1/Issuse23/PassionforPeople.asp.

———. *The Divine Art of Soul Winning.* Chicago: Moody, 1970.

Sanderson, Leonard. *Personal Soul Winning.* Nashville: Convention Press,
1958.

Sankey, Ira David. *My Life and the Story of the Gospel Hymns.*
Philadelphia: P. W. Zeigler Co., 2002.

Scarborough, L. R. *A Search for Souls.* Nashville: Sunday School Board of
the Southern Baptist Convention. 1925.

———. *How Jesus Won Men.* Nashville: Sunday School Board of the
Southern Baptist Convention, 1926.

———. "Lost!" Murfreesboro, TN: "The Sword of the Lord," April 13,
1973.

———. *With Christ after the Lost.* Nashville: Broadman Press, 1952.

Sharpe, Ray. "How Your Church Can Change the World."
www.thesoulwinner.org/Multiplication-in-Soul-Winning.html.

Shivers, Frank. *Soulwinning 101.* Sumter, SC: Hill Publishing, 2006.

———. *The Evangelistic Invitation 101.* Sumter, SC: Hill Publishing, 2004.

Shoemaker, Samuel Moor. "So I Stay Near the Door." www.aabibliography.com/dickbhtml/article10.html.

Simmons, M. Laird. "Biography of D. L. Moody." www.wholesomewords.org/biography/biomoody.html.

Sjorgren, Steve, Dave Ping, and Doug Pollock. *Irresistible Evangelism.* Loveland, CO: Group, 2004.

Smith, Bailey. *Real Evangelism.* Nashville: Broadman Press, 1978.

Smith, Jack R. ed. *Fifty Great Soul Winning Motivational Sermons.* Alpharetta, GA: North America Mission Board, 1994.

Smith, Oswald J. "Evangelize! Evangelize!" www.preachhim.org/poempage.htm.

———. *The Revival We Need.* www.gospeltruth.net/OJSmith/revival_we_needindex.htm.

Smith, Shelton. "Soul Winning." Murfreesboro, TN: Sword of the Lord, July 9, 2010.

Smith, Shelton. Ed. *Great Preaching on Revival.* Murfreesboro, TN: Sword of the Lord Publishers, 1997.

Sproul, R. C. "The New Genesis: The Holy Spirit and Regeneration." www.the-highway.com/genesis_Sproul.html.

Spurgeon, Charles H. *An All-Round Ministry.* www.spurgeon.org/misc/aarm.htm.

———. "Breakfast with Jesus." www.spurgeongems.org/vols34-36/chs2072.pdf.

———. *Come Ye Children.* Scotland: Christian Focus Publications, 1989.

———. *Evangelism.* Greenville, SC: Emerald House, 1998.

———. *Faith's Checkbook.* New Kensington, PA: Whitaker House, 2002.

———. *Lectures to My Students.* Grand Rapids: Zondervan, 1970.

Bibliography

———. *Morning and Evening.* Peabody, MA: Hendrickson Publishers, 2006.

———. *Only a Prayer Meeting.* Great Britain: Christian Focus Publications, 2000.

———. "Prayer and Intercession Quotes." http://www.tentmaker.org/Quotes/prayerquotes.htm.

———. "Sentence Sermons and Quotes." www.emi-missions.org/sentence_sermons.html.

———. *Sermons for Special Days and Occasions.* Grand Rapids: Zondervan Publishing House, 1966.

———. *Sermons on Soul Winning.* London: Marshall Morgan & Scott, 1963.

———. "Spurgeon Quotes on Evangelism." girdedwithtruth.org/2010/01/21/quotes-on-evangelism-by-spurgeon.

———. *Spurgeon's Sermons on New Testament Men, vol. 2.* Grand Rapids: Kregel, 1996.

———. *Spurgeon's Sermons on Soul Winning.* Grand Rapids: Kregel, 1995.

———. *Spurgeon's Sermons, Vol. 4.* Grand Rapids: Baker Books, 1999.

———. *The Metropolitan Tabernacle Pulpit, 1862.* Pasadena, TX: Pilgrim Publications, 1969.

———. *The Metropolitan Tabernacle Pulpit, 1876.* London: Passmore and Alabaster, 1877.

———. *The Soul Winner.* New Kensington, PA: Whitaker House, 1995.

Stafford, Bill. Bailey Smith Real Evangelism Conference, Indian Trail, North Carolina.

Stevens, Abel, ed. "The National Magazine, Vol. 1, July–December." New York: Carlton and Phillips, 1852.

Stewart, David J. "Billions of People Are Going to Hell." www.jesus-is-savior.com/billions_of_people_going_to_hell.htm.

Stockbower, Rian. "Piping in Sunlight."
arstechnica.com/science/news/2005/11/1896.ars.

Stott, John R. W. *Balanced Christianity.* London: Hodder and Stoughton, 1975.

———. *The Contemporary Christian.* Downers Grove, IL: InterVarsity Press, 1995.

———. *The Guilty Silence.* Downers Grove, IL: InterVarsity Press, 1967.

Strack, Jay. "Tradigital Strategy for Having a High Definition Ministry." Dallas Theological Seminary Chapel. March 24, 2006.

Strobel, Lee. *The Case for the Real Jesus.* Grand Rapids: Zondervan, 2009.

Sunday, Billy. "Present-Day Proverbs." Sword of the Lord, July 25, 2008.

Surgener, James M. *Lost!* Nashville: Broadman Press, 1988.

Sweazey, George. *Effective Evangelism.* New York and Evanston, IL: Harper and Row Publishers, 1953.

Sweeting, George. "Our Daily Bread." Grand Rapids: Discovery House, 1994.

Swindoll, Chuck. *Standing Out.* Portland: Multnomah Press, 1983.

Tan, Paul. *Encyclopedia of 7700 Illustrations: Signs of the Times.* Rockville, MD: Assurance Publishers, 1979.

———. *Encyclopedia of 7700 Illustrations: A Treasury of Illustrations, Anecdotes, Facts and Quotations for Pastors, Teachers and Christian Workers.* Garland, TX: Bible Communications, 1996.

Taylor, Hudson. "Rope Holder Quotes."
www.kneelingwetriumph.com/prayer/prayerquotes.htm.

ten Boom, Corrie. "Words of Wisdom." www.dailyshepherd.com/words-of-wisdom.

Thompson, Mary A. "O Zion, Haste."
www.cyberhymnal.org/htm/o/z/ozionhas.htm.

Torrey, R. A. *Anecdotes and Illustrations.* London and Edinburg: Fleming H. Revell Company, 1907.

Bibliography

———. "Soul Winning." books.google.com/books?id=5LaTe6d0GewC.

———. "The Importance of Personal Soul Winning." www.swordofthelord.com/onlinesermons/ImportanceSoulWinning.htm.

Towns, Elmer. *Winning the Winnable.* Lynchburg, VA: Church Leadership Institute, 1986.

Tripp, Dick. "Stories of Faith." www.christianity.co.nz/life_death9.htm.

Truett, George W. *A Quest for Souls.* New York: Harper and Brothers, 1917.

———. *We Would See Jesus.* Chattanooga: AMG Publishers, 1998.

Trumbull, Charles G. "Herald of His Coming." Vol. 64, Number 5.

———. *Taking Men Alive.* New York: Association Press, 1912.

———. "The Pioneer Personal Worker." www.krowtracts.com/articles/trumbull.html.

Unknown Author. "Children Saved from Burning Home." www.ksee24.com/news/local/91792659.html.

———. "Church Planting." www.pfwb.org/worldwitness/churchplanting.htm.

———. "Commentary on I Peter 1:7." www.preceptaustin.org/1_peter_17.htm.

———. "Editorials & Letters." Craig, CO: Craig Daily Press, 1990.

———. *Evangelism Sowing and Reaping.* www.scribd.com/doc/22786310/evangelism-sowing-and-reaping.

———. "History of the Jehovah's Witnesses." www.catholic.com/library/History_of_the_Jehovah_Witnesses.asp.

———. "Please Get My Mother In." www.ianpaisley.org/article.asp?ArtKey=mother.

———. "PS *Lady Elgin.*" secure.wikimedia.org/wikipedia/en/wiki/PS_Lady_Elgin.

———. "R. A. Torrey: A Biography." www.believersweb.org/view.cfm?ID=62.

————. "Salvation Sermon Illustrations." moreillustrations.com/Illustrations/salvation%208.html.

————. "Sermon Illustrations: Opportunity." http://hotsermons.com/sermon-illustrations/sermon-illustrations-opportunity.html.

————. "Spiritual Blindness." books.google.com/books?id=5LaTe6d0GewC.

————. "The Challenge of Evangelism." www.nwcoclawton.org/WorkshopSermon.pdf.

————. "The Pit." www.whosoever.org/v2i3/pit.html.

————. "The Price and Reward for Soul Winning." http://www.newlifecamp.com/application/uploads/assets/file_uploads/Year_2_Lesson_9_Complete.pdf.

————. "True Hero on the Titanic." blessedquietness.com/JOURNAL/housechu/harper.htm. (Documentation found in *The Titanic's Last Hero* by Moody Adams, Olive Press, 1997, which relates testimonies compiled by John Climie of Scotland in 1912.)

————. "Two Judgments." www.xenos.org/ct_outln/judge.htm.

————. "Wanted: A Burning Heart!" www.sermonindex.net/modules/articles/index.php?view=article&aid=19230.

————. "Why Church Planting?" www.e4network.org/why-church-planting.

————. "20 Years Later, Baby Jessica a Wife, Mother and Soon-to-Be Millionaire." www.foxnews.com/story/0,2933,302523,00.html.

Vines, Jerry. "How to Recognize a Soul Winner." www.sermonnotebook.org/romans/How%20To%20Recognize%20A%20Soul%20Winner.htm.

Walden, Viola. *Sword Scrapbook.* Murfreesboro, TN: Sword of the Lord Publishers, 1969.

Walton, Dave. Personal Correspondence.

Bibliography

Walvoord, John F. and Roy B. Zuck, *The Bible Knowledge Commentary.* Colorado Springs: Chariot Victory Publishing, 1999.

Warren, Rick. *The Purpose Driven Life.* Grand Rapids: Zondervan, 2002.

Washburn, A. V. *Outreach for the Unreached.* Nashville: Convention Press, 1960.

Wells, Mike and Mike Ray. "One Step at a Time Growth Series." www.fbbc.com/messages/one_step/one_step_07.htm.

White, Ellen G. *Gospel Workers.* Hagerstown: Review and Herald Publishing Association, 1915.

Whitesell, Faris, *Basic New Testament Evangelism.* Grand Rapids: Zondervan, 1949.

Whitney, Donald S. *Spiritual Disciplines for the Christian.* Colorado Springs: NavPress, 2002.

Wiersbe, Warren. *Be Free.* Colorado Springs: David C. Cook, 1975.

————. *Bible Expository Commentary.* Colorado Springs: David C. Cook, 2004.

————. *Classic Sermons on World Evangelism.* Grand Rapids: Kregel Publications, 1999.

Wiersbe, Warren and Lloyd M. Perry. *Wycliffe Handbook of Preaching and Preachers.* Chicago: Moody Press, 1984.

Wilbanks, C. E. *What God Hath Wrought through C. E. Matthews.* Nashville: Home Mission Board of the Southern Baptist Convention, 1957.

Wilkerson, David. *Bring Your Loved Ones to Christ.* New Jersey: Fleming Revell Company, 1979.

Woodbury, Carl. "Letters from Around the World." Sword of the Lord, June 11, 2010.

Zenor, Jon. "Spurgeon Gold." www.eternaltruthministry.com/2007/08/spurgeon-gold.

Other Resources by Frank Shivers

Soulwinning 101:
275 Helps in
Winning the Lost

Christian Basics 101:
A Concise Handbook for
Christian Growth

Evangelistic Preaching 101:
Great Voices of the Past and
Present on Effective Preaching

The Evangelistic Invitation 101:
250 Helps on Giving the
Evangelistic Invitation

Revivals 101:
A "How To" Church
Revival Manual

Growing in Knowledge
An interactive handbook on
basic Christian truths